American Domestic Priorities

An Economic Appraisal

Edited by
John M. Quigley
Daniel L. Rubinfeld

UNIVERSITY OF CALIFORNIA PRESS
Berkeley · *Los Angeles* · *London*

University of California Press
Berkeley and Los Angeles, California

University of California Press, Ltd.
London, England

© 1985 by The Regents of the University of California

Printed in the United States of America

1   2   3   4   5   6   7   8   9

LIBRARY OF CONGRESS CATALOGING IN PUBLICATION DATA

Main entry under title:
American domestic priorities.

  (California series in real estate economics and finance)
  Includes bibliographical references.
    1. United States—Economic policy—1981–
—Addresses, essays, lectures. 2. Intergovernmental fiscal
relations—United States—Addresses, essays, lectures.
    I. Quigley, John M.   II. Rubinfeld, Daniel L.   III. Series.
HC106.8.A435   1985   338.973   84–28013
ISBN 0–520–05521–7
ISBN 0–520–05522–5 (pbk.)

Contents

Preface

Domestic programs and their budgetary implications will be scrutinized closely during the 99th Congress and the second term of the Reagan administration. Can further cuts in these programs reduce massive federal deficits? Or must spending cuts be made either in social security entitlements or in defense appropriations? Can the Reagan administration succeed in shifting many public functions from the federal government to the states? Would such transfers affect public support for these programs? Is a shift away from federal responsibility and control desirable?

A forthright evaluation of domestic programs was conspicuously absent during the recent election campaign. Public debate about domestic priorities during the fall of 1984 was partisan and political, with ideological statements and misinformation the rule rather than the exception. In contrast, the urgency of the issue of the federal deficit, and of the unusually high interest rates the deficits cause, will now require elected officials to pay close attention to details of the domestic budget in defining public priorities for the next term. This will require facts about program operation, analysis of program outcomes, and knowledge of the budgetary consequences of policy alternatives.

This book provides the kind of analysis needed for this crucial debate about federal policy. It offers a serious and in-depth evaluation of domestic programs and priorities, with coverage of a broad range of issues, from education and welfare to urban transportation, from housing policy to environmental regulation. It supplies a framework for assessing the proposals of the New Federalism and the consequences of continued trade deficits.

This book presents the views of a group of nationally prominent economists, including many who have served in policymaking positions in the administrations of both parties. It carefully summarizes the recent history of government policies and their outcomes. The authors review program priorities and offer proposals for the future. The analysis is addressed to a wide audience and is enriched by lively commentary and discussion by economists knowledgeable about each of the substantive programs.

The authors present no unified opinion about what our domestic priorities ought to be. There is, however, a general consensus as to appropriate directions in a number of areas. The analysts clearly sense that we ought to move to less intrusive federal command and control and also to greater state involvement in a number of programs such as transportation, education, and the environment. The New Federalism receives substantial support in many areas, not involving poverty and welfare, from a group of economists who supported a stronger federal role a decade ago.

Despite this intellectual shift, the authors present convincing evidence that the Reagan program is really a federal budget-cutting exercise in disguise. They have forceful and controversial ideas about desirable reforms. They believe that substantial reductions in expenditures would adversely affect the quality of domestic programs.

The economic perspective of the authors is an important one, given the current policy debate and the budgetary emphasis. Economic analysis of the 1983 federal budget indicates that spending on national defense amounted to $201 billion, and spending on social security, veterans' benefits, and interest came to over $442 billion. With a federal budget of $820 billion and political promises not to cut defense or social security, the administration appears committed to cuts in the remaining $240 billion. It is hard to see how a deficit of roughly $200 billion can be removed by domestic cuts alone. The only options appear to be tax increases, large and growing federal deficits, or blind faith that growth in the economy will alleviate all problems.

Economists familiar with programs and outcomes clear up the often confused and confusing facts. For example, authors Sheldon Danziger and Daniel Feaster demonstrate irrefutably that poverty did increase under the first term of the Reagan administration. From 1978 to 1983 the poverty rate increased from 11.4 percent to 15.2 percent, while real dollars of federal aid to the poor decreased by more than one percent. Commentator Jennifer Wolch shows that many of those removed from the poverty rolls were in serious need of assistance—these are the "service-dependent" poor, who suffered severely during the first Reagan term. Further budgetary cuts in welfare can only exacerbate their problems, problems which cannot be cured simply by the benefits of a growing economy.

Sherman Maisel's economic analysis of housing programs clarifies the effects of current subsidy policies and of the alternative programs proposed by the administration. Housing affordability is a spreading problem, argues Maisel, despite the fact that 75 percent of federal housing subsidies go to the non-poor. John Kain claims that the most pressing domestic social problem in America is discrimination in the housing market. His detailed analysis of the 1980 Census of Housing suggests that some gains have been made in reducing residential segregation.

Campaign press releases indicated that student test scores had improved as a result of government programs. Economist Richard Murnane provides a detailed analysis of outcomes and program effects. He finds that reading skills of students have improved over the past decade, but that math and science skills have declined substantially. How can this crisis in education be resolved, especially in light of the need for budgetary savings? Murnane argues that the program and its solution lie in the labor market for teachers and suggests some important, but inexpensive, reforms to make it operate more effectively.

The economic analyses of domestic programs in this book conclude that there are real opportunities to reduce the federal deficit—by applying the principles of the New Federalism to revenues as well as expenditures in the federal domestic budget, and by reducing and redirecting intergovernmental grants. In fact, recommendations presented here suggest that a large share of the current deficit could be eliminated by such reforms. The detailed discussion and commentary that follows the papers provides thought-provoking and valuable recommendations for action.

John M. Quigley
Daniel L. Rubinfeld
Berkeley, California

Acknowledgments

This book grew out of a conference on domestic public policy held at the University of California, Berkeley, in September 1984. The conference was supported financially by the Center for Real Estate and Urban Economics at Berkeley and encouraged intellectually by the Center's director, Kenneth T. Rosen. The Center continued to play an important role in the development of this book by providing financial and administrative support during the preparation process.

A number of individuals helped in manuscript preparation. We are grateful for the extraordinary efforts of Jo Magaraci of the Real Estate Center and Michelle Dethke of the Graduate School of Public Policy.

PART ONE

The United States Federal System

An analysis of the United States federal system provides a useful framework for an evaluation of domestic budgetary programs. First, Robert Inman describes the Reagan administration's New Federalism, with its implied reallocation of functions between the states and the federal government. Edward Gramlich then addresses the fundamental normative question of federalism: Which levels of government ought to be assigned the right to levy taxes and to utilize other revenue-raising sources? In the Commentary, Henry Aaron discusses arguments for the important fiscal role of intergovernmental grants; George Break argues, against Gramlich, that the federal income-tax deduction for state and local taxes, although it may be less than efficient, does contribute to equity; and Julius Margolis provides a broad sociopolitical perspective on the rapid growth of government in the twentieth century.

CHAPTER ONE

Fiscal Allocations in a Federalist Economy: Understanding the "New" Federalism

Robert P. Inman

From its constitutional beginnings to today, the United States public economy has been committed to the concept of federalism in the provision of public services. The use of multiple layers of government, with each higher level possessing rights of control over a lower level, is a founding principle of our fiscal structure.[1] But while the constitutional commitment to a federalist system is clear, the precise structure and performance of that system are not.

Significant changes have taken place in our federalist fiscal system, both historically and in recent years. Scheiber (1966) has identified four stages of historical development of United States federalism: first, a period of "dualism" (1790–1860) in which states and the federal sector coexisted with essentially equivalent responsibility and powers; second, a time of "centralizing federalism" (1860–1933) as power began to gravitate to the federal level; third, a period of "cooperative federalism" growing out of the social programs to deal with the national crisis of the Great Depression (1933–1964); and finally, the recent period of "creative federalism" in which the federal government has taken an active policy interest in the specific problems of state and local governments. The first three periods can be characterized as times when the states (and their localities) made fiscal policy largely independently of direct federal interventions, while the recent period of creative federalism has involved the federal government directly in state and local fiscal affairs. Federal grants-in-aid and all their spending requirements, as well as the many new federal regulations

TABLE I.I

Federal and State-Local Government Expenditures

Year	Total domestic government spending* (1)	% federal (2)	% state-local (3)	Non-transfer, domestic government spending* (4)	% federal (5)	% state-local (6)	Government transfers to persons* (7)	% federal (8)	% state-local (9)
1902	$106.40	28.5%	71.5%	$103.30	29.0%	71.0%	$3.10	9.7%	90.3%
1913	140.70	25.6	74.3	137.50	26.1	73.9	3.20	7.8	92.2
1922	214.70	34.7	65.3	209.00	35.4	64.6	5.70	8.4	91.5
1932	414.70	34.1	65.8	397.30	35.5	64.5	17.40	4.8	95.2
1940	490.50	33.9	66.1	420.40	30.7	69.3	70.10	53.2	46.8
1950	588.50	35.9	64.1	412.00	19.1	80.9	176.50	75.2	24.8
1960	759.33	34.2	65.8	542.10	15.9	84.1	217.20	80.0	20.0
1970	1215.00	37.2	62.8	809.40	15.5	84.5	405.60	80.6	19.3
1980	1661.60	46.1	53.8	958.90	16.7	83.3	702.70	86.3	13.7
1983	1653.20	48.8	51.2	884.70	15.4	84.6	768.40	87.2	12.8

*1972 dollars per capita.

SOURCES: Government purchases of goods and services: 1940–1983, from Bureau of Economic Analysis (1981), tables 3.2, 3.3. 1902–1940, measured as the sum of total general expenditure less military services less public welfare less total insurance trust expenditure (federal); and total general expenditure = total public welfare less total insurance and trust expenditure (state/local), from Bureau of the Census (1975), Series Y605–637, Y682–709.

Government transfers to persons: 1940–1983 from Bureau of Economic Analysis (1981), tables 3.2, 3.3. 1902–1940 measured as the sum of total public welfare expenditure plus total insurance and trust expenditure, from Bureau of the Census (1975), Series Y605–637, Y682–709.

Price deflator for purchases of goods and services: 1932–1983 as the implicit price deflator of government purchases of goods and services, from Bureau of the Census (1975), Series E1–22, and Bureau of Economic Analysis (1984). 1902–1932, the GNP price-deflator from Bureau of the Census (1975), Series E1–22.

Price deflator of transfers to persons: 1902–1983, measured as the GNP price deflator, from Bureau of the Census (1975), Series E1–22, and Bureau of Economic Analysis (1984).

of state-local governments, have deeply affected the budgetary choices of the state-local sector.

In January 1982, President Reagan proposed a significant break with this trend toward federalization of our public economy. As originally presented in his budget message of that year, President Reagan's "new" federalism proposed: (1) that Medicaid become a fully federal program (which the administration hoped to curtail as part of its health-care-reform efforts); (2) that the states and localities assume responsibility for food stamp programs and Aid to Families with Dependent Children (AFDC); and (3) that more than sixty federal programs in education, community development, transportation, and social services be returned to the states, with the states receiving $28 billion a year from a federal trust fund to help pay for their new responsibilities. The trust fund was to be supported by federal excise taxes. Dollars paid from the trust fund would not be restricted to expenditures on the reassigned programs, however. The funds could, if a state so decided, be allocated to other state programs or to state tax relief. The intention of the president's new federalism was clear: to reduce federal influence on state-local fiscal choice.

What is less clear is how state and local governments will react to this restructuring of our current federalist fiscal system, and whether the present federal government will relinquish control and embrace the new federalism. Yet from the perspective of fiscal policy these are the central issues. Changes in federal grants and federal regulations will assuredly affect state and local governments' budgetary decisions. The relative economic and political attractiveness of the new federalism and of the creative federalism it seeks to replace ultimately rests on the actual allocations of resources. This paper offers some first (but considered) guesses as to what might happen under, and to, Reagan's reforms, and concludes that President Reagan and his supporters are not likely to be disappointed in the economic consequences of the new federalism, though they will be unhappy with its political prospects.

OUR CURRENT FEDERALIST FISCAL STRUCTURE

In order to predict the future under President Reagan's new federalism, it is important to understand our present federalist fiscal structure and how it evolved. The Reagan proposals are a significant challenge to the historical trend toward federalization of United States fiscal policy. Table 1.1 summarizes the federal and state/local government spending patterns

TABLE I.2

Federal Share of All Government Receipts

Year	All government receipts*	% federal government
1929	$430.80	33%
1940	613.30	48
1950	1119.40	74
1960	1266.90	72
1970	1548.50	69
1980	1737.70	72
1983	1732.00	68

*1972 dollars per capita

SOURCES: Government receipts, from taxes and contribution to social insurance, from Council of Economic Advisors (1984), tables B-75 and B-77.

Price deflator is the GNP implicit price deflator for government purchases from the Council of Economic Advisors (1984), table B-3.

over the past eighty years. As columns 1–3 show, the federal government share has grown steadily; today each sector is responsible for about half of all domestic public spending.[2] The major source of the growing federal share was expansion of social insurance programs—"transfers to persons"—from the mid 1930s to 1950 and again from 1960 to 1980 (Table 1.1, columns 7–9). While the federal government's responsibility for transfers was growing, its responsibility for direct provision of non-defense public goods and services was declining (Table 1.1, columns 4–6); the state-local sector is the primary producer of domestic public services. Overall, the major source of the historical growth in total government activity has been transfer programs, however, and these programs are the financial responsibility of the federal government.

A similar move toward the federal level is observed in the historical trends of government receipts measured as taxes plus contributions to social insurance (see Table 1.2). In 1929, all government receipts were $430.80 per capita (in 1972 dollars), of which 33 percent was raised by the federal government. By 1950 the federal share was 74 percent of all receipts. The federal share has declined slightly in recent years, but a comparison of the 1929 and 1983 divisions of the revenue-raising function shows essentially a reversal of roles between the federal and state-local sectors. In 1929, state-local governments were the main source of public dollars; now the federal government has assumed that role.

TABLE I.3

Federal Aid to State and Local Governments

Year	Direct federal aid to state governments*	Direct federal aid to state governments as % of state revenue	Direct federal aid to local governments*	Direct federal aid to local governments as % of local revenue
1902	$0.24	1.6%	$0.32	0.4%
1913	0.34	1.6	0.34	0.3
1922	4.89	7.9	0.44	0.2
1932	7.16	9.2	0.32	0.1
1940	15.98	15.2	6.73	4.0
1950	38.18	20.2	3.54	1.5
1960	60.79	23.2	5.64	1.8
1970	107.08	24.8	14.48	3.2
1980	143.62	26.8	48.22	13.7

*1972 dollars per capita

SOURCES: Federal aid to state and local governments: 1902–1970, from the Bureau of the Census (1975), pp. 1129–33; 1980, *Statistical Abstract of the United States, 1983*, p. 287. The price deflator is the GNP implicit price deflator for government purchases for the period 1932–1980, from the Council of Economic Advisors (1984), table B-3. For the period 1902–1932, the GNP implicit price deflator for government purchases was assumed to have the same rate of change as the general "all items" CPI, from the Bureau of the Census (1975), p. 211.

The federalization of our fiscal structure has manifested itself in other ways as well. The federal government now actively participates in state and local budgetary choices. It does so in two ways: through a carrot called grants-in-aid, and through a stick called regulation. Table 1.3 details the recent growth of federal aid to state and local governments. From a position of very modest absolute and relative importance in 1940, federal aid had grown by 1980 to a sizable real-dollar transfer—a total of $192/capita—and to over 25 percent of state and almost 14 percent of local non-debt revenues. Growth has been particularly dramatic over the last two decades, most noticeably in direct federal-to-local aid. Table 1.4 illustrates the other important features of the aid explosion. The growth has occurred in categorical formula grants and categorical projects grants rather than in block grants. *Block grants* are federal dollars targeted for broad programmatic missions—e.g., education, employment, community development. *Categorical aid* is directed at narrow program categories—e.g., school lunches, sewer construction, low-income transfers to fatherless families. Categorical aid can be given to states or localities

TABLE 1.4
Structure of Federal Grants-in-Aid

Year	Number of formula grants	Number of project grants	Number of block grants	% of federal aid distributed as formula/project	% of federal aid distributed as block/GRS
Before 1962	53	107	0	100%	0%
1967	99	280	2	98	2
1976	110	296	6	75	25

SOURCE: Advisory Commission on Intergovernment Relations (1978), pp. 25, 32.

according to a well-specified formula (*formula* grant), or states and localities may submit a specific project proposal for federal funding (*project* grant). Categorical aid often requires the state or local government to *match* the federal funds with state or local revenues. Block grants generally do not require such a match; instead, they serve as "free" money to the state-local sector.

Does such aid influence state-local fiscal allocations? The econometric evidence from over twenty years of research is quite unequivocal on the point: it does indeed (see the surveys in Gramlich 1969 and Inman 1979). Federal aid increases state and local spending on the targeted activities, and often on non-targeted activities as well. Categorical matching aid is the greatest stimulus to state-local spending. Block grants and the totally unconstrained, general-revenue-sharing aid induce the least increase in public spending. In the next section I review three recent studies which show that the impact of federal categorical and categorical matching grants on state and local budgets has been sizable. While there has been much political debate about whether these federal aid programs are good or bad for the state-local sector,[3] no one has denied that these programs have been an important influence on state-local budgetary choices.

The federal government also regulates many activities of the state-local sector, now more than ever. Figure 1.1 summarizes the growth of federal regulatory programs. Four types of regulation have been identified: *direct orders*, which must be obeyed to avoid civil or criminal penalties (e.g., the Equal Employment Opportunity Act of 1972, which bars job discrimination on the basis of race, color, religion, sex, or national origin); *crosscutting regulations*, broad federal mandates that apply to all forms of federal assistance (e.g., the Civil Rights Act of 1964); *crossover regulations*, which require performance on one policy dimension under penalty of loss of federal assistance from another, well-specified program (e.g., the 55mph speed limit required under threat of loss of federal highway assistance); and, finally, *partial pre-emptions*, in which federal law establishes a policy goal which, if not met by the state-local sector, will allow direct federal provision or enforcement (e.g., the Clean Air Act Amendments of 1970). The 1970s saw by far the greatest growth in federal regulation of the state-local sector. The results have been mixed. The Civil Rights Act is an example of significant accomplishment, but most environmental regulations have produced only modest gains in air, water, and land-use quality, yet have imposed large costs on state and local governments (Advisory Commission on Intergovernment Relations n.d., p. 22). Again, while the relative benefits and costs of federal regulation of the

FIGURE I.I
Federal Regulation of State-Local Governments, 1930–1979

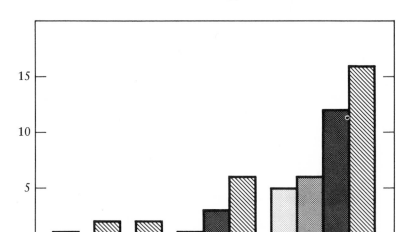

SOURCE: Advisory Commission on Intergovernment Relations (n.d.), p. 4.

state-local sector can be debated, there can be little doubt that these regulations have significantly influenced the policies and budgets of state and local governments.

We are now a federalized, federalist system. President Reagan's "new federalism" reforms strike at the heart of this centralization process. First, the two major income-maintenance programs now at the federal level— food stamps and AFDC—are to be returned to the state and local sectors. In 1983, these programs were estimated to cost the federal government $16.4 billion. A dollar shift of this magnitude will reduce the federal share of transfer to persons from 87.2 percent in 1983 (Table 1.1, column 8) to 83 percent.[4]

Second, the Medicaid program is to become fully a federal responsibility. On the surface, this adjustment appears to run counter to the defederalization intentions of the Reagan policy. The new federal Medicaid outlays, approximately $19 billion, will increase the federal share in transfers to persons, from 83 percent following the decentralization of welfare, back to 87 percent. Despite this upward adjustment in federal spending, it can be argued that the offer to take on the state's share of Medicaid is a necessary component of the new federalism package. The states and their congressional representatives will not accept the income-maintenance programs without some form of budget relief to compensate for the additional expense of these programs. Direct grant relief might be more of the same—federally funded aid for federally mandated programs. Relief could, however, be offered in the form of a federal takeover of a state responsibility. But which state responsibility? The state share of the Medicaid program is an excellent choice for three reasons: (1) the state Medicaid outlay is large and growing and a bit more than the federal dollars now spent on food stamps and AFDC, i.e., it is a "fair" trade; (2) the states have been doing a very poor job of controlling Medicaid outlays; and (3) there is a growing desire at the federal level to control federal health care costs, and Medicaid, if federalized, can more easily be included within any new federal regulations. The states do not want the responsibility of Medicaid, and for reasons not entirely related to federalism, the Reagan administration is willing to take it on. From the point of view of the new federalism, the swap of the state share of Medicaid for income-maintenance programs seems the best available trade.

Third and finally, Reagan's new federalism proposes to return to the state-local sector sixty-one existing federal-education, social-service, transportation, and community-development categorical aid programs for state administration and funding. To ease the estimated $30.2 billion financial burden imposed by these new programs, the federal government would make available to the states $27.6 billion from a federal trust fund supported by federal excise taxes. (The states' shortfall between program costs and trust fund transfers equals the states' gain from the welfare/Medicaid swap.) The intention of this exchange is to reduce federal control over state and local spending; categorical aid and its particular expenditure restrictions are dropped and replaced with unconstrained federal assistance. This federal-trust-fund aid is to be phased out, however, over four years beginning in 1988. Thus, the third component of the new federalism is intended first to reduce federal aid restrictions and then, beginning in 1988, gradually to reduce federal government spending and taxes.[5] Overall, the new federalism is: (1) to leave the federal share of transfer outlays largely unaffected but to move to the federal level those redistribution expenditures (Medicaid) that the states have found the most difficult to control; (2) to replace federal categorical aid with lump-sum aid, thereby reducing federal control over state-local spending; and finally, (3) to reduce federal spending and taxes by gradually phasing out the trust fund and its associated taxes. Or so the proponents of the new federalism hope. Whether the new federalism will in fact have these defederalizing effects is an open question.

WILL THE "NEW" FEDERALISM WORK?

While the calculations above concerning effects of President Reagan's new federalism on our fiscal system are reasonable first guesses, they are really only that—first guesses. Budget aggregates were simply moved from the federal to the state-local column and back again. Missing from such calculations is any sense that there are governments, and voters, who determine what those budget aggregates will be. Yet an analysis of such a fundamental realignment of fiscal responsibilities as the new federalism proposes must recognize that the state-local sector will react to the reforms. To predict the consequences of new federalism we must first understand the budgetary process of state and local governments.

STATE-LOCAL FISCAL CHOICE IN A FEDERALIST ECONOMY

Beginning with the early "determinants" studies of state and local spending, economists and political scientists have tried to untangle the causes of decentralized governments' fiscal choices. Analysis has proceeded from simple linear regression models of aggregate state and local spending to sophisticated maximum-likelihood estimation of utility maximization models for decisive voters in individual jurisdictions. But all these models have one element in common: they are *economic* models, with a central focus on citizen preferences and their budget constraints as causes of governmental expenditures.

Figure 1.2 illustrates the basic, and now familiar, story. A "typical" resident's preferences for public services and private goods are represented by a utility relationship over after-tax private income (y) and public goods (g), denoted $U(y,g)$. The indifference curves in Figure 1.2 rank the relative value of different combinations of y and g as represented by $U(g,y)$. Combinations of y and g on a higher indifference curve are preferred by the typical resident to those combinations on a lower indifference curve. A budget constraint will restrict the level of services which the typical resident can afford. The constraint is defined by the identity: $\hat{I} = y + p \cdot g$, where $\hat{I}$ is the typical resident's "full fiscal income" and p is the resident's "tax price" of local public goods. Full fiscal income is the sum of the resident's before state-local-tax private income (I) and the resident's

FIGURE I.2
The "Typical" Voter's Preferred Budget

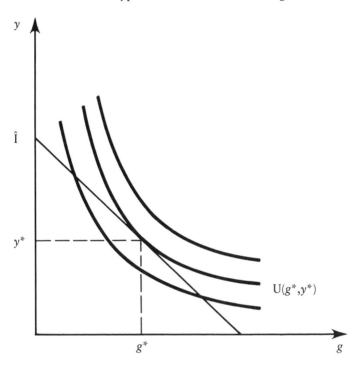

share of federal to state/local lump-sum aid per resident (z). The tax price p equals the resident's share of the tax costs of each unit of the public service, net of federal matching aid.[6]

Given preferences and the budget constraint, the typical resident will wish to buy the level of public goods that maximizes $U(y,g)$ subject to the constraint. This is point (y^*, g^*) in Figure 1.2, where the budget line is just tangent to the highest possible indifference curve. The utility maximization/budget constraint model yields a demand curve for local public goods of the following form:

(1) $g = f(p, \hat{I} | \text{Tastes})$,

where the theory predicts that $\partial g/\partial p < 0$, $\partial g/\partial \hat{I} > 0$. The taste variables (Tastes) are unique to the individual resident.

Economists are now quite comfortable with this specification of state-local fiscal choice and have applied it on numerous occasions to estimate local governments' responsiveness to various federal-government aid and tax policies. (Inman 1979 reviews these studies.) One nagging question has, however, been left unanswered by virtually every application of this approach. Who is the "typical" resident whose demand curve we are estimating? Answers have relied more on hand-waving than hard work. Empirical analyses of state-local fiscal choice have generally lacked any notion that politics, the process of conflict resolution, affects state-local fiscal allocations. Exactly whose preferences and whose budget constraints dictate the final allocations? Is the final allocation a compromise among several players, or just the preferred outcome of a "chosen" one? Who are these players? What is their standing and what are their rights within the political budgetary process? How are disagreements resolved? What happens if there is no agreement? These are political questions, and their answers require political analysis.

Introducing political considerations into the systematic analysis of budgetary choice is not a simple matter. Once we begin to study allocations involving more than one policy dimension—say, education *and* welfare spending—we confront a fundamental analytic difficulty. If there are more than two interested voters, such allocations will generally not have a stable equilibrium if budgets are decided by a simple majority-rule process, for there is no identifiable median voter in such cases (see Inman 1984). Yet state-local budgetary choices are often very stable; allocations do not change much from year to year. In an important line of new research, Shepsle (1979) has described and analyzed various legislative extensions of simple majority rule that are sufficient to produce stable fiscal allocations. The final allocations—called *structure-induced equilibria*—are conditioned by the status quo and the constitutional rules that determine legislative structures. Shepsle identifies three central structural features of legislatures: (1) a *committee structure* that identifies who is allowed to offer proposals for consideration by the full legislature; (2) a *jurisdiction structure* that defines which proposals may be considered by the committee and the legislature; and (3) an *amendment structure* that describes how the committee's proposals to the legislature may be altered. Together these structural features can insure a stable allocation. It is important to emphasize, however, and particularly for our purposes here, that a structure-induced equilibrium is a partial equilibrium, conditioned by the starting or status-quo allocation and the detailed rules of fiscal choice. Exogenous changes in the starting allocation or legislative rules because of new federal regulations or aid programs, such as the new federalism, will alter the observed equilibrium allocations.

The political theory of structure-induced equilibria allows us to specify just how such institutional changes will affect budgetary choices. The theory predicts that final fiscal allocations will be a simple weighted average of the preferred allocations of each voter. The weights depend on the status quo (denoted as $g°$, a vector of initial service levels) and the political institutional structure (denoted S, a vector of institutional variables). The allocation for service t preferred by each voter or interest group i is defined by the demand curve $g_{it} = f_{it}(p_i, \hat{I}_i | \text{Tastes}_i)$, as specified in equation (1) above, where now p_i is a vector of public-good tax prices. The resulting model of budgetary choice is therefore

$$(2) \quad g_t = \sum_{i=1}^{n} \alpha_i(g°, S) \cdot f_{it}(p_i, \hat{I}_i | \text{Tastes}_i), \quad t = 1 \ldots m,$$

where

$$\sum_{i=1}^{n} \alpha_i(.) \equiv 1,$$

and where there are $t = 1 \ldots m$ public services and $i = 1 \ldots n$ identifiable voter types or interest groups. Variables that might be included in the vector S of political structure include controlling interests (chairmanship, majority) of the legislative committees that set the agenda, jurisdiction and budgetary and bargaining rules on how dollars can be allocated, size of voting blocs within the legislature or community, political allegiance of those with veto power over final allocations (e.g., governor, mayor), and amendment rules that allow proposals to be submitted from at-large interests. The budgetary model outlined here—once it has been estimated—gives us exactly what we need to begin to analyze the effects of changes in federal dollars and fiscal structures on state-local allocations. Three recent studies (Craig and Inman 1982, Gramlich 1982, and Craig and Inman 1984) have examined President Reagan's new federalism from this perspective; their results are instructive as to the likely budgetary consequences of the proposed Reagan reforms.

THE MEDICAID-WELFARE SWAP: WHAT WILL HAPPEN TO LOW INCOME ASSISTANCE?

Gramlich (1982) and Craig and Inman (1984) have examined the likely consequences of the new federalism's proposed exchange of the food stamps and AFDC programs for Medicaid. Both studies reach essentially the same conclusion: the states will appreciably reduce their support of low income maintenance programs despite federal assumption of Medicaid and the availability of $27.6 billion in trust fund aid.

Employing an analytic framework similar to that proposed in Equation 2 above, Gramlich and Craig–Inman estimate the effects of the current fiscal structure—categorical matching aid for AFDC and Medicaid, federal provision of food stamps, and the availability of general revenue-sharing and other (nearly) unrestricted, lump-sum aid—on the state decision to provide AFDC benefits (Gramlich) and AFDC plus other low-income assistance (Craig–Inman).[7] Both studies find that dropping federal, categorical matching aid for AFDC and giving states full financial responsibility for the program will reduce spending for AFDC by at least 70 percent and perhaps as much as 95 percent. Gramlich arrives at the larger estimate when he allows for the fact that states are likely to adjust their benefit levels to those of their neighboring, fiscally competitive states. Since high benefit levels are likely to attract low-income families (see Gramlich's paper in this volume) and possibly discourage the location of richer families and firms, no state can afford high benefit levels by itself. Once the federal categorical matching aid, a strong incentive for high benefits, is removed, interstate fiscal competition dominates the allocation process, and AFDC spending is likely to fall dramatically.

Both studies conclude that low-income support from the food stamp program will also be significantly reduced. They find that state officials seem to behave as if food stamp benefits do not exist; in other words, it is a federal program and provides no direct political benefit to state politicians. A program thus ignored in the past will probably be supported only marginally under reform. The net effect of the new federalism's food-stamp transfer will be to reduce this form of assistance drastically, if not totally. Together, the transfer of AFDC and food stamps to the states is estimated to reduce the total spending on these programs by 70 percent or more.

Federal assumption of state Medicaid payments may also reduce the states' contribution to low-income medical assistance. First, as the federal government takes over the program, the previous federal Medicaid matching grant to the states is lost (i.e., the matching rate falls to zero) and state spending for low-income medical assistance declines. Second, the federal government will pay such low-income medical assistance directly to residents within the state, a possible inducement for the states to eliminate any remaining low-income medical-assistance programs. Craig and Inman (1984) estimate that the combined effect of these forces about equals the current level of state expenditures on Medicaid; that is, state welfare spending will fall by the amount of spending assumed by the federal government when it takes over Medicaid (~$19 billion).

The new federalism does offer the states financial assistance, however, and some of this relief may spill over into low income assistance. The proposed trust-fund account is to pay states $27.6 billion a year initially (less in future years). Craig and Inman estimate that trust fund aid will have no significant effect on low income assistance and may in fact depress welfare spending. Other studies (reviewed in Inman [1979]) also show no major positive effect of lump-sum aid on welfare outlays. It therefore seems safe to assume that trust fund assistance will do little to offset any decline in welfare spending.

What, then, will be the overall effect of the new federalism on state-provided low-income assistance? As we have seen, a conservative estimate is that AFDC and food stamp spending will fall by 70 percent when transferred to the state-local sector. In 1983, the federal and state governments combined spent approximately $24.04 billion on AFDC and food stamps.[8] The new federalism will reduce this total by $16.83 billion. With the Medicaid transfer, state expenditures on medical assistance for the poor will fall by approximately $19 billion, but federal spending is assumed to rise to fill this gap. There is therefore no net effect on low income assistance from the Medicaid transfer.[9] The introduction of $27.6 billion in trust fund assistance is estimated to have no effect on state welfare spending. The combined effect of the new federalism reform is therefore an estimated decline of at least $16.83 billion in aid to low-income families provided by all levels of government. From the perspective of a typical low-income family, the new federalism may mean a loss of $2406 annually, approximately a 44 percent decline in average annual benefits.[10] Clearly, the new federalism is an important fiscal reform affecting low-income households.

THE TRUST-FUND AND PROGRAM TURNBACK: WHAT WILL HAPPEN TO SERVICE PROVISION?

The sixty-one federal categorical-aid programs proposed for transfer to the states include programs in education, social services, transportation, and community development. Also included is the general revenue-sharing program. In their place the federal government will establish a trust fund that will pay to the states a lump-sum grant approximately equal to the costs of transferred categorical-aid programs. This component of the new federalism essentially substitutes unconstrained aid for categorical aid. What will happen to the provision of government services in the affected program areas?

Gramlich's (1982) analysis gives an overview of the likely effects of fiscal reform. He finds that the loss of $1 of federal categorical aid will lower state-local service expenditures by $0.38; the gain of $1 of federal lump-sum assistance will increase state-local service spending by $0.04. Gramlich's estimates of the state-local sector's response to lump-sum, revenue-sharing assistance is somewhat lower than that obtained by other researchers (see Inman 1979), but it should be pointed out that his sample covers the state-local experience to 1981 and therefore includes those governments' response to the recent pressure for fiscal responsibility and tax relief. Accepting Gramlich's estimates, we can calculate the aggregate effect of the new federalism on service provision. Turning sixty-one federal programs over to the states is equivalent to a loss of $25.6 billion in categorical aid and, since general revenue-sharing is included in the turnback program, a loss of $4.6 billion in lump-sum aid. The loss of $25.6 billion in categorical aid will reduce state-local service provision by $9.7 billion (= 0.38 × $25.60). The loss of $4.6 billion in revenue-sharing aid will reduce state-local service provision by $0.2 billion (= 0.04 × $4.60). The trust fund, on the other hand, increases federal lump-sum aid by $27.6 billion; the state-local sector's response is to increase state-local provision by $1.1 billion (= 0.04 × $27.60). The final net effect of the new federalism is to reduce state-local spending initially by $8.8 billion. This loss is equivalent to a decline of $16 per capita in services (measured in 1972 dollars) or a fall in public-service provision by the state-local sector of 2.1 percent from the 1983 service level of $768.40 per capita (see Table 1.1, column 7).

Craig and Inman's (1984) analysis of the trust-fund exchange shows a similar, though slightly larger, decline in state-local spending. Their equilibrium analysis predicts that the trust fund–program swap will reduce state taxes by 6 percent (due to relaxed matching requirements), lower state education aid and total state welfare spending by 5 percent and 33 percent respectively, and leave other state spending virtually unchanged. The states' human resource budgets seem to bear the full brunt of the spending cuts. Local government spending may rise to offset some of the decline, but the local increase will probably not match the fall in state spending.

A more detailed look at state-local education spending shows that this is exactly what happens. Craig and Inman (1982) have examined the effects of Reagan's new federalism on spending for one of the most important program areas—elementary and secondary education. Their results are suggestive of what may happen to expenditures on the other directly affected services. After estimating an econometric model of state and local school spending, Craig and Inman simulate the effects of the

TABLE I.5

The New Federalism and State-Local Education Spending

Proposal	State aid*	State tax*	Local spending*	Local tax*
Status quo (1977)	$375.58	$1025.86	$670.99	$282.34
New federalism	290.20	924.42	616.35	326.15

*Dollars per public-school enrollee.
SOURCE: Craig and Inman (1982), table 4.

new federalism in which fourteen categorical education aid programs are consolidated into a single trust-fund, or lump-sum, grant to states. Table 1.5 summarizes their results, where spending in 1977 (the last year of their sample) defines the baseline, or pre-reform, allocation. In the status quo period, the average state allocated $375.58 per public-school enrollee for state aid for education. The average state raised $1,025.86 per enrollee in state taxes, where the difference between taxes and state education aid ($650.28 per enrollee) was allocated to other, non-education state expenditures. Local school districts spent $670.99 per enrollee on education, and raised $286.34 per enrollee in local taxes to support this spending. The remaining $386.65 per enrollee of local spending was financed by state education aid ($375.58) and direct federal-to-local school aid ($9.07 per enrollee). Following new federalism reforms, Craig–Inman estimate that state support for public elementary and secondary education will fall by about 23 percent, to $290.20.

The primary reason for this decline is the same that led to a decline in welfare spending: the new federalism substitutes less constraining lump-sum aid for categorical and categorical matching aid.[11] Left on their own, states do not want to maintain spending on public education. What happens to the money now freed from the state education budget by the new federalism? The released $85.38 per enrollee (= $375.58 – $290.20) is allocated to tax relief; total state tax relief is $101.44/enrollee (= $1,025.86 – $924.42) supported in part by a fall in other (administrative?) state expenses.[12] The fall in state-to-local education aid and federal-to-local education aid reduces local school spending by about 8 percent, or $616.35/enrollee. To maintain this level of spending, local taxes must rise by 14 percent, to $326.15/enrollee. The new spending level is supported entirely by local taxes and state aid (616.35 = $326.15 + $290.20). This detailed analysis of the new federalism's effects on education reveals three important conclusions. First, education itself is not a particularly favored activity of state governments; it is federal categorical aid that keeps state funding at its present levels. Second, as the federal and state governments retreat from a fiscal responsibility for education, local school districts fill the void, somewhat; clearly, with the new federalism, financial responsibility for public education moves downward to the local level. Third, as President Reagan might have hoped, the new federalism will alter the mix of national income allocated between the private and public sectors. State taxation is lowered by $101/enrollee, while local school taxes rise by about $40/enrollee. The net result is a $61/enrollee increase in private income.

SUMMARY

It is hoped by the proponents of the new federalism that the proposed reforms will reverse the trend toward federalization of our public economy and to a large degree shift the activity of government back to the state and local levels. The analysis summarized here suggests that they will not be disappointed. The very nature of the reform reallocates responsibilities from the federal to the state-local sector, and there is nothing in the empirical research reviewed here to suggest that reforms will not be decentralizing. The states, for example, have not been held in line by federal programs so that, now unleashed, they can spend unchecked to replace one bureaucracy with another. Quite the contrary, the evidence indicates that the states will retreat from many of these categorical program areas too and, at least in the case of education, will be eager to pass fiscal responsibility down still further, to the local level.

The empirical analyses of the new federalism reveal another important consequence of reform, one which might please President Reagan even more than the move to decentralization. The new federalism will likely shrink the size of government. The exchange of Medicaid for AFDC and food stamps will markedly reduce spending on income maintenance programs and return those released dollars to state taxpayers as tax relief. The new federalism's exchange of the lump-sum trust fund aid for categorical aid also means tax relief. Craig and Inman (1982) find that, in education at least, the resulting lower level of state education spending is transferred to taxpayers as state tax relief. Local education taxes do rise, but not by enough to offset the decline in state taxation. Again, the overall size of government is reduced and taxpayers' private incomes are increased.

From the point of view of those who wish to decentralize fiscal choice and to decrease the size of government, the answer must be *yes* to the question: Will the new federalism work?

NEW FEDERALISM AS A FEDERAL ISSUE

If Reagan's new federalism will check the tide of fiscal centralization and shrink government, why then, in this era of apparent fiscal conservatism has the new federalism not been approved by the federal government? The early debates of the reform raised the obvious questions. There was much discussion about the accuracy of the administration's estimates of program costs, and the states were obviously disappointed about the projected 1988–1991 phase-out of the supporting trust fund. Would the dollar trade really be a fair one? But if a balancing of dollars was all that was at issue, we should have resolved the difference long ago. We have not. The matter runs deeper than that. The new federalism is not simply a realignment of programs between the federal and state-local sectors of government, it is a fundamental challenge to how public policy decisions are now made. Our existing, highly federalized fiscal structure did not just happen. It has evolved, I will argue, as a logical outcome of a changing federal political structure and a growing economic pressure on local governments to redistribute resources. Until the political structure changes again—and in a particular way—or until the demand for redistribution subsides, our fiscal structure will remain largely as it now stands: categorical, regulated, and centralized.

The pressure to use government as a means to redistribute resources among the members of the society is endemic to stable economies. Coalitions of potential beneficiaries form around existing, shared institutions capable of transferring dollars in their direction. Producer or consumer groups form about markets; the religious, the poor, and the ill cluster about churches; and all of us look to government for assistance. Small groups can generally organize more quickly and efficiently than large groups; while the fortunes of individual redistributive coalitions may rise or fall, such coalitions rarely die (see Olson 1982). American economic history is rich in examples of the growth and influence of redistributive coalitions (see, e.g., North 1981; Olson 1982).

With the baby boom and the explosion of home ownership and suburbanization following World War II, a new and fertile ground for the growth of such coalitions appeared—state and, most importantly, local governments. Table 1.1, column 6, illustrates the increasingly important role of the state and local sector in the provision of domestic public goods and services. The growth was particularly explosive from 1945 to 1960 as the share of the state-local sector in public-good provision rose from 69.3 percent to 84.5 percent. During this same period the number of municipal, township, and special district governments grew from 43,440 in 1942 to 56,417 in 1967.[13] The period from 1945 to 1960 saw the emergence of new redistributive coalitions with their focii almost exclusively on local government. Public employee unionization began in earnest in this period. The National Teachers Association began its slow evolution from a social and professional society to a politically active union, prodded in part by the aggressive, blatantly redistributive behavior of the newly formed American Federation of Teachers. In our larger cities, downtown business interests began to organize for the development, or redevelopment, of shopping, residential, and business centers. In the suburbs, developers lobbied for new infrastructure (paid for by tax-exempt bonds) and zoning variances. Even the large group of inner-city poor had become organized into a politically active redistributive coalition, the National Welfare Rights Organization. Each of these coalitions—public employees, business groups, the poor—turned to local governments for more—more pay, more services, more transfers. Yet the local public sector had only limited resources, and it was severely constrained by the mobility of its tax base. It was only natural that, as the brokers in the redistribution game, local officials should seek more dollars. They organized too, and in the 1960s they went to Washington as the "intergovernmental" lobby.[14] Would Washington respond?

Washington did respond—with creative federalism. The redistributive coalitions collecting about the local public sector had created a new demand for transfers. The supply of those transfers came from a United States Congress that by the mid 1960s found it particularly attractive to be responsive. Domestic policies began to assume a decidedly regional and local focus. The fiscal structure we now call creative federalism, with its extensive use of categorical aid, project aid, and federal regulations, is one consequence of this change.

Two events converged to produce this important shift. First, American voters were becoming better educated and better informed. The old political party labels were no longer sufficient to insure voter loyalty. Nie, Verba, and Petrocik (1979) found the 1960s voter to differ in important ways from the 1950s voter. There were more independents, and even those voters who wore a party label found it easy to desert the party leadership when proposed policies did not meet their demands. Second, as voters became more independent so did their congressional representatives. For exogenous reasons the strong central leadership of Lyndon Johnson in the Senate and Sam Rayburn in the House gave way in the 1960s to the less autocratic styles of Mansfield and McCormack. The 1964 Democratic landslide brought a new and active group of Democratic liberals into the House, many representing urban local coalitions. The old, fabled "conservative coalition" of Republicans and southern Democrats gave way, lost in a flurry of liberal legislation—including Medicaid, federal grants for education, urban poverty programs, and the creation of the Department of Housing and Urban Development. Much of the legislation was a response of a sympathetic Congress to the memory of a president deeply committed to social legislation.

The period 1967–1970 was one of frustration for the Democratic liberals. A fall in their numbers from the peak in 1965–1966, division within their ranks over the war in Vietnam, the election of a Republican president, and the return to importance of the conservative coalition thwarted the efforts of liberal, urban Democrats to introduce further domestic legislation. These three years proved only a temporary setback in the trend toward a more open, more locally focused Congress. Beginning in 1970, a series of procedural reforms initiated by the liberals were enacted by the Democratic Caucus and by the whole House. The intention of the reforms was to open the key leadership positions of the House—committee and subcommittee chairmanships—to more members, not just the senior, select few (for an interesting description of the process by which these reforms were introduced, see Ornstein 1975). The result was a more diffuse, younger, liberal leadership. The incentives within this more decentralized structure no longer encouraged individual representatives to look to the older leadership for signals on how to form policy. Rather, the structure encouraged offering a favored policy and bargaining with other members for its approval. And how should a representative define a policy agenda? Again, not by turning to the central leadership or to the Democratic or the Republican party. Their approval no longer won local congressional elections. The representative's policy agenda came from the local voters, for if local voters were satisfied, reelection was guaranteed (see Fiorina 1977, esp. chs. 4 and 5). The policies and budgets that emerge from such a decentralized political body will themselves be decentralized in their effects, satisfying the needs of each representative and the redistributive coalitions he or she represents.[15] When representatives are chosen from geographically prescribed areas, policies will assume a clear regional or local focus. Creative feder alism stands as a telling example of what such a political process will produce.

A decentralized congressional policy process seeking to satisfy the demands of local redistributive coalitions will necessarily design policies that will target federal dollars to local areas. Further, these dollars must be targeted to particular redistributive coalitions in a way that will assure that the congressional representative can claim credit for the transfer. Finally, if the federal dollars can be leveraged from other, non-local revenue sources such as the state, so much the better. What type of federal grants policy will achieve these objectives? The answer is categorical project aid and formula aid that uses the states whenever possible as the administrative agent but that monitors state performance closely with "pass-through" and, ideally, matching requirements. To the extent that local redistributive coalitions do not trust the states to administer the grant in their favor, the federal program will bypass the states and give dollars to local governments, or perhaps to private groups directly. Finally, since there are many congressional districts to be satisfied and each district has a different set of local redistributive coalitions, a wide range of federal grants programs are needed, with, ideally, each program capable of allocating dollars to specific local coalitions.

Not surprisingly, exactly this grants system, which we now call creative federalism, emerged over the decade 1963–1973. Table 1.4 shows the proliferation of project-aid and categorical-formula grants. Project-aid programs, the most flexible form of grant and the most susceptible to congressional direction, nearly tripled in number from 1962 to 1976 (Chernick 1979, Arnold 1981, and Plott 1968 present interesting studies of possible congressional control of project aid). The number of categorical formula grants more than doubled during this period; many of these grants employ state "pass-through" requirements and almost all have a state matching provision of some kind.[16] Further, when the states could not be trusted to target federal aid to local coalitions, direct federal-to-local programs were devised; see Table 1.3. By 1973, direct federal-to-local aid had become nearly 20 percent of all federal categorical assistance. Most of this assistance was for urban areas, bypassing state governments presumably to avoid their rural-suburban bias (see Maxwell and Aronson 1977, tables 3.1, 3.2). Finally, as the analysis predicts, almost all local governments in the country received some categorical aid. A national survey of local governments in 1974 by the Advisory Commission on Intergovernmental Relations (1978) indicated that 73.3 percent of the responding city governments received federal categorical aid, and

80.6 percent of the responding county governments received such assistance. The typical city in the survey obtained money from an average of 9.3 grants; the typical county obtained money from an average of 20.6 grants. By the mid 1970s, we had in place a federalist fiscal structure which stood as the logical outcome of the economics and politics of its time.

One anomaly in the recent history seems to run against this logic—General Revenue Sharing (GRS). In fact, however, close examination of the GRS history reveals that it was shaped by the same economic pressures and the same political structure that has given us creative federalism. When all the political maneuvering was done, the bill approved in June 1972 looked very little like the first Nixon proposal presented in August 1969. The initial Nixon plan gave 73 percent of the money to states, and those states that paid more *federal* taxes got more federal GRS aid. The GRS bill that was passed gave most of the aid to local governments (66 percent), aid given to the states contained an implicit match on *state* taxes, and the final distribution of money across local governments was effectively on the basis of population—i.e., equal funds per capita (see Nathan, Manuel, and Calkin 1975). Lastly, GRS was all *new* money for local governments; it did not replace any existing categorical aid programs. In effect, the political history of GRS proves to be just another chapter in our story.[17]

President Reagan's new federalism seeks to put an end to this tale called creative federalism. Will he succeed? The answer, I think, is *no*. The economic pressures and the political structure that produced creative federalism are still in force. The new federalism is too fundamental a change to be embraced by those who now benefit from our present fiscal structure.

Members of the House, for example, now have a wide range of categorical aid programs which direct federal resources to their favored local coalitions. As Representative John Brademas, the author of a number of categorical aid programs, commented concerning the local activities financed by general revenue sharing, "They don't even ask us to the ribbon-cutting ceremonies" (quoted in Beer 1976, p. 185). It is difficult for a member of Congress to claim credit for tax relief and general trust-fund grants—unlike classrooms, roadways, sewers, or jobs—when running for reelection. Congress prefers particularized programs (see, e.g., Mayhew 1974, pp. 53–57).

State and local officials have also shied away from Reagan's new federalism. The states, of course, were eager to give up Medicaid since it meant freed dollars, but they did not want to take on AFDC and food stamps in return. And for good reasons. State and local officials prefer redistribution to be handled at the federal level. Only in those few states with no significant low-income population will state officials prefer a decentralized welfare system. Those states can neutralize any political pressure from their small low-income group while receiving the spill-in benefits of being a low-transfer, low-tax state. Elected officials in all other states, however, will feel the pressure of having to do something for the poor at the same time that they try to control taxes on firms and mobile upper-income households. The current federal categorical welfare programs make these hard decisions for them and apply them uniformly across all the states. State officials want more lump-sum aid, but not at the price of fewer welfare aid programs and greater interstate competition (see Rose-Ackerman 1981). Local officials fear the loss of regulated, categorical aid, for the simple reason that they see less money coming their way. As Craig–Inman (1982) show for education aid, when the federal strings are loosened, the level of state-to-local support can fall significantly (see the comments of state and local officials in *National Journal* 1982).

Finally, voters have not risen to demand reform, and there are two good reasons for this. First, many voters are direct beneficiaries of categorical aid; people do not want to lose the flow of dollars to their redistributive coalition. Some voters, however, do not benefit directly from the present federalized fiscal system. They pay taxes but get no return transfers. Craig–Inman (1982) have shown that the new federalism may mean significant tax relief. Why, then, have taxpayers not formed a coalition in support of the new federalism? The answer is simply that low-spending, tax-relief coalitions are hard to put together. We all benefit a little from the hard work of a few. Yet almost no one—elected local representatives or private citizens—can afford to be one of the hardworking few for tax relief. What is required is a national coalition held together by a commitment to the coalition's central objective, even when it is in everyone's best interest to "free-ride" on the group. Such coalitions may occur once in a while—the FY1982 budget and tax cut is an example—but not often.[18]

It is not surprising, then, that the new federalism has not yet won congressional approval. Our current fiscal system is what it is because of political and economic forces which will not be easily reversed. Whether a new economic coalition of taxpayers arises and proves that it can compete effectively within a special-interest political system as another special interest remains to be seen. To date, the proponents of the new federalism have not yet succeeded in fashioning such a coalition.

CONCLUSION

A federalist fiscal structure is an ever-evolving institution, responding, as will all societal institutions, to changing economic and political pressures. Our present structure, creative federalism, is the logical consequence of a rising pressure on local governments to respond to new local coalitions, and of a congressional political system that rewards those who are most responsive to these local demands. The resulting fiscal system channels federal funds to local governments and organizations via many narrowly prescribed categorical grants closely monitored by Washington. While such a fiscal system can be rationalized historically, there are good reasons to doubt its economic logic. Too much money is being spent on too many marginally inefficient programs.[19] A cutback and a restructuring of our aid program seem in order. Reagan's new federalism is one such proposal and, as we have seen, it is likely to have its intended effects of decentralizing fiscal choice and shrinking the size of government. Gramlich (this volume) has offered a plausible alternative reform package.[20] Neither reform, however, is likely to win congressional approval in the near future, for the simple reason that what is now in place is Congress's preferred response to our present economic and political environment. Only a substantial change in that environment will lead to substantial change in our fiscal structure.

ACKNOWLEDGMENTS

This paper was written while the author was a visiting professor of economics at the University of California, Berkeley. It was financed in part by NSF grant SES-8112001 to the author and by a grant from the Center for Real Estate and Urban Economics, University of California, Berkeley. The financial support of these organizations is appreciated. Ken Shepsle, Art Frank, Dan Rubinfeld, and John Quigley were kind enough to read and comment on an earlier version of this paper, for which I am grateful.

NOTES

1. The 10th Amendment to the U.S. Constitution explicitly provides that "the powers not delegated to the United States by the Constitution nor prohibited by it to the States, are reserved to the States, respectively, or to the people." The courts, however, have historically given a broad interpretation to the ability of Congress to make laws that regulate the affairs of the states—for example, *McCulloch* v. *Maryland* (1819). Only recently have the courts shown much willingness to limit congressional control over the states: see *National League*

of Cities v. *Usery* (1976). For a useful introduction to the history of federal relations toward state and local governments, see Advisory Commission on Intergovernmental Relations (1981).

2. Federal grants given to the state-local sector are counted as state-local expenditures when spent by the state-local sector, and grants are not included in the federal spending share. Thus, grants given back to residents as tax relief are not counted as government spending.

3. George Break reports a revealing exchange between Representative Charles Goodell of New York and Anthony Celebrezze, then secretary of HEW. "What makes me tear my hair in frustration is when people like you come and say there are not controls," said Goodell, referring to federal education aid to state-local governments. Celebrezze replied: "You call it control. I refer to it as the objectives of the legislation." See Break (1980), p. 137.

4. The estimated $16.4 billion AFDC and food stamp budget averages to $32.8 per capita (1972 dollars). Cited figures are obtained by subtracting this amount from the federal transfers-to-persons and adding it to the state and local transfers.

5. The first four years of the new federalism would maintain the trust fund at $27.6 billion, but beginning in 1988 the fund would be reduced by 25 percent each year until 1991, when the fund would disappear. Since the fund is to be supported by federal excise taxes on gasoline, alcohol, tobacco, and phone services and by the windfall-profits tax, and since these taxes will be earmarked for the fund, phasing out the fund is equivalent to phasing out these federal taxes. Thus the new federalism—in addition to its effect on federal spending shares—will reduce the federal share in total government receipts. The tax effect, however, will be trivial, lowering the federal share from 68 percent in 1983 (Table 1.2) to no less than 67 percent by 1991, the final date of tax phase-out. In making this calculation I have assumed that all government receipts will grow at 6 percent per year until 1991, and on that date $27.6 billion in taxes will disappear from the federal budget and be replaced by a $27.6 billion increase in state-local taxes.

6. More formally, p equals $\{(1-m)c\}\{(1-q)(b/B)\}$, where c is the per-unit production cost of the public service, m is the federal matching share of state-local spending on the aided service, q is the resident's marginal federal tax rate, $(1-q)$ measures the share of state-local taxes actually paid (after deducting these taxes) against the resident's federal tax liability, and (b/B), the ratio of the resident's tax base to the community's total tax base, measures the resident's share of total state-local tax costs when the tax structure is proportional (as it typically is).

7. In addition to AFDC benefits, states provide funds for Medicaid, the Supplemental Security Income program (SSI), and their own state general assistance program and other targeted aid for low-income families. Craig and Inman (forthcoming) include all these state programs in their analysis.

8. The federal expenditure was set at $16.4 billion. Since 1983 state data are not yet available, our state expenditures were estimated in 1983 at $7.64 billion—the 1981 total ($6.76 billion) times one plus the increase in the government price deflator from 1981 to 1983 (1.13).

9. These calculations assume that the federal government makes no adjustment in Medicaid spending. That, however, is unlikely; see Russell (1983). Medicaid assistance is likely to be reduced as well.

10. In 1981 there were 7.115 million households receiving food stamps. Since almost all AFDC families receive food stamps, I assume the low-income target population to be 7 million families. A loss of $16.84 billion averages to $2406 per low-income family. In 1981 a typical low-income family received $1617/family from food stamps (= $11.320 billion food stamp expenditure/7.115 million food stamp families). In 1981, a typical AFDC low-income family received $282/month in benefits, $3384/year. Together, the two programs provide benefits of $5001/family, in 1981 dollars. Inflating 1981 benefits by the increase in the cost-of-living from 1981 to 1983 gives an estimate of $5514/family in total benefits in 1983. New federalism will reduce this benefit by 43.6 percent (= $2406/$5514). For another analysis of new federalism and welfare spending by the states, see Chernick (1982).

11. It must be pointed out that the Craig and Inman simulations also assume a decline

of 25 percent in total federal support. The decline in aid, however, accounts for only a small fraction of the decline in state support for local education. Simply cutting federal aid by 25 percent but retaining all categorical aid programs will reduce state aid for education by only $5/enrollee; see Craig–Inman (1982), table 4.

12. The Congressional Budget Office has estimated the administrative costs to states of federal education aid as being $0.04 per dollar of categorical assistance. In 1977, the state received approximately $41/enrollee of such aid. Thus administrative savings would be about $1.64/enrollee. However, Craig and Inman mention that for econometric reasons their tax relief estimate may be too large. Whether other state expenditures really fall by $16/enrollee, as implied by these estimates, must remain an open issue.

13. Bureau of the Census (1975), p. 1086. During this period the number of counties declined from 3050 to 3049. The number of school districts also decreased, but of course school spending and the number of school employees increased dramatically.

14. Members include the Council of State Governments, the National Governors' Conference, the National Legislative Conference (state legislative officials), the National Association of Counties, the National League of Cities, the U.S. Conference of Mayors, and the International City Management Association. For an interesting discussion of the intergovernmental lobby and federal grants policy, see Beer (1976).

15. For a theoretical model of why a diffuse, locally directed political body will produce a diffuse and locally directed set of public policies, see Shepsle and Weingast (1981) and Weingast, Shepsle, and Johnsen (1981). For one application of the theory, see Stockman (1975), who describes the "social pork barrel" in just these terms. See also Fiorina and Noll (1978), who argue that not only will decentralized legislatures produce many targeted expenditure programs, but they will also tend to create programs that are regulated and bureaucratized. Why? So that the representatives can play the role of ombudsmen for local coalitions in their relationships to the central administration.

16. *Pass-through* is the requirement that a fraction of federal-aid dollars paid to the state must be passed on to local governments. Pass-through restrictions are an important component of state-to-local aid, involving as much as 30 percent of all state-to-local aid; see Advisory Commission on Intergovernmental Relations (1980), tables A-31, A-32. Pass-through aid is an even larger share of federal-to-state aid and nearly as important as direct federal-to-local aid. Almost all the programs that use state governments use matching provisions as well. Matching aid programs became particularly popular after 1964; see Advisory Commission on Intergovernmental Relations (1978), p. 28. One implication of the model of creative federalism proposed here is that federal pass-through and matching requirements should be closely monitored at the state level to insure that dollars do flow to local coalitions, but once aid dollars have reached the local public sector, local coalitions should be allowed to spend them as they wish. In the jargon of grants analysis, federal-to-state aid should be closely monitored and not easily made fungible while state-to-local aid and federal-to-local aid ought to be highly fungible. There is some econometric evidence in support of these two propositions: see Craig–Inman (1982), who show that targeted programs do get support from states (while other programs lose), and McGuire (1978), who finds a high degree of fungibility in federal and state education aid given to local communities.

17. Samuel Beer (1976) has written this chapter. After his careful analysis of the political maneuvering behind the passage of GRS, he concludes that the "tendency [of GRS] is rather to increase the supply of public goods by subnational governments, while maintaining and enhancing the existing territorial fragmentation of power among these governments, with little regard for merit or need." In other words, GRS was just more money for the redistributive coalitions that have collected about local governments. At the same time that Nixon proposed GRS, he proposed repackaging ten categorical grants into a single block grant for cities. In 1974, the Housing and Community Development Act was approved. Under the provisions of the new act, the major urban categorical grants would be consolidated and would continue at approximately the same funding levels, and aid would be directed to the same local governments that had received assistance under the categorical programs. "Hold-harmless" provisions were included to protect local aid levels. Little was changed by this reform. To complete the historical record, it should be noted that GRS for state

government has now been eliminated, but that GRS funding to local governments remains intact.

18. The problem of forming a low-spending/low tax coalition can be cast as a classic prisoners' dilemma problem. It may well be in the interest of all of us to reduce government spending and taxes, but not one of us is willing to give up our own favorite programs for this end unless we can be guaranteed that all other voters or congressional districts will also give up their favorite programs. Such guarantees are hard to establish and often require a strong centralizing influence. Olson (1982) makes this problem a central theme in his analysis of the economic decline of nations.

19. A detailed benefit-cost analysis of our existing federal aid structure has not been performed, but there are good theoretical reasons to suspect we have too much aid and that it is allocated inefficiently. Gramlich (this volume) offers a well-structured critique of our current system. For a general analysis of why we are likely to have too much aid, see Weingast, Shepsle, and Johnsen (1981). For how a benefit-cost analysis of a grants program might be done, see my study (Inman 1978) of our present educational aid system. There I conclude that existing New York state education aid is too expensive relative to benefits provided and that the program can be significantly reduced and redesigned to achieve greater efficiency or equity. See also Gomez-Ibañez (1984) for an analysis of our current transportation aid programs.

20. A note is perhaps the right place to express my views on what our aid structure should be. I have a good deal of sympathy with the normative arguments offered by Gramlich in his paper, though I disagree on some minor points. I support Gramlich's proposal for centralizing the financing of a national floor to low-income support and allowing optional state supplementation. Once such a program is in place, I see little need for block grants or general-revenue-sharing aid to state or local governments. In program areas where significant spillovers may exist I prefer, as does Gramlich, a broadly cut categorical matching grant. Education, health care, and public housing are possible program areas. Since I see most spillovers as "merit wants," I favor a pro–low-income matching grant formula. I have examined such policies in detail for education finance (see Inman 1978). In my favorite reform package, I would also eliminate the federal deduction for state and local taxes. The resulting increase in federal taxes could be allocated to the low-income support programs or to an overall lowering of federal tax rates. Finally, I see a need for matching aid for the *maintenance* of inner-city capital stocks. This could easily be achieved by allowing our existing aid programs to reimburse maintenance as well as new construction outlays (see Gomez-Ibañez 1984).

REFERENCES

Advisory Commission on Intergovernmental Relations. 1978. *Categorical Grants: Their Role and Design.* No. A-52. Washington, D.C.: U.S. Government Printing Office.

———. 1980. *Recent Trends in Federal and State Aid to Local Governments.* No. M-118. Washington, D.C.: U.S. Government Printing Office.

———. 1981. *The Conditions of Contemporary Federalism: Conflicting Theories and Collapsing Constraints.* No. A-78. Washington, D.C.: U.S. Government Printing Office.

———. N.d. *Regulatory Federalism: Policy, Process, Impact and Reform.* No. B-7. Washington, D.C.

Arnold, D. 1981. "The Local Roots of Domestic Policy." Pp. 250–87 in T. E. Mann and N. J. Ornstein, eds., *The New Congress.* Washington, D.C.: American Enterprise Institute.

Beer, S. 1976. "The Adoption of General Revenue Sharing: A Case Study in Public Sector Politics." *Public Policy* 24: 127–96.

Bowen, H. 1943. "The Interpretation of Voting in the Allocation of Economic Resources." *Quarterly Journal of Economics* 58: 27–48.

Break, G. 1980. *Financing Government in a Federal System.* Washington, D.C.: Brookings Institution.

Bureau of the Census. 1975. *Historical Statistics of the United States, Colonial Times to 1970.* Washington, D.C.: U.S. Government Printing Office.

———. 1983. *Statistical Abstract of the United States, 1983.* Washington, D.C.: U.S. Government Printing Office.

Bureau of Economic Analysis. 1981. *National Income and Product Accounts, 1929–1976.* Washington, D.C.: U.S. Government Printing Office.

———. 1984. *Survey of Current Business.* Vol. 64. Washington, D.C.: U.S. Government Printing Office.

Chernick, H. 1979. "An Economic Model of the Distribution of Project Grants." Pp. 81–103 in P. Mieszkowski and W. Oakland, eds., *Fiscal Federalism and Grants-in-Aid.* Washington, D.C.: Urban Institute.

———. 1982. "Block Grants for the Needy: The Case of AFDC." *Journal of Policy Analysis and Management* 1: 209–222.

Council of Economic Advisors. 1984. *Economic Report of the President, February, 1984.* Washington, D.C.: U.S. Government Printing Office.

Craig, S., and R. P. Inman. 1982. "Federal Aid and Public Education: An Empirical Look at the New Fiscal Federalism." *Review of Economics and Statistics* 64: 541–52.

———. Forthcoming. "Education, Welfare, and the New Federalism: State Budgeting in a Federalist Public Economy." In H. Rosen, ed., *Studies in State and Local Public Finance.* Chicago: Chicago University Press.

Filimon, R., T. Romer, and H. Rosenthal. 1982. "Asymmetric Information and Agenda Control: The Basis of Monopoly Power in Public Spending." *Journal of Public Economics* 17: 51–70.

Fiorina, M. 1977. *Congress: Keystone of the Washington Establishment.* New Haven: Yale University Press.

Fiorina, M., and R. Noll. 1978. "Voters, Bureaucrats and Legislators: A Rational Choice Perspective on the Growth of Bureaucracy." *Journal of Public Economics* 9: 239–54.

Gomez-Ibañez, J. A. 1984. "The Federal Role in Urban Transportation." This volume.

Gramlich, E. 1969. "The Effects of Federal Grants on State and Local Expenditures: A Review of the Econometric Literature." Pp. 569–83 in *Proceedings of the 62nd Annual Conference on Taxation.* Lexington, Ky.: National Tax Association.

———. 1982. "An Econometric Examination of the New Federalism." Pp. 327–60 in *Brookings Papers on Economic Activity.*

Hamilton, B. 1983. "The Flypaper Effect and Other Anomalies." *Journal of Public Economics* 22: 347–62.

Inman, R. P. 1978. "Optional Fiscal Reform of Metropolitan Schools: Some Simulation Results." *American Economic Review* 68: 107–122.

———. 1979. "Fiscal Performances of Local Governments." Pp. 270–321 in P. Mieszkowski and M. Straszheim, eds., *Current Issues in Urban Economics.* Baltimore: Johns Hopkins University Press.

————. 1981. "Wages, Pensions, and Employment in the Local Public Sector."
Pp. 11–57 in P. Mieszkowski and G. Peterson, eds., *Public Sector Labor Markets: COUPE Papers on Public Economics*, Vol. 4.

————. Forthcoming. "Markets, Governments and the 'New' Political Economy." In A. Auerbach and M. S. Feldstein, eds., *Handbook of Public Economics*, Vol. 2. Amsterdam: North-Holland.

Jackman, R., and J. Papdachi. 1981. "Local Authority Education Expenditure in England and Wales." Pp. 47–62 in M. J. Bowman, ed., *Collective Choice in Education*. The Hague: Martinus Nijhoff.

McGuire, M. 1978. "A Method for Estimating the Effect of a Subsidy on the Receiver's Resource Constraint." *Journal of Public Economics* 10: 25–44.

Maxwell, J., and J. R. Aronson. 1977. *Financing State and Local Governments*. Washington, D.C.: Brookings Institution.

Mayhew, David. 1974. *Congress: The Electoral Connection*. New Haven: Yale University Press.

Moffitt, R. 1984. "The Effects of Grants-in-Aid on State and Local Expenditures: The Case of AFDC." *Journal of Public Economics* 23: 279–306.

Nathan, R., A. D. Manuel, and S. E. Calkin. 1975. *Monitoring Revenue Sharing*. Washington, D.C.: Brookings Institution.

National Journal. 1982. "The New Federalism." Vol. 14, 27 February 1982.

Nie, N., S. Verba, and J. Petrocik. 1979. *The Changing American Voter*. Cambridge, Mass.: Harvard University Press.

Niskanen, W. 1975. "Bureaucrats and Politicians." *Journal of Law and Economics* 18: 617–43.

North, Douglass. 1981. *Structure and Change in Economic History*. New York: W. W. Norton.

Olson, M. 1982. *The Rise and Decline of Nations*. New Haven: Yale University Press.

Ornstein, N. J. 1975. "Causes and Consequences of Congressional Change: Subcommittee Reforms in the House of Representatives, 1970–73." Pp. 88–114 in N. J. Ornstein, ed., *Congress in Change*. New York: Praeger.

Plott, C. 1968. "Some Organizational Influences on Urban Renewal Decisions." *American Economic Review* 58: 306–321.

Pommerehne, W. W. 1978. "Institutional Approaches to Public Expenditures: Empirical Evidence from Swiss Municipalities." *Journal of Public Economics* 9: 255–80.

Romer, T., and H. Rosenthal. 1979. "Bureaucrats vs. Voters: On the Political Economy of Resource Allocation by Direct Democracy." *Quarterly Journal of Economics* 93: 562–87.

Rose-Ackerman, S. 1981. "Does Federalism Matter? Political Choice in a Federal Republic." *Journal of Political Economy* 89: 152–65.

Russell, L. 1983. "Medical Care." Pp. 111–14 in J. Pechman, ed., *Setting National Priorities: 1984 Budget*. Washington, D.C.: Brookings Institution.

Scheiber, H. N. 1966. "The Condition of American Federalism: An Historian's View." Subcommittee on Intergovernmental Relations to the Committee on Government Operations, U.S. Senate, 15 October.

Shepsle, K. 1979. "Institutional Arrangements and Equilibrium in Multidimensional Voting Models." *American Journal of Political Science* 23: 27–59.

Shepsle, K., and B. R. Weingast. 1981. "Political Preferences for the Pork Barrel: A Generalization." *American Journal of Political Science* 25: 96–111.

Stockman, D. 1975. "The Social Pork Barrel." *The Public Interest* no. 39: 3–30.

Weingast, B., K. Shepsle, and C. Johnsen. 1981. "The Political Economy of Benefits and Costs: A Neoclassical Approach to Distributive Politics." *Journal of Political Economy* 89: 642–64.

CHAPTER TWO

Reforming U.S. Federal Fiscal Arrangements

Edward M. Gramlich

Economists have written any number of articles calling for tax and expenditure reform. There have been briefs for reforming the income tax, integrating it with the corporate tax, switching to a consumption tax, moving away from or toward a more progressive rate structure. There have been just as many normative treatises about expenditures—arguing for constitutional limits on total expenditures, reforming the social insurance trust funds, replacing certain expenditures with negative income taxes or vouchers. In a discipline that is alleged to emphasize the positive over the normative, public finance economists have certainly bucked the trend.

But not in one area. In contrast to many other developed countries, the United States has a very decentralized system of fiscal relationships. Over $180 billion is given as intergovernmental grants from higher to lower levels of government, and many promising revenue sources are left completely to local governments. These arrangements, loosely termed a fiscal federalism system, have not received much normative, reformist attention from economists. Politicians have certainly become aware of the potential of the federalism issue, and presidents Nixon and Reagan have both advanced well-publicized reform proposals.[1] The quasi-governmental Advisory Commission on Intergovernmental Relations (ACIR) has noticed the system and has its own reform proposals.[2] Economists have done a multitude of theoretical and empirical studies on various aspects of federalism, trying to determine optimal governmental arrangements, predicting the effects of grants or taxes, estimating the degree to which fiscal decisions are "capitalized" into property values, and the like. Unlike studies of other aspects of public finance, however, these analyses have not provided very pointed statements of what is wrong with the present federal arrangements and how they might be changed to further various goals.[3] In this paper I try to come up with such a statement.

There are obvious risks in such an attempt—one person's item to be reformed may be another person's ideal. And the theoretical basis for many of these supposed improvements is, as always, in doubt. However, a number of aspects of the present United States federal system seem unlikely to appeal either to those economists who worry primarily about efficiency or to those who worry primarily about equity. For all the positive papers analyzing the empirical impact of federalism, most of these features have not gotten the criticism they deserve from economists.

Two apologies are necessary at the outset. One is that a complete discussion of all aspects of federalism in need of major or minor reform would require a lengthy treatise. There have been two very extensive reviews of federal theory and present-day arrangements in the past decade—by Oates (1972) and Break (1980). Obviously, in one paper I cannot cover all the ground covered by these books and by countless shorter articles. I am forced to be selective both in choice of topics and in the treatment of arguments bearing on the topics. Readers desiring a more comprehensive, and undoubtedly more balanced, discussion can refer to these earlier sources. I must also mention that none of the items I single out for reform is original. I have made a stronger case for many of these measures than is typically found in the literature, but I am certainly not the first to use the relevant arguments.

The second apology is for the omission of a topic that should be fundamental to any discussion of fiscal federalism—that of reforming the structure of governments themselves. The United States has an extremely eclectic structure, with strong historical roots. Some states are large and diverse, others are small; some states conduct extensive expenditure operations of their own, other states leave these operations to localities or special districts; in some areas cities and counties overlap, in others they do not; in some areas special districts are organized to conduct functions, in others they are not; in some areas there is freedom for cities to annex suburbs, in other areas there is not. In all areas it is quite difficult to change whatever arrangements do exist. Economists such as Buchanan (1965) have developed some theories for understanding these arrangements, but there is as yet a wide gap between these theories and their practical applications. I do not even try to fill the gap here, but—as will become apparent—the optimality or lack of optimality of a set of budgetary arrangements among existing governments depends very much on the existing structures. The two questions should ideally be studied simultaneously, not separately.

THE THEORY OF FEDERALISM
AND THE UNITED STATES SYSTEM:
THE MUSGRAVE TRICHOTOMY

Twenty-five years ago Musgrave (1959) advanced his now-famous trichotomy that divided governmental functions into their allocation, distribution, and stabilization components. The Musgrave trichotomy is not always very helpful in making particular decisions—almost every tax has both allocative and distributional implications, and most expenditures do too, but it serves a useful function as an organizing device in the area of federalism.

ALLOCATION

Two separate traditions apply to public spending decisions within a federal system. Tiebout (1956) proposed a consumer choice model, according to which rational consumers would select a jurisdiction, and its menu of public goods, that would maximize consumer utility. Jurisdictions would then be led to provide the optimal menu; if not, residents would move to other jurisdictions until utility was maximized.

The second tradition follows Breton's (1965) notion of "perfect mapping" of jurisdictions. According to this notion, jurisdictional boundaries would be set to include only that set of individuals who obtain benefits from the relevant public good. In principle there could be as many jurisdictions as public goods, though in later work Breton and Scott (1978) rationalized a lesser number of jurisdictions by taking into account the costs of organizing and coordinating jurisdictions, and the costs to consumers of relocating.

These two traditions have been combined in various ways by various authors. Oates (1972) showed how jurisdiction size can be determined by the balance between two competing forces—the welfare loss from taste differences, which would argue for small jurisdictions, and the welfare gain from benefit spillovers, which would argue for large jurisdictions. His "decentralization theorem" called for public goods to be provided by the jurisdiction covering the smallest area over which benefits are distributed, so that public goods efficiencies are maximized and the effect of taste differences minimized. Breton and Scott worked out a more general theory of public goods benefits and organizational costs, but they did not formulate any general theorems, on the grounds that it might always be possible to reduce total costs by various kinds of intergovernmental transfers. Atkinson and Stiglitz (1980) built a series of models that included mobility, changes in the marginal product of labor as labor crowds into a jurisdiction, and income differences. The "results" they got were again very agnostic. Sometimes large jurisdictions were appropriate, sometimes small; sometimes there was a stable local public-goods equilibrium, sometimes not.

In light of this theoretical indeterminacy, it is no wonder that little progress has been made in attempting to determine which levels of government should provide what public services for allocation reasons. It is first necessary to adopt what seem to be reasonable simplifying assumptions and then derive the implications of the relevant model. A plausible set of such assumptions might be that organizing any new government is expensive, that mobility is costly, that changes in the marginal product of labor are small, and that income differences can be ignored (so as to focus only on considerations of efficiency). In this case one is led to the pragmatic conclusion that allocation responsibility for providing public services should be meted out to jurisdictions in accordance with Oates' decentralization theorem. But one should recognize that this conclusion is rather specialized and pertains at best only to marginal changes in the administrative structure and the pattern of production.

Turning to the actual numbers, the distribution of expenditures by function and level of government (Table 2.1) seems more or less in accord with the decentralization theorem. Those expenditures that appear to provide benefits over a wide area—national defense and energy—are conducted almost exclusively at the national level. Those that appear to provide benefits over a narrow area—elementary and secondary education and civilian safety—are carried out at the local level.[4]

The one mystery in this type of analysis involves state governments. These governments make 60 percent of all government purchases at the national or the local level, but it is not clear what public services convey benefits over as large an area as that covered by most states. I will argue below that at least some of the types of expenditure made by state governments—purchases and transfers for income support and health and hospitals—are better left to other levels of government.

Of the remaining state purchases, transportation is probably the one

TABLE 2.1

Government Expenditures by Functional Level, 1981 (billions of current dollars)

Function	Federal Government			State Governments			Local Governments	
	Purchases	Transfer, interest, subsidy	Grants	Purchases	Transfer, interest, subsidy	Grants	Purchases	Transfer, interest, subsidy
Defense & veterans	$169.3	$ 20.2	$ 1.4	—	—	—	$ 21.7	—
Civilian safety	2.1	—	0.2	$ 7.1	—	$ 0.6	116.8	—
Education	1.4	6.0	7.9	33.8	$ 2.5	62.2	19.3	—
Health & hospitals	5.9	0.7	3.4	18.5	0.1	2.2	7.3	$ 9.0
Income support	5.2	258.2	39.9	32.4	11.1	10.8	13.3	–3.5
Housing & community service	0.4	6.4	8.2	0.9	0.4	0.8	5.5	—
Recreation & culture	1.2	0.4	0.3	1.2	—	—	2.6	—
Energy & utilities	11.1	–1.4	1.1	0.4	–0.2	—	—	–2.5
Agriculture	6.7	4.9	0.8	2.0	—	—	—	—
Natural resources	4.9	—	1.1	2.0	—	0.7	1.3	—
Transportation	6.5	2.3	11.7	17.7	0.9	4.6	15.1	0.2
Post office	0.5	0.9	—	—	—	—	—	—
Economic development	1.7	–0.1	0.9	1.9	—	—	1.0	—
Labor training	1.6	0.6	5.9	3.0	0.6	—	—	1.0
Commercial activities	—	—	—	—	–1.9	—	0.1	0.2
General purpose	10.5	73.1	5.0	17.0	–2.2	11.5	25.8	1.5
Total[a]	229.2	372.2	87.9	138.0	11.2	93.4	230.0	5.9

[a] Because of rounding, details may not add to total.
SOURCE: "The U.S. National Income and Product Accounts," *Survey of Current Business*, July, 1983, table 3.16; and Levin (1983).

public service that does have natural statewide benefits, through the geographical linking of road networks. Education, specifically purchases for higher education by state university systems, may also give benefits statewide, but these benefits do not seem as "natural," since they are strongly influenced by the tuition and admissions policies followed by the state universities. Most such universities offer a large tuition reduction and perhaps relaxed admissions standards to in-state students and then find, unsurprisingly, that in-state students attend in very high numbers. One could argue that the benefits are statewide, but that begs the deeper question of whether the tuition reduction should have been granted in the first place.

To make one suggestive test of the degree of intrinsic statewide benefits, I examined data on University of Michigan (UM) freshmen accepted for admission. The results of this test, in the form of a logit regression explaining students' acceptance probabilities, are given in Table 2.2. They show that once the tuition differential has been eliminated, the probability that in-state residents who were accepted for admission will attend UM is no higher than for the accepted out-of-state residents. That sounds like an example of an unnatural statewide benefit.

DISTRIBUTION

For this governmental function, the basic theoretical analysis was done by Pauly (1973). The Pauly model determines income distribution by the interdependent utilities of individuals—higher living standards for poor transfer recipients make richer taxpayers better off. In most of his cases Pauly arrives at conclusions close to those of the decentralization theorem—that distributional policies should generally be determined by lower levels of government. Two very strong assumptions must be made to arrive at the result, however, and those assumptions are open to question.

The first assumption involves the geographical linking of utilities. The Pauly model assumes that the welfare of donors can be improved only by raising living standards in the donors' own jurisdictions, as if donors are affected by the sight of, and externalities attendant on, poor people. Some survey evidence analyzed by Ladd and Doolittle (1982) sheds doubt on this assumption. Ladd and Doolittle find that an overwhelming majority of respondents to two separate ACIR polls (1981)—respondents who are assumed to be like those who would ordinarily pay for redistribution programs—believe that the national government should retain an impor-

TABLE 2.2

Probability of Attendance as Freshman of Residents (No Alumni/ae Relatives)
Accepted by the University of Michigan, 1981

Academic ability percentile (%)	Parent's income above median?	Differential tuition reduction ($)	Probability of attending (%)	Estimated probability of attending without differential tuition reduction (%)*	Probability of nonresident attending
Top 25	yes	$2640	53%	27%	18%
Top 25	no	3090	46	21	20
Next 25	yes	3260	55	28	28
Next 25	no	3130	54	28	28
Bottom 50	yes	3370	61	35	37
Bottom 50	no	3170	59	32	41

*From a logit regression

SOURCE: "Report of the Task Force on Undergraduate Student Aid," University of Michigan, 1984, mimeo.

tant role in supporting needy people. Ladd and Doolittle interpret these results as implying that poor people throughout the nation ought to be the beneficiaries of income support programs, as if donors' preference functions contain no state-line distinction.

The other assumption involves the potential migration of beneficiaries. Even if particular states wanted to be generous, they would not be able to be if prospective beneficiaries of transfer programs were highly mobile. Mobility would raise the tax price of redistribution in all states and would prevent states from following the basic redistribution choices of their donors, for fear of attracting hordes of welfare recipients. The prevailing view seems to be that migration is not, practically speaking, a problem, because only 1 or 2 percent of transfer recipients make interstate moves in a year (see Holmer 1975). But this view is belied by transition matrix calculations given in Table 2.3 which indicate that when transfer recipients (most of whom are not working) do move, they are much more likely to move to states with more generous income-support systems. In the long run, even the low degree of mobility pointed to in the prevailing view can lead to major population shifts among the beneficiary population, as is shown in Table 2.3. This evidence provides another argument for retaining some national interest in income redistribution policies.

But it is not obvious how the national interest should be retained. Tresch (1981) views the federal aspect of redistribution policy as an either/or choice: either the national government would determine an income distribution, or a lower government would. For various reasons he favors having lower governments make the determination, and this leads him to advance a hierarchical redistribution plan. Under this plan, the national government would redistribute income among states, the states among localities, and the localities among households. Legislators at any level could vote for as much or as little redistribution as they wanted. Migration of beneficiaries and positive taxpayers alike could be stabilizing in such a system, if generous localities were entitled to greater transfers from higher levels of governments when low-income families immigrated and high-income families emigrated. But if migration were costly, this system would represent the national interest no better than a fully decentralized system, because there would be no way for national legislators representing national preferences to insure that low-income people were taken care of in particular states. Moreover, even if migration were not costly, the outcome might be socially undesirable, because it could lead to extreme differences in state and local incomes.

An alternative view is taken by Boadway and Wildasin (1984). They

TABLE 2.3

Transition Probabilities, Panel Survey of Income Dynamics (PSID) and the Decennial Census, 1970–1980

| Individual characteristic | Number | Transition probabilities[a] | | | | Initial share of AFDC or unemployment in high AFDC or unemployment state | Ultimate share[b] | Half-life (years)[c] |
| | | High AFDC or unemployment state in t | | Low AFDC or unemployment state in t | | | | |
		p_{11}	p_{12}	p_{21}	p_{22}			
AFDC recipients[d]	1220	.975	.025	.034	.966	.446	.572	45
Most unemployed workers[e]	2722	.986	.014	.018	.982	.583	.563	21
Long term unemployed[f]	525	.973	.027	.016	.984	.634	.372	16

[a]Five-year transition probabilities for AFDC recipients; one year for unemployed workers.

[b]The steady-state distribution of the relevant population, given the transition matrix. Let x be the equilibrium share of the population residing in high AFDC (unemployment) states. Then $x(1 - p_{12}) + (1 - x)p_{21} = x$, or $x = p_{21}/(p_{12} + p_{21})$.

[c]The length of time it takes for repeated multiplications by the transition matrix to give x halfway between its postulated initial value and its computed ultimate value.

[d]Non-aged female family heads receiving AFDC in period $t + 1$. Data from PSID and the Census are aggregated.

[e]Non-aged male family heads in the labor force with more than 170 hours (one-twelfth of a year) of unemployment, from PSID.

[f]Non-aged male family heads in the labor force with more than 1040 hours (one-half of a year) of unemployment, from PSID.

SOURCES: First row, Gramlich and Laren (1984), tables 4, 5. Other rows, Gramlich (1984), table 1.

do not see the national-subnational question as an either/or choice but, rather, analyze the question as a matter of benefit spillovers, where the spillover represents both the fact that donors may care about recipients from all states and the fact that when one state raises support levels and attracts migrants, other states benefit. In this logic, taxpayers outside the jurisdiction are willing to contribute to support levels in the jurisdiction, and the appropriate policy would be to allow subnational units to set support levels, partly financed by open-ended matching grants from the federal government. That, as it happens, is close to the present arrangement used in the United States for two of the main general programs for redistributing income, Aid to Families with Dependent Children (AFDC) and Medicaid. Both programs contain the added stipulation that the matching rates are more favorable for low-income states. The third main general redistribution program, food stamps, is a national program with minimum nationwide support levels.[5]

While the structure of income support programs receives extensive criticism, the Boadway–Wildasin analysis suggests that it is not so obviously in need of repair. I disagree. In the Appendix I give an analysis that shows, first, that any inefficiencies caused by migration spillovers are small, and, second, that present matching grants greatly over-correct for these inefficiencies. Yet even with these overly generous matching grants, AFDC support levels are extremely low in the states of residence of slightly more than half of AFDC beneficiaries. The basic reason is that voters in these low-benefit states appear to have little taste for redistribution, as is readily inferred from their low benefit levels in spite of generous federal matching and upward pressure from the higher support levels in other states.

That leads me to a somewhat paternalistic position, carefully spelled out in the Appendix. I would like to see a uniform national minimum standard somewhere near the level that now obtains in the states of residence of slightly less than half of the AFDC beneficiaries, roughly the Health and Human Services poverty living standard. Certainly this minimum standard could be supplemented by states, and perhaps there should even be a slight federal match for supplementation. My reason for desiring minimum standards is the simple one that I am bothered by the fact that support levels in states paying low benefits are so low. Given the numbers, there is no reasonable way to raise these support levels substantially with Boadway–Wildasin-type matching grants, and no reasonable way to justify national standards by resorting to migration inefficiencies.

STABILIZATION

The prevailing view as of a decade ago was that national governments should try to stabilize the economy by manipulating taxes and expenditures; subnational governments should not attempt to do so. Over the past decade the first statement has come under a series of withering attacks: the criticism of Mundell (1963) and Fleming (1964) that with flexible exchange rates, foreign capital flows will automatically crowd out fiscal changes; the criticism of Lucas (1972) and Sargent and Wallace (1975) that flexible prices and rational expectations render ineffective any systematic macro-policy changes; the criticism of Barro (1974) that households with long horizons expect to pay the cost of government at some point in history, and hence that the actual timing of tax liabilities (and the split between debt and taxes) has no impact on consumption. There are still unreconstructed Keynesians around (like me), but the faith in activist fiscal policy is substantially less than in former times.

Even in the fiscal activist's heyday, Oates (1972) was arguing that subnational fiscal policies were pointless. In part, his argument was based on the belief that national stabilizing fiscal policies presented a realistic alternative to subnational fiscal policy—now not so readily accepted. In part, the argument was based on a belief that the debt of subnational governments was external and that of national governments internal—a distinction now viewed as obsolete. To the extent that debt is floated on a national or worldwide capital market at a predetermined interest rate, bondholders are no better off by virtue of getting a particular interest payment, all debt is effectively external, and there is no differential advantage in having the national government float the debt.[6]

In part, the lack of faith in subnational fiscal policy was also based on a view that either the mobility of labor or goods in a country was very high. If the mobility of goods in response to spending demand was high, movements in aggregate demand throughout a country would be highly positively correlated and demand stimulation in one area would not cause extraordinary income changes there. If the mobility of labor was also high, whatever differential movements in demand might occur would inspire offsetting by changes in labor supply.

The last two rows of the transition matrix (Table 2.3) try to verify the latter of these critical assumptions, the assumed mobility of labor. Here the topic is the movement of unemployed workers, either short or long term, between states of high and low aggregate unemployment. The message is certainly to downgrade the importance of labor mobility for any but the longest run. As with the transfer recipients discussed earlier, in the short run very few workers, even when unemployed for as long as half a year, move from a high to a low unemployment state.

The upshot of all these considerations is that perhaps the question of subnational fiscal policy should be reopened. If most demand shocks these days are ultimately due to relative price shifts that benefit some areas of the country and hurt others (see Medoff 1983 for some evidence on the importance of these), if these shocks are largely transitory, if labor is immobile across regions of the country in the short run, and if currency value changes weaken national fiscal policies, then use of subnational fiscal policies may present a sensible way to decentralize responsibilities for this function of government. In another paper (Gramlich 1984) I make this argument in more detail. Most states have constitutional provisions that prevent them from running current-account-budget deficits, but they are not prevented from altering taxes and expenditures in response to income changes in their areas, and it appears to me that they should follow such policies.

TAX ASSIGNMENT

Two basic questions arise in any examination of the federal structure of taxation. The first involves the levels of taxes raised by national and subnational governments; the second, the types of tax used.

NATIONAL VS. SUBNATIONAL TAXES

While the presumption on the expenditure side of the budget is that expenditure programs should be conducted by subnational governments whenever possible, there is an opposite presumption on the tax side. Partly because of a belief that the administrative costs of levying taxes are higher for subnational than national governments, partly because of a fear of tax competition, the standard belief is that tax collection should be centralized whenever possible.

As on the expenditure side, this presumption can at least be said to be specialized, perhaps appropriate in some cases but certainly not in general. For one thing, it totally ignores a point brought out by the new "rent-seeking" literature: that inefficiencies due to lobbying for the grants may dwarf conventional economic inefficiencies. When expenditure programs are decentralized and taxes centralized, large-scale general-purpose transfers (which actually exist in other federal countries such as Canada and Australia) are needed to balance budgets at both governmental levels. These large transfers place a premium on local politicians who can lobby for grants from the federal government and very little premium on those who are effective managers of their governments—a common complaint in countries that rely heavily on tax-sharing grants (Walsh 1983). The rent-seeking literature should then alert us to a competing principle— that, as a rule, those governments that buy government services should impose their own taxes.

Moreover, the administrative cost argument given in favor of tax centralization seems quite weak. Perhaps in less developed countries it may be true that the national government can administer tax laws more effectively than can subnational governments, but there is no research supporting such a proposition in the United States. And it would be strange if such research could be found, since all states have to do to lower their own administrative costs and the compliance costs of their taxpayers is to use the federal tax base and apply their own rate.[7]

The question of competition among various governments for desirable tax bases is more complicated. In a Tiebout model with costless migration, competing governments at the same level should strive to eliminate what Buchanan (1950) called *fiscal residuals*: the difference between taxes paid to a local government and expenditure benefits received from it. The threat of tax competition among subnational governments will then limit the extent to which any of these governments can tax either industry or well-off individuals in their own community, for if these groups are asked to pay extra costs, they will simply leave the community. There is then relatively little scope for assessing redistributive taxes at any but the national level.

This innate limitation on redistributive taxes at the subnational level does not require fiscal transfers from higher to lower levels of government for redistributive spending, as long as the redistribution is done mainly by the federal government, as I have previously argued that it should be. But it could justify such transfers for spending done for allocation reasons. Gordon (1983) points out that horizontal tax competition eliminates an opportunity for a decentralized government to assess completely nondistorting taxes, if there are some factors that are in highly elastic supply to subnational jurisdictions and completely inelastic supply to the nation. In principle Gordon's point is important, but I would be more worried about it if I could determine what such productive factors are— in today's open-economy models, a routine assumption is that capital and perhaps even entrepreneurship are in elastic supply to the whole country (called the "small country" assumption, for obvious reasons). Pending illumination on this point, my tentative position on this issue is that while it is theoretically possible that principles of tax assignment would call for having certain taxes levied by national governments and accompanied by grants to the subnational governments actually doing the spending, there is no clear evidence that such an arrangement is appropriate for the United States.

Another form of tax competition would also call for more centralization of the revenue-raising function than the spending function. This form is not very common in the United States, though it exists in resource-rich countries such as Australia. It involves the vertical tax competition among all levels of government that could lay claim to taxing profitable resource deposits. Cassing and Hillman (1982) tell a story about rail freight for coal in Queensland, the most resources-rich Australian state. The federal government tries to gain its return from Queensland coal by imposing an export duty. The state of Queensland tries to gain its own return by charging exploitive rail freight rates. As the federal government raises its rates to gain revenue, the profitability of coal is reduced, as is the monopolistic freight rate Queensland can charge. Similarly, by raising its freight rates Queensland can reduce revenues available to the federal government. If the two were to compete, they would tax coal excessively and generate suboptimal tax revenues for both governments. This is one case where it would make sense to centralize taxes and have one government distribute a share of the optimal tax revenue to the other.

Whatever the resolution of these typically complex normative issues, the previously reported data on general-purpose grants suggest that there is in fact broad adherence to the levy-your-own-taxes principle in the United States. Table 2.1 shows that only $5 billion of the $88 billion in federal grants to state or local governments in 1981 were for general purposes, and only $11 billion of the $93 billion in state grants for local governments.

TYPES OF TAXES

The two basic principles for organizing a tax system are the ability-to-pay and the benefit principles. In a federal system we would expect that migration among subnational jurisdictions would be an important factor in the long run (as the tax competition argument and the evidence on AFDC benefits, described above, suggested), which in turn implies that subnational jurisdictions ultimately have only one feasible taxing ar-

TABLE 2.4

Government Revenues by Type of Tax or Grant,
1981 (billions of current dollars)

Revenue item	Federal government	State governments	Local governments
Personal income taxes	$291.7	$62.7	$25.9
Estate and gift taxes	7.0	–	–
Corporate profits taxes	67.5	13.2	0.6
Excise taxes	41.7	–	–
Customs duties	8.6	–	–
Fees and charges	6.1	19.0	8.3
Sales taxes	–	76.3	14.1
Property taxes	–	2.7	72.4
Contributions for social insurance	204.5	26.7	7.1
Federal grants	–	65.7	22.0
State grants	–	–	93.4
Total*	627.0	266.2	244.0

*Because of rounding, details may not add to total.
SOURCE: "The U.S. National Income and Product Accounts," *Survey of Current Business*, July, 1983, table 3.16; Levin (1983).

rangement, the benefit principle. If they try to make well-off individuals or industry pay taxes that will be spent in the form of programs that benefit others in the jurisdiction, these groups will move out of the jurisdiction.

It follows that in a federal system, most ability-to-pay, or redistributive, taxes will be imposed at the national level, while most benefit taxation will be done at the state or local level. An examination of actual tax data for the United States (Table 2.4) shows this to be generally the case. Income and corporate taxes, the most important ability-to-pay taxes, are imposed mainly at the national level. Contributions for social insurance, used to finance trust funds such as social security, Medicare, unemployment insurance, and the like, are also assessed at the national level. Those state or local contributions that are assessed are for pension systems for the employees of these governments, and should be viewed as a component of the wages of these employees. Those taxes that are mainly benefit taxes, fees and charges and property taxes, are assessed at the local level.[8] As on the expenditure side, the taxes of state government represent a mixed bag, with some ability-to-pay taxes, some benefit taxes, and the state sales tax, which is hard to classify.

TAX EXPORTATION

One important source of inefficiency in this division of taxing responsibility involves the possibility of exporting taxes. A standard claim on the expenditure side of the budget, routinely advanced as a rationale for categorical grants from the federal to lower governments, is that spending can be too low if some benefits from an expenditure program are realized outside the community. There is a similar, though less commonly heard, argument on the tax side (first made by McLure 1967). If taxes can be exported from a jurisdiction to individuals outside the jurisdiction, without a concomitant transfer of expenditure benefits, local citizens are not internalizing all the costs of public services, and they will spend too much on these public services. Just as we have categorical subsidies for those types of expenditures with benefit spillovers, we should in principle also assign public-service excise taxes for whatever spending is financed by exportable taxes.

The difficulties of matching expenditures and the taxes used to pay for them probably make any formal excise-tax scheme impractical, but there may be other arrangements that should be made to deal with tax exporting. One is to have the federal government assume all tax sources that can easily be exported. It is sometimes argued that this is why the federal government should take over responsibility for the corporate tax (as it largely has), but that view does not accord with prevailing views on the incidence of the corporate tax. That tax is now generally considered to be a tax on a mobile factor, capital, which would drive it, and ultimately labor, out of a jurisdiction, leaving the tax to be paid by the locationally fixed factor, land. Hence in general the corporate tax would not be exported. What would be exported are capital taxes on factors within a jurisdiction owned by outsiders (such as on resources) and excise taxes on travelers with a low price elasticity of demand.

As a practical matter, tax exporting inefficiencies do not seem to be of overriding practical importance in the United States. A recent study by Mutti and Morgan (1983) finds the revenue implications of excise-tax exporting to travelers to be very small, even for states, such as Florida, for which tourism is very important. Beyond that, though the decisions have been made on constitutional grounds, a long series of Supreme Court rulings have effectively prevented the taxation of outsiders and have thereby kept down the distortions that could have arisen from exporting (Hellerstein 1977).

Although the Supreme Court is of course concerned with legal traditions and not economic inefficiencies, there is one way an alleged constitutional restriction does cause tax exportation. As a result of court rulings in the early 1940s, the federal government now does not tax state and local bond interest payments. This treatment lowers state and local bond interest rates to about 80 percent of the rate for comparable-risk corporate securities, and subsidizes state and local investment in all communities affected by cost-of-capital. There seems to be no economic point to such a subsidy—if there are spillover benefits, matching grants can be used—and its elimination would improve the overall allocation of capital in the United States, as well as improving the equity of the federal income tax. If the subsidy really is rooted in constitutional constraints, this distortion will be with us as long as we have an income tax, though it could still be removed by moving to an expenditure tax, which taxes return to capital only when it is consumed. But there is enough confusion about the ultimate origin of the subsidy that one might also argue for another court ruling on the constitutionality of having the federal government tax state and local interest payments.

While the courts have generally tried to limit tax exporting, congressional actions have generally gone the other way. In one significant case, Congress explicitly encourages a form of tax exporting through the income-tax deduction for state and local taxes paid. This federal deduction lowers the marginal tax price for local public goods for those voters who itemize deductions, and represents exactly the sort of tax exporting that should be prevented from the standpoint of efficiency.[9]

An examination of the impact of this tax deduction within a state suggests that its effects might be considerably more pernicious than are commonly supposed. A first point is that not all state and local revenues are deductible—in general, fees and charges, the revenues that most closely conform to the benefits principle and hence cause least deadweight loss, are not deductible, while the less efficient income and sales taxes are. A second point is that only 30 percent of all tax returns claim itemized deductions. If the median, or decisive, voter in a community does not itemize, then the deduction does not affect state or local spending but merely represents an unwarranted tax break for the high-income taxpayers who do itemize.

But that is not the end of it. Although only 30 percent of *all* tax returns claim itemized deductions, it may still be that a high percentage of the tax returns filed by voters itemize deductions. Table 2.5 presents data from a survey of Michigan voters. The bottom row of the table shows that of all 2001 survey respondents, 862, or 43 percent, claim itemized deductions.

TABLE 2.5
Voters Who Itemized Deductions on Their Federal Tax Returns
(Michigan Voter Survey, 1978)

| | | | | Share itemizing | |
Residence	Respondents	Voters	Itemizers	Voters	Nonvoters
Detroit	270	164	94	.409	.255
Detroit suburbs	583	356	304	.607	.388
Lansing	54	28	21	.357	.423
Lansing suburbs	38	30	19	.533	.375
Other urban counties	242	156	107	.519	.302
Rural counties	814	514	317	.432	.317
Total	2001	1248	862	.490	.332

SOURCE: Survey data are described in Courant, Gramlich, and Rubinfeld (1980).

The difference between the 30 percent share from overall statistics and this 43 percent share is apparently due to tax returns filed on behalf of minors and others not likely to appear in a voter survey sample. The bottom row also indicates that among voters, the share of itemizers rises to 49 percent. And some of the disaggregated numbers in the table show that among voters in high-income areas, such as the Detroit and Lansing suburbs, the share rises to 60 percent.

Assume for the moment that the median voter model gives a reasonably accurate picture of how public-spending decisions are made in local jurisdictions. The numbers in Table 2.5 indicate the maximum number of voters who would be swayed by the state-local tax deduction to switch their vote in favor of higher expenditures. Using the overall statistics as an example, say that 49 percent of the voters itemize, and that voting turnout decisions are unaffected by the deduction provision. Then up to 49 percent of the voters could have their desired size of public spending increased by the tax deduction. If not too many of these voters had previously favored big governments (in which case they would have already voted for high spending), public spending would be likely to rise in the community. Reasoning in this way, we can see that the effective tax price for public spending is more likely to fall, and public spending to rise, the richer the community.

The tax price for public spending on such social investment services as education is already relatively low in these richer areas because of their high tax base. Now this basic advantage is compounded by the federal tax deduction. Indeed, a firm believer in migration will also argue that the tax deduction sets up incentives for rich people to live together so that they can export their taxes to others. It is hard to imagine a consciously designed public-policy measure having worse impacts on both efficiency and equity, in the short and the long run, than the federal income-tax deduction for state and local taxes.

INTERGOVERNMENTAL GRANTS

The other important financing mechanism in a federal system involves intergovernmental grants. As the previous numbers made clear, the United States has a very extensive grant system at both the national and the state level. While most existing grants are categorical, there are separate rationales for categorical grants and for general-purpose grants.

THE RATIONALES FOR GRANTS

Grants from higher to lower levels of government can be of a form that alters relative prices facing the recipient government, or that does not. With general-purpose grants the price structure is not altered: these grants affect community income only, and stimulate local consumption of public services according to the income effect. With open-ended categorical grants the price structure is altered: these grants lower relative prices for certain types of expenditures, have both income and substitution (price) effects, and stimulate local consumption of public services according to the uncompensated price elasticity of demand. Since the substitution effect expands spending, if anything, it is easy to establish that open-ended price reduction grants stimulate more spending on the public service in question per dollar of the federal grant.

Whether one type of grant or the other is appropriate depends on the type of problem being corrected by the grant. If there are externalities that imply that social benefits from public services exceed those realized within a community, open-ended price subsidies are appropriate—just the reverse of the tax exportation argument. If the mismatch of expenditure and revenue responsibilities described above is present, general-purpose transfers are appropriate. Indeed, Breton and Scott (1978) point out that there may be any conceivable mismatch of administrative responsibilities for taxes or expenditures at any level of government, making any set of transfers, from higher to lower governments (as most now are), or from lower to higher governments, appropriate.

But the most commonly discussed rationale for general-purpose transfers, and the one that is potentially most relevant in the United States, involves income differences across communities. Should these exist, there will be one of two outcomes. If benefit taxation is not complete, rich people will be net contributors to the public budget and poor people will receive some transfers through the public budget (in Buchanan's [1950] terms, the rich have positive fiscal residuals and the poor negative ones). If benefit taxation is complete, poor people will gain from the higher demand by rich people for public goods.[10] Either way, the tax price for public services in a community will depend on how many rich people there are or, crudely, on community income.

The argument often stops there, but it should not. Differing tax prices do not necessarily constitute a social ill, though they can if they lead poor communities to under-consume (relative to rich communities) merit public services such as education. One of many ways to eliminate these tax price differences across communities is through general-purpose transfers. But the general-purpose transfers must be compensatory, that is, they must be given in greater per-capita amounts to poor than to rich communities. And it is by no means obvious that general-purpose transfers are the best way to deal with these community income differences. Yinger (forthcoming) points out that two separate notions of equity could be applied in problems such as this: (a) fair compensation, under which all communities would have access to the same bundle of all goods; or (b) categorical equity, under which the expected expenditures on designated public services would be equalized. Under the former notion, general-purpose grants would be appropriate and would have to be given in the amount of income differences among communities. Under the latter, general-purpose grants could be given, but it would be possible to achieve the same end with fewer grant dollars by using Feldstein's (1975) variant of the power equalization approach.

Say that expenditures on public services in the ith community were determined by the linear equation

(1) $E_i = a_0 + a_1 Y_i + a_2 G_i + a_3 P_i + u_i$

where E_i is real consumption of public services, Y_i is community income (here used as a proxy for community living standards), G_i is general-purpose grants received by the community, P_i is the dollar size of price-reduction (open-ended matching) grants received by the same community, and the residual u_i refers to all other reasons why spending might differ across communities. With normal preference functions, $a_3 > a_2$; that is, the price-reduction grants would provide an added impetus to spending. If there exist what are known as "flypaper" effects, whereby general-purpose grants stimulate more spending than income, $a_2>a_1$.[11] To achieve fair compensation through general-purpose grants, $\partial G_i/\partial Y_i$ must equal -1, that is, all income deviations must be compensated dollar for dollar by larger general-purpose grants. To achieve categorical equity, it is merely necessary to insure that expected spending is equal across communities. This is done simply by taking the total derivative of (1) with respect to income, arriving at $\partial G_i/\partial Y_i = -a_1/a_2$ if equalization is accomplished through general-purpose grants, and $\partial P_i/\partial Y_i = -a_1/a_3$ if through open-ended matching grants. The first derivative is greater than or equal to -1; the second is clearly greater than -1. In these latter cases, because the price sensitivity is relied on to stimulate public spending, and because the standard is not to eliminate all spending deficiencies but only the public-services spending deficiency, less grant money is needed to achieve categorical equity.[12] Another advantage of this form of matching grants, not shown in the analysis, is that the stimulated public spending could be limited to those public services that really are merit goods.

The upshot of all this is that the usual rationales for general-purpose grants are all quite limited. One rationale could be the assignment-of-responsibilities mismatch described above, though it seems that American subnational governments are able to raise enough revenue to pay for their spending programs without resorting to obviously inefficient taxation. One could be the income-differences argument, though if the categorical-equity standard is used, categorical grants can achieve the same objective with fewer grant dollars.[13]

ACTUAL GRANTS

Table 2.6 shows real levels of intergovernmental grants at the federal level over the past decade, disaggregated by type of grant. In principle, a similar analysis of state grants to local governments should be done, but I do not show these data because nobody has developed disaggregations based on the type of grant, and those distinctions are crucial in the analysis.

The table shows that a decade ago, in 1972, there were almost no general-purpose grants, fairly large grants for income support, and even larger categorical grants for other, benefit spillover programs. Over the decade, general-purpose grants rose until 1980 because of the introduction of the Nixon administration's general-revenue-sharing program,

TABLE 2.6

Federal Grants by Type, 1972, 1980, and 1983
(billions of 1983 dollars)

	1972*	1980*	1983
General purpose	$ 1.2	$ 10.6	$ 6.5
Block	6.7	12.7	12.9
Income support	29.1	42.3	44.8
Categorical	44.2	47.3	28.8
Total	81.2	112.9	93.0

*Deflated by the national accounts deflator for state and local purchases
(1972 = 0.423, 1980 = 0.809).
SOURCE: *Budget of the United States Government, Fiscal Year 1985*, Special
Analysis H, tables H.8 and H.9.

then dropped back in real terms when the Carter administration eliminated general-revenue-sharing for state governments. Categorical grants
remained stable until 1980, then dropped back when the Reagan administration killed some of them and converted others to what are known as
block grants—grants that are nominally categorical (money has to be
spent on a designated function), but effectively for general purposes (the
designated functions are so broad, and enforcement so limited, that recipient governments can effectively do what they want with the grant
money). Income-support grants have grown from 1972 levels due to the
exploding costs of Medicaid, offset by a real drop in AFDC grants.

GENERAL-PURPOSE GRANTS

The present general-revenue-sharing program goes only to local governments, basically on a per-capita formula. There are provisions in the
law that have the effect of giving slightly more funds to poorer areas, but
the redistribution is minimal and haphazard.[14] Even if the redistribution
were effective and systematic, however, there would seem to be little cause
to retain general revenue sharing. The program violates the levy-your-
own-taxes principle described above, in a way that has never been de-
fended in terms of administrative cost saving. And even if redistribution
were a more important objective of the program than it apparently is,
open-ended matching grants with federal matching rates depending neg-

atively on community income or positively on needs could accomplish the goals of categorical equity with fewer grant dollars.

BLOCK GRANTS

These grants appear to represent a political compromise: conservatives would like to kill many categorical grant programs altogether but, lacking the muscle to do that, they settle for converting the grant to block form. As said above, this effectively makes the grant into a general-purpose grant. But the allocation of funds for the grant program is based on whatever categorical program just got cashed out—miles of highway, numbers of dilapidated houses, or whatever. Since the grants now are for general purposes, the random elements in the grant distribution formula make the funds allocation even more haphazard than for general revenue sharing. There are also excess administrative costs to maintain the fiction of the block grant. Finally, as argued above, there is no very good argument for general-purpose grants anyway. For all these reasons, these grants should either be terminated or converted to categorical-equity-matching grants for poorer communities. Block grants may provide a useful political compromise, but it is hard to see why an economist who worries about efficiency and equity would ever favor such programs.

INCOME-SUPPORT GRANTS

I argued above in favor of replacing federal grants for income support with a national program paying basic income-support levels. This should consist of a basic national benefit level (say somewhat above the present average level of AFDC and food stamps). States should be allowed to supplement this level, perhaps with slight (say 25 percent) federal matching support.

In 1983, federal matching grants for all income-support programs totalled $45 billion (see Table 2.6). States spent another $13 billion of their own funds on Medicaid and yet another $6 billion on AFDC. Were the federal government simply to assume these expenditures, federal costs would rise by about $19 billion. Then there should be some reallocations, with most of the $6 billion going to raise AFDC benefits in low-benefit states in the South. The total amount of funds devoted to AFDC can be greater than $6 billion because of the fact that Medicaid is a program much in need of cost-saving reform apart from the federal aspects focused on here, and various cost-sharing measures should be able to reduce expenditures on it.

OTHER CATEGORICAL GRANTS

Until the recent introduction of general revenue sharing, conversion to block grants, and rapid growth of Medicaid, the main form of federal intergovernmental transfer has been categorical matching grants in areas such as transportation, education, community services, environmental protection, and hospital construction. These grants appear to have as their rationale benefit spillovers across jurisdictional lines,[15] but in fact the grants are structured so that they are unlikely to achieve any such objectives.

A first fact about these grants is that legal federal matching shares are very high, averaging 80 percent across the present $29 billion of other categorical grants.[16] While there may be some benefit spillovers, at the margin the ratio of internal to total benefits for these programs seems to be much higher than 20 percent. This gives states an incentive to overspend, and overspend they probably will. To prevent grant levels from becoming very large, the federal government is forced to impose limits on the size of the grant—overall program limits enforced by the Office of Management and Budget, formula limits for individual governments or groups of governments, and agency limits for application grants. Standard indifference-curve analysis next shows that the price reduction is not effective at the margin, and that the grants have effects much like those of general-purpose grants.[17] Then budget-cutters such as David Stockman come along and argue that the grant should be either terminated or converted to block form.

This political cycle is designed to end in the termination of the categorical-grant program. Perhaps many of these grants should never have been passed—that is a question for the benefit-cost analysts. But if there is a valid spillover rationale for categorical grants, a better way to improve the grant than by simply converting it to block form and effectively killing it can easily be found. That better way is simply to lower federal matching shares until the ratio of internal to total program costs at the margin equals the ratio of internal to total program benefits at the margin.

In making such a cavalier proposal, I realize that it will often be difficult, if not impossible, to estimate the critical marginal ratio very precisely. But it should not be difficult to come closer than the 20 percent that is now the standard. My own preference would be to assume an internal share of 80 percent unless it could be shown to be significantly lower. If this is the appropriate share, a very simple demand analysis indicates that such a change should reduce federal categorical grants by about $11 billion, increase expenditures on public services with benefit spillovers, and eliminate a dead-weight loss that appears to be about 1 percent of the level of expenditures.[18]

THE REFORM AGENDA

Rather than summarize the paper, I will try to maintain its spirit by listing what seem to me to be the major problems with present-day United States fiscal federal arrangements. These problems and the proposed remedies are stated very bluntly, without even trying to list the many compromises and intermediate reforms that could work in the right direction.

1. Given the inability of the national government to stabilize demand shocks, or to stabilize them in different regions simultaneously, states should undertake limited use of stabilization policies. They can do this by creating rainy-day funds, building up these funds (running budget surpluses) in boom years, and running down the funds in recession years.

2. The federal deduction for state and local taxes paid should be abolished. This change will raise federal revenue by an estimated $26 billion (see the summary in Table 2.7), it should affect tax prices and public-spending levels relatively little in rural jurisdictions and central cities, but it should raise marginal tax prices and lower public-spending levels in high-income suburbs. I would have made a similar recommendation, for a similar reason, about the income-tax exclusion for state and local interest, but I am assuming that the provision exists for constitutional reasons, and even my reform proposals do not go that far.

3. Federal grants for income-support programs should be replaced by direct federal income-support programs with uniform national benefit levels and optional state supplementation, perhaps with limited matching support. At today's levels, a reasonable package would raise federal budget expenditures by $20 billion.

4. Federal general-purpose grants and block grants should be replaced by categorical-equity matching grants to poorer communities for merit public services such as education, health, and housing. At

TABLE 2.7

Summary of Reform Changes
(billions of 1983 dollars)

Item	Reduction in federal deficit
Eliminate deduction for state-local taxes:	26.0
Property tax[a]	8.0
Other[a]	18.0
Impose uniform national income-support benefits:	− 20.0
Raise AFDC in low-benefit states[b]	− 10.0
Assume state Medicaid expenses[b]	− 10.0
Revamp general-purpose grants:	7.5
Eliminate general-revenue-sharing[c]	4.6
Eliminate broad-based grants[c]	12.9
Introduce categorical-equity grants[a]	− 10.0
Lower federal matching share on categorical grants:	10.8
Eliminate present limited categorical grants	28.8
Introduce open-ended grants with 20% matching	− 18.0
Total impact	24.3

[a]From *Special Analysis G of the Budget*, table G.2.
[b]Author's estimate.
[c]From *Special Analysis H of the Budget*, tables H.8, H.9.
SOURCE: *Budget of the United States Government, Fiscal Year 1985*, Special Analyses G and H.

today's levels, $17.5 billion of federal grants would be saved, and perhaps $10 billion could be used for the categorical-equity grants.

5. Federal categorical grants should be altered by lowering federal matching shares to a level that better corresponds to the ratio of internal to total benefits and by eliminating limits on the size of the grant. At today's levels, such a change is likely to reduce federal budget expenditures by about $11 billion.

The measures are not advanced as a package—any one of them could be adopted with or without any of the others. If the whole package were passed, Table 2.7 suggests that all changes combined should reduce the federal budget deficit by about $24 billion—a saving equal to about one-seventh of the enormous present level of the deficit. The short-run impact of the package would be to raise income-support levels greatly for low-income people in the South; the long-run impact should be to raise support levels for all low-income people. People in low-income communities should benefit further through increased consumption of merit public services. But not everybody will be better off. For a change, high-income itemizers will be made worse off.

APPENDIX: DECENTRALIZATION OF INCOME DISTRIBUTION RESPONSIBILITIES

In the text I asserted that the twin forces of beneficiary migration and the diverse levels of AFDC benefits desired by different states argue for a more centralized system of income support. In this appendix I give the exact nature of this argument. The appendix uses real numbers and parameters from Gramlich and Laren (1984).

Suppose we had a country consisting of two states, one that preferred to pay relatively generous AFDC support levels (B_1) and one that preferred to pay very low support levels (B_2). Each state determines benefits by maximizing the utility function for its decisive voter:

(1) $U_i = U_i [Y_i(1 - T_i), B_i]$

subject to the constraint that

(2) $T_i Y_i = (1 - M_i) (B_i R_i) (B_i/B_j)^b$

where i indicates the state determining benefits, j indicates the other state, U_i the utility value for the state's decisive voter, Y_i this voter's pre-tax income (for which I will use average per-capita income), T_i the proportional state income tax rate to pay for AFDC, M_i the federal matching rate for the state, and R_i for the level of recipients per capita if state i paid the same benefits as state j. If state i benefit levels exceed those in the other state $(B_i > B_j)$, recipients would rise according to the migration-sensitivity parameter b. There are cross-state transmission effects whenever $b > 0$.

Determination of benefits in this two-state country is shown in the well-known bargaining diagram Figure 2.1. At the Nash point N each state is maximizing utility under the assumption that all federal matching rates are zero and that benefits in the other state are fixed. At this point we have, for state 1,

(3) $\partial U_1/\partial B_1 = - [R_1 (1 + b) (B_1/B_2)^b] + u_1 = 0$

where u_1 is the partial derivative of U_1 with respect to B_1, and where the partial derivative of U_1 with respect to after-tax income in state 1 has been normalized at unity. At the Nash point there is no first-order impact of changing benefits on utility, because the state has already maximized by

FIGURE 2.1
Determination of Benefits by Bargaining

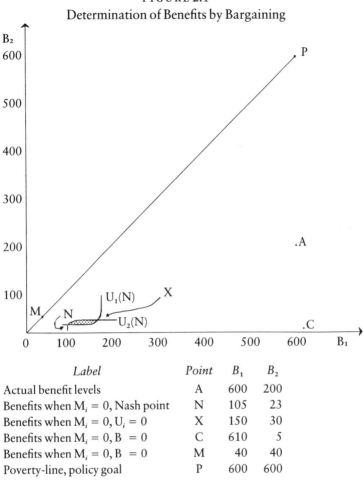

Label	Point	B_1	B_2
Actual benefit levels	A	600	200
Benefits when $M_i = 0$, Nash point	N	105	23
Benefits when $M_i = 0$, $U_i = 0$	X	150	30
Benefits when $M_i = 0$, $B = 0$	C	610	5
Benefits when $M_i = 0$, $B = 0$	M	40	40
Poverty-line, policy goal	P	600	600

equating the marginal value of benefit increases (u_1) to the marginal cost of income losses (the term in brackets). Hence the indifference curve passing through this point, U_1, is horizontal there.

But we also know that at the Nash point B_2 increases will raise U_1, because they attract AFDC recipients into state 2 and raise after-tax income in state 1 for every level of B_1. This can be seen by differentiating the utility function with respect to B_2:

(4) $\partial U_1/\partial B_2 = R_1 b \ (B_1/B_2)^{1+b} > 0$

This result shows why the U_1 curve is concave from the horizontal axis:

as B_1 is, say, raised above its optimal level at N, increasing rises in B_2 are necessary to keep the state on its indifference level.

The same results are true for state 2. The equation analogous to (3) shows that the U_2 curve is vertical at Nash point N. The equation analogous to (4) shows that benefit increases in state 1 raise utility in state 2. And the curve is concave to the vertical axis because increasing rises in B_1 are necessary to compensate for non-maximizing changes in B_2.

The fact that indifference curves cross at N implies that utility can be raised simultaneously in both states by bargaining, or by having the central government simply set benefits in both states at some level that raises utility in one state without lowering it in the other. Such a contract curve solution could be found by maximizing the joint utility function

(5) $J = wU_1 + (1-w)U_2$

for some arbitrarily specified weight w, assumed to lie between zero and one. But for reasons that will become apparent shortly, that is not going to be my argument for greater centralization. Another proposition is that the Boadway and Wildasin (1984) solution of federal matching could in principle be used to arrive at a contract curve solution, by effectively externalizing some of the cross-state gains of higher benefit levels in a state. Shortly we will also see that if this is the justification for federal matching, actual matching rates turn out to be far too generous to achieve this limited goal.

The diagram gives the area of possible gains from greater coordination as the shaded area. The northeastern limit of this area, denoted by X, can be approximated by reasoning that U_1 becomes vertical when rises in B_1 no longer raise utility in the state, that is, when B_1 is so high that u_1 is zero. Similarly, U_2 becomes horizontal when u_2 is zero. These points can be located with the equations

(6) $(\partial U_1/\partial B_1)\ \partial B_1 + (\partial U_2/\partial B_2)\ \partial B_2 = 0$

where the solution is just as before except that the derivatives are used to solve for the levels of B_1 and B_2 where the indifference curves become vertical and horizontal respectively. It can be seen from the graph that the exact crossing point is at a B_1 value less than that at which U_1 is vertical and at a B_2 value less than that at which U_2 is horizontal. I could locate this point exactly if I were willing to assume a specific form for the utility functions, but we will shortly see that such a step is not necessary.

This is all the positive theory that is required; I now try to find the various points with real-life values. The values for B_1 and B_2 will be state monthly AFDC guarantee levels for a family of four in 1981 dollars, assuming food stamps at a standard national level. Given this level, AFDC guarantee levels of about $600 would have been necessary to keep a family out of poverty status in 1981 (labeled P on the diagram).

The first step is to locate actual benefit levels in the presence of federal matching and migration. Data from Gramlich and Laren (1984) show that in typical high-benefit states, covering nearly half of AFDC recipients, B_1 ranged from $540 to $720 with a mean close to $600. In low-benefit states, B_2 ranged from $115 to $510, with a mean close to $200. These values are indicated on the diagram by point A.

Values at the Nash point N are determined from the equations given in Gramlich and Laren. Equation 9 there shows benefits to be determined in the two states by the relationships

(7a) $L(B_1) = [1/(1+cb)][Z_1 - cL(1-M_1) + cbL(B_2)]$

(7b) $L(B_2) = [1/(1+cb)][Z_2 - cL(1-M_2) + cbL(B_1)]$

where $L(x)$ denotes the log of a variable, c is the price elasticity of demand for AFDC benefits, and the Z_i terms represent the influence of all other variables. The Nash point is found by using the actual values listed above and reasonable parameter estimates from the paper ($b = 0.65$, $c = 1.8$) to evaluate the Z_i. Then these figures replace Z_i, the M_i are set at zero, and the values at point N are computed. B_1 falls from $600 to $105, B_2 from $200 to $23. The sharp drops are caused by three factors.

1. There is a sharp change in matching ratios, from $M_1 = 0.5$ and $M_2 = 0.75$ to zero.

2. The estimated price elasticity is high.

3. The estimated migration effect is high, causing the fall in B_1 to lower B_2, this to lower B_1, and so forth as in a multiplier.

Whether these estimates are believable is, of course, not as obvious. The paper finds both estimates to be highly significant, and it does confirm the all-important migration parameter with two different bodies of data.

The next step is to locate point X, the approximation for the northeastern crossing point. Because u_2 is already found to be very low (that is why the group 2 states pay so little AFDC, even when most costs are financed by the federal government), U_2 becomes horizontal when B_2 rises to 30; the same type of calculation makes U_1 vertical when B_1 equals 150. These two values are shown as point X on the graph; the true crossing point is slightly to the southwest. That these AFDC levels are so low explains why I do not use this lack of coordination argument for greater centralization: the rises in benefits due to improved coordination would not be very high.

Two other points are shown on the graph. Point C, for a closed economy, shows the solution to the model given in Equation 7 when there is no matching and when there is no migration effect. What migration does is to bring benefits in the two states together; when b is set at zero, states diverge to what might be thought of as their true preference benefit levels—close to the actual value for B_1 but close to zero for B_2. In this sense the present matching-grant system is about right for preserving the closed economy solution for the B_1 states but much more generous than is necessary for preserving the closed economy solution for the B_2 states. Finally, the point labeled M goes the other way, showing the equilibrium values for benefits when migration is infinitely sensitive to benefit disparities, as might be assumed in extreme versions of the Tiebout model. In this case benefits must be equal in the two states, by my calculation at about $40.

Hence the results here are dominated by the low intrinsic desire on the part of the group 2 states to pay benefits. These states now pay benefits of only $200 a month for a family of four, roughly one-third of the poverty line. And this in the presence of a price reduction by the federal government that averages 75 percent, a large estimated price elasticity of demand, a large migration sensitivity, and benefits in other states over three times as high. When the federal matching is eliminated to find the Nash point, benefits in these group 2 states fall to very low levels, and in the presence of the migration sensitivity, this pulls down benefits in the other states. With a Nash point anchored at this low a level, none of the normal federal policy measures aimed at improving coordination will have much effect—even at point X, benefits will be less than $30 in the low-benefit states.

To be candid, then, my policy suggestions are not aimed at preserving tastes in these low-benefit states. My goal is that benefits in all states be set at something like the poverty level of $600 per month, which also happens to be the preferred level in the high-benefit states. The much-maligned present system does bring about this result in these high-benefit states; its defects are highly overrated. But it still does fall short of my goal because of the low benefits in the other states. The easiest way to achieve the goal is simply to have the federal government establish uniform national benefit levels, with optional state supplementation.

As a final matter here, one might ask about two types of sensitivity tests. First, does the low intrinsic "taste" for AFDC benefits among low-benefit states reflect their low income? The answer is *no*. The Gramlich–Laren paper also estimates income elasticities as part of the model, and even when these are complicated by the fact that low-income states are likely to have more AFDC recipients, other things being equal, the income elasticities are extremely low. Redoing the Figure 2.1 analysis with all incomes standardized would lead to only trivial changes. AFDC benefits are low in low-benefit states for reasons that are not captured in the income term: many of these states have high incomes.

The other type of sensitivity test refers to the migration parameter b. It is already high enough that the Nash point is geometrically closer to M than to C. But it is also true that if b were underestimated for any of a number of reasons (the opposite of the usual criticism of the Gramlich–Laren paper), point X could stretch to cover point A. Unfortunately, it would take a b value close to 10 (15 times the value now estimated) to get X up to A, and close to 26 (40 times the value now estimated) to get X up to P. Theoretically, more sensitive migration could relieve the strain of the paternalistic argument for centralization: realistically, it cannot.

ACKNOWLEDGMENTS

I would like to thank the editors of the volume, along with Henry Aaron, Harvey Brazer, Theodore Bergstrom, Paul Courant, Roger Gordon, Wallace Oates, David Wildasin, and John Yinger for helpful comments. Deborah Laren and Marieka Klaiwitter produced some of the numbers, and some of the work was financed by a grant from the Sloan Foundation.

NOTES

1. Various administrations have issued numerous government documents containing these proposals. Barfield (1981) gives a good summary of them and an analysis of what happened to them.

2. The first ACIR report, *Fiscal Balance in the American Federal System*, was issued as early as 1968. Break (1980) and Barfield (1982) cover a series of subsequent reform documents.

3. One exception must be noted: Ladd (1982). While many of Ladd's arguments are similar to mine, her reform agenda is different in certain important ways.

4. In confining the benefits of elementary and secondary education to a small area, I am assuming that the primary beneficiaries of education are students and/or their parents. Once these students complete their education and move away from the area, other areas benefit from the initial area's schooling expenditures. It is difficult, however, to ascertain the extent of such benefits. For me to wade into that issue here would serve no purpose; if there

are appreciable geographical spillovers of this sort, education should be struck from the second list.

5. The numbers in Table 2.1 appear to suggest that income support transfers are given mainly at the federal level. Those numbers, however, are misleading: the federal transfer item consists of social security, unemployment, disability, and Medicare payments, all financed by social insurance trust funds where the ultimate beneficiaries (as a class) are making the contribution. These programs are not income redistribution in the sense of this class of people transferring income to other people.

6. Then Barro complicates the question further by arguing that, if the present generation will ultimately pay for government expenditures, it does not matter for consumption whether this generation pays now or later; the consumption loss implied by the external debt is offset by an equal (in present value terms) present-day consumption gain. If the present generation can escape payment by dying and not adjusting bequests, the present-day consumption gain may exceed the future consumption loss implied by the external debt.

7. Some attempts to coordinate tax policies and apply rates to the same base are discussed by Break (1980).

8. There is a great deal of dispute about exactly what sort of tax the property tax is. It can be thought of as a benefit tax to the extent that local public services are related to home values and financed by a property tax on these home values. But under certain conditions property taxes on homes or businesses may be shifted onto others and hence not be true benefit taxes.

9. Mutti and Morgan's (1983) analysis of the impact of this provision concentrates on other aspects. They work out the implications of tax importing and of having the federal government raise the revenue lost through the tax deduction by higher marginal rates on all taxpayers. Since I am concerned with the efficiency aspects of exporting, I focus only on it. Tax importing, and the higher marginal rates necessary to pay for everybody else's deduction, will be exogenous to the public-spending decisions of a particular subnational jurisdiction.

10. This statement may require some explanation. In a world of complete benefit taxation, all taxpayers are assessed Lindahl taxes. If the income elasticity of demand for public goods is positive, two poor people living together will have a lower sum of marginal benefits at each public-spending level than will a rich and a poor person living together. If the physical cost of providing public services is constant, the heterogeneous community will spend more than will the homogeneous poor community, and the Lindahl tax price of the poor person will be lower in the heterogeneous community. The poor person in the heterogeneous community gets more consumer surplus even if there is complete benefit taxation.

11. The *flypaper* moniker is occasioned by the fact that money may stick where it hits. If income rises, governments have to tax it away. But if general-purpose grants rise, governments seem to be able to cut taxes less than proportionately, and retain more of the funds for public spending. The issue is discussed at length in Mieszkowski and Oakland (1979).

12. Yinger (forthcoming) has a much more complicated model that includes need and cost factors as well. The logic used here is applicable in this more general case, but the particular allocations of grant funds will obviously change.

13. Another well-known argument is being ignored here. This is that general-purpose grants are more efficient from the standpoint of subnational governments precisely because they do not constrain subnational choices. Here I am assuming that categorical equity implies a social interest in spending on the particular service, which in turn means that subnational tastes are not the dominant concern.

14. The distribution of general-revenue-sharing funds, far and away the largest federal general-purpose transfer, is examined in Nathan, Manvel, and Calkins (1975).

15. Schultze (1974) shows how even this appearance might be viewed as wishful thinking by those with faith in the rationality of the political process.

16. This share was computed from numbers given in the *Budget of the United States, Fiscal Year 1982*, Special Analyses, p. 255.

17. A theoretical analysis can be found in Wilde (1971). An econometric analysis that gives these results is Gramlich (1982).

18. Suppose the true ratio of external to total marginal benefits was 0.2 and federal

grants were made open-ended at this matching rate. Most observers estimate the price elasticity of demand for state and local public services to be about 0.5 and the income elasticity to be very low. If so, a conversion to open-ended grants would raise state and local spending by about 0.1 and reduce (linearized) dead-weight loss by about $(0.5)(0.2)(0.1) =$ .01, or 1 percent of the present level of public spending. What this change does to grant levels is more uncertain. A rough estimate based on the numbers in Table 2.1 indicates that there is perhaps $80 billion of state and local expenditures in the functional categories in which the present $29 billion of closed-ended categorical grants (Table 2.6) is given. Converting these categorical grants to open-ended matching grants with a federal share of 0.2 will raise state and local spending to about $88 (based on the above elasticity), of which about $18 will be federal grant expenditures. In principle, the change should reduce federal grant outlays by $11 billion; in practice, I admit that everything hinges on how large state and local expenditures are in the grant categories, a number that (among others in this example) is very difficult to ascertain.

REFERENCES

Advisory Commission on Intergovernmental Relations. 1981. "Changing Public Attitudes on Governments and Taxes, 1981." S-10. Washington, D.C.

Atkinson, Anthony B., and Joseph E. Stiglitz. 1980. *Lectures on Public Economics.* New York: McGraw-Hill.

Barfield, Claude E. 1981. *Rethinking Federalism: Block Grants and Federal, State, and Local Responsibilities.* Washington, D.C.: American Enterprise Institute.

Barro, Robert J. 1974. "Are Government Bonds Net Wealth?" *Journal of Political Economy* 82: 1095–1117.

Boadway, Robin W., and David E. Wildasin. 1984. *Public Sector Economics.* Boston: Little, Brown.

Break, George E. 1980. *Financing Government in a Federal System.* Washington, D.C.: Brookings Institution.

Breton, Albert. 1965. "A Theory of Government Grants." *Canadian Journal of Economics and Political Science* 31: 175–87.

Breton, Albert, and Anthony Scott. 1978. *The Economic Constitution of Federal States.* Toronto: University of Toronto Press.

Buchanan, James M. 1950. "Federalism and Fiscal Equity." *American Economic Review* 40: 583–99.

———. 1965. "An Economic Theory of Clubs." *Economica* 32: 1–14.

Cassing, J. H., and A. L. Hillman. 1982. "State-Federal Resource Tax Rivalry: The Queensland Railway and the Federal Export Tax." *Economic Record* 58: 235–41.

Courant, Paul N., Edward M. Gramlich, and Daniel L. Rubinfeld. 1980. "Why Voters Support Tax Limitation Amendments: The Michigan Case." *National Tax Journal* 33: 1–20.

Feldstein, Martin S. 1975. "Wealth Neutrality and Local Choice in Public Education." *American Economic Review* 65: 75–89.

Fleming, Marcus. 1964. *Domestic Financial Plans under Fixed and Flexible Exchange Rates.* Washington, D.C.: International Monetary Fund Staff Papers.

Gordon, Roger H. 1983. "An Optimal Taxation Approach to Fiscal Federalism." *Quarterly Journal of Economics* 98: 567–86.

Gramlich, Edward M. 1982. "An Econometric Examination of the New Federalism." *Brookings Papers on Economic Activity* 2: 327–60.

———. 1984. "Subnational Fiscal Policy." Mimeo. Ann Arbor: University of Michigan.

Gramlich, Edward M., and Deborah S. Laren. 1984. "Migration and Income Redistribution Responsibilities." *Journal of Human Resources* 19: 489–511.

Hellerstein, Jerome R. 1977. "State Tax Discrimination against Out-of-Staters." *National Tax Journal* 30: 113–34.

Holmer, Martin. 1975. "Economic and Political Causes of the Welfare Crisis." Ph.D. dissertation. Cambridge, Mass.: MIT.

Ladd, Helen F. 1982. "Financing Public Services in the Federal System." Pp. 31–44 in *Federalism: Making the System Work*. Washington, D.C.: Center for National Policy.

Ladd, Helen F., and Fred C. Doolittle. 1982. "Which Level of Government Should Assist the Poor?" *National Tax Journal* 35: 323–36.

Levin, David J. 1983. "Receipts and Expenditures of State Governments and of Local Governments, 1968–81." *Survey of Current Business* 63: 25–38.

Lucas, Robert E. 1972. "Expectations and the Neutrality of Money." *Journal of Economic Theory* 4: 103–124.

McLure, Charles. 1967. "The Interstate Exporting of State and Local Taxes: Estimates for 1962." *National Tax Journal* 20: 49–77.

Medoff, James L. 1983. "U.S. Labor Markets, Imbalances, Wage Growth, and Productivity in the 1970s." *Brookings Papers on Economic Activity* 1: 87–120.

Mieszkowski, Peter, and William H. Oakland. 1979. *Fiscal Federalism and Grants-in-Aid*. COUPE Papers on Public Economics 1. Washington, D.C.: Urban Institute.

Mundell, Robert A. 1963. "Capital Mobility and Stabilization Policy under Fixed and Flexible Exchange Rates." *Canadian Journal of Economics and Political Science* 29: 475–85.

Musgrave, Richard A. 1959. *The Theory of Public Finance: A Study in Public Economy*. New York: McGraw-Hill.

Mutti, John H., and William E. Morgan. 1983. "The Exportation of State and Local Taxes in a Multilateral Framework: The Case of Household Type Taxes." *National Tax Journal* 36: 459–76.

Nathan, Richard P., Allen D. Manvel, and Susannah E. Calkins. 1975. *Monitoring Revenue Sharing*. Washington, D.C.: Brookings Institution.

Oates, Wallace E. 1972. *Fiscal Federalism*. New York: Harcourt, Brace, Jovanovich.

Pauly, Mark V. 1973. "Income Redistribution as a Local Public Good." *Journal of Public Economics* 2: 35–58.

Sargent, Thomas J., and Neil Wallace. 1975. "Rational Expectations, the Optimal Monetary Instrument, and the Optimal Money Supply Rule." *Journal of Political Economy* 83: 241–54.

Schultze, Charles L. 1974. "Sorting Out the Social Grant Programs: An Economist's Criteria." *American Economic Review* 64: 181–89.

Tiebout, Charles M. 1956. "A Pure Theory of Local Expenditures." *Journal of Political Economy* 64: 416–24.

Tresch, Richard W. 1981. *Public Finance: A Normative Theory*. Plano, Texas: Business Publications.

U.S. Department of Commerce. *Survey of Current Business*, various issues.

U.S. Office of Management and Budget. *Budget of the United States Government*, various issues.

Walsh, Cliff. 1983. "Reforming Federal Financial Relations: Some Radical (Or Are They Conservative?) Proposals." Paper presented at the Federal Finances Symposium, Hobart, Australia.

Wilde, James A. 1971. "Grants-in-Aid: The Analytics of Design and Response." *National Tax Journal* 24: 143–56.

Yinger, John. Forthcoming. "On Fiscal Disparities across Cities." *Journal of Urban Economics*.

CHAPTER THREE

Commentary

Henry J. Aaron

Gramlich's and Inman's articles both discuss problems of federalism, but they share only a few elements. Accordingly, I shall comment on them separately.

Gramlich's article is meaty, thought-provoking, and highly professional. No economist I can think of does a better job of integrating economic theory, statistics, and institutional realities to say something useful about practical problems. This encomium is not the prelude to devastating criticisms, but I do have some criticisms.

In the discussion of the various motives for grants, I believe that one motive (to which Inman alludes briefly) is omitted. Higher-level governments often employ lower-level governments as agents, using grants as a means of virtually drafting their administrative services. The responsibility appears to be joint, but the activity is controlled in all essential respects by the higher-level government. Such grants are best explained and appraised, in terms not of spillovers or interregional income redistribution, but of their effects on administrative efficiency. From this standpoint, narrow categories and high matching percentages are entirely rational. Better grounds for criticism would be whether the federal government should be involved in such functions, or whether administration by lower-level governments is truly advantageous.

Economists have almost completely neglected yet another motive for grants. I believe that the political leaders who fashioned the large increase in federal grants during the 1960s and 1970s thought that by offering money to hesitant states and localities on irresistible terms they could develop interest groups for activities that had previously had none and that by closely supervising how money was spent they could improve administrative processes in backward lower-level governments. In the jargon of our profession, they thought that both the preference functions and the production functions of the lower-level governments were malleable.

Economists have tackled endogenous production functions in models of learning-by-doing, but they have not carried this insight to governmental behavior. And the possibility that utility functions are endogenous to consumption has played little role except in speculations about the role of advertising and in Thomas Schelling's brilliant essays on self-control. I suggest that the history of grants-in-aid in the last quarter of a century is incomplete without both concepts. I suggest also that the endogeneity of state and local production functions and tastes for public services would go a long way toward explaining the fly-paper effect. What I have in mind is the process by which an increase in grants for a particular spending program will alter the tastes of the local politicians toward favoring more spending on that program.

My remaining comments on Gramlich's paper concern specific points. He states that there is little evidence from the distribution of expenditures among levels of government to show that there are gross misassignments of functions among levels of government. That statement is logically correct, but so is the converse—there is little evidence that functions, other than national defense, energy, and a few others, are correctly assigned. How bad are educational spillovers? How many people reside in the school district in which they received their precollege education? Where counties or states finance education, the same question applies with two words changed. Does the particular split of responsibilities for health and hospitals shown in Table 2.2 make economic sense? I do not even know how to go about answering that question.

Gramlich labels personal and corporate income taxes as the most important ability-to-pay taxes; property taxes are listed as benefit taxes; sales taxes are left unclassified, but they must be either benefit taxes or unimportant ability-to-pay taxes. Behind any such taxonomy lie implicit judgments about the value of benefits from public services that accrue to different households. Many years ago Martin McGuire and I showed that you could get virtually any result you wanted regarding the distribution of benefits from public services by selecting among plausible assumptions regarding the income elasticity of utility. For some assumed values, federal taxes were well-matched benefit taxes. For this reason I cannot assign much meaning to Gramlich's suggestion that ability-to-pay taxes should be levied at the federal level.

Gramlich suggests another principle for assigning taxes, that the federal government should take over easily exported taxes. I am not sure which taxes this rule would exclude, since even taxes borne entirely by the residents of one state may produce migration effects. Given such effects, state income taxes, for example, would have to be stricken from the list of revenue sources appropriate for state administration. The point is that all taxes place states at some disadvantage in competing for labor and capital. The degree of disadvantage depends not only on the type of tax but also on its level and structure. A poorly designed sales tax at a high rate may be more of a deterrent to business than a well-designed and well-administered corporation tax.

Gramlich's jeremiad against federal income tax deductibility of state and local taxes of all kinds is eloquent and justified. He bases his criticism on the damage such deductibility does to rational decisionmaking at the state and local levels. He might also have mentioned that deductibility, along with countless other base-narrowing provisions, raises marginal rates and increases deadweight losses to raise a given amount of revenue.

I am even more pessimistic than Gramlich on the subject of the exclusion of state and local bond interest from the federal tax base. While it is true that the interest differential between taxable and nontaxable bonds of given riskiness and maturity is only about 25 percent, the differential on short-term securities is considerably larger, in substantial measure because banks continue to hold short-term securities, as a result of their financial needs and the quaint and curious way we tax financial institutions. Furthermore, while the spread between taxable and nontaxable bonds has decreased, the volume of tax-exempt issues has mushroomed as they have become available for industrial and housing bonds. The scope for tax exemption to distort investment is thus vastly expanded. It seems safe to say that the total excess burden from the exemption of interest on state and local securities is at an all-time high.

Finally, Gramlich offers a set of recommendations regarding welfare. I found the appendix summarizing the analysis and results of another paper fascinating. The use of a bargaining model to handle migration effects of welfare payments is very clever. The most striking aspect of this analysis is that when he comes to policy recommendations, Gramlich drops the analytical framework and says that he would impose poverty-income-threshold transfer levels on both high- and low-benefit states. I cannot quarrel with the recommendation, although I do think that other aspects of the welfare program, such as work requirements, job creation, and other administrative rules are so important that benefit levels do not adequately characterize any welfare program. My point is that one can reach Gramlich's recommendation only if in Equation 5, $(1 - w)$, the weight attached to utility of residents in the low-benefit state in the social welfare function, is zero. In short, in making policy recommendations he drops his economic framework and turns—as I think he should—to value judgments.

That reminds me of two waggish laws of economics. The first states that nothing of importance in economics was ever settled by empirical analysis. The second states that nothing of importance was ever settled by theory either. I hate to think of the corollary.

I now turn the the Inman paper. He gets the big points right. The New Federalism has not been adopted and is not likely to be unless the November 1984 election is to the November 1980 election as the 1980 election was to the 1976 election, a truly awe-inspiring prospect. If it were to be adopted, the New Federalism would result in large but unevenly distributed reductions in spending by state and local governments. I do not trust the precision of his estimates (neither, I think, does Inman), because they derive from data generated by gradual year-to-year changes or from cross-sectional estimates where tastes may not have been adequately controlled. But the qualitative characterizations of those effects on outlays, i.e., big and negative, seem indisputable. The history is incomplete, however, without taking note of the effects of President Reagan's great budgetary leap backward. Even without the New Federalism, things have changed a lot. A fair amount of grant consolidation and budget reduction has occurred.

Inman's results suggest a ranking of motives on the part of the proponents of the New Federalism rather different from those he derives. He claims that the primary motives were to scale back the size of government and of federal intrusiveness, and that the achievement of these objectives was foiled by the political facts of life. States really want matching grants, not unrestricted funds, at least for welfare and other programs that help the poor. That way they can meet the requests of the teeming masses yearning to receive aid at low net marginal cost to the resident middle class. Members of Congress too were reluctant to surrender categorical grants, because each representative had one or more grants that served him or her and only a few others; logrolling did the rest.

Relegated to bit parts in this drama are two other factors to which participants in the negotiations between federal and state officials over

the New Federalism would, I think, assign primary importance. The first
is that, quite apart from any incentive effects, the New Federalism was a
raw deal for the states. They lost money right away and were promised
that after a few years they would lose a lot more. If Reaganauts had been
primarily interested in reducing the intrusiveness of government, they
could have upped the ante sufficiently to bring state officials on board.
Even if federal grants were greatly increased, it appears from both Gramlich's and Inman's calculations that total government spending could
have been cut sharply. The necessary offer was not made, because the
primary objective was cutting domestic federal spending. That the goal
of reducing federal intrusiveness may have been a rhetorical sham is
suggested by the Reagan administration's proposals for a massive increase in federal intrusiveness through regulation of state and private
behavior with respect to abortion and school prayer and by overriding
clinical and parental freedom in the treatment of infants. The fact is that
the New Federalism was a federal budget-cutting initiative, first and
foremost.

The second factor is best summarized by an ironic comment that Michael Stern, then staff director of the Senate Finance Committee, made to
me in 1977. "When it comes to welfare," Stern said, "all members of
Congress are statesmen. The welfare lobbies are so weak, most members
can and do vote their consciences." I realize that conviction as a motivation for voting has played little role in formal models, but I would suggest
that welfare is different in degree, not kind, from many other programs
included in the New Federalism proposals. Although they may not understand the Inman–Craig or Gramlich models, many members of Congress
do understand that giving less money with fewer incentives will produce
fewer effects than does more money with more incentives. Again, I think
that the Reagan administration could have swayed enough members of
Congress to accept the proposed restructuring of federalism if more
money had been put into the deal. But the desire to cut federal spending
was overmastering.

Commentary

George F. Break

Gramlich and Inman have both written excellent articles, providing much stimulus to thought and leaving little to criticize. I do have one major disagreement with Gramlich concerning the role played by federal deductibility for state and local taxes. He contends that "it is hard to imagine a consciously designed public policy measure having worse effects on both efficiency and equity counts than the federal income tax deduction for state and local taxes." In my view that feature of the federal individual income tax is both sound in principle and equity-enhancing in practice. Its effects on economic efficiency may well be generally unfavorable, but their quantitative significance has yet to be firmly established. Policy evaluation of federal deductibility is, I believe, much more complicated than Gramlich maintains, involving important, but uncertain, tradeoffs between equity gains and efficiency losses.

My argument begins with the following basic proposition concerning the role of taxes in a federal system of government: when two independent levels of government both make use of ability-to-pay taxes, the proper income tax base for each level is personal income minus the ability-based taxes of the other. This is simply a specific application of the general principle that ability to pay taxes is a function of each person's discretionary income—namely, that part of total income remaining after provision has been made for minimum survival consumption expenditures, unavoidable casualty losses, and so forth. Ability-based taxes, by definition, are compulsory transfers to the government in return for which no tangible benefits are received. Payment of such taxes to one level of government reduces ability to pay at other levels.

This is not the place to debate the relative philosophical merits of this basic proposition. Instead, let us accept it as a general principle of federal finance and discuss some of its important policy implications. Consider first a dual system of proportional income taxation, the federal rate being f and the state rate s. With no deductibility, the total nominal tax rate is $t = f + s$, and each component understates the tax rate each level of government is in fact imposing. The effective federal rate is $f^* = f/(1-s)$, and the effective state rate is $s^* = s/(1-f)$. With unilateral deductibility by either level, the total nominal tax rate is

(1) $t = f - fs + s$

For federal deductibility, which permits deduction of the state income tax from the federal base, it is convenient to concentrate on the second two terms. Taken together, $s(1-f)$ measures the net cost to state taxpayers arising from the state income tax. Taken separately, s indicates the gross rate of tax received by the state, part of which is provided by its own taxpayers $[s(1-f)]$, and part by the federal government (sf). In effect, the interaction term, sf, represents an implicit, unrestricted federal grant channeled to the state government through its resident taxpayers.

For state deductibility, on the other hand, it is convenient to concentrate on the first two terms of Equation 1. The term $f(1-s)$ now measures the net tax rate imposed on federal taxpayers, and fs is an implicit unrestricted state grant to the federal government. Double deductibility, which need not be discussed here, simply combines these two separate patterns.

Suppose, next, that each level of government wishes to operate Musgrave's Distribution Branch by levying progressive ability-based income taxes. In this joint venture the federal government is the senior partner, and states participate because there is no national consensus about the optimal degree of income redistribution to be achieved through the tax system. One would therefore expect to find considerable diversity in state Distribution Branch policies, some wishing to augment and others to offset the redistributive effects of the federal tax system. In such a fiscal environment the tax parameter of major interest to state policymakers is what I have called the incremental burden ratio, that is, the ratio of incremental state tax burdens imposed at each level of personal income to the taxpayers' after-federal-tax incomes.[1] The trouble with that ratio is its low visibility, not only to the general public but also to many state

TABLE 3.1

Federal Average and Marginal Income Tax Rates
at Selected Income Levels, 1983

Adjusted gross income (1980 $)	Average tax rate (f_i)	Marginal tax rate (f_i')	Residual income progression $(1-f_i')/(1-f_i)$
10,000	5%	15%	.89
20,000	11	19	.91
35,000	17	35	.78
50,000	22	40	.77
75,000	28	44	.78

SOURCE: John C. Weicher, "The 'Safety Net' and the 'Fairness' Issue," *AEI Economist* (August 1984): 10–11.

policymakers. In public discussions of tax policy it is the nominal state rate, or rates, that are the focus of attention. That being the case, the important question is how good, or bad, an indicator of the redistributive effects of state taxes those nominal rates are.

If there is no deductibility of one governmental level's income tax from the income tax base of the other level, neither tax is being imposed on a correctly defined base, and the nominal state tax rate is a seriously flawed indicator of the true redistributive effects of state taxes. This may be readily seen for the simple case of a proportional state income tax, levied at rate s. The incremental burden ratio at any income level i is then

(2) $IBR_i = s/(1 - f_i)$

where f_i is the average federal tax rate at income level i

Since f_i is higher at higher income levels, the IBR structure will be progressive. Combined with the average federal income tax rates shown in Table 3.1, a flat-rate state tax of 10 percent, for example, would produce incremental burden ratios that increased from 10½ percent at the $10,000 AGI level to 14 percent at the $75,000 level. With no deductibility, in short, a progressive state income tax would be more progressive than its nominal rate structure indicates, a nominally proportional tax would be progressive, and even a nominally regressive tax might be progressive.

Federal deductibility alone, which is the policy at issue here, would improve both the equity of the federal tax and the usefulness of the state nominal tax rate structure as an indicator of state redistributive policies. In this case, the incremental burden ratio is

(3) $\text{IBR}_i = \dfrac{s(1-f_i')}{(1-f_i)}$

where f_i' is the marginal federal tax rate at income level i

It will be recognized that this is simply the nominal state tax rate multiplied by one of the standard measures of income tax progression, namely, the elasticity of after-tax income with respect to before-tax income, commonly called *residual income progression.*[2]

For federal deductibility the relation between the nominal state tax rate structure and its incremental burden ratio structure may be summarized as follows:

1. $s_i > \text{IBR}_i$, since $(1-f_i')/(1-f_i) < 1$ for a progressive federal income tax.

2. Over any income range for which federal residual income tax progression is constant, the nominal state tax rate structure will be an accurate indicator of the incremental burden ratio structure. That is, the incremental burden ratio structure will be proportional when the nominal rate structure is proportional, progressive when it is progressive, and regressive when it is regressive.

3. Over an income range where residual income progression is falling—$(1-f_i')/(1-f_i)$ is rising—nominal state rates understate the progressivity of state tax policies, and vice versa.

The incremental burden ratio structure for a proportional state income tax of 10 percent, for example, may be found in the last column of Table 3.1 by moving the decimal point one place to the left.

On equity grounds alone, then, federal deductibility for state and local ability-based taxes has much to recommend it. Its efficiency rating is both more mixed and less favorable. Three main sets of effects need to be considered.

1. By lowering the net cost to federal-income-tax itemizers of state and local ability-based taxes, federal deductibility may stimulate state-local spending beyond optimal levels. Given the loose linkage between ability-based taxation and spending-level decisions and given the many ambiguities surrounding the concept of optimal government spending, this is a very difficult set of effects to evaluate. In general, it appears that policymakers face a troublesome tradeoff between federal deductibility, which may distort state-local Allocation Branch operations, and no deductibility, which, for the reasons

already given, would be likely to distort state-local Distribution Branch operations.

2. Federal deductibility biases the choice of alternative state-local financing instruments away from those that are not deductible from the federal individual-income-tax base. How strong these effects are is not clear. The biases in question could be either eliminated by repealing federal deductibility or moderated by establishing a set of matching, unrestricted federal grants based on state-local use of nondeductible taxes and user charges.

3. Federal deductibility may moderate the distorting effects that high state-local ability-based taxes have on decisions about business and household location. For federal tax itemizers, high-tax states are less unattractive than they otherwise would be, and businesses locating there can, as a consequence, attract such people with offers of lower salaries than might otherwise be needed.

Federal deductibility of state-local ability-based taxes, like most important tax issues, presents policymakers with some very hard choices. Restricting deductibility to fewer taxes (the retail sales tax has in recent years frequently been offered as a candidate for removal from deductibility status) would run the risk of seriously distorting state and local government choices among alternative ability-based taxes. Eliminating deductibility altogether would risk distorting both the operation of state-local redistributive tax policies and the location among states of households and businesses. Keeping federal deductibility intact, because it is regarded as an important structural feature of the federal income tax in a federal system of government, would risk continuation of the other distortions noted above. If deductibility is kept, its significance and equity could be improved by removing it from the official list of federal tax expenditures, thereby recognizing its basic structural function, and by moving it "above the line" into the category of "adjustments to income," thereby making it available to all federal income taxpayers.

NOTES

1. George F. Break, "Tax Principles in a Federal System," in Henry J. Aaron and Michael J. Boskin, eds., *The Economics of Taxation* (Washington, D.C.: Brookings, 1980), pp. 317–26.

2. Richard A. Musgrave and Peggy B. Musgrave, *Public Finance in Theory and Practice* (4th edition, New York: McGraw-Hill, 1984), pp. 360–63. The measure of residual income progression equals 1 for a proportional tax and is less than 1 for a progressive tax.

Commentary

Julius Margolis

The analysis of fiscal federalism within the framework of comparative statistics has great merit. However, it tells less than the full story. Five mjaor historical trends have affected the multi-level government structure of the United States: the growth of government; technological change; the decline of political parties; the revolution in the household economy, including the women's revolution; and the growth in democratization. These five trends have combined to effect the relative growth of the national government with the expansion of the locals as its agents.

THE PHENOMENAL GROWTH OF GOVERNMENT

All growing governments, whether they are unitary governments, like that of France, or highly centralized, like the Soviet Union's, are confronted by the huge bureaucratic diseconomies of trying to implement policy at a central point. France, the Soviet Union, the United States and, I would guess, almost all other nations, have set up extensive decentralized administrative structures. In the United States the degree of administrative decentralization is cloaked by the federal structure. Instead of regional divisions of federal agencies, the peripheral agencies have been the state and local governments, which are constitutionally independent of the central authorities. We find a modest degree of administrative decentralization of federal agencies and a number of regional organizations which may be created by the states but whose revenues and behavioral rules derive wholly from the federal government. More important is the way the "normal" state and local governments alter their structures and behavior so that they conform to the specifications of the feds. And of course many special districts and authorities were established with taxing powers, but their true role is to contract with the federal government, under terms specified by federal legislation, to perform services demanded by the federal government.

From a fiscal perspective, the federal government is primarily a financial intermediary, levying taxes and then transferring funds to local governments to support services performed by locally elected and controlled governments that have their own taxing and police powers. From a public service perspective, the state and local governments, when receiving federal grants or contracts, appear to be federal agents implementing federal objectives. A principal-agent model would select the federal agency rather than the local electorate as the principal in many of these operations.

When we recognize that a very large part of fiscal federalism is simply a way to adjust administrative decentralization to an American governmental structure, it becomes clear why the matching-grant formula bears no relationship to externalities. Federal loss of interest in a specific categorical program is likely to result in a budget cut rather than a search for a more efficient price.

Increasing government size fostered expertise in formulating and implementing public programs. The federal bureaucracy took the lead in sophistication of techniques and in hiring technically competent personnel. In time, the regional, state, and local bureaucracies hired their own professionals. In formal terms, programs were initiated at the federal and implemented at the local level, but in less formal terms we find a coalition of bureaucrats at all levels formed to administer these programs. Two aspects of this process are of special interest to us: increasing independence from the political process, and increasing reliance on the federal government as financier.

The coalition of bureaucracies became allied with a body of suppliers, much like the military-industrial complex, e.g., the health bureaucracies have allies in the hospitals, nursing homes, medical societies, drug companys, and instruments manufacturers, among others. And just as the military-industrial complex seems to have achieved a charmed independence from the normal political checks and balances, so has the coalition of expanding bureaus. The technical bureaucracies have come to dominate the legislative branch; at the local level they were even more influential, since they brought their own funds. The organizational power of the bureaucracies was given a powerful political boost by support from the suppliers.

The extent of these complexes of self-interested groups, dedicated professionals, and even some beneficiaries of the services is dependent on the costs of the programs, not the benefits. Herein lies an interesting observation about federalism. The set of input providers are professionalized and organized; the beneficiaries and citizenry are much less so. Of course, the political power of one coalition is not only measured in terms of its influence against the general citizenry and the specific program beneficiaries but is subject to the countervailing power of all the other coalitions competing for the limited resources extracted from the citizenry. Despite the competition among bureaus, the power in the public sector is heavily concentrated in the supply side. Although the elected leaders must eventually act to endorse or check the ambitions of the competitive bureaucracies, this model of federalism is a far cry from response to the median voters.

A second important feature of most public programs is the difference in distribution of cost versus benefits. Even for a public good, such as defense, which is spread throughout the nation, the production of weapons and training of personnel are restricted to a few production centers. Many public services such as health, education, or transportation have a very wide distribution of benefits but the production of the capital equipment is spatially concentrated. If we devised a political benefits-costs ratio, where benefits include gains to input suppliers as well as willingness to pay for outputs, the ratio for a given program would rise as we moved up the hierarchy of governments from local to national. This does not mean that local bureaus want to surrender their autonomy in exchange for a higher budget. On the contrary, there is much evidence that bureaus will resist growth if it means a dilution of independence. However, if the programs have grown due to federal initiative, coalitions already formed will resist returning funding to local levels. However, if this does happen the coalition may be able to keep a program going in the absence of direct federal support—which suggests that programs are overfunded at the federal level because of the political benefits-costs ratio and that a return of allocational decisions to the local or even the state level might bring the public decision makers closer to a social benefits-costs ratio. Another way of expressing it is that it might be of social advantage to "externalize" the costs of a public program: if the inputs of a program could be located outside the jurisdiction, then the only gain offsetting the tax costs of a program would be the value of the outputs, not the employment gains or the profits on the inputs. It seems paradoxical that even though private market failures may arise from externalities, it might be necessary to create another set of externalities to overcome public failures.

The conditions of growth in the public sector led to an excessive response to the changing trends discussed below. The coalition of suppliers greatly inflated the benefits of a program, and decentralized administration led to excessive growth at the local level. A counter-revolution should not be unexpected.

TECHNOLOGICAL CHANGE

The rapid technological changes of the past century have had a highly differential effect on local governments, since their boundaries remained relatively fixed while the pattern of land use changed drastically. Some locals became industrial enclaves, others became bedroom suburbs, and the most productive areas of the central cities turned into obsolete and high-cost producers of services for residential or business use. Thriving urban centers with great expectations were abandoned; others were depressed. This is a familiar story, but it is not clear that it had to result in the current huge fiscal disparities.

In the private market, capital equipment, labor skills, even entire industries have become obsolete. When a plant becomes obsolete it remains in productive use in the firm so long as its marginal operating costs are less than the price of the product. The capital declines in value in response to the loss of quasi-rents. Losses are taken by the owners of the capital. In time the obsolescent capital will be replaced by technologically efficient equipment, with the full faith and credit of the firm behind the credit used to finance the new equipment. The process in the public sector is very different. The city (the public plant) is expected to levy taxes sufficient to pay competitive public services (charge the same tax prices) even though the inefficient public facilities cannot attract or hold their old residential or business users. Attempting to charge the same prices (keep the high taxes) leads to abandonment and further decay. It is not surprising that, as in the case of the private firm, a higher level of organization imposes an umbrella of support over the "victims" of technological change. The (inefficient) city's costs (local taxes) are reduced through federal grants—a process similar to a firm's expecting lower quasi-rents from the older plants.

An alternative approach to shifting the problem of support of renewal of capital and labor to the central government might have been to expand the boundaries of the city containing the obsolescent resources so that the city will contain the new facilities and labor skills. However, the newer suburbs strongly resist such an expansion. Many of them might have been forced to accept annexation since they did not have the resources to support facilities, but federal support programs for new infrastructure construction obviated the need for this. One political response to the historical trend toward democratization represented by the federal support of the suburbs was a huge investment by the federal government in the resources of the central city. Boundary changes and the reassignment of responsibilities within the local units of a "regional government" might have reduced the need for federal fiscal intervention, but the drive to experiment in regional government was frustrated by problems of racial, ethnic, class, and economic differences in the urban population.

THE DECLINE OF POLITICAL PARTIES

One major instrument of political decisionmaking is the political party. If a party seeks to rule, then it must be part of a majority coalition, able to influence the agenda of the governing bodies of the central cities and the suburbs. It is the political party that is peculiarly adept at conflict resolution, at compromising among disparate interests. I would argue that we do not have real political parties in the United States at the national level; at the local level, the shadow of a party exists only in the older sections of the country. The local elections are contested by nonpartisan candidates; typically, they run in nonpresidential election years to avoid the taint of party. The ballots are structured to discourage any form of party voting. Therefore, the political capability for boundary changes and functional reassignment of tasks and fiscal resources is very limited.

THE NEW HOUSEHOLD ECONOMY

The growth of government is associated with the assumption of power—usually, by the central authority. Analysts have viewed this growth with alarm, especially when it is paired with the growth of the large and now gigantic firms. Opposing this trend has been a surprisingly large burst in economic activity in the household sector—that is, the most decentralized of all entities, the households, have been growing at a more rapid rate than the highly centralized ones. In the quarter-decade after

1950, business reproducible wealth increased by 130 percent and government reproducible wealth increased by 132 percent—while the lowly households' reproducible wealth increased by 220 percent.

A second major resource shift has been the huge decline in the number of hours of paid work over a lifetime and the dramatic increase in labor-force participation by women. The decline in paid work was a combination of a higher average age for leaving school, earlier retirement, and home production using leisure time and household capital instead of market employment. Even more sudden has been the drop in the size of the family, the reduction of the household to the nuclear family, and the woman's role shift from homemaker to fulltime member of the labor force.

Government programs have been an integral part of these changes. The first decades of life are spent in public educational institutions; the last decades of life are spent in publicly supported retirement status, with huge transfer programs to support the aged (and the younger disabled). In the postwar decades, public infrastructure was built to support private investment in suburban housing and cars. In recent decades household investment has shifted away from the house, and less complementary government investment is required. More important, especially for the debate about the new federalism, has been the transformation of women to members of the work force. Now the family pays taxes on this increased income, and the government manages the transfers. The transfer sector of the fiscal government has grown at twice the rate of collective consumption.

DEMOCRATIZATION AND EGALITARIANISM

The turbulent decade of the sixties brought into the political system neglected minorities such as the blacks, and broadened of the definition of civil rights. Equality before the law was extended to equality of public services. This revolution broke at the same time as the household revolution that surrendered to the government the role of transfers among generations, and the technological revolution that encouraged firms to locate in the suburbs near a highly skilled work force. The latter weakened the central cities and their capacity to support the revolution. The metropolitan areas had the resources to support the fiscal effects of these changes, but not the organizational structure nor political will. Local governments found it difficult to respond because of tax competition, boundaries which made it simple to avoid taxes, and a political structure biased toward property interests. We all know the history of the federal government's repeated attempts to resolve the fiscal problems of the cities.

SUMMARY

Our society has been subjected to a set of revolutions that have had a major effect on government at large and on the structure of local governments and the federal system in particular. The burden of change fell on the federal government, which relied heavily on local governments to administer programs designed and financed at the federal level. Each president from Nixon on has sought to reduce the federal role. Revenue-sharing was introduced, but the underlying structure of the relationship was not changed until the Reagan administration. If this administration succeeds in changing the balance, what will happen?

Our explanation implies that the programs will wither. The public has accepted the revolutionary changes and is willing to adopt complementary government programs. However, to continue these programs out of local resources would involve a degree of reorganization of local government that is highly unlikely, for there is no serious movement for regional governments. The federal government may well rescue the programs after the locals have failed to be responsive. There is another option: the states might continue the programs. The states seem to be the favored agency of the Reagan administration. They have been neglected by economic analysts (possibly it has been too difficult to go beyond a two-sector model) but they may be the right compromise between the fractionated locals and the overzealous federal government. The states have a stronger fiscal base, and their bureaucracies have been improved. Possibly they can prevent the counterrevolution in government from going to excessive lengths.

Distributional Programs: Education and Antipoverty

Budgetary programs that have substantial distributional implications are the focus of Part Two. Sheldon Danziger and Daniel Feaster review the recent history of income transfer programs in the federal budget, showing the nature and extent of the Reagan administration cuts. Richard Murnane evaluates public spending on primary and secondary education, considering such diverse issues as the trend in test scores, how to attract and keep good teachers in the public schools, and the reform of school finance. In the Commentary, Paul Courant raises methodological questions about the Danziger and Feaster evaluation of AFDC program trends and reflects briefly on the difficulties of achieving innovation in the provision of education. Eric Hanushek is critical of Danziger and Feaster's statistical methodology and their failure to account adequately for non-cash transfers; he also argues that we ought to reward good performance whether or not we can measure the characteristics that make for effective teaching. Focusing on the relationship between educational attainment and earning capacity, David Stern claims that recent policy has involved a shift away from reducing inequality in educational attainment toward achieving educational excellence. Finally, Jennifer Wolch cites the case of the service-dependent poverty population, who have become substantially worse off during the past few years. She suggests that to evaluate transfer programs properly it may be necessary to disaggregate the poverty population.

CHAPTER FOUR

Income Transfers and Poverty in the 1980s

Sheldon Danziger and Daniel Feaster

INCOME TRANSFERS AND ANTIPOVERTY POLICY

The primary intention of the War on Poverty was to promote employment opportunities and higher wages. The poor could then escape poverty in the same manner as the nonpoor, that is, through the private labor market, and not because of government transfer payments. Despite these hopes, income-maintenance expenditures grew rapidly. By the mid 1970s, such spending cost about three times as much in real terms as in the mid 1960s, owing to introduction of new programs and to increases in both the number of beneficiaries and the size of income-maintenance payments in existing programs. However, real transfer growth slowed in the late 1970s and then became negative in some programs as a result of the Reagan administration's budget cuts.

MEASURING POVERTY AND
THE IMPACT OF TRANSFERS

An analysis of income poverty requires the specification of both a poverty threshold and an income concept. A household is considered poor if its income falls below the poverty threshold. Different poverty thresholds and income concepts convey different information about the nature and magnitude of the poverty problem. While there are a variety of alternative thresholds and income concepts (Danziger and Gottschalk 1983), we focus here on the official poverty threshold and on two income concepts: pretransfer income and census money (post-transfer) income.

The federal government's official measure of poverty provides a set of income cutoffs adjusted for household size, the age of the head of the household, and the number of children under age 18. (Until 1981, sex of the head and farm/nonfarm residence were other distinctions.) The cut-offs provide an absolute measure of poverty that specifies in dollar terms minimally decent levels of consumption. The official income concept—current money income received during the calendar year—is defined as the sum of money wages and salaries, net income from self-employment, social security income and cash transfers from other government pro-grams, property income (e.g., interest, dividends, net rental income), and other forms of cash income (e.g., private pensions, alimony). Current money income does not include capital gains, imputed rents, government or private benefits-in-kind (e.g., food stamps, Medicare benefits, em-ployer-provided health insurance), nor does it subtract taxes, although all of these affect a household's level of consumption.[1]

So that they represent the same purchasing power each year, the official poverty thresholds are updated yearly by an amount corresponding to the change in the Consumer Price Index. For 1982, the poverty lines ranged from $4626 for a single aged person to $19,698 for a household of nine or more persons. The average poverty threshold for a family of four was $9862. According to this absolute standard, poverty will be eliminated when the incomes of all households exceed the poverty lines, regardless of what is happening to average household income.

Census income data do not distinguish between income derived from market and private transfer sources (e.g., wages, dividends, alimony) and that derived from government transfers (e.g., social security, public assis-tance). As such, census figures fail to separate the private economy's antipoverty performance from the performance of government cash-transfer programs. Households that do not receive enough money income from private sources to raise them over the poverty line constitute the pretransfer poor (a more exact title would be pre-government-transfer poor). Pretransfer poverty has received little attention, yet it reveals the magnitude of the problem faced by the public sector after the market economy and private transfer system (e.g., private pensions, interfamily transfers) have distributed their rewards.

The antipoverty effect of transfers is measured in this paper by a com-parison of pretransfer and post-transfer poverty. Cash transfers include social security, railroad retirement, Aid to Families with Dependent Children, Supplemental Security Income, general assistance, unemployment insurance, workers' compensation, government employee pensions, and veterans' pensions and compensation.[2] Pretransfer income is determined by subtracting government transfers from post-transfer income. This definition assumes that transfers elicit no behavioral responses that would cause income without transfers to deviate from observed pretransfer income. However, transfers do induce labor-supply reductions, so recipients' net incomes are not increased by the full amount of the transfer—true pretransfer income is likely to be higher than measured pretransfer income. Pre/post comparisons, therefore, like the ones made here, are likely to provide upper-bound estimates of antipoverty effects.[3]

GEOGRAPHICAL VARIATIONS IN POVERTY

Table 4.1 shows the incidence of post-transfer poverty for 1967, 1978, and 1982. We use 1967 and 1982 data because they are reported on the earliest and latest available computer tapes from the Census Bureau's annual March Current Population Survey (CPS). We chose 1978 because real cash transfers per household peaked in the late 1970s and because poverty has increased in every year since 1978.[4] The residence division of *residence not identified* is not included in the 1967 classification; it was added to preserve confidentiality after the CPS began to identify each household's state of residence.

Poverty as officially measured declined from 14.3 percent of all persons in 1967 to 11.4 percent in 1978, but increased to 15.0 percent in 1982.[5] During the 1967–1978 period, by far the largest decline was for persons living outside metropolitan areas, who had the highest rates in 1967. Poverty rates were relatively constant inside metropolitan areas during this period. Since 1978, rates have increased sharply in all locations, so that the 1982 rate is below the 1967 rate only for those living outside metropolitan areas. Central city residents now have the highest poverty rate and comprise the largest group among the poor.

As Table 4.2 shows, in the nation and in each region except the South, pretransfer and post-transfer poverty rates in 1982 were higher than they were in 1967. In the 1967–1978 period, poverty rates in the South declined more than those in the other regions; between 1978 and 1982, they rose less quickly. There is now much less variation in poverty rates across regions than there was in 1967. For example, poverty rates in the Northeast, the lowest in both 1967 and 1982, increased from 71 to 87 percent

TABLE 4.1

Incidence of Post-Transfer Poverty
among Persons, by Residence

	All persons	Inside metropolitan areas		Outside metropolitan areas	Residence not identified
		In central cities	Outside central cities		
Incidence of poverty					
1967	14.3%	15.1%	7.6%	20.3%	N.A.
1978	11.4	15.5	6.5	13.8	11.1
1982	15.0	20.3	9.2	18.1	13.6
% change, 1967–78	− 20.3	+ 2.6	− 14.5	− 32.0	N.A.
% change, 1978–82	+ 31.6	+ 31.0	+ 41.5	+ 31.2	+ 12.6
% change, 1967–82	+ 4.9	+ 34.4	+ 21.1	− 10.8	N.A.
Composition of the poor					
1967	100.0	31.2	18.7	50.1	N.A.
1978	100.0	36.2	20.9	34.7	8.3
1982	100.0	35.5	22.6	34.2	7.7
Composition of the population					
1967	100.0	29.5	35.2	35.3	N.A.
1978	100.0	26.5	36.5	28.6	8.4
1982	100.0	26.2	36.9	28.3	8.5

N.A. = not available.
SOURCE: Computations by authors from March 1968, 1979, and 1983 Current Population Survey data tapes.

of the United States average, while those in the South, the highest in both years, decreased from 155 to 121 percent of the United States average.

The last column of Table 4.2 shows the growing antipoverty effect of increased transfers over the 1967–1978 period and their declining effectiveness since 1978: the percentages of all pretransfer poor persons removed from poverty by cash transfers increased from 26.3 to 43.6 percent, and then declined to 37.5 percent. The pattern in each of the regions is the same. Transfers are least effective in the South in each year. Transfer benefits are much lower in the South than in other regions and some programs, notably Aid to Families with Dependent Children for unemployed parents and Medicaid for the medically indigent, are not even

TABLE 4.2
Incidence of Poverty among Persons and the
Antipoverty Impact of Transfers, by Region

	Pretransfer income	Post-transfer income	Percentage reduction in poverty due to cash transfers*
United States			
1967	19.4%	14.3%	26.3%
1978	20.2	11.4	43.6
1982	24.0	15.0	37.5
% change, 1967–78	4.1	− 20.3	−
% change, 1978–82	18.8	31.6	−
Northeast			
1967	15.1	10.1	33.1
1978	19.7	10.4	47.2
1982	22.5	13.0	42.2
% change, 1967–78	30.5	− 2.9	−
% change, 1978–82	14.2	25.0	−
North Central			
1967	16.8	11.6	31.0
1978	17.3	9.1	47.4
1982	22.6	13.4	40.7
% change, 1967–78	3.0	− 21.6	−
% change, 1978–82	30.6	47.3	−
South			
1967	27.3	22.2	18.7
1978	23.7	14.7	38.0
1982	26.8	18.1	32.5
% change, 1967–78	− 13.2	− 33.4	−
% change, 1978–82	13.1	23.1	−
West			
1967	16.1	10.9	32.3
1978	18.8	10.0	46.8
1982	22.7	14.1	37.9
% change, 1967–78	16.8	− 8.3	−
% change, 1978–82	20.7	41.0	−

–Not applicable.
*Defined as ((Post-transfer − Pretransfer)/Pretransfer) × 100
SOURCE: See Table 4.1.

TABLE 4.3

The Composition of the Federal Budget, 1965, 1981, 1986
(as percentage)

	Fiscal Year			
Category	Actual 1965	Actual 1981	Reagan's 1981 budget proposal for 1986	February 1984 CBO estimates for 1986
National defense, international affairs, and veterans' benefits and services	50.4%	29.5%	40.1%	33.0%
Transportation, community and regional development, and revenue sharing	6.5	6.0	3.7	4.3
Natural resources and environment, energy, and agriculture	5.8	4.5	2.5	3.1
Income security	21.7	34.3	32.8	31.9
Health	1.4	10.0	11.2	11.4
Education, training, employment, and social services	1.9	4.8	2.5	3.0
General government, interest, general science, space and technology, other	14.8	15.5	11.6	17.0
Offsetting receipts	− 2.5	− 4.6	− 4.4	− 3.7
Total	100.0%	100.0%	100.0%	100.0%
Total outlays as % of GNP	18.0	23.0	19.0	23.3
Total outlays in billions of current dollars	$118.4	$657.2	$912.0	$1012.0

NOTE: Some slight errors may exist due to reclassification of categories between 1965 and the present.
SOURCE: Office of Management and Budget, *The United States Budget in Brief, Fiscal Year 1975* (Washington, D.C.: U.S.G.P.O., 1975), p. 48; Council of Economic Advisers, *Economic Report of the President, January 1981* (Washington, D.C.: U.S.G.P.O., 1981), p. 315; Congressional Budget Office, *Baseline Budget Projections for Fiscal Years 1985–1989*, Part 2 (Washington, D.C.: U.S.G.P.O., 1984), p. 106.

operated by most southern states. However, as with poverty rates, the southern region's antipoverty impact of transfers converges toward the United States average.

THE REAGAN POLICY TOWARD INCOME TRANSFERS

From 1967 to 1978, real cash transfers per household increased by 67 percent and real GNP per household increased by 9 percent, whereas from 1978 to 1982 real transfers declined by 1 percent and real GNP by 7 percent (Gottschalk and Danziger 1984). How much of the recent increase in poverty is due to the retrenchment in income transfer programs initiated by the Reagan administration?

First let us review Reagan's changes in federal spending, which were designed both to reduce expenditures and to alter their composition. The first two columns of Table 4.3 demonstrate a growth in the ratio of federal spending to GNP from 18 to 23 percent and show the changes in budget shares that took place between 1965 and 1981 (the last pre-Reagan budget). The swing away from defense and toward income security, education and training, and especially health is apparent, and its reversal was the focus of the Reagan administration's reallocation of the budget. Column 3 indicates, by projecting budget shares to 1986, when all proposed changes would have been in place, the planned changes in priorities that Reagan put forward during the winter of 1981. Defense was to be expanded toward percentages prevailing in the early 1970s while education and training were to be rolled back to the lower levels of that same period. The income-security expenditure share was to be cut 10 percent and the expansion in health expenditures was to continue, but at a much more modest pace.

What actually has been enacted by Congress is somewhat different, as can be seen by comparing the third and fourth columns of the table. Column 4 presents February 1984 estimates of the 1986 budget size and shares, assuming that current laws and policies, including those proposed by Reagan *and* already enacted by Congress, remain unchanged. Obviously, he has not yet gained all his expected defense increases. The 1983 Social Security Amendments provided somewhat larger cuts in income security than was originally anticipated. This outcome was not reflected in the 1981 budget projections. The health share is projected to rise above expectations, because a proposed health-cost-containment package has not yet been fully enacted. Training costs will fall less than expected, because of a new program introduced to combat the long recession. And

TABLE 4.4

Estimated Outlay Changes in FY 1985 Due to
Reagan Administration Proposals and
Congressional Actions through FY 1984

Program	Projected outlays pre-Reagan ($ billions)	Proposed changes (% of baseline)	Enacted changes (% of baseline)
Social security	$200.6	− 10.4%	− 4.6%
Veterans' compensation	10.7	− 8.4	− 0.9
Veterans' pensions	3.8	− 2.6	− 2.6
Supplemental Security Income (SSI)	8.1	− 2.5	+ 8.6
Unemployment insurance	29.8	− 19.1	− 17.4
Aid to Families with Dependent Children (AFDC)	9.8	− 28.6	− 14.3
Total	$262.8	− 11.6%	− 6.2%

NOTE: For discretionary programs the proposed reductions are estimated by comparing the lowest outlays proposed by the administration for FY 1985 from its FY 1982, FY 1983, and FY 1984 budgets to the estimated outlays for FY 1985 under pre-Reagan policies. For entitlement programs the savings that would be attributable to enactment of all the various specific (actually or conceptually) nonoverlapping program changes proposed by the administration in its FY 1982, FY 1983, and FY 1984 budgets (and, in the case of social security, the proposal forwarded to Congress subsequent to the FY 1982 budget) are separately estimated and summed.

SOURCE: Palmer and Sawhill (1984), pp. 185–86.

the ratio of federal spending to GNP is even higher than it was in 1981, partly because not all the planned spending cuts were enacted, and partly because of the deep and prolonged recession.

On the expenditure side, then, Reagan and Congress have slowed the expansion of the welfare state and stepped up military expenditures. In dollar terms, or even in terms of shares of the budget, as Table 4.3 indicates, expenditure changes other than defense have not been large. However, it was in spending for the means-tested welfare programs that the Reagan administration differed so much from previous administrations and there that the cuts were the largest.

Table 4.4 shows the proposed and enacted percentage changes in outlays for each of the cash transfer programs included in the CPS data used in this paper. Since social security is by far the largest program, its proposed and enacted changes dominate the totals. Cash transfers in the CPS data are about 6 percent lower than they would have been had pre-Reagan policies remained constant.

President Nixon's Family Assistance Plan (FAP) and President Carter's Program for Better Jobs and Income (PBJI) were both intended to establish a national minimum-income guarantee, to extend benefits to persons who were categorically ineligible under existing programs, and to promote work incentives by keeping marginal benefit reduction rates on earnings well below 100 percent. As such they would both have raised the safety net and filled in some of its gaps, particularly in regional differences in eligibility requirements and benefit levels. But both generated fatal congressional opposition and harsh criticism from policy analysts who pointed out that these reforms and the goal of controlling social spending were incompatible.

Unlike his predecessors, Presidet Reagan succeeded in reforming welfare. The Omnibus Budget Reconciliation Act of 1981 (OBRA) reduced costs and caseloads by raising the tax rate on welfare recipients' earnings and by establishing more restrictive gross-income limits. It did not, however, lower the safety net for those who do not work. The philosophy behind the cuts was to transform certain income transfer programs from a general support system encouraging simultaneous receipt of wages and welfare to a safety net that forced a choice between work and welfare.

The administration argued that the break-even level for welfare benefits was so high in some states because of the work-incentive provisions it eliminated (the $30-and-one-third rule); many who were not "needy" were receiving welfare. Further, work incentives served more to keep families dependent on welfare than to encourage work. Welfare had become an income supplement and previous welfare reforms were, according to a Reagan advisor, attempts "by a largely liberal, intellectual elite . . . to foist on an unsuspecting public . . . a guaranteed income" (Anderson 1984, p. 25). Work effort was best secured by work requirements (proposed but not enacted), not work incentives.

Generally speaking, those who did not work lost only a small portion of their benefits. The biggest losers were the "working poor" and not the "poorest of the poor," who are not in the labor force. For example, the U.S. House of Representatives, Committee on Ways and Means (1984b) reports that in 1980, forty-six states would have provided AFDC benefits to a woman with two children and earnings at 50 percent of the poverty line; by 1984, only twenty-four would have provided benefits. For a woman with wages equal to three-quarters of the poverty line, the number of states paying AFDC dropped from 37 to 6. In addition, the latter

TABLE 4.5

Incidence of Poverty among Nonaged Households, by Sex of Head and by Region

Nonaged household head with children under 18	% pretransfer poor		% change, 1978–1982	% post-transfer poor		% change, 1978–1982	Reduction in poverty due to transfers	
	1978 (1)	1982 (2)	(3)	1978 (4)	1982 (5)	(6)	1978 (7)	1982 (8)
Male								
Northeast	7.6%	10.8%	+42.1%	5.4%	8.4%	+55.6%	28.9%	22.2%
North Central	6.2	11.8	+90.3	4.5	8.8	+95.6	27.4	25.4
South	10.6	14.4	+35.8	8.2	11.6	+41.5	29.3	19.4
West	8.9	14.0	+57.3	6.3	11.1	+76.2	41.3	20.7
All regions	8.4%	12.9%	+53.6%	6.2%	10.1%	+62.9%	26.2%	21.7%
Female								
Northeast	57.8%	56.0%	− 3.1%	46.6%	49.1%	+ 5.4%	19.4%	12.3%
North Central	50.5	58.2	+15.2	40.6	50.4	+24.1	19.6	13.4
South	53.6	55.4	+ 3.4	47.0	50.1	+ 6.6	12.3	9.6
West	46.0	49.6	+ 7.8	35.5	41.3	+16.3	29.6	16.7
All regions	52.4%	55.0%	+ 5.0%	43.2%	48.2%	+11.6%	17.6%	12.4%

NOTE: Percentage change is defined as $((X_{1982} - X_{1978})/X_{1978}) \times 100$ for poverty rates and as $((Post\text{-}transfer - Pretransfer)/Pretransfer) \times 100$ for the reduction in poverty due to transfers.
SOURCE: See Table 4.1.

woman had a negative federal tax burden in 1980 (payments from the Earned Income Tax Credit exceeded the sum of the social security and personal income taxes), but a positive burden in 1984. In 1980, this woman's disposable income would have been 108 percent of the poverty line, while by 1984 it would have dropped to 92 percent.

Robert Lampman (1974) has argued that the declaration of the War on Poverty had an immediate and far-reaching effect: it required all existing programs and proposals for policy changes to address the question, "What does it do for the poor?" The Reagan economic program asks instead, "What does it do for the incentives to work and to save?" As a result, we share Lampman's (1983) judgment that the declining rate of growth of federal revenues, the reordering of domestic versus military priorities, and the vast projected budget deficit fundamentally mean that "it is extraordinarily difficult to initiate new social spending measures in the field which the President has set. In that sense, the President's design for calling a halt to the growth of welfare statism seems to have won the day" (p. 381). If this is the case, then the comparisons of 1978 and 1982, which we make below, show too small an effect of the recent changes—they compare "what is" with "what was," rather than with "what would have been had there been no cuts."

Accepting the premise that these changes in the various programs differentially affect demographic groups, we examine changes in the anti-poverty impact of transfers for households headed by nonaged persons (less than 65 years of age) by sex of head. We disaggregate by region because of the long-standing regional differences in benefit levels and eligibility requirements in transfer programs, and we use household rates because transfer benefits generally vary with household size and income. The household measure treats all households equally, regardless of the number of persons.

CHANGES IN TRANSFERS AND THE TREND IN POVERTY

Table 4.5 shows the pretransfer and post-transfer poverty rates and their percentage changes from 1978 to 1982 and the antipoverty impact of transfers in those two years. While the regional variations noted above are evident in these data, they are much smaller than the male-female differences. In each region, households headed by women are four to five times more likely to be poor than those headed by men. In this period, however, the percentage increase in both pretransfer and post-transfer

TABLE 4.6

Components of the Antipoverty Impact of Transfers among
Nonaged Households, by Sex of Head and by Region

| Nonaged household head with children under 18 | % pretransfer poor households receiving cash transfers | | % pretransfer poor transfer recipients who escape poverty | | % change, 1978–1982 | | % total post-transfer poverty, 1982, due to changes in transfer program probabilities | % poverty increase, 1978 to 1982, due to changes in transfer program probabilities |
| | | | | | Cash transfers per household* | Post-transfer poverty gap per household* | | |
	1978 (1)	1982 (2)	1978 (3)	1982 (4)	(5)	(6)	(7)	(8)
Male								
Northeast	68%	63%	43%	36%	−29.3%	+5.6%	8.5%	25.9%
North Central	59	63	47	41	−26.8	−2.6	3.0	6.4
South	51	50	45	39	−32.6	−3.1	4.2	12.9
West	55	55	51	38	−22.5	+5.7	9.5	20.9
All regions	57%	56%	46%	39%	−28.3%	+0.6%	6.0%	14.5%
Female								
Northeast	85%	83%	23%	15%	−20.2%	+2.8%	8.2%	79.2%
North Central	77	83	26	16	−16.2	+9.3	7.6	23.2
South	74	67	17	14	−11.6	−0.1	3.4	14.0
West	76	74	30	23	−12.3	−2.9	7.3	23.8
All regions	78%	75%	23%	16%	−16.9%	+1.9%	5.9%	24.0%

* Adjusted for inflation.
NOTE: Percentage change is defined as $((X_{1982} - X_{1978})/X_{1978}) \times 100$.
SOURCE: See Table 4.1.

poverty rates was larger for men. Lower wage rates and lower labor-force-participation rates for women make women's poverty rates relatively immune to macroeconomic conditions—they are high at all stages of the business cycle.

For both men and women, the most rapid increase in the pretransfer poverty rate was in the North Central region and the least rapid was in the South. This reflects regional differences in the severity of the recent recession. Between 1978 and 1982, the unemployment rate increased from 6.1 to 9.7 percent in the United States as a whole, but from 5.3 to 11.1 percent in the North Central region and from 5.6 to 8.9 percent in the South.

Post-transfer poverty for all the groups shown increased more rapidly than pretransfer poverty (compare column 6 to column 3), which indicates that the total rise in poverty cannot be attributed to the recession. Transfers removed a smaller percentage of the pretransfer poor in 1982 than in 1978 for all groups. The antipoverty impacts shown here for the nonaged are smaller than those shown in Table 4.2 for all persons because by far the largest antipoverty impacts occur among the aged. The impacts are larger for households headed by men than for those headed by women, because men generally receive social insurance transfers, which are based on prior earnings and have higher maximum levels than the welfare transfers generally received by women.

Table 4.6 shows in greater detail some components of the antipoverty impact of transfers. Consider first the percentage of pretransfer poor households receiving transfers (columns 1 and 2) and among those households, the percentage receiving enough to raise them above the poverty line (columns 3 and 4). These two components provide additional insight into the male-female differences in the antipoverty impact of transfers. In each year and each region, poor women are more likely to receive transfers than men, but much less likely to be taken out of poverty. For example, in 1982 three-quarters of households headed by women received transfers, while only 56 percent of those headed by men received them. But only about one-fifth of the former received enough transfers to raise them above the poverty line, while about 40 percent of male-headed households were so raised.

Women are less likely to be taken out of poverty than men both because their mean poverty gaps are higher and because their average transfers received are smaller. In 1982, the mean pretransfer poverty gap for all female-headed households was $6615 and the average transfer amount for those receiving transfers was $4377; for male-headed households the corresponding figures were $5477 and $5141. In 1978, the gaps were $6489 and $5445 (in 1983 dollars) for women and men and the transfers received were $5124 and $7097, respectively. Thus, the poverty gap for women was about 20 percent higher than that for men in both years, while transfers were about 28 percent lower in 1978 and about 15 percent lower in 1982.

The probability of transfer receipt was relatively constant in all regions and for men and women over the 1978–1982 period, but the probability of escape after receipt declined for all groups. This result follows from the way the budget cuts were structured: poor households were more likely to receive reduced transfers than to be totally removed from the programs. Note that these conditional probabilities of escape after transfer receipt, already rather low, do not reflect the fact that almost half of poor male-headed households and a quarter of poor female-headed units receive no transfers at all. Although the rapid growth of transfers was a prime motivator of the Reagan budget cuts, these significant gaps in coverage and inadequate benefit levels have received little attention.

Columns 5 and 6 of Table 4.6 show that the decreased probability of escape after transfer receipt can be roughly attributed to the declining real value of transfers and not to macroeconomic conditions. The real pre-transfer poverty gap increased by less than 1 percent for all poor men and by less than 2 percent for all poor women. The gap for male transfer recipients actually declined by 3 percent; for female recipients, it increased by 2 percent. Some portion of the increased gap is due to the elimination of public employment positions previously funded through the Comprehensive Employment and Training Act (CETA) and might thus be attributed to program changes. The reduced escape probabilities therefore reflect the decline in real value of cash transfers of almost 30 percent for men and about 17 percent for women. This decline is due both to the administration's budget cuts and to the fact that benefits in programs that are not indexed to consumer prices by law (e.g., AFDC, unemployment insurance) have been falling in real terms since the mid 1970s.

The final two columns of Table 4.6 present the results of a simple statistical exercise that computes how much of the observed increase in the number of post-transfer poor households between 1978 and 1982 can be attributed to the observed declines in the probability of transfer receipt and the probability of escape after receipt. We begin by assuming that the program changes did not affect the demographic composition of households and pretransfer poverty.[6] We then multiply the number of pretransfer poor households in each group in 1982 by the corresponding 1978 probabilities shown in columns 1 and 3. This yields the number of poor households in 1982 who would have been removed from poverty by transfers if the 1978 transfer probabilities had remained constant. Subtracting from this simulated number the actual number of households removed from poverty in 1982 yields the increase in the number of poor households due to transfer program changes.

In column 7 this number is expressed as a percentage of the total number of post-transfer poor households in 1982; in column 8, as a percentage of the increase in the number of post-transfer poor households between 1978 and 1982. We find that the number of poor households in 1982 was about 6 percent higher both among those headed by men and by women than it would have been if the two probabilities had not changed.

Since the percentage increase in the number of poor households between 1978 and 1982 was so much higher among families headed by men (Table 4.5), the additional 6 percent of poor households accounts for about 15 percent of the increased male-headed poor families and about 25 percent of the female-headed poor families.[7] This differential is not surprising, since many female household heads either lost eligibility for AFDC or had their benefits significantly reduced by the new program rules. Our results are in general agreement with a recent microsimulation study released by the U.S. House of Representatives, Committee on Ways and Means (1984a), which attributed a larger percentage of the observed poverty increase among female household heads to program changes and a larger percentage among male household heads to the recession.

AN ECONOMETRIC MODEL OF THE
ANTIPOVERTY IMPACTS OF TRANSFERS

The descriptive data presented so far have not controlled for varying personal characteristics of the poor or differences in the degree of their poverty. We have thus ignored the fact that the probability that a poor household will receive a transfer or escape from poverty will depend to a great extent on household characteristics. For example, a nonworking widow with children will be eligible for social security benefits that are not affected by her other sources of income, while a nonworking divorced woman's AFDC benefits will be affected, and a poor household with income just below the poverty line is likely to receive different treatment by transfer programs than a household with little pretransfer income. In

TABLE 4-7

Predicted Probabilities of Changes in the Antipoverty Impacts of Transfers,
Nonaged Female Heads of Household with Pretransfer Income below the Poverty Line

	Probability of receiving a transfer		Probability of escaping poverty given receipt of a transfer		Unconditional probability of escape[a]		Change in number per 100 poor who escape poverty[b]
	1978 (1)	1982 (2)	1978 (3)	1982 (4)	1978 (5)	1982 (6)	1978–1982 (7)
Variation by race and Hispanic origin[c]							
White	.783	.764	.238	.184	.186	.141	− 4.5
Black	.878	.845	.069	.055	.060	.046	− 1.4
Hispanic	.901	.831	.142	.046	.128	.038	− 9.0
Variation by marital status for white female head[a]							
Never married	.885	.811	.176	.129	.156	.104	− 5.2
Divorced or separated	.704	.705	.162	.152	.114	.107	− 0.7
Widowed	.961	.949	.670	.603	.643	.572	− 7.1

Variation by region for white female head[e]							
Northeast	.865	.787	.298	.259	.257	.204	− 5.3
North Central	.768	.837	.288	.176	.221	.147	− 7.4
South	.708	.624	.081	.129	.058	.080	+ 2.2
West	.802	.794	.367	.227	.294	.180	− 11.4
Variation by distance from the poverty line for white female head[f]							
0.25	.795	.778	.215	.166	.171	.129	− 4.2
0.75	.537	.501	.693	.709	.372	.355	− 1.7

[a]Defined as the product of the probability of receipt by the pretransfer poor $(\frac{R}{P})$ from column 1 or 2 and the conditional probability of escape given receipt $(\frac{E}{R})$ from column 3 or 4; thus the unconditional probability of escape for a pretransfer poor household equals $(\frac{E}{P})$.

[b]Defined as the difference between the probabilities in columns 6 and 5 multiplied by 100.

[c]Evaluated using 1978 and 1982 coefficients from Table 4.8 and 1982 race-specific means for all independent variables for both years.

[d]Evaluated using 1978 and 1982 coefficients from Table 4.8 and 1982 means for white female heads for all independent variables (except marital status) for both years.

[e]Same as d, but including marital status and excluding region.

[f]Same as d, but including marital status and excluding distance from the poverty line.

order to examine more closely the antipoverty impacts of transfers, we
have estimated a two-equation econometric model of the antipoverty
impact of cash transfers.

We do not attempt to model the macroeconomy or the labor market
here. Rather, just as in our descriptive analysis, a household's pretransfer
income is assumed to be exogenous. The statistical model we use can be
termed a probit equation with sample selection. At a given time (in this
case 1978 or 1982), a pretransfer poor household has the potential to
receive a transfer, and, if one is received, to escape poverty. The following
functions describe these potentials:

(1) $y_1 = X\beta + \varepsilon_1$

(2) $y_2 = Z\delta + \varepsilon_2$

where y_1 is the potential to receive a transfer and y_2 is the potential to
escape poverty.

The specification and estimation of this model are discussed in the
Appendix. The first regression included all households with pretransfer
incomes below the poverty line; the second, only those households which
were pretransfer poor and which receive any cash transfers.

The regression coefficients derived from this model allow us to control
for changes in personal characteristics since 1978, changes that could not
be incorporated in the decomposition analysis of Table 4.6. Table 4.7,
columns 1 and 2, shows several series of predicted probabilities of transfer receipt for pretransfer poor nonaged female household heads for 1978
and 1982. Columns 3 and 4 show the predicted conditional probabilities
of escape from poverty given receipt. These probabilities are computed
by evaluating the regression coefficients at the 1982 weighted sample
means for all the independent variables except the one that is allowed to
vary in each panel of the table. Columns 5 and 6 are the unconditional
probabilities of escape, the products of the probabilities shown in columns 1 and 3 and columns 2 and 4, respectively. The final column shows
the 1978–1982 change in the number of poor households per 100 poor
households who escape poverty. It is merely the difference between columns 6 and 5 multiplied by 100. Since we have held personal characteristics at their 1982 means and allowed the coefficients to vary, we now have
a "true" measure of the change in the number of poor households due to
changes in the antipoverty impact of transfer programs.

For example, the first panel shows that in 1982, 76.4 percent of all
white female heads received transfers and 18.4 percent of the recipients

escaped poverty. If the transfer system had not changed since 1978, then 78.3 percent of the 1982 population of female heads would have received them and 23.8 percent would have escaped. The probabilities of receipt for blacks and Hispanics are higher than for whites in each year, but their probabilities of escape are much lower. This is primarily because whites are more likely to receive social insurance transfers, which are on average higher than welfare transfers. For whites and Hispanics, the declines in the escape probabilities are the bigger of the changes in the two components. The last column shows that if the transfer system were as effective in 1982 as it was in 1978, there would be 4.5 percent fewer white, 1.4 percent fewer black, and 9 percent fewer Hispanic households headed by women in poverty. What is most striking is how low the probabilities of escape are for these women in each year.

The second panel shows that transfers have a much greater antipoverty impact for widows than for other female heads; they are more likely to receive transfers and much more likely to escape poverty. This is due to their receipt of social security survivor's benefits, which are on average much higher than other transfers.

The variation by region shows the familiar pattern: the lowest probabilities of receipt and escape in the South, but regional convergence. The variation by distance from the poverty line is as expected: the poorest have a greater probability of receipt but a smaller probability of escape. The percentage decline in the number who escape is not affected by distance from the poverty line.

These results are consistent with those of our statistical decomposition. Since 1978, changes in transfer programs have reduced their antipoverty effectiveness. These declines, however, are relatively small in contrast to the increased antipoverty impacts of the 1967–1978 period (see Table 4.2).

IMPLICATIONS FOR ANTIPOVERTY POLICY DURING THE MID 1980s

Gottschalk and Danziger (1984) have projected that the aggregate poverty rate will remain above the 1978 rate through the late 1980s even if the economy continues to grow as fast as the Reagan administration expects. A return to "full" employment would substantially reduce poverty rates for nonaged men but would have a much smaller impact on the aggregate rate, because this group represents an increasingly smaller portion of the total poverty population. Thus, if poverty is to fall, the economy must grow and there must be a renewed antipoverty initiative directed at curbing the "feminization of poverty." About half of these households headed by women with children remain poor (Table 4.5), even though about three-quarters of such households receive income transfers (Table 4.6). And both our statistical decomposition and our econometric analysis show that these households have been adversely affected by the recent program changes.

It is beyond the scope of this paper to present a comprehensive strategy to lower poverty among families headed by single women. But we can offer a few suggestions. First, AFDC guarantees, which have fallen on average by more than a third in real terms since 1970, should be indexed to the same price index used to update the poverty threshold, and a national minimum AFDC benefit should be introduced. The indexation of social security benefits and the introduction of a national minimum benefit in the Supplemental Security Income program are the key reasons that poverty for the aged declined throughout the 1967–1982 period. These changes would have a particularly large impact on poverty in the South, where benefits were initially low and where they have eroded the most in recent years.

Second, a targeted employment program that allows recipients to mix work and welfare should be introduced. The Supported Work Demonstration project (Manpower Demonstration Research Corporation 1980) provides an example of the antipoverty possibilities of such a program. Danziger and Jakubson (1982) used Supported Work data to simulate the national effects of implementing such a program. They found that over 80 percent of the AFDC participants would have been poor if they merely had access to current transfer programs, whereas only 35 percent would have been poor if they also had access to the jobs program. Unlike a negative income tax, this type of employment program both increases work effort and reduces poverty.

These reforms obviously increase public spending. In contrast, a third reform is a social child-support program that attempts to minimize the need for additional public funds. Under that program, every adult who cared for a child and did not live with the child's other parent would be eligible for a support payment that would be financed by a percentage-of-earnings tax on the absent parent. If the tax on the absent parent fell below a fixed minimum level, because the parent's earnings were too low, the support payment would be raised to that level by government funds. Even if total government AFDC expenditures were maintained at current levels, the program could reduce poverty because of the additional revenue raised from absent parents (Oellerich and Garfinkel 1983).

What are the prospects for new antipoverty initiatives? While, by elect-ing Reagan, the voters clearly called for a retrenchment of the welfare state, they have shown no enthusiasm for the recent large increases in poverty. And even though the Reagan administration has reduced the scope of transfer programs, it has not abandoned their primary goals—the provision of minimum levels of cash, nutritional, medical, housing, and educational assistance for a substantial portion of the population.

During its first year in office, the administration proposed drastic cut-backs in most social programs. But because so many households are direct beneficiaries of at least one program, widespread voter and congressional opposition developed. This was particularly true for pro-grams with the broadest range of recipiency across the income distribu-tion (e.g., social security, educational financing program for college stu-dents). As a result, only a small portion of the cuts were in programs whose benefits were widely distributed. The large cuts were in income-tested welfare programs that provide benefits only for those toward the bottom of the income distribution. But because they serve fewer recipi-ents, and because the benefits of the poorest were least affected, budgetary savings as a percentage of the total budget were small.

These cuts came, however, on top of a deep recession, and those events together raised poverty rates back to the levels of the late 1960s. This increase now limits the administration's ability to obtain enactment of additional cuts in transfer programs.[8] Indeed, it is now clear to the admin-istration that the technical and political problems that make large distri-butional changes difficult are synergistic. In its defense of the fiscal year 1984 budget proposals, the U.S. Office of Management and Budget (1983) stated that "entitlement programs develop vast networks of de-pendency that cannot be precipitously altered without unacceptable so-cial and human costs. As a consequence, their claim on the budget and national economy . . . can be reduced only slowly . . ." (ch. 3, p. 9). Unfortunately, there remains a large gap between a decision to refrain from asking for further transfer cuts and one to propose increased anti-poverty expenditures.

APPENDIX: SPECIFICATION OF ECONOMETRIC MODEL

Let y_1 be the potential to receive a transfer and y_2 be the potential to escape poverty. Then

$$(1) \quad y_1 = X\beta + \varepsilon_1$$

(2) $y_2 = Z\delta + \varepsilon_2$

However, only y_1^* and y_2^*, indicators of y_1 and y_2, are observed

(3) $y_1^* = \begin{cases} 1 \text{ if } y_1 > 0 \\ \\ 0 \text{ if } y_1 < 0 \end{cases}$

and y_2^* is observed only if $y_1^* = 1$.

(4) $y_2^* = \begin{cases} 1 \text{ if } y_2 > 0 \text{ and } y_1 > 0 \\ 0 \text{ if } y_2 \leq 0 \text{ and } y_1 > 0 \\ \begin{matrix} \text{unobserved} \\ \text{or undefined} \end{matrix} \text{ if } y_1 \leq 0 \end{cases}$

There is some ambiguity surrounding the domain of ε_2. In what is termed the "sequential-decision" model by Maddala (1983), ε_2 is only defined if $y_1^* = 1$ (or $\varepsilon_1 > -X\beta$). The likelihood function, $\pounds$ (given that the ε_i are normally distributed), is

(5) $\pounds = \prod_{i=1}^{n} \Phi(X\beta)^{y_1^*} [1 - \Phi(X\beta)]^{(1-y_1^*)} [\Phi(Z\delta)^{y_2^*} \{1 - \Phi(Z\delta)\}^{(1-y_2^*)}]^{y_1^*}$

where Φ is the standard normal cumulative distribution function.

The estimation of this model can be accomplished in two steps. First, to get estimates of β, estimate a univariate probit on the indicator y_1^* for those who are pretransfer poor. Then to get estimates of δ, estimate a univariate probit on the indicator y_2^* only on those pretransfer poor who received a transfer. This procedure allows conditional inference on the probability of escaping poverty, but it does not allow the likelihood of escaping poverty to affect the probability of receiving transfers. If there are unobserved characteristics that affect both probabilities, then the estimates will be biased. Consider, for example, the unobserved variable "knowledge of how the system operates." A household head who scores high on this variable will be both more likely than one who scores low to receive a transfer at all, and more likely to receive a larger transfer and hence to escape poverty.

This correlation can be incorporated by changing the assumption on the domain of ε_2. While the situation is still one of sequential decision, ε_2 is defined for the entire population but is only observed when $\varepsilon_1 > -X\beta$. This is a censoring problem which can easily be handled with the additional assumption that

$$(6) \begin{pmatrix} \varepsilon_1 \\ \varepsilon_2 \end{pmatrix} \sim \text{Biv. Normal} \left(\begin{pmatrix} X\beta \\ Z\delta \end{pmatrix}, \begin{pmatrix} 1 & \varrho \\ \varrho & 1 \end{pmatrix} \right)$$

The estimation can no longer be done in two steps. The likelihood function is now

$$(7) \quad \pounds = \prod_{i=1}^{n} [1 - \Phi(X\beta)]^{(1-y_1^*)} F(X\beta, -Z\delta, -\varrho)^{y_1^*(1-y_2^*)} F(X\beta, Z\delta, \varrho)^{y_1^* y_2^*}$$

where Φ is as before and F is the bivariate normal cumulative distribution function.

Another way to think of the problem is to examine the log likelihood and define three mutually exclusive subsets of the sample. Let A be those for whom $y_1^* = 0$, that is, those who do not receive a transfer. Let B be those for whom $y_1^* = 1$ and $y_2^* = 0$, those who receive a transfer but are not removed from poverty. And let C be those for whom $y_1^* = 1$ and $y_2^* = 1$, those who both receive a transfer and escape poverty. The log-likelihood function, L, can then be expressed as

$$(8) \quad L = \sum_{i\varepsilon A} \ln[1 - \Phi(X\beta)] + \sum_{i\varepsilon B} \ln[F(X\beta, -Z\delta, -\varrho)] + \sum_{i\varepsilon C} \ln[F(X\beta, Z\delta, \varrho)]$$

The preceding models analyze only whether transfers remove a poor household from poverty. Since transfers are continuous, the model could be rewritten to focus on the extent to which transfers alleviate poverty. Let T equal the amount of transfers, and rewrite Equations 1 and 2 as

$$(9) \quad y_1 = X\beta + \varepsilon_1$$

$$(10) \quad T = Z\delta + \sigma\varepsilon_2$$

where σ is a scale parameter.

The likelihood function would then be

$$(11) \quad \pounds = \prod_{i\varepsilon A} [1 - \Phi(X\beta)] + \prod_{i\varepsilon B} \int_{-X\beta}^{\infty} \frac{1}{\sigma} G\left(\varepsilon_1, \frac{T - Z\delta}{\sigma}\right) d\varepsilon_1$$

We have estimated weighted regressions for both the univariate (Equation 5) and bivariate (Equation 7) models for nonaged female household heads with children. In the second specification, there was strong evidence against the hypothesis that $\varrho = 0$. We report those results in Table 4.8. (The other results are available on request. Because of high computational costs we did not estimate these models for male-headed households or any models reflecting the specification of Equations 8 and 11.) The first stage of Equation 7 included all households with pretransfer

TABLE 4.8
Determinants of the Antipoverty Impact of Transfers,
Nonaged Female Heads of Household with Pretransfer
Income below the Poverty Line

Independent variables	Probability of receiving a transfer		Probability of escaping poverty given receipt of a transfer	
	1978	1982	1978	1982
Constant	1.209	0.925	− 0.844	− 1.539
	(0.205)	(0.162)	(0.153)	(0.194)
Black	0.043	0.078	− 0.281	− 0.379
	(0.132)	(0.118)	(0.125)	(0.138)
Hispanic	− 0.067	− 0.129	− 0.148	− 0.551
	(0.203)	(0.117)	(0.195)	(0.230)
Family size 2	− 0.022	− 0.197	0.194	− 0.083
	(0.134)	(0.108)	(0.145)	(0.139)
Family size 5 +	0.121	0.426	− 0.326	− 0.082
	(0.139)	(0.124)	(0.147)	(0.175)
Region				
North Central	− 0.369	0.183	0.141	− 0.222
	(0.160)	(0.143)	(0.158)	(0.181)
South	− 0.554	− 0.483	− 0.304	− 0.576
	(0.152)	(0.140)	(0.184)	(0.173)
West	− 0.252	0.021	0.251	− 0.089
	(0.178)	(0.158)	(0.178)	(0.172)
Residence				
Central city	0.253	− 0.059	−	−
	(0.134)	(0.120)		
Suburban	− 0.013	− 0.131	−	−
	(0.146)	(0.132)		
SMSA not identified	− 0.180	− 0.305	−	−
	(0.202)	(0.171)		
Age				
<25 years	− 0.138	0.119	− 0.393	− 0.032
	(0.186)	(0.143)	(0.202)	(0.177)
25–34 years	− 0.130	0.224	− 0.367	− 0.041
	(0.123)	(0.109)	(0.155)	(0.151)
55–61 years	0.494	− 0.344	− 0.123	− 0.138
	(0.512)	(0.295)	(0.215)	(0.326)
62–64 years	0.097	− 0.132	− 0.191	− 0.146
	(0.533)	(0.572)	(0.386)	(0.713)

Continued on next page

TABLE 4.8—*continued*

Independent variables	Probability of receiving a transfer		Probability of escaping poverty given receipt of a transfer	
	1978	1982	1978	1982
Completed schooling				
<9 years	0.315	0.292	–	–
	(0.182)	(0.146)		
9–11 years	0.251	0.319	–	–
	(0.120)	(0.115)		
13–15 years	–0.062	–0.597	–	–
	(0.163)	(0.141)		
16+ years	–0.558	–0.597	–	–
	(0.298)	(0.286)		
Has disability	0.224	0.261	–0.367	0.585
	(0.185)	(0.158)	(0.189)	(0.156)
Student	0.014	–0.130	0.251	0.304
	(0.232)	(0.178)	(0.287)	(0.248)
Marital status				
Never married	0.664	0.343	0.309	–0.017
	(0.180)	(0.128)	(0.178)	(0.168)
Widowed	1.224	1.097	0.796	1.424
	(0.241)	(0.176)	(0.179)	(0.166)
Ratio of pretransfer income to poverty line	–1.463	–1.523	2.644	1.949
	(0.171)	(0.143)	(0.219)	(0.305)
ϱ	–0.893	0.763	–0.893	0.763
	(0.108)	(0.206)	(0.108)	(0.206)
Number of (unweighted) observations	1030	1293	827	988
Log likelihood	–663.4	–822.5	–663.4	–822.5

– Coefficient not estimated.

NOTE: The constant in columns 1 and 2 refers to a pretransfer poor white household head of a family of three or four persons, living outside a metropolitan area in the Northeast region who is 35–54 years of age, has completed twelve years of school, is not disabled or a student, and is divorced or separated. In columns 3 and 4 residence and education are omitted from the equations.

Asymptotic standard errors appear below coefficients in parentheses.

SOURCE: Computations by authors from March 1979 and March 1983 Current Population Surveys.

incomes below the poverty line. The dependent variable took the value of 1 if the household received any cash transfers, 0 otherwise. In the second stage, we included only those households that were pretransfer poor and received cash transfers. The dependent variable took the value of 1 if the household was removed from poverty by the transfers, 0 otherwise.

We weighted the log-likelihood function by the CPS sample weights so that the estimated equation would accurately reflect the published (weighted) variable means. The weights were adjusted so that the number of observations shown at the end of Table 4.8 is the number of unweighted observations. The procedure is the same as Manski and Lerman's (1977) correction for choice-based sampling. The fact that weighted and unweighted means for the dependent variables differ raises the possibility that the CPS sample stratification is in some way correlated with transfer receipt or low income. Examining this possibility is beyond the scope of this paper.

The independent variables were sets of dummies for the household head's race or Hispanic origin, household size, regional and metropolitan residence, age, education, and marital, disability, and student status. Also included was the ratio of pretransfer income to the poverty line. The probability-of-receipt equation included all the variables listed. Tunali (1983) shows that at least one restriction is necessary for identification of the model. Therefore, we omitted the residence and education dummies from the second equation. Education and residence are expected to affect one's knowledge of and access to transfer programs and thus to influence participation, but not to affect the amount of the transfer received and hence the probability of escape from poverty.

The general pattern of results—though not the relative magnitudes of the coefficients—is similar for each year. For example, ceteris paribus, the probability of receiving transfers increases with family size, is lowest in the South, higher for those with a disability, highest for widows, and lowest for Hispanics. Not surprisingly, those among the poor who are closest to the poverty line are least likely to receive transfers, but if they do receive transfers they are much more likely to escape poverty. The probability of receiving enough transfers to escape poverty is lowest in the South, and highest for widows and whites.

ACKNOWLEDGMENTS

This research was supported in part by the Graduate School Research Committee at the University of Wisconsin–Madison. Christine Ross provided valuable research assistance. The authors benefited from the comments of the editors and the conference discussants and participants.

NOTES

1. The omission of in-kind transfers biases estimates of transfer recipiency downward and biases estimates of the incidence of post-transfer poverty upward. Plotnick and Smeeding (1979) show that in 1974 an additional 2 to 3 percent of the population received in-kind transfers for food, housing, and/or medical care, but did not receive cash transfers. On the other hand, some have suggested that direct taxes should be subtracted from money income if in-kind transfers are added. According to the Census Bureau data provided to the U.S. House of Representatives, Committee on Ways and Means (1984c), in 1982 federal and state income and payroll taxes increased the number of poor people by 3.175 million, while food stamps and public housing reduced the number of poor by 2.799 million. However, if a value for medical care transfers is added, then the net effect of adding the major in-kind transfer benefits and subtracting taxes is to reduce the poverty count by 8.328 million persons if in-kind transfers are valued at their market costs, or by 2.155 million persons if they are added at the value that recipients would be willing to pay for them (U.S. Bureau of the Census 1984).

2. Because of the way the data are reported, public employee pensions are counted as a government transfer, like social security retirement benefits, not as a component of post-transfer income, like private pensions.

3. For example, consider an individual who earns $3000. Assume that after the passage of a public assistance program, with an income guarantee of $3000 and a tax rate of 50 percent, the person reduces hours of work and earns $2500. A transfer of $1750 is now received and total income is $4250, but the individual's final income is only $1250 higher. Because pretransfer income is in the absence of transfers an empty category, we and the authors of most other studies measure the redistributive effect as the difference between pretransfer and post-transfer income ($4250 − $2500), not as the increase in final income. Plotnick's (1984) simulation study shows that, in the absence of transfers, pretransfer poverty in 1974 for nonaged families would have been 12.4 percent rather than the observed 13.9 percent. Since post-transfer poverty was 11.4 percent, the simulation reduces the estimated antipoverty effect of transfers from 18 to 8 percent.

4. See Gottschalk and Danziger (1984) for an analysis of the relationship between macroeconomic conditions, income transfers, and poverty.

5. These patterns would not change if in-kind transfers were valued and added to cash income. See Danziger and Gottschalk (1983) for a discussion. The patterns are also the same in the 1983 data, released after this paper was completed. Poverty was 15.0 percent in 1982 and 15.2 percent in 1983.

6. If program changes, such as elimination of public jobs, increased pretransfer poverty, then our estimates are too low.

7. At the conference, Paul Courant suggested that we focus explicitly on changes in the antipoverty impact of transfers under Reagan by using data for the 1980 to 1983 period (the 1983 data became available shortly after the conference). Such a comparison also reduces the variation in economic conditions between the two chosen years. We reproduced the data in Tables 4.5 and 4.6 for 1980 and 1983 and found that our overall results were not altered by this refocus. For example, column 8 of Table 4.6 in the text shows that the changes in transfer programs accounted for about 14.5 percent of the increase in the number of poor male households and 24.0 percent in the number of poor female households between 1978 and 1982. Between 1980 and 1983, the corresponding percentages are 17.3 and 29.9. Given the high computational costs, we did not think it necessary to reestimate the econometric model.

8. In fact, the Tax Reform Act of 1984 made several policy changes, not sought by the administration, which will raise the incomes of many poor female household heads somewhat. First, welfare recipients who receive child-support payments may keep the first $50

per month. Current law allows no such income disregard. Second, beginning in 1985 the maximum earned income-tax credit is increased from $500 to $550 and the eligibility ceiling is raised from $10,000 to $11,000. Third, the OBRA changes of 1981 raised the AFDC benefit reduction rate to 100 percent after four months of work. The 1984 act introduced a $30 per month disregard for months five through twelve.

REFERENCES

Anderson, Martin. 1984. "The Objectives of the Reagan Administration's Social Welfare Policy." Pp. 15–27 in D. Lee Bawden, ed., *The Social Contract Revisited: Aims and Outcomes of President Reagan's Social Welfare Policy*. Washington, D.C.: Urban Institute Press.

Danziger, Sheldon, and Peter Gottschalk. 1983. "The Measurement of Poverty: Implications for Antipoverty Policy." *American Behavioral Scientist* 26: 739–56.

Danziger, Sheldon, and George Jakubson. 1982. "The Distributional Impact of Targeted Public Employment Programs." Pp. 210–26 in Robert Haveman, ed., *Public Finance and Public Employment*. Detroit: Wayne State University Press.

Gottschalk, Peter, and Sheldon Danziger. 1984. "Macroeconomic Conditions, Income Transfers and the Trend in Poverty." Pp. 185–215 in D. Lee Bawden, ed., *The Social Contract Revisited: Aims and Outcomes of President Reagan's Social Welfare Policy*. Washington, D.C.: Urban Institute Press.

Lampman, Robert. 1974. "What Does It Do for the Poor? A New Test for National Policy." *Public Interest* 34: 66–82.

———. 1983. "Review Article: Economic and Social Policies under the Reagan Administration." *Journal of Social Policy* 12: 378–86.

Maddala, G. S. 1983. *Limited Dependent and Qualitative Variables in Econometrics*. Cambridge: University of Cambridge Press.

Manpower Demonstration Research Corporation. 1980. *Summary and Findings of the Supported Work Demonstration*. Cambridge, Mass.: Ballinger.

Manski, Charles, and Steven Lerman. 1977. "The Estimation of Choice Probabilities from Choice-Based Samples." *Econometrica* 45: 1977–88.

Oellerich, Donald, and Irwin Garfinkel. 1983. "Distributional Impacts of Existing and Alternative Child Support Systems." *Policy Studies Journal* 12: 119–30.

Palmer, John, and Isabel Sawhill, eds. 1984. *The Reagan Record*. Cambridge, Mass.: Ballinger.

Plotnick, Robert. 1984. "The Redistributive Impact of Cash Transfers." *Public Finance Quarterly* 12: 27–50.

Plotnick, Robert, and Timothy Smeeding. 1979. "Poverty and Income Transfers: Past Trends and Future Prospects." *Public Policy* 27: 255–72.

Tunali, Insan. 1983. "A Common Structure for Models of Double Selection." Social Systems Research Institute Paper 8304. Madison: University of Wisconsin.

U.S. Bureau of the Census. 1984. *Estimates of Poverty including the Value of Noncash Benefits, 1979 to 1982*. Washington, D.C.: U.S. Government Printing Office.

U.S. House of Representatives, Committee on Ways and Means. 1984a. *Effects of the Omnibus Budget Reconciliation Act of 1981 (OBRA) Welfare Changes and the Recession on Poverty.* WMCP 98–33, 25 July 1984. Washington, D.C.: U.S. Government Printing Office.

———. 1984b. *Families in Poverty: Changes in the "Safety Net."* 98th Congress, 2nd Session, Committee Print 98–37. Washington, D.C.: U.S. Government Printing Office.

———. 1984c. "Tax Policy under Reagan Increases Number of Poor." News release, 31 July 1984.

U.S. Office of Management and Budget. 1983. *Budget of the United States Government, Fiscal Year 1984.* Washington, D.C.: U.S. Government Printing Office.

CHAPTER FIVE

An Economist's Look at Federal and State Education Policies

Richard J. Murnane

Schooling in the United States is an extraordinarily decentralized activity. Over 15,000 school districts make decisions about what salaries and benefits to offer teachers and how to allocate students and teachers to schools and classrooms. Over two million teachers decide where to apply for teaching positions, whether to request transfers, and whether to leave the profession. Over 40 million students decide how to respond to the varied academic demands placed on them. All in all, there are a tremendously large number of actors in the schooling sector who can and do respond to the incentives they face and whose responses influence the amount of learning that takes place in our schools. A central theme of this chapter is that in analyzing federal and state education policies, it is critical to examine how policies alter these incentives and to review carefully what we know about these actors' responses to changes in incentives.

One consequence of the decentralization of United States schooling is enormous variation in the quality of education provided in different school districts and, for that matter, among schools within a district. A second theme of this chapter is that evaluations of public policies should focus on how they affect the entire distribution of educational achievement, not only on how the policies affect "average achievement." In particular, it is important to consider how policies affect the education of children who in the past left the schools not only with the preexisting characteristics of minority group membership or low family income, but also without cognitive skills.

The strategy I employ in developing a framework for analyzing government education policies has three steps: first, I assess trends in educational outcomes; second, I summarize what is known about the causes of these trends; and third, I attempt to map the causes to policies. I encountered a number of problems in carrying out this strategy. First, the only systematic outcome data available are students' scores on tests of cognitive skills. These test scores do provide significant information about the skills of students in our schools. However, the linkages between these scores and life outcomes such as income are not extremely tight in the United States (cf. Jencks 1972).

Second, the arrows connecting trends to causes in many cases are very faint, if not invisible. One reason is that the design of the National Assessment of Educational Progress (NAEP), the testing program that provides the best test-score data, precludes identification of the school district or even the state in which any individual student lives. As a result, the NAEP data cannot be used to evaluate whether specific policies or educational programs affect children's test scores.

Third, linking causes to policies is very hazardous in an environment in which so many factors influence children's achievement, and the same policy (e.g., federally sponsored compensatory education) results in very different educational programs at different sites.

With these caveats explicit, I proceed.

TESTSCORE TRENDS AND EXPLANATIONS

SAT SCORES

Over the period 1963–1980 the average score of high school seniors taking the College Board's Scholastic Aptitude Test (SAT) of verbal ability fell in an almost unbroken trend from 478 to 424. The average SAT math score fell over this period from 502 to 466 (O'Neill 1984). While the declines up to 1970 are explained in large part by changes in the composition of the test-taking population, these changes do not explain the declines during the 1970s (*On Further Examination* 1977). These trends, a cause for real concern, have been emphasized in many of the recent reports criticizing the quality of United States education (e.g., *NCEE* 1983).

In assessing explanations for the decline, it is important to keep in mind that the scores measure the skills of students who have completed twelve years of education. Consequently, any set of SAT scores tells us more about what was happening during the previous twelve years than it tells us about the factors affecting student skills in the year the tests were taken. Thus, to explain the declines in scores during the 1970s, we must look for changes that took place primarily during the 1960s.

One category of explanation for the SAT score declines focuses on changes in the world outside the schools, including a sense of disillusion arising from the Vietnam War, an increase in TV watching, and a higher rate of marital dissolutions (*On Further Examination* 1977). A second category includes changes directly related to formal schooling. The best-documented schooling change contributing to the score decline is a reduction in the number of academic courses students take. This decline was the result, in part, of an attempt during the 1960s and early 1970s to tailor high school education to the needs and preferences of individual students. Subsequent research (Bryk et al. 1984; Coleman et al. 1982; Harnischfeger and Wiley 1984) supports the link between the number of academic courses students take and their scores on standardized tests.

In the four years since the SAT scores bottomed out in 1980, the average SAT scores have risen slightly (from 424 to 426 on the verbal section and from 466 to 471 on the math section: Ranbom 1984). Also, during the period 1976–1983, the gap between the average score of black students and that of white students on both the SAT verbal and math tests declined slightly. In 1976, the ratio of the average score of black students to that of white students on the SAT verbal tests was 0.736; in 1983, it was 0.765. The comparable numbers for the SAT math test are 0.718 and 0.762 (Wainer 1984). Why have the SAT scores started to rise again—albeit slowly? Why has the black-white gap closed somewhat? To answer these questions, we need to learn about the early schooling experiences and the achievement of the students who took the SAT tests in the early 1980s.

NATIONAL ASSESSMENT OF EDUCATIONAL PROGRESS

The National Assessment of Educational Progress (NAEP) is a federally sponsored testing program under which large samples of American children, aged 9, 13, and 17, are tested in a range of subject areas. The first tests were administered in 1970, and a new round of tests is given every three to four years, depending on the subject area. These test scores provide the best available evidence on the skills of students of different ages attending United States schools.

Reading

The reading skills of American children were assessed by NAEP in the school years ending in 1971, 1975, and 1980. The trends in the scores differ by age group. The scores of 17-year-olds show a reduction over the decade in inferential comprehension skills (making inferences from material presented in short passages) and stability in literal comprehension skills (locating information contained in the text) (NAEP 1981b). Since ability to make inferences is tested in several parts of the SAT, the decline in the inferential comprehension scores on the NAEP tests lends support to the conclusion that the SAT score decline over the 1970s reflected a real reduction in certain skills in the test-taking population and was not simply an artifact of a changing test-taking population.

The trend in the reading scores of 9-year-olds during the 1970s is very different from the trend for 17-year-olds. In fact, the trend for younger children provides quite encouraging data on recent changes in United States education. Over the decade the test scores of 9-year-olds increased significantly. Moreover, black children experienced the greatest gains, resulting in a closing of the black-white achievement gap. The scores of 13-year-olds increased in one skill area (literal comprehension) and remained stable in the other skill areas. As a group, the 13-year-old black children made greater gains than the white children (NAEP 1981b).

One explanation proposed for the gains in the skill levels of younger children, especially black children, is compensatory education. During the 1970s, Title I of the Elementary and Secondary Education Act of 1965 provided federal funds to local school districts to improve the basic skills of educationally disadvantaged children. It took local school districts several years to learn how to use the new categorical funds and to direct them to targeted children. However, by the mid 1970s, most local school districts complied with the regulations mandating that the funds be used to provide extra services to educationally disadvantaged children (Goettel et al. 1977).

The educational effectiveness of Title I programs has proved difficult to evaluate, since local districts design and implement quite varied programs. However, recent evidence suggests that the program has been effective in improving the skills of the target group—primarily low-achieving children in the primary grades (Anderson 1982; NAEP 1981a).

Mathematics

NAEP assessed students' skill levels in mathematics in the school years ending in 1973, 1978, and 1982. Over this period the average math skills of 9-year-old children were stable. The scores of 13-year-olds fell between the first two assessments and rose between the second and third assessment. As a group, black children gained more than white children. The scores of 17-year-old children fell between the first two assessments and were stable between the second and third assessments (NAEP 1983).

Why have students' mathematics skills remained stable or declined during the 1970s, while skill levels in reading increased during this period? One explanation is that a shortage of qualified mathematics teachers during the decade hindered student learning (more on teacher shortages below).

Science

Students' skill levels in physical and biological sciences were assessed in the school years ending in 1970, 1973, and 1977. Scores in physical sciences declined over the period between the first and third assessments for all age groups. Seventeen-year-olds also experienced a decline in biology test scores over this period. The biology scores for 9- and 13-year-old children declined between the first two assessments and rose between the second and third assessments (NAEP 1978).

Why the dismal record in science achievement in the 1970s? One proposed explanation is a shortage of qualified science teachers. A second is reduced emphasis on the teaching of science, brought about in part by the increased emphasis placed on the teaching of reading and math—the basics (NAEP 1978, p. 17).

SUMMARY OF TRENDS AND THE ROLES OF SCHOOL FACTORS

There have been significant improvements over the 1970s in the reading skills of younger children, especially those of black children. We do not yet know whether the gains of younger children achieved over the 1970s will be retained by these children during the 1980s (a cohort model that bodes well for the future) or whether the evidence should be interpreted as simply that our educational system as currently constituted is more successful in raising the skill levels of younger children than those of older children (a life-cycle model). There is limited evidence to support each hypothesis.

Although compensatory education has apparently been effective in raising the basic reading skills of disadvantaged children in the primary grades, it has not led to improved reading scores for 17-year-olds. There are two reasons for this. First, most compensatory education programs are directed at younger children. Second, most children who benefited from compensatory education in their early years in school were not yet 17 in 1980 and so were not included in the NAEP samples.

Overall, the evidence indicates that compensatory education cannot be understood as analogous to a vaccination—something given to young children that sustains them for an extended period of time without further treatment. A better metaphor appears to be a vitamin pill—a treatment that is effective but must be continued.

The most compelling explanations for the test-score declines in science deal with teacher labor-market conditions, which have changed so markedly over the last fifteen years that even a summary of the changes requires a section of its own.

STATUS OF THE TEACHER LABOR FORCE

CHANGES IN LABOR-MARKET CONDITIONS DURING THE 1970S

During the 1970s, a variety of conditions combined to make it more difficult for local school districts to attract and retain talented teachers. The first of these conditions was a decline in student enrollments. Between 1970 and 1980 the number of students attending United States public elementary and secondary schools fell from 46.1 million to 40.2 million, a drop of 13 percent (*The Condition of Education* 1983, p. 14). This enrollment decline drastically altered career opportunities for teachers. Many teachers were "riffed" during the 1970s, to use the term common in teacher circles for layoffs resulting from reductions in force. Opportunities for transfers to more desirable schools, a traditional method of gaining improved working conditions, disappeared (Murnane 1981). Involuntary transfers necessitated by school closings increased, often causing disruption of school programs.

For many teachers and for college students training to become teachers, the layoffs, transfers, and lack of job opportunities were sources of great disillusionment and reassessment. Job security was one attribute the teaching profession had in the past always offered, and it had compensated to some extent for low salaries. Now even this had disappeared.

A second, related factor affecting teacher labor markets during the 1970s was a decline in the real wages of teachers. Between 1971 and 1981, the average salary of public school teachers rose from $9269 to $17,602. However, real salaries (in 1981 dollars) fell from $20,212 to $17,602 during this period, a reduction of 13 percent. In part, the decline in real wages was the result of teachers' unions trading salary increases for continued employment of their members. Their success in this regard is reflected in the decrease in the average student-teacher ratio from 22.5 to 18.8 over the years 1970–1980 (*Digest of Education Statistics 1983*, as reported in O'Neill 1984).

The lack of jobs and the decline in real wages provided strong signals to college students making career decisions. One response to these signals was a reduction in the number of students in United States colleges and universities graduating with education degrees, from 177,000 in 1971 to 101,000 in 1982. The figures on the number of graduating students prepared to teach—that is, fulfilling minimum requirements for certification—are even more dramatic, with the number falling from a peak of 317,254 in 1971–1972 to 140,639 in 1980–1981 (*Teacher Supply and Demand* 1983). Between 1970 and 1982, the percentage of full-time freshmen indicating that they planned to choose elementary or secondary school teaching as a probable occupation fell from 19.3 percent to 4.7 percent (*Condition of Education* 1983, p. 218).

There is some evidence to suggest that another part of the response was a reduction in the quality of the pool of graduates planning to enter the teaching profession (Schlechty and Vance 1981). In part, this may have been the result of more able students choosing more financially attractive occupations. The increased career opportunities for women during this period may have led many women, who in earlier decades would have taken a low-paying teaching position, to take advantage of new opportunities in higher-paying occupations. The quality of the pool of applicants for teaching positions may also have fallen as schools of education, attempting to retain enrollments during a period of declining demand for their services, lowered admission standards (Weaver 1978).

In one respect the responses of students during the 1970s to the decline in the attractiveness of the teaching profession are not only what one would expect to happen in a market economy in which individuals are free to choose occupations; they are also desirable in the sense that these responses to market signals are the mechanisms through which labor is redistributed from declining industries to growing industries. There are three reasons, however, for concern. The first is the issue of quality, mentioned above. A second is that public school enrollments are expected to rise again, beginning in 1985, as the offspring of the post–World War II baby boom generation enter the nation's schools (Frankel and Gerald 1981, p. 15). This will result in an increased demand for teachers. Given the lag in the supply response, the teacher glut of the 1970s may be replaced by a widespread teacher shortage in the late 1980s. A third concern deals with variation in demand and supply conditions across subject areas—in particular, with the shortage of qualified teachers of mathematics and science.

THE SHORTAGE OF MATH AND SCIENCE TEACHERS

Teaching has never been a financially attractive occupation for college graduates trained in mathematics or science. For example, in 1974, graduates trained in mathematics who entered business or industry earned starting salaries that were on average 36 percent higher than beginning teacher salaries. By comparison, graduates trained in the humanities who entered business or industry in 1974 earned salaries that were 7 percent higher than beginning teacher salaries. Thus for graduates trained in the humanities, salaries offered in teaching in 1974 were almost competitive with alternatives—if a teaching position was available. This was almost equally true in 1981, when the average salary differential between business and industry, on the one hand, and teaching, on the other, was 12 percent for humanities majors. But for graduates trained in mathematics, the attractiveness of teaching relative to industry or business fell drastically during the 1970s. In 1981, the average salary differential was 61 percent (Bacharach et al. 1984, p. 66).

One consequence of this trend is that while there was a surplus of teachers overall during the 1970s, many areas of the country experienced a shortage of math and science teachers. Moreover, this shortage has become increasingly acute. Local school districts deal with the shortage of math and science teachers in a variety of ways, in part due to variation in state licensing regulations. However, a recent survey (*Impact of Teacher Shortage* 1983) identified the following responses, with the most prevalent responses listed first.

• Arrange for persons to get emergency certification.

• Use teachers certified in other subject areas.

• Increase class size.

• Cancel courses.

These responses "solve" the shortage problem by lowering the quality and quantity of math and science instruction, and thus probably contributed to the decline in the NAEP math and science scores between 1970 and 1980.

Salary trends may also help to explain why NAEP test scores in biology were more stable over the 1970s than the physical science scores were. For biology majors entering business or industry, average starting salaries were 12 percent higher than starting teacher salaries in 1974, and 31 percent higher in 1981. For graduates trained in other natural sciences, the comparable numbers are 39 percent and 86 percent (Bacharach et al. 1984, p. 66). Thus, school districts may have found it easier to find qualified biology teachers than qualified physical science teachers during the 1970s.

What should be done about the math and science teacher shortage? A central issue in considering policy alternatives is the role of certification requirements. To obtain a teaching certificate (a license to teach) in most states, college students must devote a significant part of their course work during their junior and senior years to education courses. One cost of this requirement is a reduction in the number of subject-area courses taken. For students who would like to teach math or science for a few years but who want to retain the option of moving on to a higher-paying position in business or industry at a later time, this is a heavy loss. With less preparation in math or science than other students majoring in these areas, they may be at a significant competitive disadvantage if they do decide to leave teaching.

Seen from this perspective, raising the salaries of math and science teachers above those of other teachers—a proposal that has been debated for many years (cf. Kershaw and McKean 1962)—may be less effective than policies that would make it easier for graduates who have majored in math or science to try teaching. I do not intend to imply by this argument that nothing is learned in education courses or that no special pedagogical skills are needed to teach effectively. What I do mean is that there are many alternative ways to acquire these skills, including supervised on-the-job training complemented perhaps by formal in-service instruction. Certification requirements that effectively make college students choose between preparation for teaching or intensive preparation in math or science may keep many talented potential teachers out of the classroom.

SUMMARY

When we look to explicit public policies to explain the educational problems of the 1980s, it is easy to neglect the importance of two implicit policies of the past:

- Letting teachers' salaries deteriorate relative to alternatives during a period in which alternative employment opportunities for women improved markedly.

- Requiring that aspirants for teaching positions specialize in education during college to the extent of reducing alternative career options, especially in technical areas.

Improving the quality of United States education in the 1980s will require reversal of these implicit policies.

FEDERAL EDUCATION POLICIES

POLICIES PRIOR TO THE REAGAN ADMINISTRATION

The federal role in funding elementary and secondary education in the United States has always been small. In 1950, the federal government contributed only 2.9 percent of the funds spent on United States public elementary and secondary education. Over the next thirty years the federal role did grow; by 1980 the federal contribution had increased to 9.3 percent of total expenditures (*Condition of Education* 1983, p. 42).

The major event marking a more active federal role was passage of the Elementary and Secondary Education Act of 1965 (ESEA). Title I of ESEA provided $1 billion to local school districts for compensatory education. By 1980, Title I funding had increased to $3.4 billion (O'Neill and Simms 1982). Correcting for inflation, the 1980 funding level provided a 30 percent increase in real expenditures over the 1966 funding level.

The regulations governing use of Title I funds mandate that recipient districts spend as many non–Title I dollars on low-achieving children participating in Title I programs as they spend on other children. In addition, Title I funds must be used exclusively to supplement the educational resources made available to Title I–eligible children; the funds may not be spread across all children. Gaining compliance with these regulations was a significant problem in the first years of Title I, when many districts treated Title I funds as general aid. By the mid 1970s, however, most of the 14,000 school districts receiving Title I funds complied with the regulations (Goettel et al. 1977). As summarized above, there is also limited evidence that Title I has been effective in improving the education of the target population and in reducing the achievement gap between black and white children.

Title I was the largest federal categorical grant program, but it was not the only one. In fact, the number of categorical grant programs directed to disadvantaged children grew markedly over the 1970s. Since children eligible for participation in the federal programs are concentrated in certain geographical regions of the country, especially in urban areas and in the South, one consequence of the increase in the number and size of these programs was that federal aid also became concentrated. For example, in 1980 Mississippi received federal funds amounting to $380 per public school student, while Nevada received $134 per student (*Condition of Education* 1983, pp. 16, 42). A second consequence of the increase in the number of categorical grant programs, each of which had its own compliance regulations, was that fulfilling the varied and sometimes conflicting requirements created significant administrative problems for some school districts (Hill 1979).

FEDERAL EDUCATION PROGRAMS
UNDER THE REAGAN ADMINISTRATION

The theme underlying President Reagan's treatment of education during his first two years in office is that education is a responsibility of state and local governments and federal involvement should be reduced. This theme was manifested in the Educational Consolidation and Improvement Act of 1981 (ECIA), significant provisions of which included:

• Chapter II of ECIA consolidated twenty-nine categorical programs into one block grant program. (The largest of the consolidated programs was the Emergency School Aid program, which provided funds for districts coping with desegregation-related problems.)

• The total budget authority for Chapter II was set at $456 million, approximately 24 percent less than the funds provided under the twenty-nine categorical programs. Chapter II funds are distributed to states on a per-student basis, with all students having equal weight in the formula.

• The regulations governing use of Title I (now Chapter I) funds were reduced, as were reporting requirements.

It is still too early to determine how the Reagan administration's policy changes will influence the distribution of student achievement. Among the fears of advocates for the disadvantaged is that the program changes will result in a significant reduction in the quality of education provided to minority group children and children from low-income families. They fear that the gains reported by NAEP in the achievement of black children, especially in the primary grades, where Title I programs concentrate, will not continue in the years ahead (*A Children's Defense Budget* 1984). The reason this may happen, they argue, is that the elimination of the categorical programs and the reduction in the reporting requirements for compensatory education programs will result in a transfer of funds once devoted to programs for the disadvantaged to general educational use, to other public services, or to tax relief. They cite the experience of the early years of Title I as indicating the need for strong regulations to assure that resources intended for the disadvantaged actually reach them. I find these arguments compelling because they are consistent not only with the early Title I experiences but also with the evidence on local school districts' responses to state aid. As discussed below, the evidence is that local districts tend to use unrestricted state aid to substitute for locally raised revenues, thereby permitting tax relief, instead of using the aid to increase school services (Carroll 1979).

Although we do not yet have evidence on the consequences for student achievement of the Reagan administration's education policies, we can predict that the consequences of ECIA will vary from state to state. One reason is that some states (e.g., California) have significant compensatory education programs with their own accountability and reporting requirements. In these states relaxation of the federal reporting requirements will probably not lead to resource reallocation. Other states appear more ready to let local districts determine the use of Chapter I funds, and there are strong political pressures to treat such funds as general aid. A second reason is that the distribution of political power in big cities (the primary recipients of Title I funds) varies enormously across the country. Cities with leaders elected with strong support from minorities will use Chapter I funds differently from cities whose officials are dependent on other constituencies. Thus, one general consequence of the Reagan administration's policy changes is to make the quality of education received by disadvantaged children more sensitive to where the children live and go to school.

PROPOSED CHANGES IN FEDERAL EDUCATION POLICIES

An underlying theme of this chapter is that a paramount goal of federal and state education policies should be to provide all children in the United States, no matter where they live, with strong basic cognitive skills. The question is how federal education policies can further this goal, while remaining sensitive to the following realities.

- Local school districts tend to treat education block grants as general aid to be spread across all students or to permit tax relief.

- School districts that participated in a variety of categorical grant programs often found the regulations conflicting and the burden of compliance onerous.

- Local school districts did learn to comply with the regulations mandating that Title I compensatory education funds be targeted to low-achieving children.

- Title I appears to be at least partly responsible for the improvement over the 1970s in the reading skills of minority group children in the primary grades.

- Concern about the size of the federal deficit prevents a dramatic increase in federal education funding.

I suggest the following policy changes. First, the reporting and accountability requirements of Title I that were relaxed under Chapter I of ECIA should be reinstated. The first ten years of experience with Title I demonstrated both the difficulty of targeting aid to disadvantaged children and the success of the regulations in achieving this goal.

Second, a significant part of the funds currently provided to states as block grants under Chapter II of ECIA (perhaps 50 percent of the FY1983 funding level of $451 million) should be directed to low-achieving children by adding the funds to the Chapter I compensatory education program. These additional funds could permit the program to serve more of the primary-school-aged eligible children and possibly permit expansion in some districts to middle-school-aged eligible children. Such an expansion of an existing program would not create new compliance burdens.

Reallocating funds from Chapter II to Chapter I does redistribute federal funds to districts with large concentrations of low-income children. Given the evidence supporting the effectiveness of Title I, this reallocation is consistent with a federal goal of providing all American children, no matter where they live, with the basic cognitive skills they will need to fulfill their potential.

CHANGES IN THE REAGAN ADMINISTRATION'S
EDUCATION POLICIES

When President Reagan appointed Terrell Bell to be Secretary of the Department of Education, the appointment was accompanied by a mandate to eliminate the department. This was consistent with the philosophy that the federal government should minimize its involvement in elementary and secondary education. During the second half of Reagan's first term, this attitude changed as education became a campaign issue. Secretary Bell became one of the most visible cabinet members. He commissioned a panel to study United States education and publicized the panel's report, *A Nation at Risk*, published in April 1983. This report was highly critical of United States education, as is reflected in the oft-cited statement on its first page: "The educational foundations of our society are presently being eroded by a rising tide of mediocrity." In May 1984 the Department of Education published *The Nation Responds*, which summarizes efforts of state and local governments and the private sector to improve educational quality. The tone of the document is one of the federal government exercising leadership.

Two sets of facts are necessary to set the record straight. First, the education policies that President Reagan advocates, school prayer and tuition tax credits, are very different from the recommendations made in *A Nation at Risk*. Second, most of the "responses" by states cited in *The Nation Responds* were started several years before the publication of *A Nation at Risk*. Thus, to understand the governmental policies that have been most instrumental in shaping United States education, we must redirect our attention from Washington to the states.

STATE SCHOOL FINANCE POLICIES

In contrast to the Reagan administration's philosophy that education decisions should be left to units of government closer to the people, state governments in recent years have increased their role, relative to local governments, both in funding public education and in regulating it.

STATE AID POLICIES

In the five years between the 1977–1978 and 1982–1983 school years, state support for public education increased by 62 percent (14 percent in real terms), resulting in an average state expenditure of $1611 per pupil in the 1982–1983 school year. (This average conceals extreme variation from state to state: per pupil state-aid levels of $189 in New Hampshire, $3081 in Delaware, and $5920 in Alaska [Augenblick and Van de Water 1983]). Among the reasons for the increases in state aid were changes in state aid formulas brought about by court challenges.

Until the early 1970s, most states distributed aid to local school districts on something close to a per-student basis. As a result, state aid policies did little to alter the variation in per-pupil spending levels caused in part by differences in community wealth, defined both in terms of size of the property tax base and the personal income of residents. This changed during the 1970s as existing systems of school finance in many states were successfully challenged in court cases, the first and best-known of which was the Serrano case in California. In most states in which challenges were successful, the courts mandated that the state legislature devise a state aid plan that reduced the relationship between community wealth and per-pupil spending.

The most popular of the reform plans was labeled the Guaranteed Tax Base (GTB) plan or District Power Equalizing. Under a GTB plan, a property-poor community's per-pupil expenditure level depends only on the property tax rate that the community sets, not on the amount of revenue raised. For communities in which the per-pupil property tax base is smaller than the guaranteed tax base, the state provides aid equal to the difference between the revenue raised and the revenue that would have been raised had the community's chosen tax rate been applied to the GTB.

The attraction of the GTB concept is that it has the potential to equalize "opportunities" while retaining, to a significant degree, local control of education spending. Communities are free to choose a tax rate. Communities valuing education highly can retain a high level of education spending by choosing a high rate.

In essence the GTB plan reduces the price of education for communities with low per-pupil tax bases. Thus, the effect of a GTB plan on the distribution of per-pupil spending across districts in a state depends on the sensitivity of spending levels to price. GTB plans equalize spending if property-poor communities respond to the lowering of price by purchasing more education.

To date, the evidence from the states that have adopted GTB plans is that the plans have not resulted in a significant equalization of per-pupil spending across districts. The reason is that property-poor communities responded to the GTB incentives, not by purchasing more education at the now lower price but, rather, by continuing to purchase the same amount of education and using the increased state aid to lower property taxes. Thus, the net effect of GTB plans has been drastically to increase state aid levels and to equalize property tax rates across communities, but not significantly to equalize education spending levels across districts (Carroll 1979).

The final word has not been spoken on the effects of GTB plans. The incentives present in the plans actually implemented by states differ in important respects from the incentives embodied in the model plan.

- Hold-harmless clauses provide continued aid to districts with high tax bases.

- Underfunding has led some states to put a cap on the amount of aid they will provide to property-poor districts that set high tax rates.

- Cost-of-education adjustments in some states benefit districts that do not have high costs but, rather, choose to pay high teacher salaries in order to attract high-quality teachers (Carroll 1979; Brazer et al. 1982).

Despite these qualifications, it seems clear that the main lesson from the first ten years of school finance is that GTB finance plans which lower the price of education to property-poor communities, but leave the communities free to choose between more spending on education or lower tax rates, will not produce an equalization of per-pupil spending levels across school districts and will not result in all districts spending enough to provide their students with a strong basic academic program.

In my view, states should concentrate on designing policies that provide all districts with the resources to develop strong basic academic programs. A corollary to this emphasis is that states should deemphasize concern with equalizing expenditure levels across districts, even if this means that the quality of extracurricular activities varies across districts. The primary reason for this suggestion is that affluent districts can and do subvert equalization policies in countless ways. For example, if the state places a cap on per-pupil spending in local districts (a necessary condition for full equalization), affluent districts form non-profit civic foundations to support extracurricular activities so that the entire school budget can be used to pay for core activities. This means that the quality of the educational services is superior in the affluent districts even though the levels of per-pupil spending listed on the books are no higher than in other districts.

A foundation formula can achieve the goal of providing all districts with the resources to develop a strong basic academic program. Under this type of formula the state mandates that every district set a tax rate at least equal to a state-specified minimum. In return, the state guarantees that every district will have the funds to spend a specified amount per student on education (the foundation level). If the local revenues raised by applying the required minimum tax rate to the local tax base do not generate sufficient funds to support the foundation level of spending, the state provides a grant in the amount of the deficit. If the foundation level is set suitably high—and this is the crucial step—this type of state aid formula can achieve the goal of assuring that all school districts have the resources needed to develop a strong instructional program. One way to keep the foundation level high is to mandate that it be set equal to a given percentage (perhaps 90 percent) of average per-pupil spending on education in the state.

STATE POLICIES TO IMPROVE TEACHING

By the late 1970s, many states became concerned when they realized that although state spending for education was rising rapidly, performance did not appear to be improving. This led to a variety of state efforts to tie education aid to new regulations aimed at improving the quality of instruction provided in schools and increasing the effort levels of students and teachers.

TOUGHER CERTIFICATION REQUIREMENTS

Many states have recently increased the requirements for obtaining a teaching certificate (a license to teach in a public school). One common change has been an increase in the amount of *formal training* a teacher must complete before being eligible for certification. A second change is that applicants for teaching positions must score above a minimum grade on a *standardized exam*—seven states use the National Teachers Exam for this purpose (*Condition of Education* 1983, p. 66). A third type of new requirement is that teachers undergo on-the-job *observation and evaluation* before receiving certification. Such "performance-based certification" requirements have been introduced in Florida, Georgia, New Mexico, and Oklahoma (Ordovensky 1983).

In attempting to understand the effects of increasing certification requirements, it is useful to ask what model of local-school-district behavior would justify such state actions. One model that is not consistent with such actions is that local school districts are motivated to hire effective teachers, are competent to choose such teachers from the pool of applicants, offer high enough salaries to attract a talented pool, and can and will dismiss an incompetent teacher if they make a hiring mistake. If all districts in a state fit this description, then no state teacher-certification requirements would be necessary. Such school districts could examine applicants' college transcripts and evaluate the quality of their academic preparation. They could judge whether the applicants' test scores are high enough to offer promise of intellectual skills. They could evaluate the performance of the teachers they hire and dismiss those who are not able to improve their performance sufficiently to meet minimum standards.

Among the alternative models of local school district behavior that could justify the regulations are that local districts are motivated to hire teachers on the basis of criteria other than potential teaching effectiveness, such as political connections. Or district administrators could be incompetent in making hiring decisions. Or district administrators trying to hire effective teachers could be hampered by salaries so low that competent teachers do not apply.

Tougher teacher certification requirements may improve the quality of teachers employed by such districts by preventing the hiring of incompetent teachers with political connections. They may aid local school officials in gaining taxpayer support for higher teacher salaries by highlighting the inability of the district to attract competent teachers at existing salaries. These accomplishments could justify tough certification requirements if a large percentage of school districts in a state fitted the description of districts in need of help or if the requirements had no adverse affects on other districts. It is not possible to evaluate how large a percentage of the school districts in a state need state certification requirements to influence their hiring practices.

Tougher teacher certification requirements do, however, adversely affect school districts that want to hire the most effective teachers they can find, have administrators competent to choose among applicants, and pay reasonable salaries (cf. Benham 1980). Consider state-mandated increases in the formal training college students must complete before being eligible for teacher certification. These increased requirements raise the cost of becoming a teacher. In some cases, the cost increase may result from the student having to stay in school longer. In other cases, the cost may be in terms of narrowing the set of colleges the student may attend. For example, many liberal arts colleges, attended by only a few students who want to become teachers, find it unfeasible financially to offer all the courses needed for state accreditation. Thus, the student who wants to try public school teaching may not be able to attend a college that in other respects offers an attractive academic program. In still other cases, the cost may be that increased course requirements for certification may reduce opportunities to take other courses. These foregone courses might have enhanced students' competitive positions in applying for jobs in other industries if they decide to leave teaching, or have difficulty finding a desirable teaching position, due to enrollment declines and layoffs. Such an argument may seem farfetched, for most discussions of teaching emphasize the need to attract talented college graduates to a teaching career. High attrition rates during the first years on the job are a reality among public school teachers in the United States, however—in fact, they have always been a reality (Charters 1970). Consequently, attempts to improve teaching would be more effective if they focused less on how to attract talented college graduates for a lifetime and more on how to attract talented graduates for a few years. (Indeed, many high-quality private schools recruit teachers with exactly this model in mind.) Seen from this perspective, increased course requirements for certification may significantly reduce the pool of applicants for teaching positions and make it more difficult for school districts to find talented teachers.

Strict state requirements for teacher training may also reduce the quality of teaching in public schools by hindering innovation and diversity in training programs. In most states, the first step in the teacher certification process is for the applicant to complete a prescribed course of study in a teacher training program accredited by the state. For a program to be accredited, it must offer the courses that satisfy the state requirements. This would not be a serious limitation, perhaps, if there were strong evidence that a particular set of courses provided the best training for prospective teachers. The evidence is of a quite different nature, however. Studies of the determinants of teacher effectiveness show no relation between preparation and teaching effectiveness, as measured by student test-score gains. For example, there is no evidence that teachers majoring in education are more effective than teachers majoring in other subject areas (Murnane 1983). This should not be interpreted as indicating that preparation does not matter; rather, researchers' ability to identify effective training programs is limited by the similarity among programs mandated by state regulations. It does imply, however, that state policy should encourage innovation in teacher training, rather than demand compliance with a tightly defined set of standards.

How might states promote innovation in teacher training and encourage talented college students to try teaching, while still monitoring the hiring actions of troubled school districts? I would like to offer the following immodest, three-part proposal.

First, the state should require that all college students interested in becoming teachers pass an examination testing basic literacy skills and minimum subject-matter competence. Students should be allowed to take this test at any time during their college years. The purpose of the test would be to provide information to students about minimum cognitive skills needed for teaching. Those students who did not possess these skills could either work to acquire them while in college or choose an alternative occupation rather than devoting their time and their institution's resources to teacher training. I want to emphasize that this exam is only intended to test potential teachers' basic cognitive skills. It is not intended to distinguish between competent and incompetent classroom teachers. In fact, a recent study that found a statistically significant *negative* relationship between teachers' scores on the National Teachers Exam and their students' test-score gains serves to highlight the limitations of written tests as indicators of teaching effectiveness (Summers and Wolfe 1977).

Second, all colleges and universities in the state should be allowed to design their own teacher training programs and attempt to recruit students and to place their graduates in teaching jobs. Under such a system, school district personnel officers would find it worthwhile to keep track of the performance of teachers trained in specific programs and to recruit more teachers graduating from programs that had provided effective teachers in the past. Placement officers in teacher training programs would have incentives to give honest appraisals of their graduates' potential, given that school districts would turn away from programs whose graduates turned out to be less capable than was advertised.

Third, the state should observe and evaluate teachers' performance in the classroom during their second year of teaching. (Teachers need one year on the job to overcome initial fears and frustrations.) The teacher must pass the performance-based evaluation test to gain certification. The evaluation system could be similar to that recently introduced in Georgia, where each rating team consists of one teacher and one administrator from the applicant's district, and one state official, all trained in evaluation.

I do not underestimate the well-documented problems involved in any system of evaluating teachers' performance (cf. Wise et al. 1984). Such a performance-based certification system would not assure that all school districts employ only effective teachers. There is not sufficient consensus on the definition of effective teaching to achieve that result, even with the best of evaluators. However, such a system could provide as much assurance as existing certification requirements that troubled districts do not employ incompetent teachers. Moreover, this proposal, by encouraging innovation in training and by making it easier for college students to try teaching, would increase school districts' ability to find competent teachers.

What would happen if such a market for teacher training were allowed to develop? All districts would be able to recruit better teachers as the quantity and quality of applicants increased. A second, less agreeable consequence is that districts with high salary scales and good working conditions would attract the most talented graduates from the best programs, while districts with low salaries and difficult working conditions would be able to attract only less able students and those graduating from weaker programs. Would the resulting distribution of teachers be a reason to scrap the proposal? I think not, because the pattern is the same under the existing regulatory system. The only real difference would be that the differences in the quality of the teaching staffs of different school districts would be more noticeable, because the range of quality in the overall applicant pool would be greater. Viewed from this perspective, the problem is how to make teaching more attractive in districts that are not able to attract and retain high-quality teachers. Licensing requirements that contract rather than expand the pool of applicants for positions in such districts are not the answer.

One other consequence of such a market system would be that some existing teacher-training programs would lose students. They would resist the changes, and possibly prevent deregulation of the certification requirements. I do not believe, however, that deregulation of teacher training would inevitably lead to the demise of schools of education, although it would lead to changes in what they do. An optimistic, but I believe plausible, scenario is that many education schools would swallow hard and then transform themselves into lean, mean competitors with liberal arts programs. They would concentrate on substance and on developing leadership, supervision, and other people-managing skills, and would claim (correctly) that a few years in teaching is superb background for many other careers. They would create a new market niche between the "major in business and commerce" and the liberal arts degree.

One criticism that might be made of my three-part deregulation proposal is that by expanding the number of applicants competing for teaching positions, it would reduce pressure for salary increases and thereby damage the profession. I do not believe that this criticism is valid. In the long run, the salaries of public school teachers and the prestige of the teaching profession will increase markedly only if taxpayers and employers believe that teachers provide high-quality education. My proposal, by making it easier for talented college graduates to enter teaching and for school districts to recruit able teachers, will improve the quality of teaching in our schools and thereby will ultimately benefit the teaching profession.

COMPENSATION FOR TEACHERS

Merit Pay for Teachers

Several states are providing incentives to local school districts to institute merit pay programs. For example, the state of Florida has appropriated $80 million for 1984–1985 to support merit pay for teachers (*The Nation Responds* 1984, p. 45). A large part of the attraction of merit pay is that it appears to offer a means of increasing the compensation of the best teachers without incurring the large cost of raising the salaries of all teachers.

The apparent attractiveness of merit pay is drawn into question by knowledge of its history, however. Merit pay is an old idea, dating back to 1908 in the United States. The history of merit pay plans is that they do not last very long: the typical life span is three or four years (*Merit Pay for Teachers* 1979). Moreover, the temporal and geographical nature of the evidence prohibits blaming union resistance for this brevity. Case studies indicate that the reasons plans were terminated include negative effects on teacher morale and cost of administration. Even teachers picked by their peers as likely recipients of merit pay because of their superior teaching oppose the idea (Jackson 1968).

Insight into the problems of merit pay can be gained by examining the incentives in a system in which teachers are paid according to their students' average performance on specified tests. (This is one of the criteria for teacher merit approved by the state of Florida [*The Nation Responds* 1984, p. 45]). Such a system provides incentives for teachers to devote instructional time to the skills needed to do well on the test, and to minimize time spent teaching other skills. Many teachers feel that the types of skill that can be measured on tests are only a small subset of the skills that constitute a good education. As a result, they oppose an incentive structure that fosters time allocations they see as diminishing their effectiveness as teachers.

A related problem concerns the incentives for teachers to allocate their time among children according to a strategy that maximizes their salary. To the extent that teaching time is a private good—time spent with one child decreases the amount of time available for another child—the goal of maximizing the average test-score gain of students in a class provides incentives to allocate time so that the marginal test-score gain resulting from the last unit of time spent with any child is equal across children. Another way to say this is that this compensation system provides incentives to minimize time spent with children who do not reward increased teacher attention by achieving test-score gains. Again, many teachers feel that these incentives conflict with their desire to help all children in their class to learn.

In an ongoing study, a colleague and I are attempting to learn more about the potential for merit pay by examining how it works in five districts that have used merit pay for a number of years. (Of course, the longevity of merit pay in these districts makes them quite atypical.) The preliminary evidence suggests the following conclusions.

1. The districts in which merit pay survives for an extended period of time are districts in which the uniform salary scales are above the regional average and working conditions are good. In other words, merit pay is used to supplement the pay of teachers in already high-paying districts.

2. These districts do not use student test-score gains as criteria for merit pay.

3. These districts weight teachers' activities outside the classroom heavily in determining who gets merit pay. For example, taking on heavy committee assignments, taking additional courses, and providing leadership in community activities are important in determining who gets merit pay. In other words, merit pay in these districts is more like extra pay for extra work than it is rewarding the most effective classroom teachers (Murnane, forthcoming).

Overall, the evidence from our ongoing work indicates that merit pay may be a small part of an attractive compensation package in well-running school districts with high uniform salary scales. The evidence does not suggest that it is an effective strategy for improving the quality of teaching in troubled school districts.

State-Sponsored Mini-Grants

State-sponsored mini-grant programs for teachers provide a means of stimulating teachers' effort levels and encouraging the development of new teaching ideas without the perverse effects present in most merit pay programs. The assumptions underlying the mini-grant idea are two. First, good teachers have many ideas for innovative projects but lack of funds often frustrates their attempts to implement these ideas. Second, teachers, like everyone else, desire and need recognition for excellent work. Thoughtfully designed mini-grant programs have the potential for stimulating the development of innovative teaching projects, by providing financial support. They can also provide teachers who have good ideas and an entrepreneurial spirit with recognition for their efforts.

Such programs might work as follows. The state announces the availability of funds to support small grants (e.g., $500–$3000) to support the development or execution of any idea that holds promise for improving teaching or enhancing students' experiences. Individual teachers or groups of teachers submit short proposals explaining and defending their ideas. The proposals are evaluated by a committee consisting of teachers and state officials. Awards are announced publicly. At the end of the award year, recipients submit a short summary explaining what they did with the grant money and what they accomplished with the grant. Among the important design provisions of the grant program are that there be sufficient funds to support a large percentage of proposals that hold promise and that there be no quota on the number of teachers in any school or school district who could be awarded grants.

Grant programs such as that described above have been tried in a number of states (e.g., Massachusetts), in many cases supported by funds from Title IV-C of ESEA. Evaluations of these programs are quite encouraging. They are relatively simple to administer. They have, at relatively low cost, provided support for a range of interesting activities. Moreover, they have provided recognition and support to a large number of teachers (McDonnell and McLaughlin 1980).

Salary Increases

A number of states are taking action to raise teachers' salaries. While this alone will probably not improve the quality of teaching in our schools, evidence on teacher labor markets (cited above) suggests that salary increases will be necessary to improve the quality of education in many school districts.

One critical question states face is what strategy to employ to help districts attract effective teachers. I would argue that, as stated above, a state-aid formula based on the foundation concept with a high foundation support level is an effective means of insuring that all districts have the resources to hire effective teachers.

An alternative strategy adopted by some states is to mandate statewide minimum salary levels for teachers. I do not believe that this is a good policy. Labor-market conditions for teachers vary widely among the school districts in any state; consequently, the salary that a district must offer to attract effective teachers varies widely. Districts with good working conditions that are located in or near desirable residential locations can attract talented teachers at lower salaries than other districts. Mandating that these districts offer high salaries reduces the districts' flexibility in using resources in a manner that most efficaciously builds a solid instructional program. Similarly, in districts with poor working conditions, using scarce resources to improve the conditions under which teachers work may be a more effective strategy for attracting talented teachers than raising salaries would be. (Many private schools successfully employ this strategy.) In summary, state policy should concentrate on insuring that all school districts have the resources to attract effective teachers; it should not mandate how much of these resources should be devoted to teachers' salaries.

STATE POLICIES TO STIMULATE STUDENTS' EFFORTS

In recent years, states have undertaken a number of actions aimed at stimulating students' effort levels and enhancing their achievement. A number of states have increased course requirements, especially the number of math and science courses required for high school graduation. For example, in 1982 California passed legislation requiring that, effective in the 1986–1987 school year, high school students must complete two years of mathematics and two years of science before graduating. These new requirements are much less stringent than those recommended by *A Nation at Risk*. Their significance is indicated, however, by the fact that only 40 percent of the students graduating from California high schools in 1983 satisfied these new requirements (Harnischfeger and Wiley, 1984). Other states have passed more stringent requirements. For example, effective in the 1986–1987 school year, Florida high school students must complete three years of science and three years of mathematics before graduating (*The Nation Responds* 1984, p. 43). Another common, and more controversial, state initiative is the introduction of minimum competency examinations, which students must pass to graduate from high school. Seventeen states have introduced such exam requirements (*Condition of Education* 1983, p. 64).

Presumably, the impetus for these new state policies is concern about declining test scores and the correlation between test scores and the number of academic courses students take. Certainly, the hope is that the requirements of more course work and the successful completion of a basic skills exam will stimulate students (and teachers) to work harder and achieve more. The danger is that the new requirements will elicit other, less desirable responses, such as students dropping out of school and teachers teaching tested skills at the expense of skill development in areas not tested on the minimum competency exams (Madaus 1982).

To date, there is almost no evidence on the effects of the new requirements. We simply do not yet know the responses the new requirements elicit from students and teachers, or whether these responses increase achievement. It does seem safe to conjecture, however, that the responses will depend on the extent to which students find that meeting the stiffer requirements results in rewards commensurate with the additional work. One factor that will influence this judgment, and consequently students' responses, are graduates' labor-market experiences. It seems unlikely that students will increase effort levels to earn a now harder-to-get high school diploma unless they find that labor markets reward the extra effort with improved employment opportunities. It is not possible to predict these labor-market responses; alternative models of the operation of labor markets yield different predictions (compare Smith and Welch 1977 with Thurow 1975).

A second factor that will influence students' responses to new academic requirements is the quality of teaching in the new required courses. If competent teachers are not found to teach the new required math and science courses, adolescents may well discover responses less socially desirable than working harder.

A third factor that will influence responses is the treatment of students who fail the graduation exam. Introduction of an exam requirement will be more likely to enhance the effort levels of low-achieving students, instead of inducing them to drop out, if failure leads to significant remedial instruction and additional opportunities to take the exam. These conditions are more readily met if the exam is administered early in a student's high school years, perhaps in grade 10, instead of in grade 12.

SPECIFIC QUESTIONS TO ASK

This chapter has evaluated a wide range of federal and state education policies and has made a number of recommendations for policy changes. I stand behind these recommendations and argue that they are the right directions to move in attempting to provide all American children with a good education. It is important to keep in mind, however, that the consequences of any policy will depend on the details of the policy and on the composition of the package of which the particular policy is a part. It is not possible in such a broad-brush essay to analyze the significance of particular policy details and packaging, but I would like to suggest that in analyzing any particular state or federal policy, it is useful to ask the following three sets of questions.

1. What model of local-school-district behavior underlies the policy? Does the policy assume that local districts are incompetent or constrained by local politics? How will the policy affect the options of districts that are competent and have taxpayer support for developing a high-quality education program?

2. Does the policy make teaching more, or less, attractive as an occupation? What responses from teachers might the policy evoke? Does the policy make it more, or less, difficult for college students to prepare to teach, at least for a few years?

3. Does the policy offer rewards to students commensurate with the increased demands made upon them? What happens to students who do not meet the demands?

ACKNOWLEDGMENTS

I appreciate the first-rate research assistance of Marc Moss and Patrick J. Murnane. I would also like to acknowledge helpful conversations with Jeanne Chall, Mary E. Curtis, Harold Howe, Francis Keppel, Marvin Lazerson, Jerome Murphy, Richard Nelson, Barbara Neufeld, and Carol Weiss. I would particularly like to thank Edward Pauly, who read several drafts of this essay and provided many important ideas.

REFERENCES

Anderson, Judith I. 1982. "Measuring the Effectiveness of Title I: A Summary of the 1979–80 State Title I Evaluation Reports." Paper presented at the annual meeting of the American Educational Research Association, New York, March.

Augenblick, John, and Gordon Van de Water. 1983. *State Support for Education, 1982–83.* Denver: Education Policy/Planning Service.

Bacharach, Samuel B., David B. Lipsky, and Joseph B. Shedd. 1984. *Paying for Better Teaching: Merit Pay and Its Alternatives.* Ithaca, N.Y.: Organizational Analysis and Practice.

Benham, L. 1980. "The Demand for Occupational Licensure." Pp. 13–25 in S. Rottenberg, ed., *Occupational Licensing and Regulation*. Washington, D.C.: American Enterprise Institute.

Brazer, Harvey E., Deborah S. Laren, and Frank Yu-Hsieh Sung. 1982. "Elementary and Secondary School Financing." Pp. 411–46 in H. Brazer, ed., *Michigan's Fiscal and Economic Structure*. Ann Arbor: University of Michigan.

Bryk, Anthony S., Peter B. Holland, Valerie E. Lee, and Ruben A. Carriedo. 1984. *Effective Catholic Schools: An Exploration*. Washington, D.C.: National Catholic Education Association.

Carroll, Stephen J. 1979. *The Search for Equity in School Finance: Summary and Conclusions*. Santa Monica: Rand Corp.

Charters, W. W. 1970. "Some Factors Affecting Teacher Survival in School Districts." *American Educational Research Journal* 7: 1–27.

A Children's Defense Budget: An Analysis of the President's FY 1984 Budget and Children. 1984. Washington, D.C.: Children's Defense Fund.

Coleman, James S., Thomas Hoffer, and Sally Kilgore. 1982. *High School Achievement*. New York: Basic Books.

The Condition of Education 1983. 1983. Washington, D.C.: U.S. Department of Education.

Darling-Hammond, Linda, and Arthur E. Wise. Forthcoming. "Beyond Standardization: State Standards and School Improvement." *Elementary School Journal*.

Digest of Education Statistics 1983. 1983. Washington, D.C.: U.S. Department of Education.

Frankel, Martin M., and Debra E. Gerald. 1981. *The Projections of Education Statistics to 1990–91*, Vol. 1. Washington, D.C.: National Center for Education Statistics.

Goettel, Robert J., Bernard A. Kaplan, Martin E. Orland, Pascal D. Forgione, Jr., and Sheila D. Huff. 1977. *A Comparative Analysis of ESEA, Title I Administration in Eight States*. Syracuse, N.Y.: Syracuse Research Corp.

Harnischfeger, Annegret, and David E. Wiley. 1975. *Achievement Test Score Decline: Do We Need to Worry?* Chicago: Cemrel.

———. 1984. *Time and Learning in California Schools*. Sacramento: California Testing Program.

Hill, Paul. 1979. *Do Federal Programs Interfere with One Another?* Santa Monica: Rand Corp.

The Impact of Teacher Shortage and Surplus on Quality Issues in Teacher Education. 1983. Washington, D.C.: American Association of Colleges for Teacher Education.

Jackson, Philip W. 1968. *Life in Classrooms*. New York: Holt, Rinehart and Winston.

Jencks, Christopher, Marshall Smith, Henry Akland, Mary J. Bane, David Cohen, Herbert Gintis, Barbara Heyns, and Stephen Michelson. 1972. *Inequality: A Reassessment of the Effect of Family and Schooling in America*. New York: Basic Books.

Kershaw, Joseph A., and Roland N. McKean. 1962. *Teacher Shortages and Salary Schedules*. New York: McGraw-Hill.

McDonnell, Lorraine M., and Milbrey W. McLaughlin. 1980. *Program Consolidation and the State Role in ESEA Title IV*. Santa Monica: Rand Corp.

Madaus, George F. 1982. "Competency Testing: State and Local Level Responsibilities." *Educational Measurement: Issues and Practice*, Winter.

Merit Pay for Teachers. 1979. Arlington, Va.: Educational Research Service.

Murnane, Richard J. 1981. "Teacher Mobility Revisited." *Journal of Human Resources* 16: 3–19.

———. 1983. "Understanding the Sources of Teaching Competence: Choices, Skills, and the Limits of Training." *Teachers College Record* 84: 564–69.

———. Forthcoming. "The Rhetoric and Reality of Merit Pay: Why Are They Different?" In Henry C. Johnson, ed., *Merit, Money and Teachers' Careers*. Lanham, Md.: University Press of America.

National Assessment of Educational Progress (NAEP). 1978. *Three National Assessments of Science: Changes in Achievement, 1969–77*. Denver: Education Commission of the States.

———. 1981a. *Has Title I Improved Education for Disadvantaged Students? Evidence from Three National Assessments of Reading*. Denver: Education Commission of the States.

———. 1981b. *Three Assessments of Reading: Changes in Performance, 1970–80*. Denver: Education Commission of the States.

———. 1982. *Reading, Science and Mathematics Trends: A Closer Look*. Denver: Education Commission of the States.

———. 1983. *The Third National Mathematics Assessment: Results, Trends and Issues*. Denver: Education Commission of the States.

National Commission on Excellence in Education (NCEE). 1983. *A Nation at Risk: The Imperative for Educational Reform*. Washington, D.C.: U.S. Department of Education.

The Nation Responds: Recent Efforts to Improve Education. 1984. Washington, D.C.: U.S. Department of Education.

O'Neill, Dave A. 1984. *Education in the United States, 1940–1983: A Survey of Trends and Current Concerns*. Special demographic analysis. Washington, D.C.: U.S. Bureau of the Census.

O'Neill, June A., and Margaret C. Simms. 1982. "Education." Chapter 11 in J. L. Palmer and I. S. Sawhill, eds., *The Reagan Experiment*. Washington, D.C.: Urban Institute.

On Further Examination: Report of the Advisory Panel on the Scholastic Test Score Decline. 1977. New York: College Entrance Examination Board.

Ordovensky, Pat. 1983. "Evaluations Sort out Good, Bad Teachers." *USA Today*, 8 June, p. 3A.

Ranbom, Sheppard. 1984. "S.A.T. Scores Up 4 Points, Biggest Jump in 21 Years." *Education Week*, 26 September, p. 1.

The Reagan FY1985 Budget Series: Education. 1984. Washington, D.C.: Federal Budget Report.

Schlechty, P. C., and V. S. Vance. 1981. "Do Academically Able Teachers Leave Education? The North Carolina Case." *Phi Delta Kappan* 63: 106–112.

Smith, James P., and Finis Welch. 1977. "Black-White Wage Ratios, 1960–1970." *American Economic Review* 67: 323–38.

Summers, Anita A., and Barbara L. Wolfe. 1977. "Do Schools Make a Difference?" *American Economic Review* 67: 639–52.

Teacher Supply and Demand in Public Schools, 1981–82. 1983. Washington, D.C.: National Education Association.

Thurow, Lester C. 1975. *Generating Inequality.* New York: Basic Books.

Wainer, Howard. 1984. "An Exploratory Analysis of Performance on the SAT." *Journal of Educational Measurement* 21(2): 81–91.

Weaver, W. T. "Educators in Supply and Demand: Effects on Quality." *School Review* 86: 552–93.

Wise, Arthur E., Linda Darling-Hammond, Milbrey W. McLaughlin, and Harriet T. Bernstein. 1984. *Teacher Evaluation: A Study of Effective Practices.* Santa Monica: Rand Corp.

CHAPTER SIX

Commentary

Paul N. Courant

The methodology of economics is powerful at showing where there is no role for government; where it shows that there is a role to be played, the methodology is not very useful as a guide to designing programs to permit that role to be performed effectively. Thus, when we consider issues of social concern, we have a lot to say about what should not be done, and we have something to say about where things should be done, but we say very little about how things should be done, except that perhaps they should be done some other way. It seems to me that if we are to present useful prescriptions for social policy, we need methods that can be used to tell us what the governmental role might be and how to play it. I suggest that we devote more attention to figuring out what rules might meet the ends of "rough justice" and, if I may, "rough efficiency," and less time bemoaning the fact that what we see is not defensible under rigorous rules of evaluation. Put another way, I think that our method often biases us toward getting the right answer to the wrong problem. And our answer is usually "no."

The paper by Danziger and Feaster is relatively straightforward: reasonably good data are used to examine a well-defined question. We come away with some new knowledge about how recent policy has affected poverty, according to the official definition of poverty. The results do not change the way we think about policy, but they add to our understanding.

The article by Murnane is very different in character. While its title implies a focus on recent policy changes, its coverage is much broader. It starts with the now familiar, depressing statistics on SAT scores over the past two decades, and attempts to focus the diverse literature on elementary and secondary education on the question of why those scores fell and what might be done about it. I learned a great deal about the literature from Murnane's article, but this literature is remarkably unhelpful in providing guidance as to what should be done. I must also confess to some confusion regarding the objectives of public education. Thus, much of what I have to say about this paper will be quite speculative. I note here, however, that in my opinion, Murnane often draws too much from the literature (e.g., inferring that Title I is effective because over a decade the ratio of black to white test scores has improved somewhat) and sometimes too little (e.g., if Murnane's own work shows that teacher training has no effect on teaching effectiveness, why is he so careful not to conclude that education courses are a waste of time?).

ANTIPOVERTY EFFECTS OF TRANSFER PROGRAMS

Danziger and Feaster measure the effectiveness of antipoverty programs by comparing pretransfer income and post-transfer income. As the authors know well, this approach is strictly accurate only if there are no behavioral responses to the programs themselves. Thus, the measure is an upper bound on the effectiveness of government programs. They cite a study suggestion that the upper-bound estimate of the effect of transfer programs is indeed an upper bound, but a very poor estimate. According to Danziger and Feaster, their method of calculation overstates the reductions in poverty attributable to transfers by a factor of more than two (for 1974 data). If antipoverty programs cause disincentives of this magnitude, it may be worth pursuing some other approach.

A second difficulty with the Danziger and Feaster paper is that they use the census definition of income, under which non-cash transfers are not included. Perhaps their results would not change using a more comprehensive income definition, but the details, especially with regard to sex, might change—given that AFDC eligibility often implies Medicaid eligibility and that it is relatively difficult for male-headed households to receive such assistance in many states.

Another cause of some disquiet arises from the years chosen for comparison—1978 and 1982, years that are at radically different positions in the business cycle. The year 1978 was unusually good, and 1982 unusually bad. A comparison of policy effects should not depend so heavily on statistical controls for the business cycle. The business cycle also varies by region. The North Central region has always been very cyclical, and so, no doubt, have been its poverty numbers. A sample of cycles, rather than just one peak to trough, would be desirable.

no doubt, have been its poverty numbers. A sample of cycles, rather than just one peak to trough, would be desirable.

Perhaps more important is the interpretation of the descriptive statistics and associated analysis. The authors first state that the probability of escape from poverty, given receipt of transfers, was essentially unaffected by the recession. Later in the discussion, they show that 15 percent of the increase in the number of persons poor in male-headed households (and 24 percent of the increase for female-headed households) can be attributed to program changes. Do we then infer that the remaining 85 percent and 76 percent are due to the recession? If so, their first statement is misleading.

The most striking results that emerge from the analysis are: (1) women are more likely to receive transfers, and less likely to be removed from poverty by them; (2) households with incomes far below the poverty line are more likely to receive transfers and less likely to be removed from poverty by them. Blacks are less likely to be removed from poverty than whites, conditional on receipt of transfers. The authors attribute this finding to the fact that whites are more likely to receive social insurance payments, which are more generous than welfare payments. Might it also be the case that whites are more likely to be near the poverty line in the first place?

I think the authors' assumption that 1978 policies would have stayed in effect, or even become more generous, had Mr. Reagan not been elected is probably wrong. My own experience in and around the White House in 1980 indicates that even the moderate welfare reform that was official administration policy at the time was not pursued seriously.

Danziger and Feaster say that the primary goals of transfer programs are the "provision of minimum levels of cash, nutritional, medical, housing, and educational assistance for a substantial portion of the population." Unfortunately, the analysis is really only about cash programs and about poverty lines, rather than about "minimum levels of assistance." This article simply does not tell us how much the Reagan changes have affected the living standards of the poor in general, or even of those poor who receive transfers. Instead, we know a tremendous amount about the effect on their cash incomes.

I find little to quarrel with in the authors' policy prescriptions. Surely if we have defined a minimum standard, we ought to index it. If targeted employment programs are cost-effective (all that is indicated in the text is that they could eliminate a lot of poverty, and costs are not discussed), they may be worth pursuing. The Garfinkel plan, essentially a national tax-transfer scheme from absent fathers to present mothers, has always appealed to me, in part because it is a program with antipoverty impact that does not require poverty as a condition for either receipt or contribution.

If it is really true that pretransfer incomes would be as much higher, in the absence of programs, as is implied by Plotnick's results, there should be large potential efficiency gains in the design of antipoverty programs. If over half the effect of antipoverty programs now is to reduce pretransfer incomes, surely we should start thinking about radical changes in program design, especially if current programs are not well adapted to respond to the feminization of poverty. Are there specialized training or workplace rules that affect women differently from men, and that involve interventions in labor markets so that women will be helped by economic growth more than they have in the past?

ELEMENTARY AND SECONDARY EDUCATION POLICY

If our measures of the effectiveness of income redistribution programs suffer because Consumer Population Survey data are incomplete and the poverty line is not a perfect welfare index, the situation for evaluation of education policy is far worse. Nothing in Murnane's paper vitiates Hanushek's conclusion that we do not know much about the production function for education.[1] Even worse, we do not have social agreement on what we want, beyond vague phrases like "excellence" and "equality of opportunity," goals that may often be in conflict. We do have a sense that the schools are not doing especially well at promoting either goal and that there is some problem with incentive structures at the level of school and classroom. "Merit pay," the economist's natural solution to the problem, needs to become far more than a slogan if it is to have any effect, and Murnane's own work indicates that schools' organizational structure limits its potential. So we have a good that we cannot measure, produced by a process that we do not understand, coupled with a general sense that things are not going well. What's a policymaker to do?

Murnane's major policy proposals are in the area of teacher certification. He argues that current certification requirements in many states raise the opportunity cost of becoming a teacher by preventing the prospective teacher from acquiring training that can be used for anything else. I would add, as a sometime counselor of undergraduates, that another reason why some students stay away from education courses is that the courses themselves are not very interesting. Why would a student with relatively good scientific aptitude choose to enter an education curriculum as a college junior when by studying chemistry she or he will have a better time in school and have more opportunities, at higher pay, two years hence?

Murnane's suggestion that states experiment with certification requirements is very promising. Indeed, in light of the econometric evidence that education courses have nothing to do with classroom performance, the case for trying this kind of approach seems overwhelming. The problems are essentially political. It is not news that education courses accomplish little, yet they have been around for a long time, and both teacher-training schools and teachers' unions seem to be natural constituencies for their maintenance. When essentially all of the institutional experts in an area have a clear interest in maintaining a policy, it is not going to be easy to abolish it, even if the social interest in doing so is large.

The preceding example is one where the preferred policy involves reducing the state's role in education policy. There are many such examples, leading us to the question of just what we believe the state ought to be doing in this area. Murnane advances a number of reasons for state regulation of local boards, and in all cases that bear on personnel policy the reasons cited make sense only if local boards are incompetent. Moreover, to the extent that education is a private good, it is hard to find a role for state government, much less for federal. Indeed, it may be hard to find a role for government at any level.

Such a conclusion seems to miss the point. Traditionally, it has been argued that there *is* a public-good aspect to elementary and secondary education, that it is important that there be some common core of knowledge and literacy, and (perhaps) that there be some socialization toward a common set of values. Moreover, there may be some information economies in the choice of curriculum ("experts" can help to guide families regarding the returns to the acquisition of specific kinds of training). Surely a set of school curricula can be established which are likely to be beneficial in most contingencies (arithmetic and literacy in English are surely two elements of such a set). In any of these cases, it would seem that the state does have a role to play in defining a required curriculum and in requiring some minimum performance level in that curriculum. But the state's role here would be quite removed from the details of day-to-day school operations or personnel policy. Promulgation of output standards, coupled with some incentive system to induce schools to meet those standards as they saw fit, would seem to be appropriate.

There is some scope for regulation of a more detailed kind. However, the system is currently overregulated from the top and leaves little room for innovation. The "best and the brightest" face real barriers to entering teaching; in addition, once people become established as teachers, union rules make it virtually impossible to fire the bad ones and reward the good ones. While the latter problem will always exist, and the internal dynamics of any collective enterprise are such that strict adherence to the marginal-productivity doctrine of wages, individual by individual, probably causes serious morale problems, it should be possible to introduce considerably more flexibility into the training and promotion of teachers than is currently the norm.

A tennis coach once told me, "Always change a losing game." He was a public school teacher, and a good one. I suggest we apply his advice to public schools themselves.

NOTES

1. Eric A. Hanushek, "Throwing Money at Schools," *Journal of Policy Analysis and Management* 1 (1981): 19–42.

Commentary

Eric A. Hanushek

POVERTY AND WELFARE

The article by Danziger and Feaster is excellent. It attempts to disentangle the various factors affecting changes in poverty over the recent past and, most important, to consider separate demographic and geographic groupings of the poor. In order to separate technique from conclusions, their analysis is done in several ways.

From the analytic viewpoint, I think two related issues are particularly worth considering. These involve the concentration on poverty thresholds and, relatedly, the definition of poverty. The development of an agreed-upon measure of poverty has been very important in the history of social policy. The definition evolved from the early work of Mollie Orshansky and was refined somewhat over time. No one believes the current definition is a perfect measure of the welfare (or misery) of families, but it has provided a yardstick against which intertemporal as well as cross-sectional changes can be identified, quantified, and analyzed. The Census Bureau provides data on poverty regularly; programs use poverty definitions to determine eligibility; and social scientists make a living interpreting the incidence of poverty. Nevertheless, it is important to reflect on the usefulness of poverty measures in the Danziger/Feaster analysis. One interpretation of their approach is that they have taken an inherently continuous variable, that of income, and introduced errors into it to arrive at the dichotomous variable of poverty. To add to this, it is now well known that linear regression models have certain conceptual difficulties when applied to dichotomous dependent variables. Therefore, we frequently turn to some nonlinear method of estimation such as probit analysis, which can be thought of as a device for inferring what the underlying continuous probability distribution of a variable looks like given the realized values of the probability process—that is, the dichotomous observed values. Unfortunately, the estimation theory surrounding probit analysis is not as well developed as that for linear regression analysis. The estimation appears to be quite sensitive to data problems such as correlations of the exogenous variables or errors-in-variables. Moreover, the method is quite expensive, thus inhibiting some lines of inquiry.

The Danziger/Feaster analysis has pursued such a strategy: it takes a continuous variable (income), transforms it into a discontinuous variable (poverty), and then estimates models of its incidence and the effects of different variables on poverty within a probit context. Moreover, the focus of their analysis is the antipoverty impact of governmental transfers and how this might have changed between 1978 and 1982. Perhaps for symmetry, they have measured transfers simply in terms of receipt; the magnitude of such transfers is ignored.

While their concentration on poverty status conforms to the now-standard poverty data presented by the Bureau of the Census and while this makes for a more "state of the art" article that can introduce interesting likelihood functions, it makes little analytical sense to me. The obvious alternative is to analyze the income position of families and how transfers of different amounts affect that. Such an effort might still require estimating a probit model of the probability of receiving a transfer. That, however, would be a simple probit instead of their simultaneous probit. The one concession the authors have made to the continuous nature of the problem is to include a measure of distance below the poverty line in their models of the probability of escape from poverty. Not surprisingly, this is an important predictor. They never discuss the alternative of using the natural measure of income, even though this would greatly simplify their estimation and might—although it is difficult to know a priori—affect the results of their analysis.

A related point about interpretation involves noncash transfers. While this has recently become a very heated political issue, the underlying conceptual issue is quite straightforward. Many transfers to the poor are not in the form of cash but instead come as food stamps, subsidized housing, or medical insurance. Although it is hard to tell the difference between cash and food stamps—the Federal Reserve shreds food stamps just as it does worn-out dollar bills—poverty measures take no account of noncash transfers.

In truth, this is just one part of a much larger measurement question. Presumably we want to measure the welfare of families; thus, to the extent that food stamps, housing programs, and the like contribute to their welfare, they should be counted. Conversely, to the extent that taxes or high living costs of a particular area detract from welfare, they should also be included in the analysis. To be sure, the measurement issues are large, particularly in the case of in-kind provision of items that are not tradable and are not close to cash. For example, the value of Medicare in improving the welfare of families is difficult to estimate. Some effort, however, should be made to incorporate noncash factors, since these have become an increasingly important component of our income support system. Major means-tested noncash benefit programs rose from $5 billion in 1965 to $47 billion in 1982 (in constant 1982 dollars). The aggregate programmatic changes should make it obvious why it is so important to include noncash items in any intertemporal analysis of poverty.

The desirability of including such items is perhaps even greater in a cross-sectional analysis. Two families with equal cash income are obviously not equally well off if one family pays taxes and the other does not, particularly when pretax income is the standard, as it is in poverty estimates. As social security taxes have grown and as inflation has reduced the effective beginning point of the income tax schedule, taxes have become increasingly important to the working poor. (By recent estimates, the personal-income-tax threshold for 1984 falls 17 percent above the poverty cutoff for a family of four.) Thus, neglecting taxes introduces a systematic distortion between working and nonworking poor. Similarly, there is a distortion between those in subsidized housing and those not, between those receiving Medicaid and those not, and so forth.

Much of the recent (and heated) discussion about whether to include noncash benefits in the definition of poverty has revolved around its potential effect on the perception of poverty and the transfer programs that explicitly mention poverty in eligibility rules. There is no denying, however, that these noncash items are valuable in improving individual welfare and, therefore, that they should be included to the extent possible in analyses of the low-income population.

A related issue that has received less public attention is the potential effect of geographical differences in the cost of living. As one who regularly commutes between Rochester, New York, and Washington, D.C., I can testify that prices do differ around the country. This is obviously more important for stationary items—say, houses—than for mobile ones—

say, hamburgers. (There are, correspondingly, benefits that exist in one area but not in another—for example, the lack of good Thai restaurants in Rochester). These differences surely affect true welfare, but little attention is ever given to them. While this may be a case where the perennial "lack of data" excuse comes into play, I basically believe a crude correction is better than none at all. For example, the now-defunct Bureau of Labor Statistics (BLS) budget estimates could provide a rough standardization for 1978 and 1982.

Finally, with respect to the analytical issues, there is always interest in the conventional poverty statistics. For this reason, it might be useful to provide the aggregate summary of the results in poverty terms, after doing the analysis in income or adjusted-income terms.

The reaction to the Danziger/Feaster article from a Washington and a policy perspective is somewhat clearer. The proposals to provide cost-of-living adjustments for transfer programs do not seem to lead anywhere. First, though motivated by a current poverty problem, this policy would only affect the rate of change of future poverty; inflation would not in the future lead to implicit cuts in benefit levels of transfers, and thus would not have the direct antipoverty bias of a nonindexed transfer system. Unless the policy were applied retroactively, anyone poor today would remain poor in the future as well, regardless of the inflation rate. Second, if in fact inflation is controlled—a primary goal of recent policies—the change to indexing would have no effect. Finally, cutting cost of living adjustments (COLAs) is one of the more popular deficit reduction proposals, in part because it is a way of identifying large expenditures. Therefore, while not impossible, new COLA plans seem somewhat unlikely.

Establishing national minimums for AFDC levels has some appeal in view of regional poverty statistics and locational distortions introduced by different welfare levels. Nevertheless, the case for a national minimum is not really developed, leaving one to wonder whether the argument is entirely based on regional paternalism. Obviously, it has some large budgetary implications.

EDUCATION

Murnane has put together a comprehensive picture of educational policies along with some provocative ideas for thought and policy. Everyone from the serious educational researcher to the educational decision-maker to the casual reader is bound to get something from this paper.

Having said that, I must point out the most startling feature of educational research and policy today: almost any assertion or policy suggestion is permissible. There is little requirement to present evidence to support a position; indeed, little systematic evidence is available. This lack of evidence is convenient because there is little chance of any assertion being refuted.

I point this out in part because Murnane is guilty of making unsupported assertions; in fact, he is forced to do so if he wishes to make a broad assessment in the area of education. Perhaps because we share many of the same biases, however, I find Murnane's assertions frequently plausible and always sensible. This stands somewhat in contrast to a variety of major studies and commission reports that have recently been issued. They have provided us with assertions, recommendations, and pronouncements that represent individual opinions. With a few exceptions, they do not represent new evidence about the character of the educational process; about how the various components of our educational sector interact; or about how regulations, financial incentives, and schools interact.

The general perspective that Murnane brings to analyzing school policies might be characterized as an economist's standard view of deregulation. He focuses particularly on the certification requirements imposed by all states. I believe that his arrow is aimed at a good spot. Indeed, this is perhaps a classic case of regulation and a classic example of why economists often recommend deregulation.

Our knowledge about the educational production process is quite imprecise. States have quite generally imposed certification requirements with absolutely no knowledge of what characteristics make for effective teachers or classrooms. A major effect of these certification requirements, which are typically phrased in terms of specific teacher-training courses, has been to impose constraints on entering the teaching profession. In particular, individuals who take a standard liberal-arts or science curriculum in college will not have the required education courses and thus will be ineligible for teaching. (A secondary effect has been the artificial support of teacher-training institutions that, in the absence of such requirements, might find it difficult to compete for students.) This may be an important factor in preventing high-caliber people from entering teaching. It may also have a differential effect by school subject matter (because of varying opportunity costs).

Murnane advocates ways of circumventing the teacher-training requirements. I find his notions appealing, but I think they are too limited.

A plethora of restrictions emanate from state laws, state regulations, local regulations, contract provisions and, to a lesser extent, federal laws and regulations. These restrictions have their supporters, but support is seldom based on evidence of performance in schools. There is little reason, therefore, for Murnane to draw a box around certification and to leave the larger matter out of consideration. If the argument is built entirely on some idea of political feasibility, I suspect that there is no cost in broadening the scope. All these regulations have their own constituency built on the strongest of all bonds—individual labor-market advantages created by regulations.

It is surprising that Murnane makes no mention of labor unions in this discussion. Unions are, of course, key actors in many of the discussions. They are direct participants in a majority of local contracts, where many binding regulations concerning personnel and school organizations are imbedded. They are indirect actors in state regulations, in schools of education, and so forth. The policies that Murnane suggests would very likely lead to resistance from unions, and the natural extensions would almost certainly be ones of considerable conflict with unions.

One reason educational policy is in its current (perpetual) state of chaos, I assert, is that attention has been focused on the wrong set of questions. For the most part, people have been concerned with what characteristics of teachers determine, or simply indicate, good teaching ability and—having discovered that—how these characteristics can be developed. These are appealing questions; if they could be answered, we could undoubtedly make much better educational decisions. The answers might in particular provide a basis for teacher certification requirements and other regulatory devices. However, it appears that answering these questions is beyond our current capability. This does not imply that we cannot improve matters. A more natural approach would be to reward good performance itself, instead of factors that tend to be correlated in the population with good performance. On this score, Murnane's paper is particularly interesting. He provides some insights into merit pay and what can be gleaned from past experience. This indeed seems to be a productive way to proceed. Unfortunately, we currently lack definitive studies of merit pay, so this area again comes down to listing hypotheses and the few shreds of available evidence.

Poverty and education have been the focus of consistent attention for the past twenty years. They have, since the War on Poverty, been the subject of governmental policy attention. Two things seem clear at this time. First, both issues remain unresolved. Second, with current skepticism about the effectiveness of many governmental programs and with current pressures against the expansion of governmental outlays, new ways of looking at problems and dealing with them are called for. Both of these articles do implicitly contain some such ideas, although evidence of the effectiveness of the specific suggestions of each is scant.

Commentary

David Stern

Direct transfers in cash or kind are the most cost-effective way for governments to provide an adequate standard of living for households that lack sufficient income from their own labor, capital, or private transfer payments. But government transfers to the poor, especially in cash, are politically unpopular in this country. Danziger and Feaster found that even in 1978, when transfer payments by all levels of government had risen to 10.1 percent of the GNP—up from 5.7 percent in 1960—more than three out of four nonaged poor households were not receiving enough cash from governments to raise them above the poverty line. They found that under the Reagan administration, cuts in transfer programs reduced the antipoverty impact to the point where, in 1982, cash transfers failed to lift more than four-fifths of the nonaged poor households over the poverty line.

Giving "a hand, not a handout" is in this country a more popular strategy for helping the poor. Governments at all levels sponsor programs to increase the earning capacity of poor people or of their children. If these programs reduce the number of people whose pretransfer earnings are insufficient, then, obviously, they reduce the need for transfer payments. Examples of such programs are insurance on loans to businesses owned by members of disadvantaged minority groups, employment training for low-income people, agricultural extension services for small farmers, and educational assistance for students from poor families.

Of the various programs that affect the distribution of earning capacity, education is the largest in dollar outlays. I focus here on education as a means of enabling more people to earn adequate incomes. I will review some evidence that policy in the past two decades has had some effect in reducing inequality of educational attainment. However, since 1980, policy has shifted away from concern for economic inequality toward an emphasis on educational "excellence." To achieve higher standards of academic performance, central and local policymakers are changing the incentive structure for teachers and students. I suggest here how new incentives can motivate efforts to improve educational performance without abandoning the goal of reducing economic inequality.

EDUCATION AS AN EQUALIZER: THE 1960s AND 1970s

If putting more money into the pockets of poor people were the sole goal, education would not be an efficient means. Ribich showed in 1968 that a dollar spent on compensatory education at the elementary or secondary level produces less than a dollar increase in the present value of lifetime earnings of children from low-income households. Jencks and his colleagues in 1972 assembled a great deal of evidence to argue that the link between education and income is too weak for schooling to be useful as a means of altering the income distribution. On the other hand, economists of the human-capital school (Mincer 1974; Chiswick 1974) have demonstrated that more of the variance in earnings can be explained by a model that includes years of work experience in addition to years of schooling, and their findings suggest that schooling may be complementary to learning on the job. Even so, most of the variance in individual earnings cannot be attributed to differences in educational attainment.

Furthermore, public policy cannot control educational attainment directly. Dollars for schools must first be converted into instructional programs, which may or may not increase students' learning (see Hanushek 1981). Any gain in students' learning then may or may not lead to higher educational attainment and earnings. It would be surprising if the eventual increase in earnings produced by an additional dollar of spending on schools were as much as half a dollar in present value. This cost-ineffectiveness is simply the price we pay for trying to change the distribution of pretransfer income rather than using cash transfers directly.

Of course, cash transfers themselves produce less than a dollar of net income gain per dollar of transfer payment, because they induce recipients to spend less time in paid work. The Seattle and Denver income-maintenance experiments found that a thousand-dollar lump-sum grant would cause husbands to reduce their paid work by 47 hours a year

(Keeley et al. 1978, table 4). At the then-minimum wage of $2.00 an hour, this translates to an earnings reduction that is less than 10 percent of the thousand-dollar transfer. For wives, the earnings reduction is less than 40 percent of the transfer, and for female heads of households it is 23 percent. These reductions are not negligible, but they still leave much more than half of the transfer as a net gain in recipients' income.

The rationale for using education rather than cash grants to combat poverty is largely moral and political, not economic. Some low-income adults may be seen as "undeserving" of public aid, but children cannot be held responsible for their families' lack of money. In 1965 this kind of moral argument, combined with the self-interest of the education lobby and representatives of low-income communities, helped to produce a winning political coalition in support of federal aid for schools in low-income neighborhoods (see Timpane 1978). The result was Title I of the 1965 Elementary and Secondary Education Act. This was, and still is (as Chapter I of the 1981 Educational Consolidation and Improvement Act), the largest item in the federal budget for elementary and secondary education. It is also the biggest single source of money for compensatory education of low-income children.

The moral and political forces that produced Title I of ESEA also directed the attention and resources of states, school districts, and individual teachers toward the educational needs of low-income students during the 1960s and 1970s. Sixteen states provided categorical funds for disadvantaged students, and another eight gave extra weight to disadvantaged students in allocating general-purpose aid to local districts (Simms 1984). Many high schools created new curricular options, such as granting academic credit for work experience, to encourage attendance by students who otherwise would have been likely to drop out (Abramowitz and Tenenbaum 1978). Even within individual classrooms, there is evidence from this period that teachers tended to give extra attention to slower students (Brown and Saks 1981). An equalizing tendency was evident from the center to the periphery of the educational system.

There is also evidence that a certain degree of equalization was actually achieved. The latest, and largest, evaluation of the federal Title I program itself found evidence of definite gains by participating students, relative to other low-income students (Carter 1984). More generally, effects of efforts toward equalization at various levels are evident in data from the National Assessment of Educational Progress, which tested students at ages 9, 13, and 17. Achievement in mathematics was tested during the 1977–1978 and 1981–1982 school years; reading was tested in 1974–

1975 and 1979–1980. Changes in average achievement were more positive for blacks and Hispanics than for whites. Changes were also more
positive for students whose parents lacked high school diplomas than for
students whose parents had some schooling beyond high school. These
differences occurred in both reading and mathematics, and in all three
age groups.

Similarly, data from the Current Population Survey in 1959, 1969, and
1979 show that illiteracy in the population aged 14 and over declined
more steeply for blacks than whites. Among whites aged 14 to 24, the
percentage of illiterate fell from 0.5 in 1959 to 0.2 in 1979. Among blacks
aged 14 to 24, illiteracy fell from 1.2 percent in 1959 to 0.2 percent in
1979.

High school dropout rates among blacks also fell dramatically: from
30.0 percent of the 14-to-34 age group in 1970 (31.2 percent of the 18-
and 19-year-olds) to 17.9 percent in the 14- to-34-year-olds (19.3 percent
of the 18- and 19-year-olds) in 1981. In comparison, between 1970 and
1981 white dropout rates in the 14-to-34 age group declined from 15.2
only to 12.1 percent. And among 18- and 19-year-old whites the dropout
rate actually rose slightly, from 14.1 to 15.5 percent (Grant and Eiden
1980; Grant and Snyder 1983).

These numbers indicate movement toward more equal educational
attainment between blacks and whites, between students whose parents
had different amounts of schooling, and between students whose parents
had different levels of income. This does not necessarily mean that the
distribution of income among these students will be any more equal than
it was among their parents, but it does mean that education was doing
more to reduce the likelihood that children of poor parents would grow
up to be poor themselves.

ENTER "EXCELLENCE" (AGAIN)

Schools in the 1960s and 1970s were not always champions of the
poor. In many communities, new programs for low-income children were
born out of struggle and acrimony (Ravitch 1982; Stern and Timar
1982). But whether schools resisted, accommodated, or actively promoted change, they were part of it.

Since 1980, however, the same political and moral sea change that
allowed economic policy to produce a 10 percent unemployment rate,
make the income tax less progressive, and reduce cash transfers for the
poor has also affected educational policy. Federal budget cuts have re-

duced the number of economically disadvantaged children receiving compensatory services by an estimated 500,000 to 900,000 since 1981 (Simms 1984). Instead of reducing inequality, achieving "excellence" is now the top priority.

In 1982 and 1983 dozens of reports viewed with alarm the performance of American students and educators. The first and clearest of these reports was *A Nation at Risk* (National Commission on Excellence in Education 1983). It complained that "the ideal of academic excellence as the primary goal of schooling seems to be fading across the board in American education" (p. 14). After reviewing evidence of declining educational performance, the report listed its findings about aspects of the educational process that have contributed to the decline. First among the findings:

> Secondary school curricula have been homogenized, diluted, and diffused to the point that they no longer have a central purpose. In effect, we have a cafeteria-style curriculum in which the appetizers and desserts can easily be mistaken for the main courses. . . . This curricular smorgasbord, combined with extensive student choice, explains a great deal about where we find ourselves today. . . . Twenty-five percent of the credits earned by general track high school students are in physical and health education, work experience outside the school, remedial English and mathematics, and personal service and development courses, such as training for adulthood and marriage. (pp. 18–19)

The Commission on Excellence recommended tougher standards for high school graduation, more time on academic subjects, and various measures to strengthen the teaching profession. This program, in various versions, quickly swept the country. By the fall of 1983, twenty-six states had adopted more stringent requirements for high school graduation, and the remaining twenty-four states were all actively considering proposals to do the same (*Education Week*, 7 December 1983).

The renewed insistence on high academic standards immediately prompted expressions of concern about abandoning the struggle against inequality. Harold Howe (1984, p. 24), formerly United States Commissioner of Education, urged policymakers "to give equity a chance in the excellence game. Unless we find a way to do this, our 'excellence' will be so flawed that it will haunt us." He charged that "a major component missing" from most of the recent commission reports "is any recognition of the importance of motivation" for students. He warned that the "recommendations for more homework, more demanding courses, longer school days, and more tests are likely to be implemented in ways that further increase the number of dropouts." As someone else put it, "If a kid isn't clearing six feet, what's the point of raising the bar to six feet and two inches?"

The current stress on excellence is much like the response after Sputnik in 1957. Then, too, schools were charged with lack of academic rigor (see Conant 1959; Rickover 1963). Curricular reforms in science and mathematics were designed to produce more and better scientists and engineers, in the hope of restoring America's technical supremacy. Now, again, new resources are being earmarked for education in science and mathematics, to preserve the nation's technical edge against foreign competition. But these priorities and programs in the 1960s and 1970s came to be regarded as elitist. For instance, Gallup polls in 1971 and 1972 found large majorities of the general public agreeing that "the schools spend too much time in preparing students for college and not on occupations which don't require a college degree," and approving of "schools reducing the amount of classroom instruction to make greater use of educational opportunities outside the school" (Timpane et al. 1976). Work experience and other items now regarded as educational junk food were just what the public ordered ten or fifteen years ago.

Political tides may turn again. Today's educational reforms may once again be denounced as elitist and unfair to children whose home environment puts them at a disadvantage even before they enter school. American education has oscillated between these poles for at least a century (see Edson 1983). But oscillation is not progress, and changing the direction of policy entails considerable transaction costs as old programs are dismantled and new ones put in place. Are current reforms merely another swing of the pendulum, or will they produce some lasting improvement?

INCENTIVES AND INFORMATION

There do seem to be one or two new things under the sun. One is the systematic attention now being given to the incentive structure in education. Another is the development of better technology for managing information.

Neither revenues of school districts nor compensation of staff usually depends on actual performance. Possibly local taxpayers are willing to pay more for schools they think are doing a good job, but this is a clumsy mechanism for quality control. Furthermore, states now pay a larger share of the nation's school costs than localities pay themselves. Most grants by states to school districts are allocated simply on the basis of enrollment or attendance, sometimes with a correction for a district's own ability to pay, but they do not depend on any measure of what students learn. Some state grants, along with federal grants, are categorical awards for specific purposes such as compensatory education, vocational classes, or special services for handicapped students. But categorical grants "throw money at" problems; they are paid whether results are achieved or not.

For teachers, it has long been recognized that public schools do not offer incentives like those provided for employees in a typical private enterprise. To begin with, most business firms can adjust levels of compensation to attract qualified applicants for particular jobs and can even tailor compensation packages for individuals. Once hired, individuals can be fired if they perform below standard, and if they perform above standard they may well be rewarded with additional pay (Henderson 1979). In contrast, compensation of public school teachers, almost everywhere in the United States, is governed by a salary schedule in which the only two factors that determine differences in pay are experience and training. The level of the salary schedule and the precise amount of increments for experience and training do vary from district to district and change from time to time. But local administrators do not have the power to make adjustments as they see fit. Availability of revenues from the federal and state governments, the politics of local school boards, and collective bargaining (which covers a much larger proportion of public school teachers than of employees in the private sector) all exert powerful influences on salary decisions. As a result, compensation does not serve as a flexible tool for recruitment, motivation, and retention of employees in public schools, as it does in private business.

Lack of incentives has been a problem in other parts of the public sector. The past fifteen years have seen considerable experimentation with management techniques, including new compensation schemes, to make government work better. Productivity has been improved in street repair, garbage collection, police and fire protection, hospitals, libraries, public utilities, and other public services (National Commission on Productivity and Work Quality 1975; National Center for Productivity and Quality of Working Life 1977; Greiner et al. 1977). However, among the hundreds of cases described in the literature on improving productivity in the public sector, examples of incentives for teachers have until very recently been extremely rare.

Why have public elementary and secondary schools been particularly inhospitable to incentive plans? One obvious reason is that teachers' unions have consistently opposed any differentiated compensation except that based on experience and training. One of the unions' arguments against merit pay is that if administrators had the power to decide which teachers deserved extra pay, the decisions would sometimes be arbitrary and capricious. Underlying this objection to merit pay is the basic technical problem of deciding which teachers are more productive—a problem which would exist even if there were no teachers' unions. The problem was well summarized in a report by the Committee for Economic Development (1976) on improving productivity in government:

> [P]roductivity in education is difficult to measure both because many of the goals of education are intangible and because complex outside factors come into play. A decline in reading scores does not necessarily indicate a drop in the productivity of public schools; it might also reflect a change in the composition of the school population. However, a sustained rise in reading scores does not necessarily indicate better teaching; it might result from increased enrollment of students from family backgrounds that stimulate learning. (p. 56)

It is possible—with sufficient good data—to control for students' characteristics by means of statistical regression analysis or other procedures. But the multiplicity, subtlety, and long-range nature of educational goals still create a problem. Explicitly or implicitly, performance incentives emphasize some goals more than others. This was evident in the federally sponsored demonstration of educational performance contracting in 1970–1971 (Gramlich and Koshel 1975).

Finally, even if the technical problem is somehow solved, a political problem will remain—and this, too, would arise even if teachers' unions did not exist. The problem is, if some teachers are better than others and are given higher pay in recognition of that fact, how to justify, and explain to parents, why the better teachers are assigned to some students rather than others.

Currently the problem of incentives for teachers is receiving an extraordinary amount of attention. Present shortages of qualified math and science teachers, and impending shortages of teachers in the elementary grades due to the echo of the baby boom, are one theme of current discussion. Comments by the National Commission on Excellence in Education (1983) on the desirability of rewarding good teachers, followed by President Reagan's strong statements in support of merit pay, have also generated much debate. In response to both concerns, teachers' unions are currently reexamining their positions on differential compensation.

In 1983 Florida and California both established merit-pay programs for outstanding teachers. In both plans, a winning teacher receives a cash bonus of several thousand dollars a year for one to three years. The selection process is controlled by the state in Florida, while in California it is carried out locally. In California the "mentor teachers" also have extra responsibilities for curriculum development and supervision of new teachers.

Merit pay for individuals has the well-known drawback of encouraging individuals to try to look good at their coworkers' expense; for instance, teachers may try to have troublesome students assigned to other classrooms, or they may undermine other teachers in relations with parents or supervisors.

Conversely, merit pay for individuals does not encourage collaboration, and some collaboration among teachers can benefit students. Teachers can collaborate by coordinating curricular content across classrooms, enforcing consistent standards for student conduct in the common areas of the school (auditorium, hallways, cafeteria, school yard), communicating information to and from parents, supervising extracurricular activities, sharing ideas about individual students, and teaching each other new instructional techniques. This last kind of collaboration may be especially important for improving performance, because there is ample evidence in the research literature that certain instructional practices are relatively effective (see Bloom 1984; Levin et al. 1984) but diffusion of these practices is very slow. Incentives for teachers ought to encourage such diffusion, not impede it further.

For reasons such as these, Florida and California have moved quickly to supplement their individual merit-pay programs with "merit school" plans, which would provide incentives to teachers in groups. Florida passed the necessary legislation in 1984. In California, state superintendent Bill Honig has begun distribution of "report cards" on each public school in the state, but legislation providing money to merit schools had not passed as of December 1984.

These incentive plans hold considerable promise for motivating schools toward "excellence" while promoting equal educational opportunity. Awards to schools can be based not only on average achievement test scores but also on measures of performance by disadvantaged students: average scores in the bottom quartile, for instance, or low dropout rates. Schools with students at lower socioeconomic levels can be given bigger bonuses for achieving the same growth in students' learning as schools with students from more prosperous families.

Such refined incentive formulas require a good deal of data on individual schools. Because computers have become relatively cheap and widespread, these data are now much more readily accessible than they were a decade ago. Most states now have, or can easily construct, machine-readable files containing current data on test scores, enrollments, and some socioeconomic characteristics of students in each school. Indeed, the recent development of statewide data bases creates a temptation for state reformers to impose incentive systems that are too centralized. Incentive formulas are likely to seem more legitimate and less artificial if they are negotiated locally (see Stern 1984). States can encourage or require local districts to establish incentive plans. Making use of an "educational management information system" (Davis et al. 1984), incentives can motivate simultaneous progress toward higher standards and less educational inequality.

In the very short run, schools may face a real tradeoff between raising standards and reducing inequality. For instance, with a given staff it may not be possible to offer both advanced and remedial instruction. Such a tradeoff may also exist along some theoretical long-run frontier where, even with the best technology, resource constraints force a choice between helping the high achievers or the disadvantaged. However, most schools are a long way from this frontier. The task of educational improvement is to move schools toward the frontier by speeding diffusion of more effective practices. Creating new incentives may do that.

In theory, some sort of voucher plan could also provide the right incentives. But a bare-fisted, free-market voucher system, with price competition and *caveat emptor*, is likely to produce market segmentation along geographic and socioeconomic lines (Stern and Timar 1982). If publicly supported schools are to reduce the likelihood that children of poor parents will grow up poor themselves, a voucher system would have to be of the regulated, compensatory sort designed by Jencks et al. (1970).

Finally, it is important to reiterate that education by itself cannot eliminate poverty. As argued here, the commitment to compensatory education for children of the poor does not have to be dropped in the current quest for educational excellence. Compensatory education can give these children a better shot at getting good jobs. But educational policy cannot guarantee that there will be enough good jobs to go around.

REFERENCES

Abramowitz, Susan, and Ellen Tenenbaum. 1978. *High School '77*. Washington, D.C.: National Institute of Education.

Bloom, Benjamin. 1984. "The 2 Sigma Problem: The Search for Methods of Group Instruction as Effective as One-to-One Tutoring." *Educational Researcher* 13 (6): 4–16.

Brown, Byron W., and Daniel H. Saks. 1981. "The Microeconomics of Schooling." Chapter 5 in David C. Berliner, ed., *Review of Research in Education*, vol. 9. Washington, D.C.: American Educational Research Association.

Carter, Launor F. 1984. "The Sustaining Effects Study of Compensatory and Elementary Education." *Educational Researcher* 13 (7): 4–13.

Chiswick, Barry R. 1974. *Income Inequality*. New York: National Bureau of Economic Research. 1974.

Committee for Economic Development. 1976. *Improving Productivity in State and Local Government*. New York: Committee for Economic Development.

Conant, James B. 1959. *The American High School Today*. New York: McGraw Hill.

Davis, Otto A., Harry R. Faulk, and Holly H. Johnston. 1984. "An Educational Management Information System" (draft). Pittsburgh: School of Urban and Public Affairs, Carnegie-Mellon University.

Edson, C. H. 1983. "Risking the Nation: Historical Dimensions on Survival and Educational Reform." *Issues in Education* 1 (2 & 3): 171–84.

Gramlich, Edward M., and Patricia P. Koshel. 1975. *Educational Performance Contracting*. Washington, D.C.: Brookings.

Grant W. Vance, and Leo J. Eiden. 1980. *Digest of Education Statistics 1980*. Washington, D.C.: National Center for Education Statistics.

Grant, W. Vance, and Thomas D. Snyder. 1983. *Digest of Education Statistics 1983–84*. Washington, D.C.: National Center for Education Statistics.

Greiner, John M., et al. 1977. *Monetary Incentives and Work Standards in Five Cities*. Washington, D.C.: Urban Institute.

Hanushek, Eric A. 1981. "Throwing Money at Schools." *Journal of Policy Analysis and Management* 1: 19–41.

Henderson, Richard I. 1979. *Compensation Management*. Reston, Va.: Reston Publishing.

Honig, Bill. 1984. "Setting the Course for School Reform." *Education Week*, 18 April.

Howe, Harold, II. 1984. "More-of-the-Sane Reform Will Not Achieve Both Excellence and Equity." *Education Week,* 23 May, p. 24.

Jencks, Christopher, et al. 1970. *Educational Vouchers*. Cambridge, Mass.: Center for the Study of Public Policy.

———. 1972. *Inequality*. New York: Basic Books.

Keeley, Michael C., et al. 1978. "The Estimation of Labor Supply Models Using Experimental Data." *American Economic Review* 68: 873–87.

Levin, Henry M., et al. 1984. "Cost Effectiveness of Four Educational Interventions." Project Report 84-All. Stanford, Calif.: Institute for Research on Educational Finance and Governance, Stanford University.

Mincer, Jacob. 1974. *Schooling, Experience, and Earnings.* New York: National Bureau of Economic Research.

National Center for Productivity and Quality of Working Life. 1977. *Improving Government Productivity: Selected Case Studies.* Washington, D.C.: NCPQWL.

National Commission on Excellence in Education. 1983. *A Nation at Risk.* Washington, D.C.: U.S. Government Printing Office.

National Commission on Productivity and Work Quality. 1975. *Employee Incentives to Improve State and Local Government Productivity.* Washington, D.C.: NCPWQ.

Ravitch, Diane. 1982. *The Troubled Crusade.* New York: Basic Books.

Ribich, Thomas I. 1968. *Education and Poverty.* Washington, D.C.: Brookings.

Rickover, Hyman G. *American Education, a National Failure.* New York: Dutton.

Simms, Margaret C. 1984. "The Impact of Changes in Federal Elementary and Secondary Education Policy" (draft). Washington: Urban Institute.

Stern, David. 1984. *Toward a Statewide System for Public School Acountability: A Report from California.* Berkeley, Calif.: Policy Analysis for California Education, University of California.

Stern, David, and Thomas Timar. 1982. "Conflict and Choice in Public Education." *Education and Urban Society* 14: 485–510.

Timpane, Michael. 1978. "Federal Aid to Education: Prologue and Prospects." Pp. 1–20 in Michael Timpane, ed., *The Federal Interest in Financing Schooling.* Cambridge, Mass.: Ballinger.

Timpane, Michael, et al. 1976. *Youth Policy in Transition.* Santa Monica, Calif.: RAND.

Commentary

Jennifer R. Wolch

The view of welfare and education problems and policies provided by these two papers is discouraging, because the problems are worsening and because substantial increases in public resources to solve them are not likely to be forthcoming. Sheldon Danziger and Daniel Feaster find that the extent of poverty has grown over the past half-decade, with women as a greater percentage of the poor. Largely because of social spending reductions, government cash transfers are now less effective in relieving households in poverty. Richard Murnane provides a similarly depressing picture of problems in public education and the retreat from the federal role in education that had been established during the 1960s. In my commentary I raise questions that focus on the nexus of urban structure, poverty, and educational attainment.

EDUCATION AND THE CITIES: QUESTIONS FOR RESEARCH AND POLICY

Murnane and others regard the shortage of adequate teachers as one of the most pressing problems for public education policy, suggesting that shortages are due to relatively low teacher salaries. In fact, the salary differentials are astounding. Clearly, governmental arrangements for education mediate this situation, as do teacher unions. Nevertheless, public education has historically been remarkably responsive to the labor requirements of the economy (Bowles and Gintis 1976; Katz 1981). This implies that if the problems in primary and secondary education were of greater concern to the private sector, we might see more progress toward overcoming them. Is the failure to commit more public resources to education, particularly for teachers' pay, indicative of fundamental changes in the economy, and as a result, in national as well as urban and regional labor markets? And is the failure to solve the problems of scarce teacher resources in inner-city schools related to central-city labor markets that appear to be dominated by services and labor-intensive industries which require only low-skill, low-wage labor from their nonprofessional/nontechnical workforce?

As Braverman (1978), Bluestone and Harrison (1982), and others argue, recent advances in production technology have been accompanied by a reduction in the demand for highly trained labor and thus in the need for high-quality educational services. Moreover, the industrial and occupational mix in metropolitan areas has shifted in the past decade; skilled and unskilled blue-collar jobs have been lost, while service-sector employment has increased dramatically (Phillips and Vidal 1983). The slackening of demand for skilled labor is most acute in the inner city, where—apart from the downtown office sector, which employs highly skilled professional and technical workers—labor markets are characterized by growing demand for low-wage clerical workers, and for unskilled workers for service firms and small-scale, labor-intensive manufacturing companies (Scott 1982). Many of these unskilled jobs pay very poorly; clerical jobs often do not provide median family incomes for workers, and many service jobs do not guarantee sufficient income to keep families out of poverty (Phillips and Vidal 1983). Since the marginal return on educational inputs in the inner city is typically lower than in suburban and more affluent central-city neighborhoods, any cost-benefit calculus might discourage heavy investment of public resources in inner-city education.

These factors raise troubling questions about the potential of less expensive policies such as minimum high-school-graduation requirements. Unless higher scholastic requirements are justified by the promise of better jobs and/or higher incomes, students are unlikely to make the extra effort. Can today's urban economy supply the variety and numbers of employment opportunities for students who meet additional requirements, or can policy levers succeed in creating such jobs? If not, we may be making the same mistake that befell job training programs of earlier years, i.e., assuming that the demand for labor will rise to meet an added quantity and improved quality of labor. The changing character of the urban economy and the mix of job skills demanded do not encourage these assumptions. High-school graduates may not find meaningful jobs awaiting them; instead, they could be relegated to low-wage, unskilled positions, sporadic employment, or unemployment.

We face deepening divisions of class and race and growing disparities in the quality of life offered by neighborhoods in United States cities. Would the low-cost policy options open to state and local policymakers, such as minimum high-school-performance requirements or tougher teacher-certification programs, help or hinder this situation? The former policy may serve to increase dropout rates, particularly among inner-city minority youth. The latter policy typically increases the costs of becoming a teacher, thereby decreasing the supply and increasing the interdistrict competition for qualified staff. The losers in such a competition are likely to be poor, low-paying districts, exacerbating already severe deficits of teacher resources. The implications of such policies for income inequality and the extent of urban poverty must be explored further. If we do not undertake this task, the preeminent urban service and amenity—education—is likely to suffer from ever greater geographical disparities in quantity and quality, hindering the ability of central cities to maintain middle-income population groups.

THE URBAN POOR:
SERVICE-DEPENDENT SUBPOPULATIONS

Danziger and Feaster analyze the declining effectiveness of anti-poverty cash transfers. A major gap in this analysis, however, is the exclusion of in-kind transfers and services, and the change in their antipoverty effect for subgroups of the poverty population who may be differentially reliant on in-kind assistance. As a means of bridging this gap and refocusing the discussion on urban dimensions of the poverty problem, it is useful to document the changing situation of in-kind service programs for the mentally ill, physically handicapped, retarded, ex-offenders, substance abusers, and the needy elderly. Unlike those supported by cash transfers and primary in-kind programs such as Medicaid and food stamps (mostly the AFDC population), these *service-dependent* groups not only rely on cash transfers and the major in-kind programs but also use a host of human services: community health and mental health care, vocational rehabilitation, sheltered workshops, adult day care for the elderly or retarded, juvenile diversion programs, crisis management services, nutritional assistance, drug- and alcohol-abuse treatment, job training programs, and residential treatment services.

Estimates of the service-dependent population are substantial, whether *dependency* is defined by various rough measures of "need" or by indices of program utilization. A lower-bound estimate of the population is the fraction of those receiving Supplemental Security Income who also receive services through the Title XX Social Service Program. In 1979, the last year for which data are available, almost 40 percent of the SSI population received Title XX services (U.S. Department of Health and Human Services 1981). Applying this proportion to the 1982 SSI population (because of cutbacks, the proportion actually receiving services is no doubt somewhat lower) yields a service-dependent population of about 1,489,000 persons, 13.4 percent as large as the AFDC population (U.S. Department of Commerce 1984).

A large portion of the service-dependent population now living in cities was formerly institutionalized (Wolpert and Wolpert 1976). These service-dependent poor concentrated in old, deteriorated parts of inner cities typically close to downtown. On the one hand, they were attracted by cheap housing—often large dwellings converted to congregate use—and by availability of urban services first developed there under the auspices of Great Society programs. On the other hand, they were pushed away from better-off neighborhoods and suburban jurisdictions. These communities mounted opposition campaigns aimed at systematically excluding the dependent poor and those public and voluntary service agencies that support them.

Just as with the wider poverty population, the problems of these groups have always been troubling. Since deinstitutionalization got underway in earnest, community-based services have been inadequate, as have been cash aid programs (see, for example, U.S. General Accounting Office 1977). Reagan administration cutbacks of in-kind services and cash assistance have created even greater problems for service-dependent populations, especially in states such as California, where tax limitations have curbed state and local spending.

In some cities the perils of being poor have intensified not only because of funding reductions but because of the changing economic and physical environment of the city. Anecdotal evidence from several United States and Canadian cities, as well as empirical research in California, suggests that the inner-city districts where the community-based dependent populations are concentrated have become the targets for private gentrification and public urban-renewal programs, market dynamics themselves prompted by the changing nature of the urban economy—mainly the growth of downtown service activities and skilled white-collar employment. As a result, dependent populations are being displaced to even less supportive environments. Their service networks are also being dispersed, unable to maintain their vital activities due to shrinking public resources which by and large have not been replaced by private philanthropy.

SAN JOSE: A CASE STUDY

A study of the service-dependent population in San Jose, California, illustrates the urban dynamics of the service-dependent poor (Wolch and Gabriel forthcoming). Following deinstitutionalization of the mentally ill, retarded, and other groups in California during the late 1960s, a ghetto of service-dependent persons developed in downtown San Jose. By the mid 1970s, an area housing 15 percent of the city's population contained over 1800 residents in 140 board-and-care or rehabilitation facilities (83 percent of the city's total); 13 alcoholic halfway houses; 11 boarding homes for the aged; 4 job corps facilities; and a home for felons. A third of the city's SSI population lived in the same district, along with social security and AFDC recipients in much higher proportions than the city average.

This pattern of ghetto development changed after the mid 1970s. Growth in high-technology and service employment in the southern Bay Area combined with limited residential development to create a serious job/housing imbalance. The result was rapid home-price inflation and revived interest on the part of prospective homebuyers in downtown San Jose. New businesses were also increasingly drawn to San Jose. Local officials sought to encourage the changing economic functions of their city's core area by pursuing an aggressive downtown redevelopment program entailing massive new urban public facilities, transportation links, and office and residential construction.

Local officials saw the presence of service-dependent populations and their facilities as a barrier to successful revitalization. This change in attitude placed added political pressure on service operators, forcing them either to relocate or to close their facilities. These actions coincided with state and federal budget reductions. Proposition 13 cost Santa Clara County 92 human service positions, $42 million in human service funding, and two key service units; the Reagan cuts led to a loss of 363 social services positions from the county, forced regulatory changes that reduced the caseload of in-home support services for the aged, blind, and disabled by 24 percent and reduced services to over half the remaining cases, and reduced benefits to 12 percent of the county's AFDC recipients, many of whom were removed from the program. The 1982–1983 budget for social services dropped by 20 percent, general assistance funds fell by 34 percent, and alcoholism services were curtailed by 19 percent.

The results of service cutbacks, program closures, and gentrification and renewal are already visible in San Jose. Between 1979 and 1982, a dozen facilities were closed or relocated; the size of the service-dependent population housed in community care facilities downtown fell by 20 percent; the number of cash transfer recipients there fell between 1 and 10 percent; and the number of people receiving food stamps and Title XX Social Services fell 32 percent and 65 percent, respectively.

Where are these service-dependent poor going? While there is limited hard evidence, it appears that in San Jose and other urban areas, clients are increasingly misassigned to services. For instance, more community-based mental patients seem to be taken into the criminal justice system or into purely custodial medical care. And more of the dependent are home-less. According to recent estimates, for example, there are about 25,000 to 30,000 homeless people in Los Angeles, a third of whom are either physically or mentally disabled (U.S. Committee on Banking, Finance and Urban Affairs 1984). Finally, at least in California, a return of clients to large-scale institutions may be in the offing. This is indicated by initia-tives to build more penitentiaries, and by Deukmejian administration proposals to reaccredit all state mental hospitals so that their service costs can be reimbursed by the federal government (via Medicaid and Medi-care). This of course could dramatically reduce the fiscal incentives for state and local communities to provide community-based care, which in turn could mean sending more people to institutions.

The example of the service-dependent poor in San Jose indicates that evaluation efforts which disaggregate the poverty population may be necessary in order fully to understand the dynamics of program changes and spending reductions. Groups reliant on in-kind services as well as cash transfers appear to be distinct from other welfare populations. Fur-thermore, urban conditions interact with social program changes, and so both must be assessed as to their implications for the well-being of the poor.

PROSPECTS FOR SOCIAL POLICY

I am not optimistic about the prospects for changing expenditure prior-ities in this country, at least in the short run. Danziger and Feaster recommend that AFDC grants be indexed and that a targeted employment program be established for welfare recipients, but both entail major federal expenditures. And while the authors may be right when they argue that further social spending reductions are unlikely because of political resistance, it is equally improbable that either cash or in-kind transfer programs for the poor will expand.

The problems of the service-dependent poor cannot be solved by indexing cash aid or by providing expanded employment programs. This group faces two sets of problems: income and service inadequacy, and residential displacement. Policy solutions to these problems will require increased spending for local and metropolitan service delivery coordination and planning, and also greater expenditures for more and better human services, neither of which is apt to be forthcoming either from states or localities or from the federal government.

In the education area, the direction of federal programming is more uncertain. As Murnane indicates, Reagan administration initiatives in education policy may be a sign of renewed federal dedication of resources for solving education problems. Alternatively, they could simply be symbolic, election-year responses to public concern about education that do not fundamentally alter the administration stance of reducing the federal role in education.

In summary, urban poverty and education are worsening. The absolute size of the poverty population (in particular, the number of women in poverty) is growing and public programs are insufficient to ameliorate this situation; dilemmas of educational reform and school resources persist with no ready solutions. The changing structure of urban economies exacerbates the situation, reducing the attractiveness of low-cost education policies such as minimum high-school-graduation requirements. It also darkens the outlook for the service-dependent poor, as employment dynamics lead to downtown gentrification and renewal and a displacement of clients and human services from the urban core. Dedication of additional public resources to overcome difficulties in education, income maintenance, and other spheres of social life is improbable given the political-economic environment of the 1980s. I suspect that these challenges for public policy will still be with us as we enter the next decade.

REFERENCES

Bluestone, B., and B. Harrison. 1982. *The Deindustrializating of America*. New York: Basic Books.

Bowles, S., and H. Gintis. 1976. *Schooling in Capitalist America: Educational Reforms and the Contradictions of Economic Life.* New York: Basic Books.

Braverman, H. 1974. *Labor and Monopoly Capital: The Degradation of Work in the Twentieth Century.* New York: Monthly Review Press.

Katz, M. B. 1981. "Education and Inequality: A Historical Perspective." Pp. 111–25 in D. Rothman and S. Wheeler, eds., *Social History and Social Policy.* New York: Academic Press.

Phillips, R. S., and A. Vidal. 1983. "The Growth and Restructuring of Metropolitan Economies." *Journal of the American Planning Association* 49: 291–306.

Scott, A. J. 1982. "Production System Dynamics and Metropolitan Development." *Annals of the Association of American Geographers* 72: 185–200.

U.S. Committee on Banking, Finance and Urban Affairs, Subcommitee on Housing and Urban Development. 1984. "Homeless in America—II." Hearing before the Subcommittee on Housing and Urban Development. Committee on Banking and Urban Affairs, House of Representatives, 98th Congress, 2nd session, Jan. 25. Washington, D.C.: U.S. Government Printing Office.

U.S. Department of Commerce, Bureau of the Census. 1984. *Statistical Abstract of the United States, 1984.* Washington, D.C.: U.S. Government Printing Office.

U.S. Department of Health and Human Services, Office of the Secretary. 1981. *Annual Report to the Congress on Title XX of the Social Security Act, Fiscal Year 1980.* Washington, D.C.: U.S. Government Printing Office.

U.S. General Accounting Office, Comptroller of the United States. 1977. *Returning the Mentally Disabled to the Community: Government Needs to Do More.* Washington, D.C.: U.S. Government Printing Office.

Wolch, J. R., and S. A. Gabriel. Forthcoming. "Dismantling the Community-Based Human Service System." *Journal of the American Planning Association.*

Wolpert, J., and E. Wolpert. 1976. "The Relocation of Released Mental Hospital Patients into Residential Communities." *Policy Sciences* 7: 31–51.

PART THREE

Urban Programs: Transportation and Housing

Two of the federal domestic programs that have the greatest effect on urban areas are transportation and housing. Jose Gomez-Ibañez argues for a reduction of the federal role in transportation. Sherman Maisel sets an agenda for housing policy that includes a substantial federal role in providing aid to new home purchasers and to low-income renters. John Kain suggests that federal support for fair housing has helped to mitigate the effects of racial discrimination in housing and that a recent trend toward black suburbanization may provide a glimmer of hope for the future. In the Commentary, Michael Goldberg uses the Canadian experience to support his contention that the federal government's role in housing and urban affairs should be smaller than Maisel advocates. Theodore Keeler questions Gomez-Ibañez's conclusions on the grounds that the benefits of urban highways far outweigh the costs and that the costs of fixed rail systems are substantial. Richard Muth disagrees with both Kain and Maisel, maintaining, first, that fair housing policies are not responsible for reported declines in housing segregation and, second, that there is little need for a federal role in housing policy. Melvin Webber faults Gomez-Ibañez for concentrating on the auto-transit dualism, suggesting that the appropriate dichotomy in most modern metropolitan areas is that between large-vehicle and small-vehicle systems.

CHAPTER SEVEN

The Federal Role in Urban Transportation

Jose A. Gomez-Ibañez

The federal role in urban transportation increased in size and scope after World War II. In the late 1950s and early 1960s, federal involvement was largely limited to grants for urban segments of the Interstate Highway System, but by the late 1960s and early 1970s it included aid for other types of urban highways and for mass transit as well. At first, federal assistance was confined to aid to capital expenditures, but it gradually broadened to include some operating and maintenance expenses. By 1980, federal aid accounted for as much as 40 percent of all government capital spending on urban highways, 80 percent of capital assistance for urban mass transit, and 30 percent of mass-transit operating subsidies.

The Reagan administration proposed to reduce federal aid for urban transportation significantly, by restricting highway aid largely to the Interstate Highway System, by phasing out operating aid for mass transit, by reducing transit capital aid, and by allocating transit capital grants by formula rather than project by project. Congress rejected most of these proposals in 1982, when it restored or substantially increased funding for many of the existing programs.

While some of the proposals made by the Reagan administration may be undesirable, the idea of forcing local governments to assume more responsibility for decisions about the level and mix of urban transportation spending has merit. The rationale for extensive federal involvement in urban transportation is weak, and several of the federal programs, particularly grants for Interstate Highway construction and mass transit capital projects, probably distort local transportation decisions. Reduced

TABLE 7.1
Recent Trends in Urban Travel

	Urban population (millions)[a]	Vehicle-miles of highway travel (billions)[b]			Urban mass transit trips[c] (millions)	% metropolitan commuters using public transport[d]
		Urban highways	Rural highways	All highways		
1940	74.4	150.0	152.2	302.5	10,504	
1950	96.8	218.2	240.0	458.2	13,845	18.7%
1960	125.3	331.6	387.3	718.8	7,521	
1965		423.9	463.8	887.6	6,798	
1970	149.3	574.6	539.5	1,114.1	5,932	12.0
1975		729.4	600.7	1,330.1	5,643	8.4
1980	167.1	847.1	673.7	1,520.9	6,447	7.7
1981		863.4	686.9	1,550.3	6,278	
1982		901.8	690.7	1,592.5	6,038	
% change						
1940–50	+30.1%	+45.5%	+57.7%	+51.5%	+31.8%	
1950–60	+29.4	+52.0	+61.4	+56.9	−45.7	
1960–70	+19.1	+73.3	+39.3	+55.0	−21.1	
1970–80	+11.2	+47.4	+73.9	+36.5	+ 8.7	

[a]U.S. Bureau of Census, *Statistical Abstract of the United States, 1984* (Washington, D.C.: U.S. Government Printing Office, 1984), p. 32. The 1940 data is for the coterminous United States only.

[b]Federal Highway Administration, *Highway Statistics Summary to 1975* (Washington, D.C.: U.S. Government Printing Office, n.d.), pp. 73–84.

[c]American Public Transit Association, *Transit Fact Book*, various years.

[d]Estimates for 1960 from U.S. Bureau of the Census, *1960 Census of Population.* Vol. PC-1: *Detailed Characteristics: United States Summary* (Washington, D.C.: U.S. Government Printing Office), p. 801. Estimates for 1970 calculated from U.S. Bureau of the Census, *1970 Census of Population.* Vol. PC-1: *General Social and Economic Characteristics: United States Summary* (Washington, D.C.: U.S. Government Printing Office), p. 415. 1975 estimates from U.S. Bureau of the Census, *Statistical Abstract of the United States, 1978* (Washington, D.C.: U.S. Government Printing Office, 1978), p. 657.

federal aid for highways and mass transit might impose temporary financial hardships, but in the long run most urban areas would probably be better off.

DEVELOPMENT OF FEDERAL PROGRAMS

URBAN HIGHWAY AID

Early Federal Aid

Federal highway aid began in 1913 but was largely confined to rural roads until after World War II.[1] The first highway program apportioned federal funds among the states to cover up to one-half the construction costs of rural post roads, roads over which the mail was carried. In 1921 the federal program was restructured and federal aid was restricted to two types of highways: primary or interstate highways, and secondary or intercounty highways. Each state, in consultation with the federal government, could designate a small portion of their highway mileage as part of these federal aid systems. Highway aid was apportioned among states on the basis of a formula that considered population, land use, and rural-post-route mileage.

Until the Depression, urban highways were specifically excluded from federal aid mileage. Public works relief legislation in 1932 and 1933 provided some temporary funding for urban highway construction since many of the unemployed were city dwellers, and in 1934 the prohibition on including urban mileage in primary or secondary systems was eliminated. Not until the Federal Highway Aid Act of 1944 was specific authorization made for urban highways. This act established three distinct categories of federal-aid highways: primary and secondary rural highways (which were to receive 45 and 30 percent of all aid, respectively) and urban extensions of the primary and secondary routes (which were to receive only 25 percent of the aid).

The Postwar Construction Boom

Pressures to increase highway spending mounted after World War II as postwar prosperity fostered automobile ownership and use. During the 1940s and 1950s urban highway traffic grew at almost double the rate of the urban population, as higher incomes encouraged travelers both to increase the number of trips they made and to make more of them by automobile rather than mass transit (Table 7.1).

Federal aid for urban highways became available on a large scale in 1956, when the federal government responded to the rapid traffic growth by funding the Interstate and Defense Highway System. Under the Interstate program, federal grants paid 90 percent of the construction costs of a congressionally designated system of 42,500 miles of limited access highways. The system was initially conceived as serving intercity travel and bypassing major cities but, under pressures from urban interests, about 20 percent of the final system was located in urban areas. Urban mileage accounted for an even larger share of Interstate program expenditures, since the urban segments were often wider and more costly than their rural counterparts. Unlike the primary and secondary road programs, Interstate grants were to be distributed to the states on a project-by-project basis rather than by formula. In 1970 Congress also established a new federal-aid urban system, instructing the states to designate for the new system mileage that supplements (but does not overlap) the older urban extensions; aid for the urban system is allocated to states on the basis of urban population. Thanks largely to the Interstate program, the federal share of highway capital spending by all levels of government grew from only 10 percent in 1950 to around 40 percent in the 1960s. While in 1950 federal grants were almost exclusively for rural roads, by the 1960s and 1970s many federal highway dollars were spent in urban areas.

Disenchantment with Highways

During the 1960s many social and environmental costs of highway construction and automobile use became apparent. The first focus of concern was the social and aesthetic costs of expressway construction, particularly in urban areas. In response, Congress in 1962 required that metropolitan areas receiving federal highway aid prepare a comprehensive land use and transportation plan, which included consideration of mass transit alternatives. These regulations were substantially strengthened in 1969 by passage of the National Environmental Policy Act, which required the preparation, with public comments and hearings, of an environmental impact statement for any federally funded project. In 1973 Congress also allowed local governments to trade in the federal funds designated for locally contested segments of the Interstate System for use on mass transit improvements, as long as the United States Secretary of Transportation certified that the contested segment wsa not essential to the national Interstate System. By 1980, over 8000 miles of urban

Interstates had been opened to traffic, although in almost every metropolitan area controversial segments remained unfinished.

The 1960s and 1970s also saw the development of federal programs to regulate the safety, air pollution emissions, and fuel economy of new motor vehicles. In 1965 Congress established the National Highway Traffic Safety Administration, with authority to set safety standards for new cars and to order manufacturers to recall and correct defective vehicles. Air pollution was the next focus of concern, as the problems caused by automotive emissions of hydrocarbons, carbon monoxide, and nitrogen oxides became more noticeable in major urban areas. The Clean Air Act of 1970 required 90 percent rollback in the emission rates of these pollutants from new automobiles by the 1975 model year. High costs and technological uncertainties forced several extensions of the deadlines and a relaxation of the nitrogen oxide target to a 75 percent rollback, but by the 1982 model year the goals set by the Clean Air Act were achieved. Finally, the oil crisis of 1973–1974 stimulated Congress to pass a law requiring that average new-car fuel economy be improved in stages from 18 mpg in model year 1978 to 27.5 mpg in 1985. United States automakers were in compliance with the schedule as of model year 1984, although weakening gasoline prices were making it more difficult to induce customers to buy fuel-efficient models.[2]

The level of highway construction and investment peaked during the late 1960s. Although nominal highway spending continued to increase during the 1960s and 1970s, capital outlays failed to keep pace with the rapid inflation in building costs (see Table 7.2). The decline in real spending was due in part to the heavy reliance on federal and state fuel taxes to finance highway improvements. Since fuel taxes are assessed in cents per gallon, real receipts fell with rapid inflation and the automobile fuel-economy improvements of the 1970s.

The scope of federal highway aid expanded in the 1970s, despite the spending decline. Highway maintenance became a major concern toward the end of the 1970s, as many of the highway pavements and structures built in the decades immediately following World War II began to reach the end of their useful lives. Until the 1970s, federal highway aid could only be used for new construction or for major reconstruction projects in which the road was widened or substantially rebuilt. In 1976 Congress responded to the maintenance crisis by expanding the definition of highway construction to include "resurfacing, restoration, and rehabilitation" (3R) and establishing a separate program of grants for Interstate 3R projects. In 1970 Congress also established a special aid program for

TABLE 7.2

Highway Expenditures by All Levels of Government

	Millions of current dollars[a]				Millions of 1980 dollars[b]			
	Capital	Maintenance	Admin., police safety	Total	Capital	Maintenance	Admin., police safety	Total
1940	1,450	610	128	2,188	14,057	6,073	785	20,915
1950	2,297	1,423	298	4,018	12,170	7,574	993	20,737
1960	6,290	2,640	810	9,740	27,710	9,202	2,104	39,016
1965	8,368	3,289	1,275	12,932	32,709	10,019	3,048	45,776
1970	11,575	4,720	2,578	18,873	32,529	11,038	4,599	48,166
1975	14,261	7,070	4,209	25,540	24,039	11,162	5,910	41,111
1980	19,961	10,928	6,784	37,673	19,961	10,928	6,784	37,673
1981	18,820	11,713	7,225	37,758	19,403	10,775	6,784	36,784
1982	19,472	12,816	7,240	39,528	21,710	10,777	6,244	38,731
% change								
1940–50					− 13.4%			− 0.8%
1950–60					+127.7			+88.1
1960–70					+ 17.4			+23.4
1970–80					− 38.6			−21.2

[a]Federal Highway Administration, *Highway Statistics Summary to 1975*, pp. 122–36; and Federal Highway Administration, *Highway Statistics* (Washington, D.C.: U.S. Government Printing Office, various years), table HF-10.

[b]Capital costs adjusted using the Federal Highway Administration's highway construction price index; maintenance costs deflated with the Federal Highway Administration's highway operations and maintenance price index; other costs deflated using the GNP price index.

bridge repair and reconstruction on the federal aid highway systems, activities that had been exclusively state-financed.

Urban highway traffic has continued to grow despite the slowdown in highway construction, higher fuel prices, and increased regulation of new car pollution and fuel economy. Traffic growth was slightly lower in the 1970s than in earlier decades, probably largely because the growth in urban population also slowed during that decade. As in the previous decade, urban traffic increased about four times faster than the urban population during the 1970s (see Table 7.1).

URBAN MASS TRANSIT AID

Almost as rapid as the growth in urban automobile use was the decline of urban mass transit ridership in the 1940s and 1950s, falling from a wartime high of 18 billion trips per year to 7 billion trips in 1960. In an attempt to stem the ridership loss, in the 1940s and 1950s many large metropolitan areas began to provide government aid to their mass transit systems, and several metropolitan areas planned new rail systems. The rapidly deteriorating financial condition of mass transit strained local resources, however, and by the early 1960s had led to strong pressure for federal assistance.

Federal aid began in 1964 with a small program of capital grants that would finance up to two-thirds of the cost of a capital project.[3] Funds were allocated for specific projects at the discretion of the Secretary of Transportation. Funding for the capital grant program expanded rapidly during the 1970s, reaching levels of almost $3 billion per year, and in 1973 the maximum federal share was raised to 80 percent of costs. Federal grants were used to finance local government buyouts of ailing private bus companies, replacement or refurbishing of much of the existing transit rolling stock and equipment, construction of several new rail systems, and extensions to many of the existing rail systems.

In 1974 Congress established a new federal transit grant program to fund operating expenses, partly in response to pressure from metropolitan areas that felt they did not benefit greatly from the capital grant program, either because their rail systems predated federal aid or because they were too small to consider rail seriously. Funds from the new grant program could be used for capital as well as operating expenses, although in practice almost all was used for operating aid. The federal grants had to be matched by an equal amount of state or local aid if operating expenses were being subsidized, but the federal share could be as high as

TABLE 7.3

Passenger Revenues and Government Assistance for Mass Transit, 1940–1982[a]

	Passenger contributions to operating expenses			Estimated assistance by all levels of government ($ mil.)		
	Operating expense ($ mil.)	Passenger revenues ($ mil.)[b]	% covered by fares	Operating	Capital	Total
1940	661	737	111%	n.a.	n.a.	n.a.
1950	1386	1452	105	n.a.	n.a.	n.a.
1960	1377	1407	102	n.a.	n.a.	n.a.
1965	1454	1444	99	n.a.	n.a.	n.a.
1970	1996	1707	86	318[c]	200[c]	518
1975	3752	2002	53	1408	1609[c]	3017
1980	6711	2663	40	3705	3434[c]	7139
1981	7632	2784	36	4321	3682[d]	8003
1982	8324	3152	38	4587	3181[d]	7768

[a]Unless otherwise noted, all statistics are from American Public Transit Association, *Transit Fact Book*, various years; and U.S. Bureau of the Census, *Statistical Abstract of the United States, 1984* (Washington, D.C.: U.S. Government Printing Office, 1984), p. 624.

[b]Figures shown are operating revenue, largely fare receipts but including small amounts of miscellaneous revenues from rentals and other sources.

[c]From John Pucher, Anders Markstedt, and Ira Hirschman, "Impact of Subsidies on the Costs of Urban Public Transport," *Journal of Transport Economics and Policy* 17 (1983): 156. Pucher estimates higher levels of operating subsidies than the American Public Transit Association does because he includes the cost of certain services rendered, such as city payment of transit police.

[d]Estimated based on the federal grant approvals in Table 7.4 and assuming a 20 percent local matching share of project costs.

80 percent for capital projects. In a significant departure from the original capital-grant program, the operating grants were allocated among urbanized areas according to a formula based on population and population density instead of at the discretion of the Secretary. Federal operating aid grew steadily from around $200 million in 1970 to nearly $1 billion in 1980.

Transit aid from all levels of government increased so rapidly during the 1970s that sometime in the middle of that decade government aid became a more important source of revenue to the industry than passenger fares (Table 7.3). Passenger fares had been enough to cover operating costs and make a small contribution to capital expenses through the 1950s, despite the fact that the industry was contracting. In 1964 passenger receipts fell below operating expenses for the industry as a whole and by the 1980s covered only about 40 percent of operating costs and made no contribution to capital expenses. Government aid grew from $518 million in 1970 to $7.8 billion in 1982, and the federal share of all aid grew from 26 to 53 percent, as shown in Table 7.4.

The influx of government aid was not enough to restore mass transit ridership to its former levels. The steady postwar decline in nationwide mass transit ridership was reversed between 1974 and 1980, when patronage grew by 15 percent, but in 1981 it began to fall once again. The most important urban travel market is commuting, since work trips dominate rush hour travel and are key contributors to traffic congestion and other urban transportation problems. Public transportation's share of commuting trips in all metropolitan areas fell steadily from 19 percent in 1960 to 12 percent in 1970 and 8 percent in 1980 (Table 7.1). As of 1980, mass transit captured more than 10 percent of the commuter market only in a dozen of the largest, densest, and oldest metropolitan areas, where high levels of traffic congestion and parking fees discourage auto ownership and use. Only in one metropolitan area (New York) does transit's share of the commuting market exceed 20 percent.[4]

The performance of the first new rail systems—opened in San Francisco in 1972 and Washington in 1976—was particularly disappointing; construction costs soared far beyond original projections and the ridership gains were smaller than originally forecast. These results failed to discourage local interest in new rail systems, however, in part because federal aid was available to fund up to 80 percent of construction costs. To force local governments to consider smaller and more cost-effective alternatives, in 1976 the federal government required that cities applying for rail grants submit an analysis of non-rail alternatives, including low-

TABLE 7.4

Federal Share of Outlays by All Levels of Government
for Highways and Urban Mass Transit

	Federal highway capital grants[a]		Federal mass transit capital and operating grants[b]		
	As % of capital outlays	As % of all hwy outlays	Fed. share of capital aid	Fed. share of operating aid	Fed. share of all aid
1940	12%	8%	0%	0%	0%
1950	17	10	0	0	0
1960	39	25	0	0	0
1965	45	29	n.a.	0	n.a.
1970	38	24	67	0	26
1975	39	22	80	21	48
1980	41	22	80	30	53
1981	39	20	n.a.	n.a.	n.a.
1982	30	18	n.a.	n.a.	n.a.

[a]Obtained from comparing federal highway expenditure data in Table 7.5 with the highway expenditures by all levels of government in Table 7.2.

[b]John Pucher, Anders Markstedt, and Ira Hirschman, "Impact of Subsidies on the Costs of Urban Public Transport," *Journal of Transport Economics and Policy* 17 (1983): 156.

cost express bus systems. Federal regulations also restricted new rail starts in each metropolitan area to one major corridor at a time, rather than to an entire system of many lines. In 1978 these regulations were strengthened to limit federal liability in the case of construction cost overruns and to specify in more detail the types of low-cost, non-rail alternatives that had to be considered.

POLICY UNDER THE REAGAN ADMINISTRATION

By the time President Reagan took office in 1981, federal grants had increased to cover roughly 20 percent of all government highway aid and 50 percent of all transit aid (Table 7.4). The Reagan administration initially proposed dramatic changes in urban transportation policy as part of its "new federalism" initiative. The theme of the new federalism was to return responsibility for largely local programs, such as urban transportation, to state and local governments. The Reagan administra-

TABLE 7.5

Federal Expenditures and Authorizations
for Major Highway Aid Programs, 1940–1986 (millions of dollars)

	Interstate	Primary	Secondary	Urban	Grade crossing and bridge	Total
Expenditures (CY)[a]						
1940			139		30	169
1950			389		12	401
1960	1,601		856		4	2,461
1965	1,601		957		30	3,802
1970	3,246		1,073		110	4,431
1975	3,157		1,952		503	5,613
1980	4,384	1,681	433	993	638	8,129
1981	3,805	1,654	394	806	694	7,353
1982	3,313[b]	1,670	391	791	784	6,949
Authorizations (FY)[c]						
1983	6,207[d]	1,883	650	800	1,790	11,845[f]
1984	7,100[d]	2,147[e]	650[e]	800[e]	1,840	3,126[f]
1985	7,500[d]	2,382[e]	650[e]	800[e]	1,940	13,869[f]
1986	7,875[d]	2,505[e]	650[e]	800[e]	2,240	14,701[f]

[a] Federal Highway Administration, *Highway Statistics Summary to 1975* (Washington, D.C.: U.S. Government Printing Office, n.d.), and *Highway Statistics* (Washington, D.C.: U.S. Government Printing Office, various years), table FA-3.

[b] Interstate expenditures include $348 for resurfacing in 1982.

[c] Provided by the Surface Transportation Assistance Act of 1982.

[d] Figures include $1,950, $2,400, $2,800, and $3,150 million for Interstate resurfacing in 1983–1986 and $257, $700, $700, and $723 million for Interstate highway substitution in those years.

[e] From 1984 on, 40 percent of all primary, secondary, and urban funds must be spent on resurfacing.

[f] Includes funds of $515, $589, $597, and $631 million in 1983–1986 to resume minimum highway aid allocations for states.

tion proposed both to reduce the level of federal highway aid and to restrict it to highways, such as the Interstate System, in which the federal interest was clearest. Federal gasoline taxes would be lowered (to the levels necessary to fund the smaller program) and state governments would be encouraged to increase their own fuel taxes as needed. For mass transit, the Reagan administration proposed to eliminate federal aid for operating expenses, reduce federal aid for capital projects, and allocate

TABLE 7.6
Federal Expenditures and Projected Budget Levels
for Major Mass Transit Aid Programs, 1965–1982 (millions of dollars)[a]

	Capital grants		Interstate transfers	Operating & capital formula grants	Total federal grants
	Discretionary	Formula			
Expenditures (CY)[b]					
1965	51	–	–	–	51
1970	133	–	–	–	133
1975	1197	9	81	143	1430
1980	1655	431	701	1121	3908
1981	1925	361	660	1130	4076
1982	1635	298	612	1056	3600
Projected budget (FY)[c]					
1983	1464	–	560	1433[d]	3457
1984	1692	–	412	2047[d]	4151
1985	1250	–	295	2387[d]	3932
1986	1110	–	250	2389[d]	3747

[a]Excludes small research, training, and demonstration grant programs.
[b]Grant approvals by the Urban Mass Transportation Administration reported in U.S. Bureau of the Census, *Statistical Abstract of the United States, 1984* (Washington, D.C.: U.S. Government Printing Office, 1984), p. 624.
[c]Edward Weiner, "Devolution of the Federal Role in Urban Transportation," U.S. Department of Transportation, photocopied draft, March 1984, table 2.
[d]Consolidated block grants, part of which can be used for operating expenses.

capital grants on the basis of a formula rather than at the discretion of the Secretary of Transportation.[5]

The administration achieved some of these goals in its first year in office. The FY1982 budget reduced federal transit aid below FY1981 levels and left highway aid unchanged despite inflationary pressures. The administration also imposed a moratorium on federal aid for starts of new rail mass transit systems or extensions, although funding would continue for projects already under construction.

These victories did not last long. Frustrated by the Reagan administration's moratorium on new rail starts, the House and Senate appropriating committees began to order the Urban Mass Transportation Administration (UMTA) to fund the planning, engineering, or construction of new rail systems in specific cities. The FY1982 appropriations conference report earmarked federal planning grants for six projects and construction grants for five others (two in Miami), while the FY1983 report earmarked funds for alternatives analysis of seventeen projects and engineering or construction of eleven. If all these new rail projects are built with federal aid, the cost to the federal treasury will be between $12 and $19 billion.[6]

During 1982 pressure also grew within the administration and Congress to increase highway spending as a means to alleviate the deterioration of the nation's highways and bridges and to combat unemployment from the 1981–1982 recession. To gain support from urban areas for increased highway spending, Congress proposed to increase mass transit aid as well.

The Surface Transportation Assistance Act, passed in December 1982, greatly increased federal funding for highways and restored the cuts to mass transit. The law raised the federal gas tax from 4 to 9 cents per gallon, the first increase since 1959. Four cents of the increase is dedicated to the Federal Highway Trust Fund to finance a near-doubling of 1982 levels of highway aid (Table 7.5). The remaining cent of the new gas taxes is earmarked for a new Federal Mass Transportation Trust Fund, which will be used to finance the discretionary capital grant program. Additional transit funding is authorized out of general revenues for new operating and capital formula grant programs and total transit aid is restored to the 1981 funding levels (Table 7.6). The Reagan administration's only victories were in the composition of the spending authorized by the act. Only highway aid for Interstate and rural primary systems is increased, for example, while funding for rural secondary and urban extensions was held constant. Transit operating assistance is also to be gradually lowered.

EVALUATING HIGHWAY AID

BENEFITS AND COSTS OF POSTWAR HIGHWAY EXPANSION

Although some benefit-cost analyses have been made for isolated high-way projects, there have been no recent and reliable attempts to measure the benefits and costs of the federal urban highway program as a whole.[7] A comparison of highway user tax receipts with highway expenses suggests, however, that the benefits of the postwar boom in urban highway construction, partly financed by federal aid, have on the whole exceeded the costs.[8]

User Payments as Benefit Measures

Motorists pay a variety of special taxes to use the highways, including gasoline taxes, tolls, and vehicle registration fees. Since motorists are willing to pay at least this much (and maybe more) for highway use, these user charges provide a minimum estimate of the benefits motorists receive from highway investments. In theory, a particular segment of the highway system might be deemed worthwhile if users pay enough in highway taxes to cover the costs that segment imposes on society.[9]

Estimating the user component in highway taxes involves differentiating between special charges made for highway use and general taxes levied on consumption or personal property. The commonly used rule for making such separations is to regard a tax as a highway-user charge if collected from highway users or on motor vehicles but not on most other comparable goods or services. By this rule, highway-user charges clearly include federal gasoline, vehicle, spare parts, and excise taxes; state motor vehicle and driver registration fees; and special highway-user taxes on trucks. State gasoline and motor vehicle sales and property taxes are not necessarily included, since many states or localities levy sales or personal property taxes on a variety of other goods, although typically at lower rates. Estimates of United States highway-user-charge receipts derived by following this separation principle are shown in Table 7.7 in current dollars for the years 1956 through 1975.

Government Highway Expenditures

The costs of the urban highway system include both direct government highway expenditures, such as highway construction and maintenance outlays, and the externalities or social damages that highway users impose on others in the form, for example, of automobile air pollution and noise. Table 7.7 also shows estimates for 1956 to 1975 of direct highway expenditures paid by all levels of government, but excluding any external social costs of highway use. The estimates assume that all government highway capital expenses are amortized over the life of the facilities using a 5 percent real discount rate—thus, for example, the 1975 costs include charges for the depreciation of capital investments made in previous years. Capital outlays include all expenditures for the purchase of right-of-way (including relocation assistance), grading and drainage costs, construction of bridges and tunnels, and paving costs. Operating expenses include routine maintenance, snow removal, mowing, painting, and similar activities as well as highway administration, research, safety, and law enforcement. Outlays for all police assigned to traffic and highway safety duties, as well as correctional expenses attributable to enforcing traffic laws and curtailing automobile theft, are included as highway law enforcement costs.

Most highway expenses and user revenues can be attributed to particular parts of the highway system, such as urban or rural roads or Interstate and non-Interstate highways. Some costs and revenues, such as the administrative expenses of highway agencies or annual vehicle registration fees, are, however, not clearly assignable. These costs and revenues amount to about one-quarter of the total and are allocated, somewhat arbitrarily, to the different highway types according to the vehicle mileage occurring on those highways.

For the national highway system as a whole, highway user charges exceeded direct government costs by 50 to 80 percent in the 1950s and 1960s, but fell to rough parity with costs by 1975. If a more conservative 10 percent discount rate is used instead of 5 percent, revenues exceeded expenses by about 25 percent in the 1950s and 1960s but fell short of costs by about an equal amount in the 1970s.[10] The ratio of revenues to expenses fell largely because total amortized highway outlays increased in real terms (although current capital investment has declined), while user revenues did not keep pace with inflation.

Most of the shortfalls between highway user revenues and direct gov-

TABLE 7.7

Highway Expenditure and User Revenues, 1956–1975 (millions of current dollars)

	1956		1960		1965		1970		1975	
	Expense	Revenue	Expense	Revenue	Expense	Revenue	Expense	Revenue	Expense	Revenue
All Areas										
Interstate	571	2,328	892	3,122	1,496	4,476	2,249	5,339	2,826	3,911
Federal primary	3,576	5,817	3,864	7,121	4,032	8,772	4,503	8,496	5,081	6,830
Federal secondary	2,140	2,938	2,515	3,555	3,032	4,411	3,864	4,560	4,704	3,704
Other	6,401	7,483	6,723	8,766	7,070	10,215	7,738	9,222	8,692	6,749
Total	12,688	18,566	13,994	22,564	15,630	27,874	18,354	27,617	21,303	21,194
Urban Areas Only										
Interstate	315	805	457	1,069	725	1,609	1,092	2,270	1,378	1,711
Federal primary	1,202	1,743	1,289	2,241	1,315	3,029	1,446	3,682	1,744	3,337
Federal secondary	263	568	313	703	371	975	494	1,431	680	1,357
Other	3,403	5,399	3,526	6,266	3,573	7,270	3,777	6,909	4,308	5,267
Total	5,183	8,515	5,585	10,279	5,984	12,883	6,809	14,292	8,110	11,672
Rural Areas Only										
Interstate	256	1,523	435	2,053	771	2,867	1,157	3,069	1,448	2,200
Federal primary	2,374	4,074	2,575	4,880	2,717	5,743	3,057	4,814	3,337	3,493
Federal secondary	1,877	2,370	2,202	2,852	2,611	3,436	3,370	3,129	4,024	2,347
Other	2,998	2,084	3,197	2,500	3,497	2,945	3,961	2,313	4,384	1,482
Total	7,505	10,051	8,409	12,285	9,596	14,991	11,545	13,325	13,193	9,522

SOURCE: From John R. Meyer and José A. Gomez-Ibañez, *Autos, Transit, and Cities* (Cambridge, Mass.: Harvard, 1981), pp. 200–203. Calculated by Meyer and Gomez-Ibañez from data in Kiran Bhatt, Michael Beesley, and Kevin Neels, *An Analysis of Road Expenditures and Payments by Vehicle Class, 1956–1975* (Washington, D.C.: Urban Institute, 1977), pp. 115, 143, 195, 196.

ernment highway expenditures occur in rural rather than urban areas and on roads other than the Interstate and other federal aid systems. For the urban Interstates and urban extensions of the federal primary and secondary systems, user revenues were double or triple direct government expenses in the 1950s and 1960s and still exceeded expenses by 30 to 50 percent in 1975.

Even though collectively urban highway users may pay their capital and operating costs, the users of highways in the centers of large dense metropolitan areas probably do not. Costs of constructing and maintaining a lane-mile of highway are much higher in the downtowns of large metropolitan areas than they are in the suburbs or in small metropolitan areas.[11] The number of lanes in an urban highway is dictated by peak period rather than off-peak travel needs, moreover, so there is substantial reason to assign most of the costs of constructing and maintaining that capacity to peak users only. While highway construction maintenance and administration costs in 1975 averaged only about 1.3 cents per vehicle mile on all urban Interstates, for example, studies suggest that the cost of serving peak-hour users on expressways in the central business districts of Boston and San Francisco were as high as 10 to 30 cents per vehicle mile in the mid 1970s.[12]

While the capital and operating expenses attributable to peak-period and downtown motorists are much higher than average, the highway-user taxes paid by these motorists are only moderately higher. In 1975, tax receipts from all urban highway users—mainly in the form of the gasoline tax—averaged about 1.7 cents per vehicle-mile. Because of congestion, peak-period and downtown users probably consumed a bit more fuel and therefore paid perhaps 10 to 20 percent more taxes per mile than average. The differential between peak and off-peak highway-user tax payments is therefore far smaller than the differential between peak and off-peak highway capital and operating costs on major downtown highways.

In short, while urban highway users as a whole, and urban Interstate users in particular, supply more highway tax revenue than the government pays directly in highway expenditures, many peak-hour motorists in the centers of very large urban areas probably pay less than their share of highway costs. Since user taxes actually paid may be viewed as a lower-bound estimate of benefits (many highway users might well be willing to pay more rather than do without), it seems likely that the benefit/cost ratio for many urban highways exceeds unity (still ignoring social externalities for the moment). Even high-cost downtown urban expressways might be able to generate receipts in excess of costs if special tolls were charged, but this is speculative.

External Social Costs

These results probably are not substantially changed by including the external social costs of highway use, such as air and noise pollution, the aesthetic blight of urban highways, and the social costs of relocation and land takings. Although most of these external costs are extremely difficult to measure, estimates of the costs of motor-vehicle air and noise pollution have been made. A study of urban transportation in the San Francisco Bay Area estimated the property, health, vegetation, and materials damage of air pollution from the average car in the 1968 fleet at 1.29 cents per vehicle-mile (in 1973 dollars). Because of federally mandated reductions in new-car emissions rates, the same study estimated that a 1972 model automobile in San Francisco had air pollution costs of only 0.48 cents per vehicle mile. A 1982 model automobile that achieved the nearly 90 percent reduction in emissions over 1970 levels would generate air pollution costs of only 0.1 to 0.2 cents per vehicle mile.[13] Similar estimates of the effects of traffic noise on neighboring businesses and residences suggest that noise costs probably averaged less than one-tenth of a cent per automobile mile in the mid 1970s.[14]

Estimates are unavailable for several other social costs of highways, the most notable being uncompensated costs to households and businesses relocated by highway construction, and the visual or aesthetic blight of highways. These costs are probably substantial for some poorly designed and badly sited urban highways constructed in the 1950s and 1960s. Federal regulations mandating relocation assistance, environmental impact statements, and increased citizen involvement in highway planning have probably reduced these uncompensated damages substantially on highways built after the 1960s.[15]

The external social costs of urban automobile use in the mid 1970s probably averaged about 0.5 cents per vehicle mile based on air and noise pollution alone, and perhaps as much as 1 cent per vehicle mile if an allowance for other unestimated social costs is included. Combined with the 1.3 cent-per-vehicle-mile average cost of constructing and maintaining highways, these figures imply that urban highway users probably on average only slightly underpaid their costs during the mid 1970s. The rough parity of highway user receipts and costs suggests that many of the urban highways constructed with federal aid during the postwar period were worthwhile, especially when it is remembered that user fees are a minimum estimate of user benefits. The principal exceptions are likely to be extremely high-cost highways designed to accommodate rush hour traffic in the centers of major metropolitan areas.

Future Highway Needs

Several forecasts of future urban highway spending needs have been prepared, the most sophisticated of which are the Federal Highway Administration (FHWA) biennial reports to Congress on highway needs. The FHWA estimates that highway capital spending on all roads (urban and rural) should be increased by about 50 percent over the levels of the late 1970s and early 1980s in order to restore the roads to what it terms minimum tolerable conditions; a 40 percent increase is needed merely to prevent further deterioration.[16] Such increases would restore real highway capital spending to the peak levels of the mid and late 1960s (see Table 7.2). The composition of capital spending would shift to emphasize the repair and reconstruction of existing pavement and structures instead of major widening or alignment improvement projects.

The FHWA's highway needs forecasts are limited, however, in that they are based on common highway engineering practices or rules of thumb rather than detailed benefit-cost analysis. The FHWA presumes, for example, that additional lanes are needed on an urban Interstate highway segment when the peak-hour traffic volumes exceed 85 percent of the roadway's maximum hourly capacity. Similarly, the FHWA assumes that repaving is needed on an urban Interstate when the Pavement Serviceability Index (PSI), a physical index of pavement roughness, falls below 3.2. There is some evidence that the volume-to-capacity standard used by the FHWA may, on average, recommend more highway widening than benefit-cost analysis would call for, while the FHWA's pavement standard— again, on average—may recommend too little repaving. For urban highway segments with widening and paving costs much higher or lower than average, moreover, the simple uniform standards used in the FHWA forecasts are almost certainly misleading.[17]

Despite the shortcomings of its forecasts, the FHWA was almost certainly correct in recommending a substantial increase in highway investment over late 1970s levels. Given the slowdown in real highway capital spending in the 1970s, the net value of highway investments has undoubtedly been declining, despite continuing growth in urban (and rural) traffic volumes. If the postwar highway investments were, on the whole, worthwhile, then comparable—or perhaps greater—levels of investment are probably justified for today's higher traffic volumes.

THE MERITS OF FEDERAL INVOLVEMENT

The Rationale for Federal Aid

Whatever the appropriate level of urban highway investment, one key issue is why the federal government should be so heavily involved. Since 70 percent of the United States population lives in urban areas, the majority of the country clearly has a strong interest in urban highways. At least in theory, however, our federal system reserves powers and responsibilities to state and local governments unless some compelling and distinct national interest is involved. This devolution of resonsibilities is based both on democratic ideals and the pragmatic argument that those who are closest to a problem often know best how to solve it.

The principal rationale for federal highway aid programs has been the national interest in an intercity transportation system that serves long-distance or interstate as well as local traffic. When federal highway aid began in 1916, the road system was largely unpaved and road construction and maintenance were the responsibility of county governments. The counties were notorious for their failure to cooperate in improving roads that served more than one county, perhaps because their dependence on property tax revenues made it difficult to finance improvements that served more than local needs. An interconnected road system would benefit all, it was argued, by promoting interstate commerce and reducing the social and political isolation of rural communities. The federal government gave highway aid directly to state governments, on the theory that states would have more interest than counties in promoting an intercity highway system.[18]

While federal intervention may have been needed to promote an interconnected higway system seventy years ago, it may be unnecessary today. Thanks in part to early federal aid, each state now finances and administers its own system of trunk highways, leaving county and city governments responsible mainly for local or secondary roads. Federal aid may not be necessary even to induce states to build a coordinated interstate highway system. In the decade before the Interstate System was funded, for example, many Eastern and Central states cooperated in the construction of an interconnected system of limited-access toll expressways that allowed motorists to travel between New York and Chicago or Boston and Albany without ever having to stop for an intersection or traffic light. Toll financing had eliminated the problem of using local taxes to support interstate travel and by 1956, when Interstate funding ended the boom, around 12,000 miles of toll expressways had been built, started, authorized, or projected.[19]

To the extent that there is a distinct national interest in the highway system, it applies more clearly to roads that primarily serve long-distance and interstate rather than local travelers. Although Interstate System planners rationalized the inclusion of urban segments on the grounds that interstate traffic often originates or terminates in urban areas, urban expressways probably have a limited claim to federal aid, since their design is largely dictated by peak-hour local commuting traffic.

Perhaps the strongest argument for a federal role is in the areas of highway research and demonstration projects. Research on pavement durability, highway planning techniques, and highway safety measures is of potential benefit to all states. Since no single state captures all the benefits, there is little incentive for a state to fund research alone. The federal government, however, can consider the benefits to all states in designing its research program.

Incentives under Federal Aid

If state and local interests predominate in urban highways, federal highway aid may distort state and local highway decisions in undesirable ways. It is extremely difficult to predict what the urban highway system might have looked like without federal aid, much less whether the system would have been better or worse. The design of the federal aid programs offers some simple clues about the degree to which state and local choices might be altered. The broader the category of highway projects eligible for aid and the lower the funding levels, the more likely federal aid will merely serve to reduce state or local taxes and leave highway spending decisions largely unchanged. Conversely, the more restrictive the eligibility and the greater the funding, the more likely it is that federal aid, if accepted, will alter local choices.

According to this test, federal aid for the primary, secondary, and urban systems probably had little effect on postwar state and local highway decisions. Although states can designate only a fraction of their highway mileage as eligible and federal funds must be matched by an equal amount of state or local aid, the level of federal aid probably falls far short of current expenditures on these systems. In 1980, for example, federal primary, secondary, and urban systems aid accounted for only $2 billion of the $9 billion spent for capital outlays on state-administered highways (excluding the Interstates).[20] The ratio of spending to federal aid was probably even lower in urban areas, since the federally aided mileage is still disproportionately rural.

The Interstate program offers potentially strong incentives to distort state and local choices, however, and efforts to reduce or offset these incentives have been only partially successful. Only segments of the 42,500-mile congressionally designated Interstate System are eligible for aid, and each segment must meet strict federal design standards governing access control, lane width, curvature, ramp length, and other features. In return, the federal government will pay up to 90 percent of the cost of constructing the segment, no matter how expensive the project. (Only allowable, highway-related costs can be reimbursed, of course, and competitive bidding must be used.)

These strong financial incentives led early critics to fear that state and local highway agencies would overlook the environmental costs and social disruption of highway construction and build many unnecessary Interstate segments. Although blighting and disruptive highways were probably built, as noted earlier, the majority of urban Interstate mileage appears to have been worthwhile. The rapid rates of expressway construction and planning in the years immediately preceding the start of the Interstate program also suggest that some, though certainly not all, of the limited-access highways might have been constructed anyway. Finally, federal regulations requiring comprehensive transportation planning, environmental impact statements, and public hearings have helped to reduce the problem of blighting and disruptive highways by increasing the opportunities for citizens to block or delay highway projects.

Recently a new problem has emerged, due to the combination of the strong financial incentives of the Interstate program and the federal regulations mandating increased citizen involvement. To overcome local opposition to the construction of environmentally or socially sensitive urban Interstate segments, state highway officials are now encouraged to incorporate costly design features that are largely paid for by the federal government. Two extreme examples of this new problem are the West Side Highway in New York City and the Central Artery in Boston. Both of these downtown elevated expressways are now part of the designated Interstate system but were built before Interstate aid was available and consequently do not meet Interstate design standards. Part of the West Side Highway collapsed in 1973, and the Central Artery deck is nearing the end of its expected structural life. Local groups oppose reconstructing the highways in their current form, since they are ugly and blighting; in any case, a reconstruction project would be ineligible for Interstate funding unless federal officials granted a design variance. New York's solution (which was approved by federal transportation officials but has been delayed by an environmental lawsuit) is to build four miles of new Interstate offshore in the Hudson River, with 230 acres of landfill for housing and parks to serve as a buffer between the highway and existing neighborhoods. Boston's proposal (which is pending federal approval) is to depress one mile of the highway along the original alignment, with decks to support overhead development. These offshore and depressed highways would cost around $1–2 billion each, four times more than reconstruction. The added costs appear to be far larger than the estimated environmental or aesthetic benefits to be gained.[21]

If these two highways can be rehabilitated only at such high costs, they may not be worth maintaining at all. But the availability of 90 percent federal funding—coupled with complaints from local politicians and congressional delegations if federal officials attempt to review local designs more closely—have made local officials unwilling to consider less grandiose schemes.[22] The Interstate program, in short, may have shifted from building some urban highways that were excessively disruptive and blighting to building some that have been overly beautified.

Financial Effects on Urban Governments

Federal highway aid may not only distort local choices, it also may fail to alleviate long-term financial pressures on local governments to any significant degree. The availability of federal highway aid reduces the need to raise state and local taxes, to be sure, but the aid is financed by federal highway user taxes paid in part by urban residents. Since the federal highway aid program is heavily oriented toward rural roads, federal highway-user tax payments probably significantly exceed federal highway grants in most urban areas. Although detailed urban/rural data are not available, data on federal highway receipts and expenditures by states for the period from 1956 through 1982 show that the ratio of federal highway grants to federal user tax payments was below the national average in virtually every highly urbanized state and that almost all the states with above-average grant-to-tax payment ratios were rural.[23]

These simple calculations also ignore the fact that federal highway aid may encourage state and local governments to build projects whose costs exceed their benefits. If the benefits from the West Side Highway project are less than the costs, for example, then the federal aid for that project is worth less to New York than its nominal value. In short, many heavily urbanized states would probably be financially better off if they could substitute their own state or local fuel and vehicle taxes for federal highway taxes and highway aid.

EVALUATING TRANSIT AID

THE EXPERIENCE WITH TRANSIT SUBSIDIES

Three arguments are usually offered in support of government assistance to mass transit. First, mass transit aid is said to reduce the level of automobile use and thereby to alleviate traffic congestion, the demand for costly urban highways, and automotive air and noise pollution and energy consumption. Second, subsidies to mass transit are thought to promote more concentrated, downtown-oriented forms of metropolitan development, with possible attendant infrastructure or energy savings. Finally, transit assistance is expected to benefit low-income households, the elderly, and children—those too poor, too old, or too young to drive or own an automobile.

Reducing Auto Use

The failure of transit aid programs in the 1970s to increase transit ridership significantly was discouraging, especially given the rapid increase in government aid during the decade. Where transit ridership did increase, moreover, only a fraction of the new riders were former auto users; thus, the cost per auto trip avoided was often extremely high.

The new rail systems provided the most dramatic examples of the difficulties of reducing auto use at reasonable cost. Both the San Francisco Bay Area Rapid Transit (BART), opened in 1972, and the Washington D.C. Metrorail, opened in 1976, had anticipated that fares would cover at least operating costs and, in the case of BART, make some small contribution to construction costs as well. Construction and operating costs on both systems proved to be higher than anticipated, however, even adjusting for inflation, while ridership was overprojected by nearly a factor of two.[24] In 1976, the average fare on BART was 72 cents, while the operating cost per rider was about $1.95 and the total public subsidies—operating and capital—amounted to $3.76 per rider. Since only 35 percent of all BART riders were former auto users (the remainder being former bus patrons or persons making new trips), the subsidy per auto trip avoided amounted to at least $10.74.[25]

Metrorail has fared slightly better, perhaps in part because it is still under construction and only some of the most productive segments have been opened to date. When the commitment to build Metrorail was made in 1969, the cost of the planned 98-mile system was set at $2.5 billion. The 31-mile Phase III system, which was in operation by late 1979, alone cost over $3 billion to build (in 1980 dollars), and the cost to complete the entire system (since expanded to 101 miles) is now climbing toward $12 billion.[26] With the Phase III system, total costs amounted to $2.73 per rail trip in 1980, two-thirds of which was for capital.[27] Metrorail Phase III did reduce rush-hour auto trips to the downtown core by 4 percent.[28] Since only 36 percent of all Metrorail riders were former auto or taxi users, however, the Metrorail capital cost per auto trip removed from the road amounted to $5.21, while the total cost (operating plus capital) might have been as high as $7.58.[29] As the outer extensions of the system are opened, the cost per rider and per auto trip diverted are likely to increase.[30]

Operating aid also brought disappointing ridership gains, despite the fact that the average operating subsidy per rider increased from 5 cents in 1970 to 76 cents in 1982. The small ridership increase was caused in part by the absorption of much of the aid in reduced productivity and higher unit costs rather than in fare reductions or service improvements. Between 1970 and 1982 the average wage for transit drivers grew 40 percent more than inflation, for example, while labor productivity, as measured in annual vehicle hours of service per full-time employee, fell by 20 percent.[31] The rapid cost increases meant that the average real fare declined by only 19 percent from 1970 to 1982, while the number of vehicle miles of service offered by the transit industry increased by only 13 percent.[32]

Even where operating aid led to significant fare reductions or service improvements, the ridership increases were often relatively small. In the Boston metropolitan area, for example, government operating subsidies for mass transportation increased from approximately $80 million in 1971 to $233 million in 1980, while passenger revenues remained relatively constant at $50–60 million per year. The operating aid was used to maintain existing service and keep the fare at 25 cents, despite rapid inflation in operating costs. Inasmuch as the consumer price index more than doubled bwteen 1971 and 1980, retaining the 25-cent fare amounted to reducing the fare by half (in real dollars) over the course of the decade. Despite this substantial decline in price, ridership remained stable or declined slightly throughout the 1970s. In late 1980 and 1981, when financial realities finally forced Boston officials to raise fares, the response in ridership and auto usage was also relatively small.[33] When bus fares increased by 100 percent and rail fares increased 50 percent in August 1981, for example, ridership fell by only 10 percent and car usage in the metropolitan area increased by at most 0.5 percent.[34] Boston temporarily retained some mass transit riders by avoiding a fare increase during the 1970s, but the cost of doing so amounted to around $2 to $3 in added subsidy per passenger trip saved.[35]

About a dozen metropolitan areas significantly increased their transit ridership during the 1970s, sometimes at a relatively modest subsidy cost of 50 cents or so per added rider. In most cases, however, fare reductions and service improvements were not the only factors contributing to the ridership gains. A few cities allowed their transit service to deteriorate greatly before public subsidies began; thus the increase was significant only compared to the very small base. In several other cities, policies to discourage auto use—such as parking taxes or controls, priority for buses in traffic, or exclusive bus lanes—appear to have contributed greatly to increasing patronage.[36]

In short, the experience of the 1970s showed that it is difficult to expand transit patronage—and reduce auto use—much beyond transit's traditional markets. Transis has always been best in serving commuters to the downtowns of large and congested metropolitan areas, such as New York, Chicago, San Francisco, and Boston. The combination of high downtown parking fees and slow traffic speeds makes transit competitive with the automobile for these trips, particularly if transit can be protected from the congestion with either an exclusive rail or bus right-of-way or bus priority in traffic. The irony is that where transit contributes most to the alleviation of auto problems, it is probably least in need of government assistance. Where traffic congestion is severe and parking charges high, transit can offer relatively competitive service without significant government aid.

Concentrating Urban Development

The supporters of the new rail transit systems hoped they would lead to more concentrated forms of urban development as well as reduced auto use. A review of the experience of new rail systems in San Francisco, Washington, Montreal, and Toronto and major rail extensions in other cities suggests, however, that rail service is not sufficient to insure intensified development around suburban or outlying stations. A variety of other complementary factors are needed, including rapid economic and population growth in the metropolitan area and support from the community and local land use policies. In Toronto, for example, clusters of high-rise apartment buildings and retailing appeared around outlying stations, in part because rapid metropolitan growth encouraged new construction and local officials offered powerful zoning incentives for development around stations. With BART and Montreal's Metro, by contrast, there was little development around suburban stations, due in part to slower growth, community opposition, and difficulties of land assembly.[37]

The principal land-use effect of these new rail systems appears to be in facilitating downtown high-rise office development. San Francisco, Toronto, and Montreal have experienced rapid downtown development since their new systems were completed; Washington, D.C., and Atlanta, where partial systems are now in operation, show signs of similar trends. Other non-rail factors probably contributed, however, since the downtown office booms often pre-dated the subway openings and other cities without new rail systems experienced similar developments.

If new rail systems promote downtown offices but leave suburban development dispersed, their land-use effects are similar to those of the radial expressways that transit advocates often oppose. By increasing the accessibility of the downtown to the suburbs, the rail system promotes more concentrated employment in the downtown and the displacement and dispersal of residences into the suburbs. The overall effect is probably to increase rather than reduce the average length of the commuting trip and to turn the downtown and its immediate neighborhoods into areas that are active during the day and have few residents and associated nighttime activities.[38]

Helping the Poor

The experience of the 1970s also suggests that transit aid is not always an efficient or effective way to help poor people.[39] Transit accounts for only a modest fraction of the trips poor people make. Although poor households are more dependent on mass transit than rich households, in 1977–1978 mass transit accounted for only 6.9 percent of the trips made by metropolitan residents with household incomes below $6000, a figure not much different from transit's 3.4 percent share of trips by metropolitan residents of all incomes.[40] While 85 percent of all metropolitan households owned at least one car in 1977–1978, a surprising 54 percent of households with incomes below $5000 and 83 percent of households with incomes between $5000 and $10,000 owned autos.[41]

Poor people make up a small fraction of all transit riders, moreover. Travelers with 1977–1978 household incomes below $6000 accounted for only 25 percent of all transit trips in metropolitan areas, for example.[42] The share of subsidy that goes to poor transit riders is probably even smaller, since low-income ridership tends to be concentrated on services where the subsidy per rider is relatively low. Subsidies per rider are typically three to four times higher on commuter railroad services than they are on buses or subways, for example, yet only 9 percent of all commuter rail trips were made by persons with 1977–1978 household incomes below $6000, while 38 percent were made by travelers with incomes above $25,000.[43] Within rail and bus systems, transit subsidies tend to be higher for long-distance and peak-hour travelers, because the costs are higher while fares typically are not. Poor people ride much shorter distances than average because they live closer to the city center; the poor also travel disproportionately in the off-peak hours since many are unemployed.[44]

Transit subsidies could better help the poor, of course, if they were targetted directly at poor travelers or the services they use. Virtually every transit system offers discount fares for handicapped and elderly persons, but these discounts help only slightly: 75 percent of the metropolitan poor are neither handicapped nor elderly.[45] A more promising possibility is to subsidize poor users directly; poor persons might be issued discount fare identification cards or, to avoid the possible stigma of an identification card, could be sold monthly transit passes or a supply of transit tokens at a discount price. Targetting the subsidies to services such as bus, off-peak, and short-distance that poor people tend to use is less efficient but would be an improvement over the existing system. The federal government has sponsored several successful demonstrations of the possibilities of direct subsidies to poor people, but so far the practice has been adopted only in a handful of cities.[46]

THE PROBLEMS OF FEDERAL AID

The Federal Rationale

The rationale for federal involvement in urban mass transit shares many of the weaknesses of the rationale for federal aid to urban highways. The argument most often cited in the early 1960s debates over the initial federal capital grant program was the need to counterbalance federal highway aid. The federal and state highway trust funds, all financed with dedicated gasoline taxes, were thought to have induced state and local governments to channel too much capital spending into highways and too little into mass transit. Transit had declined because of undercapitalization, the argument continued, and federal transit aid was needed to correct the imbalance.[47]

The failure of the transit investments of the 1970s to increase ridership significantly suggests that undercapitalization was probably not a major cause of the decline of mass transit patronage. Rising real household incomes, suburbanization of jobs and residences, and other demographic trends probably played more important roles in the postwar patronage losses. Even if local governments had seriously overinvested in highways and underinvested in transit, a massive new transit aid program may not have been the correct answer. By subsidizing both the highway and transit modes the federal government might reduce the balance between transit and highways only at the risk of overcapitalizing transportation in general. Reducing or eliminating the federal highway aid program might have encouraged more balanced spending on all forms of transportation.

Discretionary Capital Grants and the Rail Starts Problem

Whether mass transit was ever undercapitalized, the federal discretionary transit capital grant program now appears to encourage overcapitalization. The transit capital grant program has many of the same features as the Interstate Highway program. The federal government will pay up to 80 percent of the cost of a transit capital project (after 1982, 75 percent). Since grants are allocated for specific projects at the discretion of the Secretary of Transportation, moreover, there is no clear limit to the assistance a city may receive; the use of aid for one project does not preclude aid for others.

State and local governments have an obvious incentive to use the discretionary capital grant program to substitute federally paid capital costs for locally paid operating expenses.[48] For example, one early study examined the possibility that transit authorities might save on bus maintenance costs by using federal capital grants to retire buses earlier than they would otherwise. That study never investigated whether transit authorities actually engaged in this practice but estimated that if they did, the waste would amount to more than 20 percent of the value of the federal capital grants.[49]

Since most federal capital grants have been spent on rail transit, a most troublesome possibility is that local authorities may substitute federal capital grants for local operating expenses by building rail instead of bus systems. Among the advantages often cited for new rail systems is the potential for reducing labor costs by replacing several bus drivers with a single train operator. There are some offsets, of course, such as the added costs of maintaining track, signals, power distribution systems, stations, and other facilities not normally found on a bus system. In some situations, however, rail may offer savings in operating costs even though total costs, including capital, are higher.

The availability of federal aid has been a strong factor in the recent revival of rail transit. Rail systems are often classified as either heavy or light: on heavy rail systems, such as a conventional subway or metro, passengers board from platforms and power is distributed by a third rail; on light rail systems, such as streetcars or trolleys, passengers may board from street level and power is distributed by overhead catenary. From the 1930s through the late 1950s, rail transit mileage declined steadily in the United States as many cities replaced their streetcar lines with buses.[50] When the federal capital grant program began in 1964, five United States metropolitan areas had rail systems that pre-dated World War II, Cleveland had opened a new heavy rail system in 1958, and San Francisco had already begun the construction of BART. Between 1964 and 1984, almost every older rail system extended its lines, four cities opened new heavy rail systems, one opened a new light rail system, and another five cities began building new light rail systems. As of 1984 at least 13 more cities were in various stages of designing or planning new rail systems, while virtually every existing rail system was planning extensions to existing lines (Table 7.8). While most of the rail construction in the 1960s and 1970s involved heavy rail systems, almost all the cities building or planning new systems in the 1980s are considering light rail.

Several studies have compared the operating and capital costs of using buses and heavy rail to serve metropolitan commuting trips. To insure that the cost comparisons are meaningful, these studies attempt to make the quality of service on the two modes comparable. While it is difficult to make the services exactly equivalent, the cost studies usually insure that the ratio of seated to standing passengers is the same on rail and bus and that bus travel times are comparable to heavy rail by, for example, operating the buses on an exclusive busway or an expressway whose access ramps are controlled to prevent congestion. The cost studies generally show that the bus is less expensive than heavy rail in radial corridors with

TABLE 7.8
Status of United States Rail Transit Systems, May 1984

	Miles in service[a]		Miles under construction		Further extensions in planning[b]
	Heavy	Light	Heavy	Light	
Systems built before 1940					
New York	259	4			yes
Chicago	97		2		no
Philadelphia	53	88			yes
Boston	42	35	8		yes
Pittsburgh		24[c]			yes
New Orleans		7			yes
New systems (year opened)					
Cleveland (1958)	19	13[d]			yes
San Francisco (1972)	71	30[d]			yes
Washington (1976)	48		14[e]		yes
Atlanta (1979)	16		9		yes
San Diego (1981)		16			yes
Baltimore (1983)	8		6		yes
Miami (1984)	10		11	2[f]	yes
Systems under construction (scheduled opening)					
Buffalo (1984)				6	yes
Portland (1986)				15	yes
Sacramento (1986)				18	no
San Jose (1988)				20	yes
Detroit (?)				?	yes

Systems in planning[b]

In final design:
    Los Angeles
In alternatives analysis:
    Columbus
    Milwaukee
    Minneapolis–St. Paul
    St. Louis
    Seattle

In systems planning:
    Cincinnati
    Dallas
    Denver
    Honolulu
    Houston
    Orlando
    San Juan

[a]All mileage except Philadelphia from F. K. Plous, Jr., "A Streetcar Named Desire," *Planning* 50 (June 1984): 15–23.

[b]As estimated by the U.S. Urban Mass Transportation Administration, "New Starts Pipeline as of May 1984," photocopy, n.d.

[c]Portions of the Pittsburgh light rail system are currently being rebuilt.

[d]The light rail systems in Cleveland and San Francisco pre-date World War II.

[e]A total of 101 miles is planned in Washington, D.C.

[f]A 1.9-mile automated people mover is under construction in Miami.

weekday peak-hour travel volumes below 15,000 transit passengers. When the peak travel volumes exceed 30,000 transit passengers, heavy rail is less expensive, and between 15,000 and 30,000 passengers the choice is usually determined by local conditions, such as the availability of a relatively free-flowing expressway that buses can use.[51] Radial corridor volumes above 15,000 persons per peak hour probably are found only in metropolitan area with populations of at least several million, with high population densities and a strong downtown.[52] Of the metropolitan areas that opened or began construction of heavy rail systems in the 1970s, probably only San Francisco and Washington, D.C., have corridor volumes that exceed the minimum heavy rail threshold. Even in those metropolitan areas, moreover, a careful bus-rail cost comparison would probably suggest much smaller heavy rail systems than the ones opened or planned.

The high cost of the heavy rail systems built in the 1970s stimulated interest in light rail systems in the 1980s. Unfortunately, there has been very little analysis of the comparative costs of light rail and bus.[53] Light-rail proponents argue that it can be much cheaper than heavy rail because it can operate safely on city streets where building an exclusive right-of-way or subway would be expensive. Because the right-of-way need not be grade-separated, the argument continues, a light rail system does not need nearly as high corridor volumes to bring its per-passenger costs down to reasonable levels. If the light rail system is not grade-separated, however, the comparison bus service probably can also avoid expenditures for exclusive busways or similar facilities. Whether the savings in rail costs outweight the savings in bus costs may depend greatly on local conditions. Many of the metropolitan areas now building or planning light rail systems have such modest populations and densities as to make construction of even light rail systems very risky.

The high construction costs of some of the new rail systems built to date lend credence to the view that the total costs of many of these systems are greater than those of comparable bus systems. Even more striking is the possibility that at least some of the new rail systems may have increased rather than reduced locally paid operating costs. San Diego's new light rail system, for example, is widely touted as a success because farebox receipts cover 80 percent of its operating expenses, compared to only 40 percent on the San Diego bus system. The rail system consists of a single sixteen-mile line connecting the downtown with the southern suburbs and the United States–Mexican border, and it offers faster terminal-to-terminal travel times than the two bus routes it replaced.[54] The original bus routes were among the most heavily patronized in the San Diego system, however, and their farebox receipts exceeded operating expenses. Had the bus routes enjoyed the partially grade-separated right-of-way of the rail system, their travel times probably would have been comparable to rail and their operating profits even greater.[55] Comparisons of bus costs for other larger rail systems are more difficult, since it is harder to identify the specific bus services they replaced. The steady increases in operating deficits in many of the metropolitan areas that recently opened rail systems suggests that the operating savings over buses may have been small.

Federal regulations requiring analysis of low-cost alternatives and restricting new rail starts to one line at a time have not been effective in limiting new rail construction.[56] The 1976 requirement for alternatives analysis is credited with eliminating Denver's heavy rail proposal and reducing the size of the Buffalo light rail plan (when bus systems were found to offer comparable service at a fraction of the cost). Although the analysis requirement probably has discouraged or reduced the scale of other proposals, since the Denver and Buffalo decisions federal officials have not turned down any rail proposals after alternatives analysis, and the number of cities engaged in rail planning has increased.

As in the case of highways, the complexity of urban transportation planning helps to limit the effectiveness of federal rail transit regulations. Forecasting rail and bus patronage is a difficult art, for example, since ridership projections are sensitive to the detailed spatial distribution of future jobs and residences, which is itself uncertain. The non-rail alternatives can also appear relatively costly and unattractive if they are poorly or unimaginatively designed. Although experience has shown that many of the rail analyses overestimated patronage and understated costs, it is often difficult to demonstrate conclusively before the fact that a forecast is unreliable. Given the subtle judgment involved in accurately forecasting ridership and costs or designing alternatives, it is difficult for UMTA's small staff to detect or correct the potential errors in the alternatives analysis.

These problems are often further compounded by strong political support for rail from local officials and their congressional delegations. Local officials displeased with UMTA decisions are often quick to bring congressional pressure to bear on the agency, particularly when the UMTA position seems petty or unreasonable. The FY1982 and 1983 congressional earmarking of rail funds for specific cities is perhaps only the most extreme example of this problem.

In May 1984 the UMTA administrator announced that future rail-start decisions would be based on the added cost per new transit rider attracted, using a low-cost bus alternative as the baseline for measuring added rail costs and ridership. The hope is that the figures will embarrass Congress and discourage future earmarking for particularly cost-ineffective rail projects. The cost-per-rider estimates will be based on data from the alternatives analyses, however, which will increase the need for UMTA to monitor the quality of these studies.[57]

Incentives of Operating Aid

The principal debate over federal operating assistance focuses on the extent to which it either substitutes for state or local aid or distorts state and local decisions in undesirable ways. Federal assistance was originally restricted to capital expenses in 1964, for example, partly out of fear that operating grants would reduce incentives for transit managers to control labor costs and improve productivity. Capital grants do not eliminate these incentives altogether, of course, since they free local resources that otherwise might have been absorbed by capital needs for operating expenses. With operating aid, however, the incentives might be more direct and obvious.

The relationship between operating aid and efficiency has received increasing attention because of the rapid inflation in transit operating costs during the 1970s. A careful study of the real (net of general inflation) increase in United States bus transit operating deficits between 1970 and 1980 found, for example, that increasing real labor compensation rates or declining labor productivity accounted for 48 percent of the deficit growth, while real fuel-cost increases accounted for only 11 percent of the deficit growth, service expansions only 19 percent, and fare reductions only 22 percent.[58] Several cross-section and time series studies of transit agencies have also found that higher levels of government operating subsidies are strongly associated with higher wage levels and lower labor productivity. Correlation does not prove causation, however, and none of these studies has been able to demonstrate conclusively that higher subsidies caused operating cost increases rather than vice versa.[59]

A more recent concern is the possibility that federal operating grants may encourage expansion of transit service into markets where transit has little chance of capturing significant ridership. Many smaller metropolitan areas greatly expanded their transit service during the 1970s even though low levels of auto congestion and low population densities make it difficult to attract ridership. Some larger metropolitan areas greatly increased suburban and crosstown services, where the possibilities for attracting additional patronage at reasonable subsidy costs is probably also limited.

The cost inflation and the expansion of underutilized services encouraged by federal operating aid may well be centered on small, low-density metropolitan areas. State and local government aid accounts for 70 percent of all operating assistance for the United States transit industry as a whole, far less than the 50 percent minimum match required for federal grants. The formulas for distributing federal operating aid also provide less assistance per rider to many of the largest and most transit-oriented metropolitan areas; in the big Eastern and North Central cities such as New York, Chicago, Boston, and Philadelphia, federal aid accounts for less than 20 percent of all operating assistance. In many smaller and low-density metropolitan areas, federal aid is at the 50 percent limit and its potential effect on service and efficiency decisions is much greater.[60]

Federal officials have rejected suggestions that they monitor the services or efficiency of operating grant recipients, in part for lack of simple and reasonable standards. The best remedy would probably be to increase the local matching requirement or to change the formula to favor the larger, transit-oriented cities more. The operating aid formulas were changed in 1978 and 1982 to increase the large cities' share of funding, but the need for broadly based congressional support has insured that many small, low-density metropolitan areas still receive a disproportionate share of aid.[61]

Financial Effects on Urban Governments

Federal transit aid is targeted far more heavily at urban areas than federal highway aid, and urban taxpayers almost certainly receive more in federal transit grants than they pay in federal taxes to support the program. In 1980, for example, 34 states—all predominantly rural—received less than $10 per capita in federal transit aid, while only 8 states—all with cities that were building or expanding rail systems—received over $20 per capita.[62] Since all federal transit aid was financed out of general revenues in that year, the federal tax burden for the program is probably far more equally distributed and urban areas are the net gainers.

As in the case of highways, however, the benefits to urban residents from a federal transit grant may be smaller than the dollar value of the grant. To the extent that federal grants encourage too many rail transit extensions, expansion of underutilized services, or reduced productivity, the value of the grant to the recipient may be significantly lower than its dollar value. Capital grants may cause additional financial strains for urban governments if the capital projects increase rather than reduce local operating costs. The experience of the San Diego light rail system suggests, for example, that the construction of some rail systems may burden local governments with increased transit operating deficits.

The financial effects of federal transit aid also probably should not be viewed separately from those of federal highway aid. If urban representatives in Congress trade their support for highway aid in return for rural support for transit aid, then it would be impossible to eliminate or reduce the federal highway program without making comparable reductions in the federal transit programs. One recent study of the state-by-state allocations of federal transportation grants and taxes suggests that the urban bias of transit aid is not enough to offset the rural bias of highway aid. Of ten highly urbanized states, only two received more in highway and transit grants than they paid in federal highway and other taxes to support the programs. Almost all the states that received more in federal highway and transit grants than they paid in federal taxes were rural.[63]

THE FEDERAL ROLE RECONSIDERED

The Reagan administration's proposals to reduce the federal role in urban transportation represented a significant redirection in federal policy. Despite the unsympathetic reaction from Congress, a reduced federal role might have proven beneficial not only for the federal taxpayer but for urban residents.

The rationale for federal involvement in urban transportation is much less compelling now than when that involvement began. Federal highway aid began early in 1916 because of a national interest in establishing an interstate and interconnected highway system. This concern always applied more clearly to rural than urban highways and has been far less compelling since the development of strong state highway agencies than it was under the old county road system. Federal transit aid was rationalized in part as a needed counterbalance to federal highway aid, but in retrospect reduced federal highway aid might have been a more sensible remedy.

Several of the federal urban transportation programs begun in the postwar period appear to distort local transportation decisions in undesirable ways. Interstate highway aid and discretionary mass-transit capital grants create the greatest problems, since both have low state and local matching requirements and are distributed for specific federally approved projects rather than by formula or for a broad range of potential uses. The Interstate highway grants probably encouraged the construction of some highways that were excessively blighting during the 1950s and 1960s and now may be encouraging the construction of highways that are excessively beautified. The transit capital-grant program appears to encourage excessive spending on transit, particularly in the form of new rail systems.

Some of the federal aid programs are relatively less distorting, particularly the federal urban-systems-highway grants and, to a lesser extent, the transit operating and capital formula grants. In both cases, the funds can be used for a relatively broad range of transportation activities, and state and local spending usually exceeds the minimum federal matching requirements. These less distorting programs account for an increasing share of federal transit funding but a declining share of federal highway aid.

A reduction in federal highway and transit aid might leave urban residents financially better off, as long as it was accompanied by a reduction in federal tax rates. On average, urban dwellers probably pay more in federal highway taxes than they receive in federal highway aid. Although the federal transit program reduces this imbalance somewhat, even when the transit program is included urban residents pay more in federal tax than they receive in transportation aid. This calculation exaggerates the benefits urban dwellers receive from federal aid, moreover, since it ignores the possibility that federal aid encourages at least some projects whose costs far exceed their benefits. If estimates of the benefits from federally supported urban transportation projects were available and could be compared with the federal taxes urban residents pay to support these programs, the case for a reduced federal role might be even stronger.

NOTES

1. For histories of federal highway aid see U.S. Congressional Budget Office, *Highway Assistance Programs: A Historical Perspective* (Washington, D.C.: U.S. Government Printing Office, 1978); Philip M. Burch, Jr., *Highway Revenue and Expenditure Policy in the United States* (New Brunswick, N.J.: Rutgers, 1962); Gary T. Schwartz, "Urban Freeways and the Interstate System," *Southern California Law Review* 49 (1976): 406–513; Jonathan Lewis Gifford, "An Analysis of the Federal Role in the Planning, Design, and Deploy-

ment of Rural Roads, Toll Roads, and Urban Freeways," Ph.D. dissertation, University of California at Berkeley, 1983.

2. For a review of the accomplishments of these federal programs see John R. Meyer and Jose A. Gomez-Ibañez, *Autos, Transit and Cities* (Cambridge, Mass.: Harvard, 1981); and Lawrence J. White, *The Regulation of Air Pollutant Emissions from Motor Vehicles* (Washington, D.C.: American Enterprise Institute, 1982).

3. For histories of federal transit aid see Meyer and Gomez-Ibañez, *Autos, Transit and Cities*, pp. 37–55; George W. Hilton, *Federal Transit Subsidies* (Washington, D.C.: American Enterprise Institute, 1974); and Michael Rossetti and Douglas Lee, "Legislative History of Federal Operating Assistance for Mass Transit," U.S. Department of Transportation, Transportation Systems Center, Cambridge, Mass., June 1983.

4. Philip N. Fulton, "Public Transportation: Solving the Commuting Problem?" paper presented at the Transportation Research Board annual meeting, Washington, D.C., January 1983, p. 6.

5. For a description of the initial Reagan administration proposals see Rochelle L. Stanfield, "The New Federalism Is Reagan's Answer to Decaying Highway and Transit Systems," *National Journal*, 12 June 1982, pp. 1040–44; and Neal R. Pierce and Carol Steinbach, "Cuts in Transit Aid May Hurt But Could Have a Silver Lining," *National Journal*, 4 April 1981, pp. 568–72.

6. Unpublished Urban Mass Transportation Administration estimate.

7. The only comprehensive benefit-cost analysis, by Ann Friedlaender, dates from the early 1960s, when only about half of the Interstate System was completed: see Ann F. Friedlaender, *The Interstate Highway System: A Study in Public Investment* (Amsterdam: North-Holland, 1965).

8. This section summarizes material originally presented in Meyer and Gomez-Ibañez, *Autos, Transit and Cities*, pp. 188–208.

9. Whether it is desirable to set user fares exactly at, below, or above average highway costs depends on whether there are economies of scale in the construction and operation of highways; see ibid., p. 191.

10. Ibid., p. 198.

11. U.S. Federal Highway Administration, *The States and Conditions of the Nation's Highways*, report by the U.S. Secretary of Transportation to the U.S. Congress, Committee Print No. 97–2, 97th Congress, 1st session, January 1981, pp. 142–43.

12. Meyer and Gomez-Ibañez, *Autos, Transit and Cities*, pp. 199–205; Theodore Keeler and Kenneth A. Small, *Automobile Costs and Final Intermodal Cost Comparisons*, vol. 3 of *The Full Costs of Urban Transport*, ed. Theodore E. Keeler, Leonard A. Merewitz, and P.M.J. Fisher (Berkeley: University of California, Institute of Urban and Regional Development, 1975).

13. Keeler and Small, *Automobile Costs*, pp. 52–55; U.S. Federal Highway Administration, *Final Report on the Federal Highway Cost Allocation Study*, report by the Secretary of Transportation to the U.S. Congress (Washington, D.C.: U.S. Government Printing Office, 1982), pp. E-41 to E-53.

14. Meyer and Gomez-Ibañez, *Autos, Transit and Cities*, pp. 172–76, 207; U.S. Federal Highway Administration, *Highway Cost Allocation Study*, pp. E-46 to E-53.

15. Alan A. Altshuler and Robert W. Curry, "The Changing Environment of Urban Development Policy," *Urban Law Journal* 10 (1976): 1–47.

16. The FHWA published reports provide estimates that exclude local roads and thus are not directly comparable to the figures given in table 2 of this report. The U.S. Congressional Budget Office reports some figures from unpublished FHWA estimates that include local roads: see U.S. Congressional Budget Office, *Public Works Infrastructure: Policy Considerations for the 1980s* (Washington, D.C.: U.S. Government Printing Office, 1983), p. 9.

17. Jose A. Gomez-Ibañez and Mary M. O'Keeffe, "The Benefits from Improved Investment Rules: A Case Study of the Interstate Highway System," report to the U.S. Department of Transportation, forthcoming.

18. Gifford, "The Federal Role in Roads"; Burch, *Highway Revenue and Expenditure*

Policy; and John B. Rae, *The Car and the Road in American Life* (Cambridge, Mass.: MIT, 1972).

19. Rae, *The Car and the Road*, pp. 173–82.

20. See Table 7.2 in this paper and U.S. Federal Highway Administration, *Highway Statistics, 1980* (Washington, D.C.: U.S. Government Printing Office, 1981), p. 39.

21. See Meyer and Gomez-Ibañez, *Autos, Transit and Cities*, pp. 176–77; David Segal, "The Economic Benefits of Depressing an Urban Expressway: The Case of Boston's John Fitzgerald Expressway," paper presented at the annual meeting of the Transportation Research Board, Washington, D.C., 1981.

22. Regina Herzlinger, "Costs, Benefits and the West Side Highway," *The Public Interest* no. 55 (Spring 1979): 77–98.

23. For the nation as a whole, the ratio of federal highway grants to user tax payments was 1.07, thanks largely to interest earned on balances in the federal highway trust fund. Amoung highly urbanized states, the ratio of grants to user tax payments was 1.00 for New York State, 1.05 for Illinois, 1.03 for Pennsylvania, 0.97 for Massachusetts, 0.88 for Indiana, 0.84 for Michigan, 0.82 for New Jersey, 0.81 for California, and 0.80 for Indiana. See U.S. Federal Highway Administration, *Highway Statistics, 1982* (Washington, D.C.: U.S. Government Printing Office, 1983), p. 50.

24. For BART see Melvin M. Webber, "The BART Experience—What Have We Learned?" *The Public Interest* no. 45 (Fall 1976): 85.

25. Webber, "The BART Experience," pp. 85–97.

26. Phase II costs are unpublished estimates supplied by Daniel Brand of Charles River Associates, Boston, Mass., August 1984.

27. In FY1980, Metrorail carried 93.2 million trips at an operating cost of $79.4 million, or $0.85 per trip. Assuming the capital costs to have been $3 billion, a 5 percent real discount rate, and a 40-year average expected life for the investment, the capital costs per ride amounted to an additional $1.88. See U.S. Urban Mass Transportation Administration, *National Urban Mass Transportation Statistics: Second Annual Report, Section 15 Reporting System* (Washington, D.C.: U.S. Government Printing Office, 1982), pp. 2–50 and 2–176. It is unclear whether Metrorail resulted in any significant savings in bus transit costs. The number of bus miles operated by Metrobus dropped by about 8 percent between 1975–1976 and 1979, but the number of bus passengers dropped by 6 percent during that period as well. It may be that the reductions in bus service along the new rail routes just equaled the increases in bus service along the new rail stations. A 2 percent reduction in 1980 Metrobus operating costs would have amounted to only $3.2 million, or 3 cents per Metrorail rider. See Robert T. Dunphy and Robert E. Griffiths, *The First Four Years of Metrorail: Travel Changes*, report no. DOT–1–82–5 to the U.S. Urban Mass Transportation Administration, September 1981, p. 60.

28. Dunphy and Griffiths, *Travel Changes*, pp. 35, 70.

29. These calculations assume one auto trip saved per auto or taxi passenger who shifts to rail, an obviously optimistic assumption.

30. A 1976 study by the U.S. Library of Congress and the Congressional Research Service argued that the additional costs were high and the added patronage low from expanding Metrorail beyond a basic 41-mile system. A 1978 analysis prepared for the Metropolitan Washington Council of Governments disagreed, although only relatively minor reductions in mileage from the original 101-mile system were considered. See U.S. Library of Congress and Congressional Research Service, *Washington Area Metrorail*; Peat, Marwick, Mitchell, and Company, "Metrorail Alternatives Analysis: Final Report," report to the Metropolitan Washington Council of Governments, August 1978.

31. John Pucher, Anders Markstedt, and Ira Hirschman, "Impact of Subsidies on the Costs of Urban Public Transport," *Journal of Transport Economics and Policy* 17 (1983): 159–60.

32. Fares are deflated using the GNP price deflator.

33. Rail rapid transit fares were raised to 50 cents in July 1980, raised again to 75 cents in August 1981, and then rolled back to 60 cents in May of 1982. Bus fares were kept at 25 cents until August 1981, when they were raised to 50 cents.

34. (Boston) Central Area Transportation Planning Staff, *Final Environmental and Socioeconomic Impact Report of the MBTA Fare Increase* (Boston: Central Transportation Planning Staff, 1982), pp. 63, 69.

35. Assuming that the fare increase would eventually bring at least $40–50 million per year in added farebox revenue.

36. For a list of the metropolitan areas where transit's share of work trips increased during the 1970s see Fulton, "Public Transportation," pp. 5–6. For detailed case studies of seven cities see Urban Mass Transportation Administration, *Increasing Transit Ridership: The Experience of Seven Cities* (Washington, D.C.: Urban Mass Transportation Administration, 1976).

37. For a review of the experiences of several cities with new rail systems, see Robert L. Knight, "The Impact of Rail Transit on Land Use: Evidence and a Change in Perspective," *Transportation* 9 (1980): 3–16.

38. For a comparison of the development incentives offered by expressways and rail transit, see John R. Meyer and Jose A. Gomez-Ibañez, *Autos, Transit and Cities*, pp. 104–122; Jose A. Gomez-Ibañez, "Using Transportation Policy to Shape Metropolitan Development," forthcoming in *Transportation Research*, vol. 2, 1984.

39. For a more complete discussion of the problems of poverty and transportation see Meyer and Gomez-Ibañez, *Autos, Transit and Cities*, pp. 230–53; and Jose A. Gomez-Ibañez, "Transportation and the Poor," pp. 143–70 in *The State and the Poor in the 1980s*, ed. Manuel Carballo and Mary Jo Bane (Cambridge, Mass.: Auburn House, 1983).

40. John Pucher, Chris Hendrickson, and Sue McNeil, "Socioeconomic Characteristics of Transit Riders: Some Recent Evidence," *Traffic Quarterly* 35 (1981): 466.

41. J. Richard Kuzmyak, *Household Vehicle Ownership*, report no. 2 of the *1977 Nationwide Personal Transportation Study* (Washington, D.C.: U.S. Government Printing Office, 1980), pp. 66.

42. Households with 1977–1978 incomes below $6000 account for 16 percent of all persons and 22 percent of all households in metropolitan areas; see Pucher, Hendrickson, and McNeil, "Transit Riders," p. 464.

43. Ibid., p. 464.

44. Ibid., pp. 468, 470.

45. Only 14 percent of the elderly and 40 percent of the handicapped were poor as of 1977, although the poor were probably disproportionately represented among the elderly and handicapped mass transit riders. For statistics on the size of the poor, elderly, and handicapped groups and their mobility problems see Meyer and Gomez-Ibañez, *Autos, Transit and Cities*, pp. 234–46.

46. See Bruce D. Spear, "User-Side Subsidies: Delivering Special Needs Transportation through Private Providers," paper presented at the annual meeting of the Transportation Research Board, Washington, D.C., January 1982.

47. For examples of this argument see Lyle C. Fitch and Associates, *Transportation and Public Policy* (San Francisco, Calif.: Chandler, 1964); Thomas E. Lisco, "Mass Transportation: Cinderella in Our Cities," *The Public Interest* no. 18 (1970): 52–74. The contrast between the overcapitalization and the demographic hypotheses was shown most clearly in George W. Hilton, "The Urban Mass Transportation Assistance Program," pp. 131–44 in *Perspectives on Federal Transportation Policy*, ed. James C. Miller, III (Washington, D.C.: American Enterprise Institute, 1975); and George W. Hilton, *Federal Transit Subsidies* (Washington, D.C.: American Enterprise Institute, 1974).

48. The advent of federal operating aid in 1974 did not change this incentive, since the allocation formulas insure that the size of an urban area's operating grant is only slightly and indirectly influenced by capital projects. Under the original 1974 operating grant formula, funds were allocated to urbanized areas on the basis of population and population density, so the receipt of capital grants did not influence operating aid. Congress changed the operating aid formulas in 1978 and again in 1982 to allocate some aid according to transit ridership and vehicle mileage. By changing levels of rail and bus patronage or mileage, therefore, a capital grant may alter the level of operating aid.

49. William B. Tye, "The Capital Grant as a Subsidy Device: The Case Study of Urban Mass Transportation," in *Transportation Subsidies*, pt. 6 of *The Economics of Federal Subsidy Programs*, U.S. Congress, Joint Economic Committee (Washington, D.C.: U.S. Government Printing Office, 1973), pp. 796–826.

50. American Public Transit Association, *Transit Fact Book 1981* (Washington, D.C.: American Public Transit Association, 1981).

51. Several studies came to similar conclusions about the travel volume necessary to support rail transit. See John R. Meyer, John F. Kain, and Martin Wohl, *The Urban Transportation Problem* (Cambridge, Mass.: Harvard, 1965), pp. 299–306; Keeler and Small, *Automobile Costs*; and J. Hayden Boyd, Norman J. Asher, and Elliot S. Wetzler, *Evaluation of Rail Rapid Transit and Express Bus Service in the Urban Commuter Market*, report prepared by the Institute for Defense Analyses for the U.S. Department of Transportation (Washington, D.C.: U.S. Government Printing Office, 1973). A recent study by Boris Pushkarev and Jeffery Zupan argues that rail transit dominates bus at lower volumes than those reported here. Don Pickrell has demonstrated, however, that several of Pushkarev and Zupan's key assumptions appear unduly favorable to rail. See Boris Pushkarev and Jeffery Zupan, *Urban Rail in America: An Exploration of Criteria for Fixed-Guideway Transit*, report no. UMTA–06–0061–80–1 to the U.S. Urban Mass Transportation Administration (Washington, D.C.: U.S. Mass Transportation Administration, 1980); and Don H. Pickrell, "How Many More Subways Does the U.S. Need?" paper presented at the annual meeting of the Association of Collegiate Schools of Planning, New York, October 1984.

52. Meyer and Gomez-Ibañez, *Autos, Transit and Cities*, p. 52.

53. Boris Pushkarev and Jeffery Zupan do compare bus and light rail costs in their recent study but, as noted in note 51, their results appear to derive from some questionable assumptions.

54. T. J. McGean et al., *Assessment of the San Diego Light Rail System* (Washington, D.C.: U.S. Urban Mass Transportation Administration, report no. UMTA–IT–06–0248–84–1, November 1983), pp. 5–29.

55. Jose A. Gomez-Ibañez, "Light Rail Transit: The Record to Date," photocopy, July 1984, pp. 13–14.

56. For a description of the federal requirements and their limitations, see David M. Kennedy, "UMTA and the New Rail Start Policy," draft case, John F. Kennedy School of Government, Harvard University, 1984.

57. For a description of the proposed system and initial reactions see "Mass Transit: The Expensive Dream," *Business Week*, 27 August 1984, pp. 62–69.

58. Don H. Pickrell, "The Causes of Rising Transit Operating Deficits," report no. MA–11–0037 to the U.S. Urban Mass Transportation Administration, John F. Kennedy School of Government, Harvard University, 1983.

59. See P. H. Bly, F. V. Webster, and Susan Pounds, "Effects of Subsidies on Urban Public Transport," *Transportation* 9 (1980): 311–31; Robert Cervero, "Cost and Performance Impacts of Transit Subsidy Programs," paper presented at the Transportation Research Board Meetings, Washington, D.C., 1982; Pucher, Markstedt, and Hirschman, "Impact of Subsidies," pp. 155–76; John Pucher, "Effects of Subsidies on Transport Costs," *Transportation Quarterly* 36 (1982): 549–62; and Shirley C. Anderson, "The Effect of Government Ownership and Subsidy on Performance: Evidence from the Bus Transit Industry," *Transportation Research* 17A (1983): 191–200.

60. U.S. Urban Mass Transportation Administration, *National Urban Mass Transportation Statistics, 1982 Section 15 Annual Report* (Washington, D.C.: U.S. Government Printing Office, 1983), pp. 3–15 to 3–22.

61. For estimates of the distribution of operating aid to selected cities under the 1974, 1978, and 1982 formulas, see John Pucher, "Distribution of Federal Transportation Subsidies," *Urban Affairs Quarterly* 19 (1983): 191–216, esp. pp. 196 and 209.

62. The eight include the District of Columbia ($258 per capita), Maryland ($69), Massachusetts ($63), New York ($40), Georgia ($37), New Jersey ($28), Illinois ($27), and Pennsylvania ($23). See John Pucher, "The Distribution of Federal Transportation Subsidies," *Urban Affairs Quarterly* 19 (1983): 200.

63. The ratio of federal transportation grants to taxes in the states was 1.7 in Massachusetts; 1.1 in New York; 0.9 in Illinois; 0.8 in Pennsylvania, Michigan, and New Jersey; 0.7 in Indiana and Rhode Island; and 0.6 in Ohio and California. See Pucher, "Distribution of Federal Transportation Subsidies," p. 202.

CHAPTER EIGHT

The Agenda for Metropolitan Housing Policies

Sherman Maisel

Virtually every country, including the United States, has over the years developed a wide range of governmental housing policies. The stated goals are to insure each household the opportunity to live in a decent house in a suitable environment at a cost that would leave sufficient income available for other needs. Governments have also been concerned with the efficiency of housing production, the damage to the industry and to the housing market from cyclical swings in output, and the availability and use of credit. At the local level, deterioration of neighborhoods and central cities impose large-scale costs on individuals. Such changes cannot be reversed by private action. They require government programs.

In the past fifty years the United States government has built up an exceedingly complex, extensive, and expensive mélange of programs in such spheres as assistance to low-income families; community development and slum clearance; mortgage insurance and guarantee; secondary market institutions and operations; tax subsidies for homeownership and rental housing; policy development and research; equal opportunities; and consumer protection.

In seeking to plan an agenda for the future, we must examine the main factors that brought these programs into existence. Were they based on the peculiar institutional requirements of housing, or were they primarily the result of industry and bureaucratic pressures? Are they the remains of logical reactions to past needs that have far outlived their usefulness, or will they continue to be useful? How can their efficiency be improved?

RECENT DEVELOPMENTS AND
THE FUTURE HOUSING AGENDA

When the Reagan administration came into office, it resolved to change existing housing policies. It was concerned that housing was taking too large a share of the government's budget, of national saving, of capital investment, and of the money available in the credit markets. It believed that "the genius of the market economy, freed of the distortions forced by government housing policies and regulations . . . can provide for housing far better than Federal Programs."[1]

To implement its program, the administration called for reductions in several types of government expenditures on housing. It advocated curtailing or halting much governmental effort in credit markets. It appointed the President's Commission on Housing, chaired by William F. McKenna. The April 1982 report of this commission is frequently cited as the basic documentation and philosophical basis for the Reagan administration's housing agenda.

The commission identified major problems: (1) affordability of decent houses for low-income families and first-home buyers; (2) a shortage of rental units; (3) a cyclical shortage of jobs and disturbingly large losses and bankruptcies among building contractors; and (4) hard times, losses, bankruptcies, and market disruption in the housing finance industry, particularly among savings and loan associations and savings banks.

The commission recommended that government programs be reoriented in order to address these problems directly. Instead of federal programs, the country ought to rely on the private sector; encourage free and deregulated housing markets; promote an enlightened federalism with minimum government intervention; and recognize the government's continuing role in meeting the housing needs of the poor.[2]

Its specific recommendations, on the whole, were far from earthshaking. For political reasons, both nationally and within the commission, it failed to recommend action with respect to the most expensive programs. Contrary to its stated philosophy, it urged increased federal intervention in others. Basically, it proposed:

1. That government programs aimed at increasing the supply of dwellings be replaced by a voucher program, which would subsidize people rather than structures.[3]

2. That most government programs for homeowners' mortgage insur-

ance and in the secondary market be removed or reduced, but that
the government aid in the development of new mortgage
instruments.

3. That the thrift industry be restructured and both housing finance
and building undergo deregulation.

4. That the tax-expenditure programs for homeownership be continued.

5. That the tax incentives for mortgage lending be expanded and new
subsidies be introduced.

6. That federal intervention be reduced except when the federal government believed that states and localities were misusing their powers in spheres such as zoning, building codes, rent controls, and due-
on-sale clauses. In such cases, the general concept of federalism
should be put aside and the federal government should increase its
intervention.

On the whole, the administration has adopted this agenda, although the
eagerness with which it has pursued particular recommendations has
varied greatly.

I believe that both the commission's proposals and the administration's
agenda are faulty. It is true that the government urban programs are large
and expensive and that in credit markets they have far-reaching effects.
However, the administration's agenda does not deal with the most expensive programs—tax expenditures for homeowners and for mortgage
lenders. Its suggestions with respect to neglecting construction and pri-
vatizing credit appear flawed. It aims at curtailing aid to communities
without a careful evaluation of the costs and benefits. While it emphasizes
decentralized decisionmaking, its recommendations and laws go in the
opposite direction. Most of the suggestions for local action are rehashes
of suggestions that have been made repeatedly for over fifty years. It is
hard to explain why, if they are truly efficient proposals, they have never
been adopted. The agenda is weak because it is based on insufficient
analysis, poor economic theories, and perverse views of proper government actions with respect to income distribution. It neglects significant
factors in the housing sphere.

In the following analysis I argue that there are major reasons why
government intervention in the housing market may improve both individual and national welfare. Both economic theory and history argue
against the view that a private housing market can do as well as or better

than one aided by government policies. In the housing sphere, market results may be improved by government policies.

Proper analysis must examine the areas of possible improvement. A logical agenda must consider whether the implementation of government programs is likely to be successful. The amount of government expenditure for each proposal must also be analyzed to judge whether the nation is getting its money's worth or whether particular programs should be cut back or abolished. The competition between housing and other investments should be compared to see whether any clear evidence exists that investment or use of financial or real resources has been excessive. The results of such analysis can be improved if they start and are carried forward from a neutral intellectual base.

From the following analysis, I conclude that some of the commission's proposals make sense, while others should be altered or forgotten.

1. The problem of the ill-housed should be recognized as one caused primarily by households that are poor because they are out of the employment market. On the whole, income too low to afford housing occurs mainly among a few specific groups in the economy, namely, the elderly, families with female heads, and some very large families, principally among minorities. In some of these cases, the type of housing needed can be so specialized that it may require new construction.

2. Currently a problem also exists for moderate-income first buyers and for some tenants just above the poverty line in high-cost localities. The problem arises from inflation, with a resulting mortgage tilt, and also from high real interest rates. These needs can be attacked through improved credit programs to shape cash flows to real costs, through better targeting of tax expenditures, and through more attention to community development.

3. By far the most expensive program is the aid to homeownership through tax expenditures. Not only are these programs expensive, they are perverse: the higher one's income, the larger is the public's contribution. Similarly, tax aids for existing rental units tend to be as large as or larger than for new ones. Only slight effort has been made to limit subsidies to new supply. Tax expenditures are an extremely difficult political problem; still, no agenda for the future should neglect the most expensive of housing programs.

4. The government's attack on many of the credit programs seems ill

advised. These programs perform an important function in reducing risks and increasing the efficiency of the market. Most are self-supporting or could easily be made so. An initial purpose of most of these programs was to aid in the stabilization of production. This logical goal appears to have been forgotten, but it should be reemphasized. Still, most of the pressure for abolishing these programs seems to arise from a misapplication of political dogma. Unless pragmatic, not theoretical, reasons are advanced for terminating successfully functioning programs, they should be continued. However, attempts should be made to improve their efficiency and to see that they serve the needs of the overall economy rather than a few industry groups.

5. Finally, the programs to aid communities and for housing renewal and rehabilitation should be given more complete analysis. Economic theory appears to support such expenditures. It is not obvious why they should be a principal target of budget-cutting. Whether cuts or increases are proper depends on an analysis of their efficiency and what may be gained from existing or better-structured programs.

FEDERAL EXPENDITURES FOR HOUSING

In the United States as elsewhere, the unique features of housing have led to numerous governmental programs aimed at solving capital cost and financing problems, reducing cyclical instability, and aiding in the maintenance and rehabilitation of declining communities. The Department of Housing and Urban Development (HUD) lists over seventy programs it currently administers.[4] This list is far from complete; many of the most expensive and significant programs lie outside HUD's jurisdiction.

Table 8.1 shows that in 1984, the various housing programs entail budget and tax expenditures of about $60 billion. This is 5 percent of the nearly $1180 billion contained in the federal budget plus tax expenditures. Clearly, a reexamination of the housing agenda should play a significant role in any formulation of government policies. The expenditure numbers in Table 8.1 are not exact, nor are the categorical breakdowns; tax expenditures are subject to significant estimating errors, and many programs serve dual purposes. The relative orders of magnitude would not, however, change much if other existing procedures were used.

TABLE 8.1
Costs and Commitments of Federal Government to Housing Programs
(billions of dollars)

	1983 (actual)	1984 (estimated)	1985 (estimated)
Tax expenditures	41.7	44.7	48.2
Low-rent assistance	12.1	12.5	12.2
Community development	4.3	4.3	4.3
Housing credit, loans, insurance, guarantees			
Annual transactions	120.5	125.2	139.5
Total outstanding	480.0	530.0	580.0

SOURCE: Tables 8.4, 8.6, 8.7, 8.8.

Similar problems arise in estimating the federal presence in credit markets. Table 8.1 excludes some of the credit transactions that relate to intragovernmental loans used to minimize the budget costs of certain assistance programs. It also excludes Government National Mortgage Association (GNMA) guarantees that duplicate other government insurance and guarantees. However, a fair amount of duplication still remains, because a considerable portion of the portfolios of the Federal National Mortgage Association (FNMA) consists of government-insured and government-guaranteed loans.

HOUSING COMPLEXITY AND EXPENSE

Housing remains a universal problem because it is an expensive necessity. It takes a major share of both national and individual resources. It plays a critical role in the ups and downs of inflation. The Reagan housing agenda was initially based on a fear that housing was playing a deleterious part in the national economy. Supply-side economics emphasized the lack of investment in plant and equipment as a key factor explaining the decline in growth during the 1970s, and blamed the unfair or undesirable competition by housing for economic resources for some of this failure to invest elsewhere.

Houses require a great deal of capital, and the annual payments for housing services are large compared to the income of many families. The cost of an average new dwelling unit is currently over $80,000, or more than three times the income of the average family. The amount of capital required for housing competes directly with other demands on total national saving (capital), such as plant and equipment or lending to the government to fund the public debt. In 1983, residential construction was 27 percent of total private fixed investment, compared to a peak of 42 percent in 1950, 35.5 percent in 1963, and 34.5 percent in 1972. It reflected, however, a considerable recovery from the 20 percent share in the severe recession year of 1982.

Very few homeowners or landlords can accumulate the capital needed for such large investments; it must be borrowed from those who have saved. Lending on residential mortgages is by far the largest activity in credit markets. In mid 1984, outstanding residential mortgages exceeded $1.4 billion, or more than 23 percent of the total outstanding private domestic debt. The task of raising this capital and lending it on a sound basis to millions of individuals occupies a fair share of the time of financial institutions. The market is complex, consisting of both general-purpose and specialized institutions operating in both the primary and secondary markets. Its demand for funds affects—and in turn is influenced in differing degrees by—all other financing activities.

In addition, the size and individual location of each dwelling create specialized needs for the organization of the housing industry and its methods of production. Houses are large, heavy, complex, composed of a large number of materials and subassemblies. Dwellings must be attached to individual sites, which involves a difficult, time-consuming, decentralized development and construction process.

The demand for construction fluctuates widely. Because of the amount of capital required, most of which must be borrowed and repaid over long periods, demand is strongly influenced by changes in interest rates and the availability of credit. Because the additions to supply in any year are small compared to the existing stock, changes in the demand for existing units greatly affect construction demand. Demand is met through a highly competitive decentralized reaction of numerous builders. The supply process is quite lengthy, particularly when the planning, financing, and permit process is included. Thus supply can greatly exceed demand, or can fail to meet it.

As a result of these forces, the number of dwellings started per quarter has varied by well over 100 percent in the course of individual business cycles. For example, the rate of starts at the beginning of 1982 was only about 40 percent of the rate at the end of 1978. By spring of 1983, the rate had increased by over 100 percent. Similarly, residential construction was over 5.9 percent of the GNP at the end of 1977, falling to about 2.8 percent in mid 1982.

These forces together affect the structure of the housing industry in two ways. First, the industry's organization allows comparatively rapid adjustment of production to the market. Firms have minimal investments in fixed plant or equipment. Relations with labor, material suppliers, and subcontractors tend to be temporary and to allow for large swings in the level of production. Resources are shifted in and out of the industry with comparative ease. The costs of this flexibility are high wages, high peak profits, and relatively unspecialized techniques and equipment. Most observers believe that costs are raised in direct proportion to the degree of fluctuation. Second, even if no cyclical requirements existed, the industry's organization would be heavily influenced by the complexity of its product and the need to produce houses attached to individual sites in disparate local markets. House-building primarily consists of transportation of large volumes of heavy materials to and on specific lots. The land must be specially prepared. The assembly process is complicated by the variety of materials and the physical dispersion of sites.

The degree of rationality with which the industry has adjusted to its unique tasks has been debated for over eighty years. The government has engaged in various minor programs aimed at changing the structure of the industry. President Reagan's commission placed great emphasis on such programs and urged that the dictates of federalism be pushed aside, if necessary, to enforce centralized deregulation on states and localities. I know of no evidence to support the popular belief that the industry has not adjusted in the most efficient manner. No one has been able to show where greater efficiencies would come from or why they have not been introduced if they exist.

The issue of cyclical stability is also debated. Many observers feel that if demand could be stabilized, the costs of production could be reduced. Some of the existing industry features are efficient only because of the need to adjust to wide swings in demand. Because of the need to build in flexibility and to avoid fixed costs, productivity is reduced. Wages and other payments to the factors of production are high to compensate for unemployment, which tends to reach levels well above those of other industries. Because prices shoot up in periods of excess demand, income becomes maldistributed. Excess factor prices recede slowly, if at all, in the following recessions. A more stable environment might lead to significant changes in these areas.

TABLE 8.2

Housing Costs as a Percentage of Income
(United States, inside SMSAs, 1981)

| | Number of households (thousands) | | | % households | | | |
	Income below $8500	Income above $8500	Total	Income below $8500	Income above $8500	Total
Owner-occupied						
Housing costs under 30% of income	1,112	20,341	21,453	36%	87%	81%
Housing costs 30% of income or more	1,949	2,974	4,923	64	13	19
Not reported or calculated	633	2,086	2,719	–	–	–
Total	3,694	25,401	29,095	100%	100%	100%
Renters						
Gross rents under 30% of income	1,504	9,920	11,424	21%	74%	55%
Gross rents 30% of income or more	5,622	3,775	9,397	79	26	45
Not reported or calculated	538	358	896	–	–	–
Total	7,664	14,053	21,717	100%	100%	100%

SOURCE: U.S Department of Housing and Urban Development, *National Housing Survey* (Washington, D.C.: U.S. Government Printing Office, 1981), H–150–81, Part B, table A-1.

In contrast, some argue that it is good national policy to concentrate instability in the housing sphere. Fluctuations in construction have only minimal effects on the availability of shelter, since movements in vacancies offset most variations in the rate at which new units come into the market. Only an extremely long period of subnormal activity in construction leads to overcrowding.

While disagreements are possible, my own view is that the country would be better off if housing production were more stable. If the economy requires sectors that can release resources in periods of excess demand, it would be better if the instability were shared more equitably with other industries. Shelter costs would be lower and welfare higher with a more stable housing production, leading to improvements in productivity and a more even distribution of income.

Because housing capital requirements are so large and because the structure of the industry is unique, in most economies it has been thought of as a major problem. Over the years the industry's structure has been under constant attack. Because it differs so greatly from others, it has been assumed—but never proved—to be faulty. However, emphasis on housing's competition for both real and financial resources is a new issue. While the scarcity of resources was always of concern in developing economies, most industrialized nations in the past viewed the macroeconomic problem of housing as one of fluctuating rather than excessive demand. Traditionally, their primary concern was over affordability, either directly, that is, the costs were too large a drain on the income of individual households, or indirectly, that is, too many families lived in substandard dwellings since they could not afford the cost of adequate houses.

Table 8.2 illustrates one measure of the affordability problem. It shows the number and percentage of households in 1981 who reported spending more than 30 percent of their income for housing (mortgage payments, property taxes, and utilities for owners; gross rent for tenants).

The required payments for housing services are large, and they are far from constant either in absolute terms or relative to household incomes. Current service costs depend on the real mortgage rate (a function of real interest rates, the costs and risks of mortgage lending, and changes in relative housing prices). They also must cover depreciation (low, in most cases) and basic maintenance. In addition, utility expenses, which grew rapidly with the acceleration in energy prices, must be covered. Finally, houses are taxed for local services which may or may not be related to

TABLE 8.3

Percentage of United States Families Able to Afford a New House

Year	Median price, new home	Effective interest rate	Terms of mortgage (years)	Median monthly Payment[a]	Median monthly family income	% affording median house[b]
1970	$23,400	8.45%	25.1	$180	$ 728	60%
1975	39,300	9.01	26.8	310	983	48
1980	64,600	12.66	28.1	632	1589	32
1984	81,000	13.40	27.3	832	1958	32

[a]Based on 75% mortage and 2% property taxes.
[b]Assuming mortgage and property payment not to exceed 30% of income.
SOURCE: Derived by author from U.S. Census and Federal Home Loan Bank Board data.

their shelter function. Offsetting some of these expenses are potential subsidies, either direct or through income-tax deductions.

In the past decade, the cost of many housing services rose at a more rapid rate than family incomes. The price of housing units rose relative to other prices. In the 1970s, inflation and tax subsidies made real interest rates extremely low or even negative for many families. In the 1980s, underlying real interest rates shot up. Risks inherent in real-estate lending became more obvious, raising real mortgage rates even more. Energy prices rose extremely quickly to record levels. Income-tax changes lowered the tax subsidy to homeownerships, while raising it for rental units.

As real housing costs increased rapidly, real household incomes stagnated. Median real household incomes in 1984 are well below the amounts earned in past peak income years such as 1969, 1973, and 1978. Furthermore, the national poverty rate has been increasing. In 1983, it was at the highest level in eighteen years. Increased costs and decreased incomes have meant that affordability of housing has become a critical national issue.

The degree to which affordability affects households, however, varies widely depending on their income and also on whether they already own a dwelling or are entering the market for the first time.

Difficulties occur primarily among tenant families—particularly those who are poor. More than 45 percent of all tenants reported that they paid over 30 percent of their income for rent in 1981 (Table 8.2). The percentage of poor in this category was nearly 79 percent. While rents as a share of income fall as incomes rise, affordability was also a problem for moderate-income families.

Table 8.3 measures changes in affordability for home purchasers. It indicates the percentage of families who could meet mortgage payments and property taxes on the median newly built house if they allocated no more than 30 percent of their income for this purpose. Under this standard, the percentage of families who could afford a new house fell from about 60 percent in 1970 to 48 percent in 1975, and to 32 percent in 1980. It reached a low of 27 percent in 1981. With interest rates below their 1981 highs and incomes rising faster than house prices, the index returned to 32 percent in 1984—just more than half of its 1970 level.

Such simple indexes tend to be arbitrary. Definitions differ, as do the underlying data.[5] Tastes change. With rising incomes families can spend more for housing. The percentage of income the average family devotes to housing has risen and can rise further. By definition, half of the houses produced cost less than the median, while existing houses cost less than new ones. The number of potential purchasers is raised because of these lower-priced units. On the other hand, the index makes no provision for the fact that housing markets are local. For example, in California housing prices rose far more than the national average. In California, according to this index, the percentage who can afford a new house is only two-thirds of the national average, while in highest-cost localities it is less than half.

In contrast, Table 8.2 reports that even with a broader definition of expense, only about 19 percent of owner households reported spending more than 30 percent of their income for housing. This figure is much smaller because most owners bought their houses in earlier days at lower prices. On the average, owners occupy their houses for about eight years. Because mortgage expenses tend to be fixed at the time of purchase, rising incomes and inflation decrease the mortgage burden. With higher prices, owners who relocate have capital gains which reduce their mortgage requirements. In 1981, almost one-third of owner-households reported no outstanding mortgage.

This and similar analyses indicate that the problem of affordability can be divided. It differs somewhat for three separate groups: families in poverty or with low incomes and special housing needs; first-time buyers or those forced by circumstances to move from a low-cost to a high-cost locality; and the majority of families, who can afford adequate housing but who would prefer to have more income available for other uses. If the expenses of shelter were lower, they would be better off.

RENTAL ASSISTANCE FOR LOW-INCOME FAMILIES

Table 8.4 estimates that the United States government currently spends about $12 billion annually on assisting low-income families to meet their rent bills; of this, only about $2 billion is spent in rural areas. About 3.9 million households receive aid. In this table, as in the preceding ones, estimates have considerable variance. The actual subsidies have been greatly manipulated for budget purposes, making exact estimates difficult if not impossible.

The Reagan administration has recommended that the number of assisted households be limited to current totals, that expenditures be reduced, and that in the future rent vouchers be gradually substituted for existing programs: "The purpose of Federal housing programs should be to help people, not to build projects."[6] Congress has more or less acquiesced. The 1984–1985 programs call for minimum construction of

TABLE 8.4

Federal Housing Assistance Programs
(billions of dollars)

	1983 (actual)	1984 (estimated)	1985 (estimated)	Assisted units (millions)
Low-income housing (Section 8)	6.3	6.3	6.3	1.7
Public housing	2.8	2.8	2.8	1.3
Demonstration vouchers	0.2	0.2	0.2	
Rural housing programs	1.8	2.2	1.9	0.9
Other (including elderly)	1.0	1.0	1.0	
Total	12.1	12.5	12.2	3.9

SOURCE: U.S. Office of Management and Budget and Congressional Budget Office.

about 12,000 new units for public housing, Indians, and the elderly together with an expanded voucher demonstration program.

These proposals raise several issues. Why is a federal housing program necessary if it is not to deal with the supply of units? Since housing vouchers are an inefficient method of subsidizing incomes and exert a minimal impact on housing standards, what good does such a program hope to do? Table 8.2 showed that affordability is primarily a problem for the poor. In 1984, between 14 and 15 percent of the population were in poverty. Of this group, about 79 percent of renter households and 64 percent of owner households spent over 30 percent of their income for housing. This target group for housing assistance is enlarged by the need to include some families lying just above the poverty line.

Table 8.5 illustrates some of the details of the poverty class. Only about one-quarter were families with a male head under 65. Of these, a minority were fully employed. In fact, only about 10 percent of the over 12 million households in poverty had a fully employed head. The poor are concentrated among families with female or non-family heads and the elderly; these groups tend not to be in the labor force. Of the traditional families with fully employed heads included in the poverty group, most are unskilled minority workers with large households. (Data are corrected for family size.)

Initially housing assistance programs were aimed at the ill-housed one-third of the nation. However, many housing difficulties facing normal families in the past were solved by a rise in income. Current estimates are that about 7 percent of urban houses are substandard. For various tech-

TABLE 8.5
Households in Poverty, 1982
(thousands)

	Head under 65	Head 65 and over	Total
Male family head	3,398	670	4,068
Female family head	3,217	227	3,444
Total	6,615	897	7,512
Male unrelated	1,168	348	1,516
Female unrelated	1,355	1,777	3,132
Total	2,523	2,125	4,648
Grand Total	9,138	3,022	12,160

SOURCE: U.S. Bureau of the Census, *Current Population Report* (Washington, D.C.: U.S. Government Printing Office, 1984), P-60 No. 144, tables 5, 20, 23.

nical reasons, this probably overestimates the problem. Substandard housing is hard to define statistically; the Census Bureau has worked on this problem for thirty years without much success.

Because they lack potential wage-earners, most households in poverty do not have incomes that rise with growth in the economy. They cannot afford standard housing now and will not be able to do so in the future. These people constitute the hard core of both the housing and poverty problems. However, when we examine government housing programs, we note that only from 15 to 20 percent of those in poverty receive direct housing assistance. (Probably one-third of the assisted lie above the poverty line.) How is this possible? What do the other 80 percent of the poor do to obtain standard housing? About half of the unassisted poor are homeowners. Their current housing costs may be low, or they may have additional capital. The majority of the remaining poverty households have their housing paid for through Aid to Families with Dependent Children (AFDC) or other welfare programs.

The fact that so much of housing assistance comes through general income assistance rather than direct housing aid raises the basic issue of why general income supplements should not take the place of housing assistance, especially since most observers believe income supplements are preferable to categorical grants. The question is usually answered in one of two ways: (1) active lobbies insure that aid to the poor through categorical housing grants will exceed that available through income supplements; or (2) the housing needs of the poor are specialized—if government programs did not directly increase the available supply, too few standard units would be available at affordable rents. Neither of these answers furnishes a logical basis for a voucher program. If government assistance is not required to increase the supply of units available at low rents, then the basic reason for a separate housing program has disappeared. Money going to a separate voucher program might be better spent on other needed urban programs or on general relief.

TAX EXPENDITURE AND CREDIT PROGRAMS

While most debates have been over public housing and rental assistance programs, Table 8.1 showed that these programs make up only a small part of the cost of federal assistance. Most expenditure and credit programs benefit homeowners; only minor portions aid the owners of rental properties. Tax expenditure subsidies reduce costs. Credit programs make more mortgages available at reduced costs and with greater stability. They lower the costs of housing services by reducing interest rates and the costs of production. They also may make houses easier to buy by easing cash flow difficulties.

On the whole, expenditures have not been well targeted. Better structuring of tax expenditure and of credit aids could help, but the Reagan agenda proposes only a few minor improvements. It appears retrogressive in several critical spheres.

Table 8.6 shows the distribution of tax expenditures by type. As indicated in Table 8.1, these are by far the most expensive federal housing programs. Homeowners are allowed to reduce the amount of income tax they pay by deducting interest and property taxes from gross income. Tax reductions resulting from these deductions totaled $34 billion in 1983 and are expected to rise to nearly $41 billion in 1985. Special capital gains treatments, currently at nearly $3 billion, are rising steadily. The other three considerably smaller subsidies cover expenditures that go partly to homeowners and partly to reduce rents on tenant units.

Estimates of tax expenditures are subject to considerable variation depending on the assumptions used. In addition, some observers object to the entire concept of tax expenditures on the theory that the only taxes owed are those enacted into laws. They believe that exemptions should not be examined one by one. Failure to tax should not be thought of as a subsidy even if the tax law is shaped so as to aid a particular function. In addition some, incorrectly, argue that the deductibility of mortgage interest and property taxes on owner-occupied housing is no special advantage because they are deductible in any business. What this argument fails to

TABLE 8.6

Tax Expenditures of the Federal Government for Housing
(billions of dollars)

	1983 (actual)	1984 (estimate)	1985 (estimate)
Deductions on owner-occupied homes			
Mortgage interest	25.1	27.9	30.1
Property taxes	8.8	9.5	10.5
Deferral of capital gains	0.8	1.1	1.3
Exclusion of capital gains for owners over 55	1.3	1.6	1.9
Total	36.0	40.1	43.8
Exclusion of state and local bond interest	1.6	1.7	1.7
Tax breaks for mortgage lenders	2.7	1.1	0.8
Tax breaks for rental properties	1.4	1.8	1.9
Grand Total	41.7	44.7	48.2

SOURCE: U.S. Congressional Budget Office, *Tax Expenditures: Current Issues and Five-year Budget Projections for Fiscal Years 1984–88* (Washington, D.C.: U.S. Government Printing Office, 1983), table A4.

recognize is that in the other cases income from ownership must be reported and the deductions are legitimate expenses of creating the income. In the case of owner occupation, the deductions are against sources of income arising elsewhere. A subsidy occurs because we do not report the imputed income from renting the house to ourselves.

Both economic and social reasons have been advanced for subsidizing homeownership. An increase in the percentage owning and living in their own homes can increase both individual and the national welfare. Homeownership increases the efficiency with which housing capital is used: owners take better care of their own property; maintenance is cheaper because much is performed in what would otherwise be leisure time, thus increasing total available labor and the real GNP; and no management costs are incurred. The level of national savings is increased as required mortgage payments lead to forced savings, as do investments in rehabilitation and new improvements. Various social and political advantages are said to arise from the fact that owners are more stable. Homeowners tend to take a greater interest in their community. The desire to increase the value of one's house results in a more attractive and safer neighborhood.

On the other hand, the tax expenditures have been opposed on the grounds that they improperly aid housing at the expense of other investment, are not efficient, are too expensive, and are perverse in their effects on income distribution.

Government credit programs developed because households can invest in housing only by borrowing large sums of money. Furthermore, it has been clear for many years that some of the wide fluctuations in house-building arise from prior movements in the cost and availability of credit. Starting in the Great Depression, the government has offered programs that served to lower down payments and lengthen amortization periods. Other programs have decreased credit costs by widening the geographic markets for funds.

The magnitude of some of the credit programs is brought out in Table 8.7. The top part of the table shows insurance and guarantees for private mortgages and tax-exempt bonds issued by local public housing authorities. In recent years, the three government agencies involved have issued $75 to $80 billion of these guarantees per year. Guarantees outstanding total over $300 billion. The FHA programs are virtually self-supporting. The losses on VA guarantees are not large and are considered a veteran benefit offered in lieu of bonuses paid in earlier wars. Payments on the public housing bonds are part of the costs shown under housing assistance.

The second category shows portfolio loans made by the government-sponsored agencies—the Federal Home Loan Bank System (FHLB), the Federal National Mortgage Association (FNMA), and the Federal Home Loan Mortgage Corporation (FHLMC). In this period these agencies are expected to increase their portfolios by about $10 billion a year. Their outstanding portfolios total about $150 billion. In addition, these agencies plus the Government National Mortgage Association (GNMA) are expected to issue about $100 billion in bonds, certificates, and guarantees against private mortgages. Only part of these sums are in addition to those listed above, since all of those from GNMA plus parts of the others duplicate to a large extent guarantees already given by the FHA and VA and thus are already counted. Including these in the government total is double counting.

The reasoning behind each of these programs is quite straightforward. A reduction in the price of credit can make houses more affordable. Large cyclical swings in credit availability cause major inefficiencies as well as distress for the firms and labor employed in house-building. High credit costs and periods in which credit is rationed or unavailable cause the average level of housing production to fall below the optimum. If government programs could be properly devised and administered, they would serve to improve the nation's housing standard, increase economic stability, and lower housing costs.

TABLE 8.7
Government Programs to Increase Housing Credit and Flows
(billions of dollars)

Housing credit	Transactions			Outstanding		
	1983 (actual)	1984 (estimated)	1985 (estimated)	1983 (actual)	1984 (estimated)	1985 (estimated)
Mortgage insurance and guarantees						
FHA	44.6	46.6	49.2	157.0	—	—
VA	15.5	18.6	22.9	122.0	—	—
Low-cost public housing	14.3	14.7	14.7	29.0	—	—
Total	74.4	79.9	86.8	308.0	—	—
Portfolio loans						
FNMA	18.1	13.5	15.0	75.2	79.3	79.6
FHL banks	−10.3	2.8	5.4	60.4	63.3	68.7
FHLMC	1.7	2.4	4.2	6.9	9.3	13.5
Total	9.5	18.7	24.6	142.5	151.9	161.8
Mortgage pools and guarantees						
FNMA	17.5	13.0	17.4	23.8	33.6	46.7
FHLMC	19.1	13.6	10.7	54.2	67.8	78.5
GNMA	61.8	68.3	71.4	159.9	204.3	249.7
Total	98.4	94.9	99.5	237.9	305.7	374.9

SOURCE: U.S. Office of Management and Budget, *The Budget for Fiscal Year 1985, Special Analyses,* and U.S. Congressional Budget Office, *An Analysis of the President's Credit Budget for Fiscal Year 1985, Staff Working Paper,* March 1984.

The basic idea that the government could lower credit costs and increase credit stability has led to the growth of the programs shown in Table 8.7. The FHA–VA insurance and guarantee programs have at times underwritten nearly half of all housing starts. In recent years, they have also been prominent in helping finance the resale of existing units. The direct purchases, mortgage pass-throughs, and other funds furnished through GNMA, FNMA, FHLMC, and FHLB have dominated the mortgage market.

Before the introduction of the government programs, housing credit for individuals required large down payments and involved expensive risk premiums and high transaction costs. It depended on loans primarily from local institutions, whose source of funds fluctuated widely. This meant that the supply of mortgages was cyclical. The government programs introduced standardized instruments. They enabled shares in residential mortgages to be bought in a manner similar to the purchase of bonds. As a result, risks to lenders were reduced significantly and major credit markets were opened to mortgage borrowers. In theory, the government agencies also were to furnish credit so as to stabilize production. In fact, policies primarily attempted to increase availability as rapidly as possible. Stabilization was of secondary importance.

OWNERSHIP COSTS

While expensive to the government, the programs to aid homeownerships were extremely successful through the 1970s. Homeownership rose steadily, from an estimated 44 percent in 1940 to 65 percent in 1981. The FHA–VA programs gave the initial impetus to increasing ownership. They reduced down payments to between 0 and 5 percent. The need to save for a down payment no longer inhibited ownership. The prime restraint became the amount of income available for mortgage payments. Initially these programs plus the growing secondary market helped solve the payment problem also. By reducing risks through better underwriting and pooling, the government was able to extend the amortization period to thirty years. Interest rates were reduced because additional funds were brought into the mortgage market and transaction costs were lowered.

Ability to meet mortgage payments gradually eroded, however, under the pressure of the mortgage tilt problem. In periods of inflation, although real interest rates and costs of shelter may not be high, many families cannot qualify for mortgage credit. This is true even though these families could afford to pay the real costs of owning and occupying a house. The risk to lenders is low, but nominal mortgage payments are high—they are front-loaded. The share of a family's income required for mortgage payments in the first year of owning a home may be two or three times their real costs and well above the share of income to be paid after twenty years. The number of people disqualified by current interest rates depends on the rate of inflation and the way loans are structured. The net effect of the mortgage tilt, however, is greatly to exacerbate the affordability problem.

Furthermore, after 1980 the real costs of housing increased. Until then, the interaction of inflation and the tax subsidy meant that owners who could benefit from the tax deductions had negative real costs. Rosen, for example, shows that for the period 1975–1979, a typical California homeowner making average mortgage payments and whose property appreciated at the average rate had a negative cost of ownership of $2,237 per year.[7] Everyone who could meet mortgage payments profited greatly by owning a home. Since this was obvious to most people, the desire to own spread rapidly.

Since 1980, nominal and real interest rates have increased. A typical family who bought between 1981 and 1984 would have had a positive real cost of $6,423 per year. Neither the tax benefits nor the various credit programs succeeded in reducing the housing burden. Most people entering the housing market without accumulated gains and savings found that affordability was a critical problem.

What, then, should the agenda be? I think the current administration's plan, continuing the tax expenditure program and reducing or abolishing most of the credit aids, is wrong. At the start of the Reagan administration, a strong argument was made that too much investment and credit were going to housing at the expense of other forms of investment. It was assumed that the housing subsidies had reduced costs by so much that expenditures were excessive. The argument appears quite weak. Housing's share of the total fixed investment has fallen, not risen. It was 37 percent of the total in the period 1950–1954 and had fallen to 24 percent for the period 1980–1983.

TAX EXPENDITURES

The claim that the tax system unduly subsidized housing at the expense of other investment has not held up well under careful scrutiny. Fullerton and Henderson state that under the 1980 tax laws, marginal tax rates on owner-occupied housing, at 19 percent, were considerably higher than on equipment, at 9 percent, but were lower than average rates on corporate assets, at 34.5 percent, and on unincorporated rental housing, at 40 percent. The 1982 tax law did not alter the marginal tax rate for owner-occupied housing, but marginal taxes were reduced still further on equipment (they became subsidized), while the rate on structures fell by 10 to 20 percent. Estimates of marginal tax rates vary depending on assumptions concerning interest rates and the rate of inflation. It is difficult to argue that housing was either aided or hindered by the total tax system in comparison with all other investments. Currently a wide divergence exists in the marginal-tax effects on different types of investment goods.[8]

Other problems with the existing tax expenditure programs are more important. While these programs did succeed in holding down real costs for most homeowners, they accomplished this goal in an extremely inefficient manner. It is not unreasonable to assume that the large amounts spent on subsidizing homeownership would bring greater benefits if the program were rationalized or if the amounts could be used to support other housing programs or, failing that, if they were used to reduce taxes or the deficit.

Tax benefits and inflation caused major disturbances in housing prices between 1970 and 1980. The negative costs of ownership increased demand. Lagging supply fostered excessive profits and undue increases in the prices of land, labor, and materials.

The tax subsidies through tax-exempt bonds and thrift institutions and those for rental housing are inefficient for other reasons. All suffer because they allow excess returns to inframarginal lenders or owners at the expense of the government, without equivalent benefits to borrowers or tenants. For example, the subsidy through excess depreciation allowances is reestablished on the sale of existing properties, yet this subsidy goes only to the previous owners. It is capitalized into owners' quasi-rents through a higher price-to-rent ratio. It does not affect rents, since these are primarily determined by the price and supply of newly constructed units.

Finally, the existing programs have a perverse effect on income, because benefits depend upon the homeowner's other income. The higher one's income, the higher the subsidy. Many elderly and moderate-income families are not able to benefit fully from the deduction because their itemized deductions prior to the inclusion of housing fall below the standard deduction. Gravelle, for example, estimates that individuals earning $17,000 in adjusted gross income would benefit from only half their potential housing deductions. She also shows that, on average, the amount of tax saving rises rapidly with income.[9] These tax incentives have another perverse feature: they are not limited to a single house, but apply equally to second or third houses, whether held for vacation or other reasons.

The form of the subsidy is unfortunate. Other countries cope with these difficulties either by counting the imputed income from owner-occupancy or, at a minimum, disallowing deductions. Reform proposals in this country have concentrated on abolishing deductions for second homes and on allowing deductions only against some standard tax rate such as 14 or 20 percent. Because a majority of voters profit in some degree from this subsidy, it has been politically sacrosanct. As a result, tax expenditures in this category have been increasing steadily. The Congressional Budget Office estimates that they will reach $68 billion by 1988.

The tax expenditure packages should be reshaped; the country is not getting its money's worth from these programs. While they are hard to alter politically, at least marginal adjustments should be possible. One approach would be to target first-time buyers more directly. Tax expenditures could be used to subsidize their savings up to a limited total. Higher tax credits could be given for those whose total deductions are limited and whose marginal tax rates are no higher than 25 or 30 percent. Actual payments or tax refunds could be authorized if the total tax expenditure for a family is below some limited amount.

CREDIT PROGRAMS

Another major thrust of the administration's program has been an attempt to curtail most of the credit programs. The administration has argued that the government was reducing efficiency by subsidizing borrowers and by interfering with the private market. I find but slight evidence to support such arguments. The government, because of its size and credit standing, has been able to reduce risks to lenders and thus has increased market efficiency; it has greatly lowered transaction costs by standardization and its own efficiency. Probably more credit has flowed to housing as a result of lower costs, but the net result should be an increase, not a decrease, in public welfare. Ideological arguments that those services efficiently provided by the government should instead be supplied by higher-cost industries do not seem valid.

The existing programs can properly be criticized for paying too slight attention maintaining stability. They have at times been pro- rather than anti-cyclical. Builders, mortgage brokers, and real estate operators have wanted the cheapest and most available credit, no matter what the state of housing demand. In response, the government programs have continued to operate at full speed even when available resources were insufficient to meet demands. When demand fell, some programs were helpful in supporting production. However, the programs' total cyclical impact has probably been negative.

An agenda for the future should pay greater attention to the needs of those who may not be able to afford housing when either nominal or real interest rates are high. This group does not include the poor; they need generalized income assistance and perhaps some construction for special-function units. It does not include most existing homeowners, since unless their income falls, they are able to meet these expenses. The program beneficiaries will be found primarily among existing tenant groups or newly formed households. Some find it difficult to purchase because their income is insufficient to cover their necessary expenses. Others want to remain tenants but find that rent increases exceed income increases. Some tenants find their dwellings deteriorating due to lack of maintenance or community decline. Finally, owners may be forced to remain in unsatisfactory units because they are unable to pay the much higher interest rates now current.

To benefit these groups, it appears logical to continue the basic government credit programs in the areas of insurance and guarantees and in the secondary market. In these spheres the government has major advantages over private entrepreneurs. Some risks, such as those of credit crunches or inflation, can best be assumed by the government. In other cases, because catastrophic events are likely to have extremely abnormal distributions, the amount of private capital needed to insure safety may be too large to be profitable. Since homeownership creates public as well as private goods, it may be worthwhile for the government to take unknown risks in order to reshape financial contracts. For institutional reasons, the reaction of financial markets to swings in credit differs widely among industries. All might gain if these swings in housing could be moderated.

Government programs have developed in the field of housing finance for these reasons. The programs have been successful in reducing required down payments and real interest rates. Now new instruments must be developed to shape payment flows more closely to expected incomes. Interest rates now carry high risk premiums, reflecting past variances and future uncertainty. These types of risks are best assumed by the government. The government should place more policy emphasis on the goal of increasing cyclical stability. Policies should not be used to make small cost reductions in boom periods; rather, the government should restrain its own lending in periods of adequate private credit to be better able to supplement credit when private mortgage flows are curtailed. Finally, more effort could be made to insure the maintenance or renewal of values through community programs. These are the subject of the next section.

EXTERNALITIES AND AIDS
TO COMMUNITY DEVELOPMENT

A third distinctive characteristic of housing is its dependence on external factors for its use and value. Because of its fixed location, the value of a dwelling is greatly influenced by its neighborhood, its environment, its public infrastructure and services, transportation, job locations, and social perceptions. The development of useful lots requires a considerable capital investment both by individual owners and the community.

The private market is simply inadequate to solve the problem of maintaining values, given the extent of external forces. Historically, a critical variable in neighborhood changes has been the migration and immigration of poor families. Central cities have grown and declined as transportation systems have altered and suburbs have been opened.[10]

Urban problems have been exacerbated by the unequal fiscal burdens and capacities of different localities. Competition among localities for development is shaped by national forces having little or nothing to do with the basic value of individual houses. Because of their durability, dwellings and communities are slow to adjust to change. Much of value can be lost if the market is not aided in its adjustment to change.

The concept of externalities provides one of the clearest justifications for government intervention in the housing area. A family's housing standard may depend as much on its neighborhood and community environment as on its house. Deterioration of neighborhoods occurs for numerous reasons: the infrastructure may be outdated; traffic and smog may reduce livability; the structures may be old-fashioned; competition from newer areas and suburbs may reduce a neighborhood's desirability. While these and similar physical features are important, it is clear that many problems arise from poor people's need for affordable houses. Low rents are feasible primarily through overcrowding and under-maintenance of dwellings. The recent gentrification of many neighborhoods containing most of the same physical features as neighboring slums shows how significant nonphysical factors can be.

The principal local development grant programs have included Community Development Block Grants (CDBG), funded at 3.47 billion dollars in fiscal year 1983, and the Urban Development Action Grants (UDAG), funded at 0.44 billion dollars. The levels of funding for CDBGs and UDAGs are estimated to be at the same levels, $3.47 billion and $0.44 billion respectively, through fiscal year 1985. Two new programs, Rental Rehabilitation and Rental Development (so-called Section 17 programs) were funded in 1984 at $0.15 billion and $0.20 billion respectively; funding estimates for 1985 are $0.15 billion and $0.12 billion.

These programs differ mainly in the rules under which the funds are distributed. Funds are available for use by local authorities on a wide range of eligible activities. Decisionmaking is primarily by the local units. The Community Development Block Grants are distributed on a formula basis, but most of the other funds are awarded through competitions based on applications for specific proposals from individual communities.

The Reagan agenda called for three types of change. The first was to reduce the funds available in real terms. This was accomplished by denying additional funds despite inflationary cost increases. The second was to reduce the amount of federal interference, specifically, to lower the pressure for earmarking funds for housing programs. The third change was to alter the programs for rental housing rehabilitation and development. Section 17 of the Housing and Urban-Rural Recovery Act of 1983 replaced Section 312 of the Housing Act of 1964 as the principal vehicle for aid to rehabilitation. Under the new act, funds could be used for new housing construction.

Some people question the use of federal funds for such specific local purposes. They ask why the federal government should spend its money for aid to localities. People could avoid problem areas by voting with their feet. If they wanted better schools or lower taxes, they could move from the central city to the suburbs, or from one state to another if they wanted fewer services and wanted to pay less. Both mobility and lack of mobility cause problems. Most of the poverty that brings about a need for development and renewal is not local; it is the result of national policies. Few localities can afford the required improvements. Raising taxes beyond some point causes a loss, not a gain, in revenue. Furthermore, it is costly to abandon useful houses and expensive urban infrastructures. The cheapest housing may result from saving existing communities. The aged and the poor lack flexibility in their choices. They may not be able to move, or the trauma may lead to illness and death. On the other hand, many of the high costs in particular localities may be created by refugees or by transients attracted to localities by federal military or other programs. Why should individual communities be forced to pay costs not of their own making? Why should we force or allow destructive downward spirals to ruin potentially valuable resources? The nation should recognize that many externalities, both positive and negative, reach well beyond the legal limits of specific localities.

Attention has been concentrated on housing assistance and credit rather than on attempts to improve communities. It is far from clear that expenditures have been allocated optimally. It is certainly possible that additional expenditures on community development and the rehabilitation and renewal of existing dwellings would do more to solve housing problems than any other approach. Existing communities have numerous advantages. The land is already developed. An infrastructure, though it may be old and deteriorating, is in place. Transportation is usually adequate, although often not to newer plants in the suburbs. Dwellings are already built; the problem is to maintain their livability while not raising their costs to moderate-income tenants.

Under the Community Development Block Grants, localities have a great deal of flexibility in their use of funds, provided that most funds are used in ways that will aid lower-income families. The largest share of funds (over one-third) is used to rehabilitate houses. The other major uses are for public improvements, public services and facilities. Economic development and planning and administration are other important uses. We have too little information to rank these expenditures with others in the housing field. It seems likely, however, that these sums are used more efficiently than those of many other programs.

CONCLUSIONS: THE AGENDA FOR THE FUTURE

Housing remains a basic problem because of the large amount of capital required, the burden on individual families, the complexity of producing new supplies, and the actual or potential deterioration of the existing stock. Little progress has been made on the side of production. Real costs have risen relative to other consumer expenditures. Fluctuations have increased rather than diminished in amplitude. No major breakthroughs have occurred in technology or in the organization of the industry.

The past twenty-five years have witnessed improvement in some spheres but retrogression in others. The costs of owning or occupying a house have risen faster than family incomes. The average family entering the market today has a harder time meeting housing expenses than was true in the past. On the other hand, the percentage of substandard houses, as measured by lack of plumbing or other equipment, or need for repairs, has declined. What has happened with respect to external forces such as neighborhoods and public services is uncertain. For a period, older neighborhoods declined drastically. Some of the worst remain; some have been destroyed. Some have been renewed with public funds, and others have undergone private renewal and gentrification.

The mélange of existing housing programs can be attributed in part to the way the housing problem was visualized over the past one hundred years and in part to happenstance. The current programs are expensive and frequently inefficient. The fact that each type of program tends to have its vociferous supporters is no guarantee of effectiveness.

The new Reagan agenda has emphasized "allowing industry to solve its problems," while imposing spending limits and a reduction of expenditures in real terms. The number of poor aided was reduced. Under current policies most families would have their assistance cut. There would be a gradual shift from other forms of assistance to vouchers. Virtually no aid would be programmed for new dwellings. The supply of units for the poor would be left to the market. Assistance to housing would be limited and would occur mainly through community development and renewal grants. Government and government-sponsored lending programs would be cut back, to leave the field free for the private market. States and localities would be urged to deregulate land and housing. They would be coerced to do so if they failed to meet federal standards.

If we were to start with a clean slate, but able to utilize most of the large sums shown in Table 8.1, how would we structure a logical program? Our program, unlike the administration's, would recognize that some of housing's most enduring problems cannot be solved by turning them over to the private market. Income distribution, reduction of credit risks, and maintaining or increasing the supply of public goods are needs best met through the interplay of market and government forces. For the poor and others who are either not able to afford market rents or who have special non-market needs, we would probably have a mixture of vouchers and new construction of specialized units for large families, for the elderly or handicapped, and in particular localities. We might attempt to substitute general income supplements for the voucher programs.

We would continue most insurance and guarantee programs. The government and government-sponsored agencies reduce risks and transaction costs and, therefore, the real costs of credit. They can meet specific needs not addressed by the private market. They can hold an open channel for housing to the money markets if normal channels close down, as has periodically been true.

Some aid would be continued to homeownership on the theory that it does increase the national welfare. Tax expenditures for homeownership should probably be a flat amount per family, or at most proportional to income. Special programs might well be established for moderate-income families, particularly to aid in their purchase of a first home.

Money saved by reducing tax expenditures might be spent to improve the urban infrastructure and to renew the existing stock, using block grants. Each locality may well be the best judge of the most effective way to maintain the existing stock: through spending on housing, on transportation, or on other types of public services. Unfortunately, as in many social spheres, we have few good measures of whether the nation is getting its money's worth. The national welfare is almost certainly raised, but we do not know the actual payoffs.

NOTES

1. U.S. President's Commission on Housing, *The Report of the President's Commission on Housing* (Washington, D.C.: U.S. Government Printing Office, 1982), p. xvii.

2. Ibid., p. xviii.

3. While this statement was generally adhered to, the commission did recommend that a housing construction program be added to community block grants. This component would be distributed based on housing needs. In addition, new construction would be authorized as a legitimate use of community development block grants.

4. U.S. Department of Housing and Urban Development, *Programs of HUD* (Washington, D.C.: U.S. Government Printing Office, 1984).

5. For other measures which give more local detail and arrive at similar conclusions see K. T. Rosen, *California Housing Markets in the 1980s: Demand, Affordability, and Policies* (Cambridge, Mass.: Oelgeschlager, Gunn and Hain, 1984), ch. 2.

6. U.S. President's Commission on Housing, *Report*, p. xxii.

7. Rosen, *California Housing Markets*, p. 42.

8. D. Fullerton and Y. Henderson, "Incentive Effects of Taxes on Income from Capital: Alternative Policies in the 1980's," Working Paper no. 1262 (Cambridge, Mass.: National Bureau of Economic Research, 1984).

9. Jane Gravelle, "Tax Subsidies to Housing, 1953–83," U.S. Congress, Committee on Banking, Finance and Urban Affairs, *Housing—A Reader*, Committee Print 98–5, p. 93.

10. A. Downs, *Neighborhoods and Urban Development* (Washington, D.C.: Brookings Institution, 1981).

CHAPTER NINE

Black Suburbanization in the Eighties: A New Beginning or a False Hope?

John F. Kain

Roughly half as many black households lived in the suburbs of America's metropolitan areas in 1980 as would be predicted on the basis of household income and family structure. And the black residents of central cities and of those few suburban communities where blacks live in significant numbers are intensely segregated. Segregation of ethnic and nationality groups rapidly decreased after they had attained levels approaching that of blacks today, but the segregation of American blacks has remained at a high level, and by some measures has actually increased.

Current and past discrimination is the principal explanation for black households' segregation. Prejudice of individual white sellers is a contributing factor, but without the active support of real estate brokers, renting agents, insurance companies, lenders, developers, homebuilders, and their associations, these individual acts would have been insufficient first to create and then to maintain this situation. Federal, state, and local governments initially supported the creation of segregated living patterns, then took a neutral stance, and only recently have begun to assist blacks in obtaining housing on a nondiscriminatory basis.

The intense residential segregation of black households with its adverse impact on black incomes, educational opportunities, housing conditions, and general welfare has long been recognized as among the most, if not the most, pressing of the nation's social problems. This recognition, and the growing political power of minorities, caused Congress to declare racial discrimination in the sale and rental of housing to be illegal. But discrimination is still pervasive. Data from the 1980 census of population and some earlier intercensal data, particularly school enrollment statistics, however, point to the emergence of a new and hopeful pattern of minority residence—the movement of small but significant numbers of black households to a large number of widely dispersed suburban communities. This paper examines these developments using 1970 and 1980 census data for the Chicago, Cleveland, San Francisco–Oakland, and San Jose metropolitan areas.

HISTORY OF GOVERNMENT POLICY

Government support of fair housing is relatively new. Early in the twentieth century, many American communities enacted zoning ordinances requiring block-by-block racial segregation. State governments, having delegated zoning powers to local governments, supported the enactment of these ordinances, which were upheld in state courts. Though declared unconstitutional by the Supreme Court in *Buchanan* v. *Warley* in 1917, these ordinances frequently remained in force and as late as the 1950s, attempts to enforce them were still being made (U.S. Commission on Civil Rights 1975, p. 4).

After the Supreme Court's decision in *Buchanan* v. *Warley*, restrictive covenants became the preferred method of enforcing racially segregated living patterns. Although they were private agreements, racial covenants were judicially enforced until 1948, when the Supreme Court ruled in *Shelley* v. *Kraemer* that their enforcement was a violation of the Fourteenth Amendment. They were still widely employed, however, and many individuals continued to observe them.

Numerous state-chartered organizations also supported racial segregation. In 1950 the National Association of Real Estate Brokers (NAREB) Code of Ethics still stated that:

> A Realtor should never be instrumental in introducing into a neighborhood, by character of property or occupancy, members of any race or nationality, or any individual whose presence will clearly be detrimental to property values in the neighborhood.

In *Twenty Years after Brown: Equal Opportunity in Housing*, the United States Commission on Civil Rights (1975, p. 39) charged the federal government with being "most influential in creating and maintaining urban residential segregation," noting that "for nearly 30 years after the first Federal housing programs were initiated, the Federal government either actively or passively promoted racial and ethnic discrimination." The commission pointed out that for fifteen years, the FHA

Underwriting Manual warned of the "infiltration of 'inharmonious racial groups' into neighborhoods occupied by families of a different race" (p. 40). Furthermore, until December 1949, following the Supreme Court's decision in *Shelley v. Kramer*, the FHA actively promoted the use of a model racially restricted covenant by builders and owners whose properties were to receive FHA insurance. The commission determined that the "policies of the four federal financial regulatory agencies responsible for the supervision and regulation of mortgage lenders also endorsed overt racial and ethnic discrimination in mortgage lending until passage of the 1968 Fair Housing Law" (p. 41). The commission reported that these agencies permitted mortgage lenders to consider minorities less desirable risks than whites, regardless of their personal or financial worth, and routinely to refuse to provide home mortgages for minorities in non-minority areas. The policy—in force until recently—of discounting all or part of a wife's income in determining eligibility for loans also worked to the particular disadvantage of blacks, since black females have higher labor-force participation rates than white females and thus make proportionately larger contributions to family incomes.

Federal administration of public housing programs also contributed to the maintenance of racially segregated living patterns. The federal Public Housing Administration (PHA) permitted local public-housing authorities (LHAs) to maintain either "separate but equal" or "open occupancy" policies. Most LHAs chose "separate but equal" and, with federal approval, created management offices for projects occupied by whites separate from those for projects occupied by blacks, and made up separate waiting lists based on race. The PHA continued to sanction "separate but equal" policies through the 1950s and into the 1960s, despite the enactment of a growing number of state and local laws prohibiting discrimination in public housing, and several court decisions that found state-enforced segregation in public housing unconstitutional.

LHAs also selected, and the PHA approved the selection of, separate locations for the units to be occupied by white and minority families. In some localities, the policies pursued by LHAs created segregated residential patterns and concentrations where they had not existed previously. In virtually all metropolitan areas, the location of public housing accentuated the concentration of minorities in central cities.

FEDERAL SUPPORT FOR FAIR HOUSING

Significant federal support for open housing began in November 1962, when President Kennedy signed Executive Order 11063 prohibiting discrimination based on race, color, creed, or national origin with respect to the sale, leasing, rental, or other disposition of residential property and related facilities. Although couched in broad terms, the order covered only housing provided through Federal Housing Administration (FHA) mortgage insurance or Veterans Administration (VA) loan guarantees and federally assisted public housing; conventionally financed housing was excluded from coverage. The U.S. Commission on Civil Rights (1979) estimated that the order covered less than one percent of the nation's housing. The order also stipulated that builders and owners of housing could be barred from participation in federal programs if they were found to discriminate. Federal aid agreements executed before 20 November 1962, however, were generally exempt.

Title VI of the Civil Rights Act of 1964 broadened the coverage of Executive Order 11063 and led to important changes in the administration of federal housing programs, particularly public housing. All housing in urban renewal areas was made subject to Title VI, as was public housing regardless of the date of the contract for assistance, as long as federal financial contributions were still being received. However, housing provided through FHA mortgage insurance and VA guarantee programs outside urban renewal areas, as well as Farmers Home Administration housing, remained exempt.

Title VIII of the Civil Rights Act of 1968, widely referred to as the Fair Housing Act, greatly expanded the federal commitment to open housing. It prohibited discrimination in the sale or rental of all housing except single-family homes and owner-occuped one-to-four-unit structures sold or rented without use of a broker and without publication, posting, or mailing of any advertisement indicating any preference, limitation, or discrimination based on race, color, religion, or national origin. Title VIII covers more than 80 percent of all housing and encompasses the activities of all segments of the real estate industry including real estate brokers, builders, apartment owners, sellers, and mortgage lenders as well as all federally owned and operated dwellings and dwellings provided by federally insured loans and grants. Prohibited activities include:

1. Refusal to sell or rent a dwelling.

2. Discrimination in the terms, conditions, or privileges in the sale or rental of a dwelling.

3. Indicating a preference, limitation, or discrimination in advertising.

4. Representation to a person or persons that a dwelling is unavailable.

5. Denial of a loan for purchasing, constructing, improving, or repairing a dwelling.

6. Discrimination in setting the amount or other conditions of a real estate loan.

7. Denial of access to or membership in any multiple-listing service or real estate brokers' organization.

Title VIII also explicitly prohibits *blockbusting*—convincing owners to sell property on the grounds that minorities are about to move into a neighborhood—and *steering*, the process of directing a racial, ethnic, or religious group into a neighborhood in which members of the same group already live and directing other persons away from this neighborhood.

While Title VIII is very comprehensive in both its coverage and the range of prohibited activities, its effectiveness has been limited by lax enforcement. The Department of Housing and Urban Development (HUD), which is responsible for the overall administration of Title VIII, may only investigate and conciliate complaints of housing discrimination. The Justice Department may initiate litigation, but only when there is a pattern or practice of housing discrimination or where issues of housing discrimination are of general public importance. In its March 1979 report on the federal fair-housing enforcement effort, the U.S. Commission on Civil Rights gave the Justice Department's Housing and Credit Section generally high marks for its litigation efforts but noted that it had brought only 300 cases since its creation in 1969 (p. 70).

In spite of its legal and symbolic importance, Title VIII has several glaring deficiencies: it does not authorize the Secretary of HUD to initiate investigations unless a complaint has been made, even if the Secretary has reason to believe the law is being violated; it makes no provisions for third parties to file fair housing complaints; it does not provide HUD with enforcement authority; it makes no provision for regular collection of data on those subject to its prohibitions; it does not explicitly authorize the use of testers; it includes too narrow a litigation authority to the Department of Justice; and it limits the awarding of attorney's fees in private litigation to those plaintiffs who are "not financially able to assume said attorneys' fees." Several efforts to strengthen the Fair Housing Act have been defeated, as have several conservative attempts to weaken it.

Decisions by federal courts have been at least as important as congressional legislation and Executive Orders in combating housing market discrimination. In *Jones* v. *Alfred H. Mayer Co.*, the Supreme Court held that in the Civil Rights Act of 1866 Congress intended "to prohibit all discrimination against Negroes in the sale or rental of property—discrimination by private owners as well as by public authorities." The Supreme Court thus, unlike Congress in the Civil Rights Act of 1968, allowed no exceptions. Subsequent decisions have established that a plaintiff can recover both punitive and compensatory damages as well as attorney's fees. Rulings supporting the awarding of attorney's fees have been crucial in enabling minorities to exercise their rights to rent and buy private housing, although use of the courts to secure these rights requires that black households know their rights under the Fair Housing law and depends on the willingness of private attorneys to bring fair-housing cases.

The Carter administration exhibited considerable ambivalence toward racial discrimination and segregation. The first drafts of Carter's 1978 urban policy statement completely ignored these issues, and the final version was not much of an improvement. In 1979, however, the Carter administration supported amendments to the fair-housing law that would have added an administrative enforcement mechanism, extended the statute of limitations from 180 days to two years, made attorney's fee awards available to all victims of discrimination, and authorized court proceedings to hold a house or apartment off the market while the discrimination claim was being decided. The bill passed the House of Representatives but failed in the Senate in December 1980, when its proponents fell five votes short of the two-thirds required to end a filibuster. In the same month the Carter administration belatedly sent to Congress an extensive set of Title VIII regulations. The proposed regulations—which did not become operative—would have provided the first comprehensive interpretation of Title VIII, covering both private market and federally assisted housing and including definitions of what constitutes discrimination and who may sue and be sued.

The Reagan administration's first fair-housing initiative was to recall the Title VIII regulations that had been submitted to Congress in the waning days of the Carter administration. Although HUD gave assurances that it would resubmit revised regulations after it had an opportunity to review them, no regulations had been proposed by the forty-fourth month of the Reagan administration.

During the Reagan administration's first thirty months, the Justice Department filed only six fair-housing cases, whereas forty-six cases were filed during the first thirty months of the Carter administration (Miller 1984). Selig (1984), Miller (1984), and others accused the Reagan administration of deliberately bringing a large number of low-impact cases, abandoning efforts begun during the Carter administration to focus the Justice Department's limited resources on a small number of high-visibility, precedent-setting cases. In addition, the Citizens Commission on Civil Rights contended that Reagan administration fair-housing cases were settled on terms that imposed much less significant penalties and fewer obligations than agreements secured in earlier cases (Citizens Commission on Civil Rights 1983).

The Reagan administration has also refused to employ the "effects test," even though federal courts and Congress have repeatedly stated that a violation of the Civil Rights Act may be proven by showing either that an intentional act of discrimination has been committed or that the actions complained of have had a discriminatory effect. Commenting on the administration's failure to use the effects test, the authors of an American Civil Liberties Union review of the Reagan civil rights record stated that "in defiance of the clear legal standard, the Reagan Administration has taken upon itself to redefine the law to its own liking" (1984, p. 7). Speaking more generally of the Reagan administration's civil rights record, these authors concluded:

> The actions described above reveal a pattern of disregard by the Executive Branch for the rule of law and the mandates of the legislature. . . . Since 1803, amendments to the Constitution and dozens of congressional and judicial decisions have reaffirmed the principle . . . that the officers of the Executive Branch do not operate with unfettered discretion, particularly when constitutional rights are at stake. Their clear duty is to carry out the laws enacted by Congress, so long as those laws are consistent with the Constitution. To an unprecedented degree, the officials of this administration have flouted that duty.

The Citizens Commission on Civil Rights added that the Reagan administration has attempted to eliminate regulations requiring localities to certify that they will comply with civil rights laws and Executive Orders on equal housing and with the nondiscrimination provisions of the Community Development Act itself (p. 63); with diluting voluntary affirmative marketing agreements; with using the Paperwork Reduction Act and regulatory reform as excuses for eliminating collection of essential data on the race and sex of beneficiaries of federal programs; and with using budget cuts and the allocation of this smaller budget to low-impact programs that further weakened HUD's already inadequate enforcement efforts.

THE EXTENT OF RACIAL SEGREGATION
AND ITS CAUSES

Racial segregation in America has two dimensions: first, vastly disproportionate numbers of blacks live in the central cities of the largest metropolitan areas and blacks are seriously underrepresented in suburban
communities; second, blacks are intensely segregated within both central
cities and suburban areas. Evidence on the first point is provided by Table
9.1. The mean (unweighted) proportion of SMSA nonblacks residing in
the suburbs of all thirty-one SMSAs in 1970 was 3.3 times as large as the
mean (unweighted) proportion of SMSA blacks. The weighted mean was
nearly twice as large as the unweighted mean, indicating that the concentration of blacks in central cities is greater in larger SMSAs than in smaller
ones. The rapid growth of suburban black populations in a number of
metropolitan areas during 1970–1980 (discussed below) reduced but did
not eliminate the gap in a number of metropolitan areas; by 1980 the
weighted-mean black/white ratio had declined to 2.54 and the unweighted ratio to 3.98.

Table 9.2 shows that black households are intensely segregated within
both central cities and suburban areas. The segregation indexes measure
the extent to which observed patterns of residence location by race differ
from proportional representation: a value of zero indicates a completely
uniform distribution—the proportion of blacks residing in every block or
census tract is equal to their proportion of the entire city or metropolitan
area population—while a value of 100 denotes complete segregation—
all blocks or tracts are either 100 percent or 0 percent black. Table 9.2
contains both block and tract indexes. Block indexes are generally regarded as better indicators of the extent of segregation, but block statistics are unavailable for many parts of metropolitan areas. Moreover, the
heavy concentration of black households in central cities and other areas
covered by block statistics and the growth in coverage of block statistics
over time means that care must be taken in using block indexes to study
trends.

The segregation indexes in Table 9.2 confirm the widespread impression that racial segregation is particularly persistent in Chicago and
Cleveland; the indexes for 1980 are insignificantly lower than the indexes
thirty and forty years earlier. By comparison, the San Francisco–Oakland
indexes are both substantially lower in 1980 and have declined steadily
since 1950. Comparisons of the Bay Area with Chicago and Cleveland,
however, may be confounded by the presence of Asian- and Spanish-

TABLE 9.1

Percentage of SMSA Populations Living Outside Central City in 1970 and 1980, by Race[a]

SMSA*	1970			1980		
	% Negro	% White	Ratio W/N	% Black	% Nonblack	Ratio NB/B
Atlanta	26.6	85.0	3.19	43.3	90.7	2.10
Baltimore	14.2	69.3	4.86	22.6	78.0	3.46
Boston	19.9	76.8	3.86	22.6	79.2	3.50
Chicago	10.4	60.5	5.81	16.2	68.1	4.21
Cincinnati	17.9	73.4	4.10	24.9	79.2	3.19
Cleveland	13.5	73.3	5.44	27.3	79.2	2.90
Columbus	8.2	51.6	6.31	7.3	54.1	7.43
Dallas–Fort Worth	12.6	53.6	4.25	15.7	63.4	4.03
Denver–Boulder	5.2	55.1	10.61	22.3	67.1	3.00
Detroit	13.2	76.8	5.83	14.8	87.2	5.90
Fort Lauderdale	68.6	59.1	0.86	67.3	73.8	1.10
Houston	18.8	43.0	2.29	16.7	51.5	3.08
Indianapolis	2.2	38.1	17.37	2.9	45.7	15.53
Kansas City	3.4	67.8	20.02	29.2	71.8	2.46
L.A.–Long Beach	31.5	57.8	1.83	42.2	57.4	1.36
Miami	59.8	76.0	1.27	68.9	80.7	1.17
Milwaukee	1.4	52.8	38.96	2.5	60.7	24.49
Minneapolis–St. Paul	6.8	63.1	9.27	16.6	71.0	4.27
New York	6.9	23.9	3.47	8.1	26.4	3.27
Philadelphia	22.6	67.4	2.99	27.8	72.6	2.62
Portland, Ore.	7.4	63.6	8.65	16.9	72.0	4.25
Riverside–San Bernardino	54.5	73.5	1.35	58.8	76.6	1.30
Sacramento	28.1	70.0	2.49	39.9	74.9	1.88
St. Louis	32.9	81.9	2.49	49.4	87.3	1.77
San Antonio	16.3	27.1	1.66	20.7	27.2	1.31
San Diego	14.6	50.3	3.44	25.6	54.6	2.13
San Francisco–Oakland	33.1	69.2	2.09	37.2	73.0	1.96
San Jose	39.4	57.1	1.45	33.3	51.5	1.55
Seattle–Everett	8.1	60.5	7.49	18.5	67.7	3.65
Tampa–St. Petersburg	23.5	58.2	2.48	28.0	71.7	2.56
Washington, D.C.	25.0	90.0	3.60	47.5	91.4	1.92
All SMSAs						
Weighted Mean	18.1	59.8	3.30	25.8	65.4	2.54
Unweighted Mean	20.9	62.1	6.12	28.2	67.9	3.98

[a]For SMSA's with populations over 1 million in 1980, census racial classification changes between 1970 and 1980.

SOURCE: U.S. Department of Commerce, Bureau of the Census, 1980 Census of Population, PC80-51-5, "Standard Metropolitan Statistical Areas and Consolidated Statistical Areas: 1980."

TABLE 9.2

Indexes of Residential Segregation for Selected Cities
and Metropolitan Areas, 1940–1980

Area and Type	1940	1950	1960	1970	1980
Block Indexes					
Chicago	95.0	92.1	92.6	93.0	91.9
Evanston	91.5	92.1	87.2	85.3	69.9
Cleveland	92.0	91.5	91.3	90.1	91.0
San Francisco	82.9	79.8	69.3	75.0	68.2
Oakland	78.4	81.2	73.1	70.4	58.6
San Jose	NA	NA	60.4	NA	49.5
Berkeley	81.2	80.3	69.4	75.4	71.6
Mean 207 Cities	NA	NA	86.2	NA	NA
All regions	NA	NA	87.7	NA	NA
North Central	NA	NA	78.7	NA	NA
Pacific	NA	NA		NA	NA
Tract Indexes					
Chicago	NA	88.1	91.2	91.2	86.3
Cleveland	NA	86.6	89.6	90.2	87.5
San Francisco–Oakland	NA	NA	79.4	77.3	68.2
San Jose	NA	NA	65.6	51.1	40.3
All SMSAs	NA	NA	75.4	69.5	NA
North Central	NA	NA	79.5	74.1	NA
West	NA	NA	76.3	65.8	NA
All Central Cities					
North Central	NA	NA	75.9	68.5	NA
West	NA	NA	76.2	62.9	NA
Same 137 SMSAs	NA	NA	75.6	75.1	NA
North Central	NA	NA	79.3	79.7	NA
West	NA	NA	77.0	71.4	NA

NOTE: For 1940 through 1970, indexes refer to Negro-White segregation. For 1980, indexes refer to Black-Non Black segregation.

SOURCES: City block indexes 1940–1960 (Taeuber and Taeuber 1965); City and SMSA tract indexes, 1960–1970 (Van Valey et al. 1977); city block indexes and SMSA tract indexes 1970 and 1980 (unpublished indexes supplied by Karl Taeuber).

origin minorities in predominantly black neighborhoods. Statistics on the percentages of central city blacks living in census tracts that were more than 50 and 90 percent black in 1970, however, also suggest that the segregation of blacks is much less intense in the Bay Area than in Chicago and Cleveland. Using the lower threshold, 93.9 percent of Chicago's and 93.7 percent of Cleveland's but only 55.5 percent of San Francisco's black population lived in census tracts that were more than 50 percent black in 1970. Furthermore, no San Francisco blacks lived in tracts that were 90 percent or more black in 1970, as compared to 77.7 percent of Chicago's and 67.4 percent of Cleveland's blacks.

Persons seeking to justify the high levels of black segregation often point to the tendency of various ethnic minorities to cluster in identifiable communities as evidence of the normality of this behavior, suggesting thereby that the residence patterns of black households are explained by blacks' preference for living with other blacks. Studies comparing the residence patterns of blacks and various ethnic groups, however, demonstrate that the other groups exhibit much less segregation than blacks. Unlike the segregation of black households, which has remained at high levels or even increased for seventy years or more, the segregation of ethnic minorities has declined steadily over time (Lieberson 1963; Taeuber and Taeuber 1964; Hersberg et al. 1971). Attitudinal surveys also fail to support the preference argument. Seventy-four percent of black Americans interviewed in a 1969 *Newsweek* poll responded that they would rather live in a neighborhood that had both whites and Negroes than in a neighborhood with all-Negro families; only 16 percent chose an all-black neighborhood (Pettigrew 1973). Moreover, between 1963 and 1969 the percentage preferring all-black neighborhoods declined, while the percentage preferring integrated neighborhoods increased. Pettigrew (1973), after reviewing eleven surveys conducted between 1958 and 1969, found that "when presented with a meaningful choice between an all-black neighborhood and a mixed neighborhood, black residents overwhelmingly favored the latter."

Sheatsley (1966) and Pettigrew (1973) also documented a steady increase in white racial tolerance. Pettigrew, for example, compared responses to identical questions included on seven National Opinion Research Corporation (NORC) polls administered between 1942 and 1968 and a second set included in five Gallup polls conducted between 1958 and 1967. In the NORC surveys, the percentage of whites indicating that it would make a difference to them if a Negro, equal to them in income and education, moved to their block had declined from 62 percent in 1942 to 46 percent in 1956, to 35 percent in 1965, and to 21 percent in 1968 (Pettigrew 1973). Similarly, 48 percent of whites interviewed in 1958 stated that they definitely or might move "if colored people came to live next door"; nine years later the percentage had declined to 35 percent. An even more recent Gallup survey revealed that the fraction of white households who said they would move if a black family moved next door had declined to only 18 percent by 1978 (American Institute of Public Opinion 1978).

A more elaborate survey of 743 white and 400 black households in Detroit (Farley et al. 1978) obtained results that are generally consistent with those summarized above. Farley and his associates found that, "freed of racial hostility, . . . most Detroit area blacks would select neighborhoods which are about one-half white and one-half black," but concluded, after finding that the whites surveyed expressed a preference for neighborhoods with smaller concentrations of blacks, that "the prospects for residential integration seem quite slim" (p. 336). The interpretation of these preference data, as well as those of other analysts with similar views, has been strongly influenced by Schelling's (1972) theoretical analyses of the relationship between black and white preferences and racial segregation. Yinger (1978, 1980) emphasizes the need to consider more than preferences in applying Schelling's findings to real-world situations.

The low incomes of blacks are an even more common explanation proffered for their underrepresentation in suburban areas and their high levels of segregation within central cities. Noting that the central-city housing stock is older and of poorer quality than the suburban housing stock, this position asserts that blacks must occupy the cheapest central city housing and cannot afford expensive suburban housing. Several careful empirical studies have examined this proposition and have found little or no support for it (Kain 1977; Pascal 1967; Schnare 1977; Taeuber 1968). Nonetheless, this myth continues to find wide acceptance.

The estimate that only half as many black households lived in the suburbs of United States metropolitan areas in 1980 as would be expected on the basis of their incomes and family characteristics is confirmed by a more detailed analysis which calculates the ratio of SMSA black households to SMSA total households in 1980 for 135 household categories (see Table A in the appendix); multiplies these proportions by the number of suburban households of each type to obtain a predicted number of suburban black households of each type; and sums the 135 categories of suburban households. The 135 income–household type categories are defined in terms of nine household-income intervals; three household types—married couple families, male householder; no wife present; and female householder, no husband present—and five age-of-householder categories. The actual number of black households residing outside the central cities of all SMSAs in 1980 was 1,846,303; the predicted number, obtained using the model described above, was 3,631,702, or 1.97 times the actual number.

The gap between the actual and predicted numbers of black households is even greater for individual metropolitan areas. Analyses for Chicago using 1970 public-use sample data, for example, indicate that the actual black population of Chicago's suburbs is only 30 percent as large as would be expected in the absence of racial discrimination (Kain 1984). The Chicago estimate was obtained using the methodology described above, except that family size was added to the list of explanatory variables.

A similar analysis for Cleveland in 1970, based on both tract and public-use sample data, used 384 types of households and roughly the same methodology to predict the residence locations of black households and nine individual nationality groups that are present in significant numbers in the Cleveland metropolitan area (Kain 1977). This analysis, prepared for the Justice Department as part of its fair-housing litigation against Parma, Ohio, obtained estimates of the actual and predicted racial and ethnic composition for each of the 440 census tracts in the Cleveland SMSA in 1970 and thereby provides a more precise indication of the extent of black segregation.

Figure 9.1 illustrates the distinctive character of black segregation. Virtually all Cleveland SMSA tracts in 1970 were either more than 70 percent or fewer than 4 percent black; 313 of the SMSA's 414 tracts were less than 4 percent black and only 61 were between 5 and 79 percent black. Most of the 61 "integrated" tracts, moreover, were actually "transitional" tracts located at the periphery of the ghetto.

In contrast to the distributions of actual percent black, 302 of Cleveland's 440 tracts were predicted to have between 10 and 19 percent black households. Only 11 tracts had this racial composition in 1970. No Cleveland SMSA tract had higher than 59 percent blacks predicted in 1970, while 70 tracts had actual black percentages greater than this fraction. The predicted proportions, then, in contrast to the actual percentages, cluster tightly around the SMSA mean proportion of blacks.

The Cleveland analysis of ethnic residence patterns demonstrates the vast difference between the tendency of various ethnic minorities to cluster in identifiable ethnic communities, and the intense segregation of blacks. While ethnic neighborhoods exist in every American city, members of ethnic minorities live in all parts of the metropolitan areas. The model used to predict the residential patterns of Cleveland's blacks, described above, is quite successful in reproducing the actual residential distributions of Cleveland's German-, Polish-, Czech-, Austrian-, Hungarian-, Yugoslavian-, Italian-, and Russian-American households (Kain 1977). Yet, as we have seen, the model has virtually no success in predict-

FIGURE 9.1

Actual and Predicted Number of Census Tracts by Tract Percent Black,
Cleveland SMSA in 1970

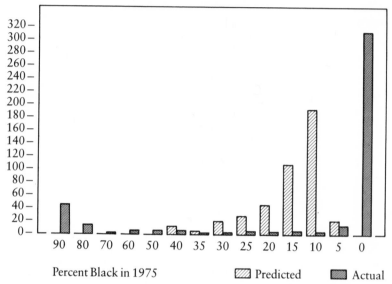

SOURCE: John F. Kain, "Race, Ethnicity, and Residential Location," in Ronald E. Grieson (ed.), *Public and Urban Economics* (Lexington: Lexington Books, D.C. Heath and Co., 1976), Table 17-2, p. 278.

ing the residence locations of blacks. Instead of providing a rationale for the segregation of blacks, the current and past experience of America's ethnic and nationality groups provides strong inferential evidence that the intense segregation of America's black households is due to a systematic and continuing denial of choice.

BLACK SUBURBANIZATION DURING THE '70s

During 1970–1980 the black populations of the nation's 239 metropolitan areas increased by 1.8 million within constant 1980 boundaries, and the black share of the suburban population of these areas increased from 4.6 to 6.1 percent (Grier and Grier 1983). Statistics on the black suburban population of the nation's large SMSAs (1980 populations of more than 1 million) (Table 9.3) indicate that the growth of suburban black populations was widespread. The suburban black populations of four of these large SMSAs grew by over 100,000, those of four more by

50,000–100,000, and of seven more by 20,000–50,000. The mean increase in the suburban black populations for all 31 SMSAs during the period 1970–1980 was 41,218, and the mean (weighted) growth, which averaged 66.8 percent, was 4.3 times as great as the growth rate of their suburban white populations, or 15.5 percent. Finally, both the unweighted average growth rate of the suburban black population and the ratio of black to white suburban growth rates are substantially greater than the weighted rates, indicating that suburban black populations grew particularly rapidly in smaller metropolitan areas.

Grier and Grier (1983) and others have correctly observed that most black suburbanization during the period 1970–1980 was attributable to the growth of established black suburban enclaves or peripheral expansion of the central city ghetto across central city boundaries. In these instances, the traditional pattern of ghetto expansion seems to be continuing, with the initial entry of black residents being followed by the withdrawal of white demand, rapid growth of the black population, and finally by the area's consolidation with the central city ghetto (Karlen 1968; Kain and Quigley 1975). This form of ghetto expansion may benefit central cities by breaking what long appeared to be a central city monopoly on black poverty, but it does little to change the expectations of either blacks or whites about the consequences of black entry on the eventual racial composition of formerly all-white neighborhoods and communities.

At the same time, analysis of recent census data reveals a quantitatively small but potentially highly important pattern of dispersed black suburban residence—a movement of small but significant numbers of black households into formerly all-white suburban communities. The finding that a fundamental change may be occurring in the residence patterns of black households is based on a fairly detailed investigation of the pattern of black suburbanization in four metropolitan areas, along with a general impression of similar developments in a number of other areas. Chicago, Cleveland, San Francisco–Oakland, and San Jose are examined in detail; statistics for San Francisco–Oakland and San Jose are combined and are reported as the Bay Area.

Table 9.4 shows that 69 of Chicago's 116 suburban communities (59.5 percent) and 16 of Cleveland's 41 suburban communities (39 percent) had fewer than 5 black households in 1970. Ten years later only 15 Chicago and 2 Cleveland suburbs had fewer than 5 black households. Similarly, between 1970 and 1980 the number of Chicago suburban communities with 10 to 49 black households more than doubled and the

TABLE 9.3
Suburban Black Population, 1970–1980 (SMSAs over 1,000,000 population, 1980)

SMSA	Suburban black population		Difference black 1970–80	% change 1980–1970		Ratio % changes, black to white
	1970	1980		Black	White	
Washington, D.C.	179,328	405,490	226,162	126.1	2.2	57.92
Los Angeles–Long Beach	295,492	398,020	157,822	53.4	5.0	10.60
Atlanta	92,479	215,914	123,435	133.5	26.2	5.10
Chicago	128,299	230,826	102,527	79.9	11.2	7.14
Miami	113,510	193,324	79,814	70.3	32.5	2.16
St. Louis	124,838	201,470	76,632	61.4	2.2	27.67
Baltimore	69,802	125,721	55,919	80.1	15.2	5.28
Philadelphia	190,509	245,529	55,020	28.9	3.7	7.79
Cleveland	44,773	94,299	49,526	110.6	(3.0)	–
Kansas City	5,134	50,485	45,351	883.3	8.8	100.52
San Francisco–Oakland	109,319	145,514	36,195	33.1	8.6	3.83
New York	123,251	156,504	33,253	27.0	(3.2)	–
Detroit	100,189	131,478	31,289	31.2	7.0	4.47
Dallas–Fort Worth	41,672	65,883	24,211	58.1	47.5	1.22
Fort Lauderdale	53,124	76,415	23,291	43.8	108.2	0.41

Riverside–San Bernardino	27,533	46,273	18,740	68.1	41.5	1.64
San Diego	9,067	26,752	17,685	195.0	47.3	4.12
Cincinnati	27,263	43,189	15,926	58.4	7.3	7.98
Houston	73,337	88,253	14,916	20.3	76.6	0.27
Denver–Boulder	2,607	17,377	14,770	566.6	57.8	9.80
Tampa–St. Petersburg	26,563	40,853	14,290	53.8	79.6	0.68
Sacramento	10,667	24,432	13,765	129.0	33.2	3.89
Boston	27,031	39,194	12,163	45.0	0.7	66.48
San Jose	7,135	14,559	7,424	104.1	7.6	13.62
Seattle–Everett	3,361	10,771	7,410	220.5	25.2	8.75
Minneapolis–St. Paul	2,184	8,310	6,126	280.5	20.2	13.91
San Antonio	9,773	15,085	5,312	54.4	21.1	2.58
Portland, Ore.	1,712	5,651	3,939	230.1	39.1	5.88
Milwaukee	1,444	3,737	2,293	158.8	10.5	15.08
Indianapolis	3,015	4,628	1,613	53.5	24.2	2.21
Columbus	8,864	9,806	942	10.6	10.6	1.00
All SMSAs						
Sum	1,913,275	3,135,742	1,277,761			
Weighted Mean	61,719	101,153	41,218	66.8	15.5	4.32
Unweighted Mean				131.3	25.0	12.65

SOURCE: U.S. Department of Commerce, Bureau of the Census, 1980 Census of Population, PC80-51-5, "Standard Metropolitan Statistical Areas and Consolidated Statistical Areas: 1980."

TABLE 9.4

Black Households in Chicago and Cleveland SMSAs and Bay Area Communities, 1970 and 1980

Number of black households in community	Chicago communities				Cleveland communities				Bay Area communities			
	1970		1980		1970		1980		1970		1980	
	No.	%	No.	%	No.	%	No.	%	No.	%	No.	%
1,000–15,000	9	7.8	19	16.4	2	4.9	7	17.1	5	7.8	11	17.2
50–999	11	9.5	39	33.6	12	29.3	14	34.1	22	34.4	40	62.5
10–49	12	10.3	28	24.1	4	9.8	13	31.7	26	40.6	12	18.8
5–9	15	12.9	15	12.9	7	17.1	5	12.2	4	6.3	1	1.6
0–4	69	59.5	15	12.9	16	39.0	2	4.9	7	10.9	0	0.0
All suburbs	116	100.0	116	100.0	41	100.0	41	100.0	64	100.0	64	100.0
Central cities	1		1		1		1		3		3	

NOTE: Percentages may not add up to 100, due to rounding.
SOURCE: U.S. Bureau of the Census, 1970 Census of Population and Housing: Census Tracts, Final Report (Chicago, Cleveland, San Francisco, and San Jose), table H-1; U.S. Bureau of the Census, Census of Housing: 1970, General Housing Characteristics, Final Report, HC(11) (San Francisco, Chicago, and Cleveland), tables 18, 23; U.S. Bureau of the Census, 1980 Census of Population and Housing: Census Tracts (Chicago, Cleveland, San Francisco, and San Jose), table H-1.

number with 50 to 999 black households more than tripled. The number of Cleveland suburbs with 10 to 49 black households tripled, although the number with 50 to 999 increased only from 12 to 14.

Suburbs in the Bay Area also experienced impressive growth in black population, although smaller percentages of Bay Area suburbs had fewer than 5 or between 5 and 9 black households in 1970; combining these two categories, only 17.2 percent of Bay Area suburbs had fewer than 9 black households in 1970, compared to 72.4 percent for Chicago and 56.1 percent for Cleveland. These data support the view that racial segregation is less intense in the Bay Area than in Chicago and Cleveland and suggest that the movement of small numbers of black households to a large number of dispersed suburban communities, evident in Chicago and Cleveland during the period 1970–1980, may have begun a decade earlier in the Bay Area.

While the data in Table 9.4 point to an important qualitative change in black residence patterns, the quantitative impact of these changes remains small. In 1980, after a decade of rapid black suburban growth, 80.0, 73.6, and 67.4 percent of all black households in the three metropolitan areas still lived in central cities (Table 9.5). Most of the remaining black residents of the three areas—11.2 percent, 10.1 percent, and 13.5 percent of all SMSA black households—lived in suburban communities with 5,000 to 15,000 black households, either well-established suburban enclaves or "transitional" communities on the boundary of the central city ghetto. Suburban communities with 10 to 49 black households accounted for only 0.2, 0.3, and 0.2 percent of black households, and communities with 50 to 999 black households for 2.0, 2.2, and 8.5 percent of the total in the three areas.

Nearly all the black suburbanization in the Chicago and Cleveland SMSAs and in the Bay Area took the form of growth of established black suburban enclaves or peripheral expansion of the central city ghetto across central city boundaries. The number of suburbs with fewer than 5 black households declined substantially, however—from 92 to 17 for the three areas combined—and the number of suburbs with 10 to 999 black households increased from 87 to 146. The 1980 black populations of newly integrated suburban communities located at some distance from the central city ghettos were only a small fraction of the total 1980 black populations of the metropolitan areas studied, but the significance of the appearance of even token numbers of black households in so many, widely dispersed suburban communities cannot be overemphasized. The difference between none and several is enormous. Each of the thousands

TABLE 9.5

Distribution of Black Households among Communities of Various Levels of Integration
for Chicago, Cleveland, Bay Area: 1970 and 1980

Number of black households	Chicago 1970	Chicago 1980	Cleveland 1970	Cleveland 1980	Bay Area 1970	Bay Area 1980
			Number of households			
Suburbs						
1,000–15,000	20,511	84,904	8,527	28,830	26,215	37,166
50–999	2,888	9,644	2,139	2,686	4,094	13,140
10–49	271	813	53	308	117	384
5–9	103	103	49	31	2	9
0–4	99	0	27	0	0	0
All suburbs	23,872	95,464	10,795	31,855	30,428	50,699
Central cities	314,640	381,601	86,474	88,795	75,075	104,626
Entire SMSA	338,512	477,065	97,269	120,650	105,503	155,325

Percent of black households in metropolitan area

Suburbs						
1,000–15,000	6.1	17.8	8.8	23.9	24.8	23.9
50–999	0.9	2.0	2.2	2.2	3.9	8.5
10–49	0.1	0.2	0.1	0.3	0.1	0.2
5–9	0.0	0.0	0.1	0.0	0.0	0.0
0–4	0.0	0.0	0.0	0.0	0.0	0.0
All suburbs	7.1	20.0	11.1	26.4	28.8	32.6
Central cities	92.9	80.0	88.9	73.6	71.2	67.4
Entire SMSA	100.0	100.0	100.0	100.0	100.0	100.0

Percent of all suburban black households

1,000–15,000	85.9	88.9	79.0	90.5	86.2	73.3
50–999	12.1	10.1	19.8	8.4	13.5	25.9
10–49	1.1	0.9	0.5	1.0	0.4	0.8
5–9	0.4	0.1	0.5	0.1	0.0	0.0
0–4	0.4	0.0	0.3	0.0	0.0	0.0
All suburbs	100.0	100.0	100.0	100.0	100.0	100.0

SOURCES: U.S. Bureau of the Census, 1970 Census of Population and Housing: Census Tracts, Final Report (Chicago, Cleveland, San Francisco, and San Jose), table H-1; U.S. Bureau of the Census, Census of Housing: 1970, General Housing Characteristics, Final Report, HC(11) (San Francisco, Chicago, and Cleveland), tables 18, 23; U.S. Bureau of the Census, 1980 Census of Population and Housing: Census Tracts (Chicago, Cleveland, San Francisco, and San Jose), table H-1.

of black residents of these communities in 1980 has dozens of black relatives, friends, and co-workers. Thus their success in overcoming the continuing discriminatory barriers provides information and encouragement for thousands or possibly hundreds of thousands of other black families, who even now may be considering a move to the suburbs. Further, the appearance of nontrivial numbers of black children in previously all-white suburban schools must have begun to change the attitudes and expectations of both blacks and whites about the likely effects of black entry into formerly all-white schools and neighborhoods.

While black entry into all-white communities adjacent to the ghetto may still signal a nearly certain transition to all-black occupancy, there are simply too few blacks to produce this outcome in the large number of widely dispersed communities that by 1980 had between 26 and 600 blacks. As both blacks and whites cease to believe that black entry necessarily leads to the creation of an all-black slum, this outcome will occur less often. Whites will continue to buy or rent housing in neighborhoods with black residents, and blacks will no longer feel they can obtain improved housing only in a few communities and neighborhoods that have come to be recognized as acceptable for black occupancy. The resulting changes in black and white expectations could produce significant decreases in racial residential segregation within a surprisingly short period.

The changes in black residence patterns discussed above represent the first hopeful signs of a solution to what until recently seemed an intractable problem. If the small gains suggested by the preceding analysis can be exploited, considerable progress could be made in solving one of the nation's most vexing and dangerous problems. The trends identified in this paper are rooted in long-term, and very likely irreversible, changes in black and white attitudes. Even so, the rate at which discriminatory practices are eradicated and blacks obtain access to previously closed segments of metropolitan housing markets will depend critically on government policy.

POLICY RECOMMENDATIONS

It is impossible to determine how much of the newly emerging pattern of black suburbanization identified in this paper is attributable to the fair-housing legislation enacted during the past two decades and to federal and state courts' growing support, during most of this period, in defending the civil rights of black Americans. Still, it is clear that these efforts have had an effect and, perhaps even more critical, that several administrations' support of civil rights has encouraged white Americans to moderate their attitudes and practices relating to racial integration. These conclusions open questions about the likely effects of the second Reagan administration.

Few would disagree with the finding that the Reagan administration has shown less support for fair housing and civil rights generally than the administrations that proceed it had demonstrated. While long-term decreases in white prejudice are likely to withstand even four more years of a Reagan administration, the extent of federal support for fair housing during the next four years could have a substantial impact on how much racial integration occurs in the next decade or two. Regardless of the outcome of the election or of the enthusiasm of the incoming administration for civil rights, efforts to devise policies to reduce housing market discrimination must be made with a clear understanding of the respective roles of income and racial discrimination.

In spite of clear evidence to the contrary, civil rights advocates and policymakers have continued to formulate policies based on the mistaken belief that the low income of black households is the primary cause of racial segregation and the serious underrepresentation of black households in suburban areas. Joel Selig, former Deputy Chief of the Justice Department's Civil Rights Division, argued that the Justice Department should concentrate on lawsuits challenging exclusionary land-use practices (1984, pp. 445–504); similarly, most legislators and policymakers would agree with the position set forth by the authors of a recent *Yale Law Review* note on racial steering:

> While the supporters of the 1968 legislation understood that only a small number of ghetto dwellers would be able to afford property in suburban areas, they believed that the fair housing title was important as an expression of the nation's concern for the well-being of its black minority. (Notes 1976).

The conclusion that "only a small number of ghetto dwellers would be able to afford property in suburban areas" was and still is incorrect. The statistics for the city of Chicago and the Chicago suburbs (Table 9.6) once again demonstrate how little the level of black income has to do with the underrepresentation of black households in suburban areas. The six categories of suburb are defined by whether the area's median household income in 1980 was above or below the SMSA median, and by the area's percentage of blacks (over the SMSA average of 18 percent; between 10 and 18 percent; or less than 10 percent). Of Chicago's suburban areas, 21

TABLE 9.6

Central City and Suburbs by Median Income and Percentage of Black Residents,
1970 and 1980 for Chicago SMSA

Classification	No. of areas	Black households as % of all households			% SMSA black households		
		Actual		Pred.	Actual		Pred.
		1970	1980	1980	1970	1980	1980
Central city	1	27.7	34.9	21.1	91.2	85.1	51.5
Suburbs							
Below SMSA median income							
24.6–71.4 % black	4	24.7	46.8	19.4	2.7	4.0	1.7
10.5–16.9 % black	5	7.4	14.6	18.4	1.7	2.7	3.4
0.0– 8.9 % black	12	1.7	3.1	18.5	0.6	1.0	5.9
Above SMSA median income							
18.2–64.9 % black	3	14.3	24.9	16.6	1.6	2.1	1.4
10.2–11.8 % black	5	1.2	10.9	15.3	0.1	0.6	0.8
0.0– 8.1 % black	93	1.0	1.9	14.8	2.2	4.4	35.3
Entire SMSA	123	15.8	18.0	18.0	100.0	100.0	100.0

SOURCE: U.S. Bureau of the Census, 1970 *Census of Population and Housing: Census Tracts, Final Report* (Chicago, Cleveland, San Francisco, and San Jose), table H-1; U.S. Bureau of the Census, *Census of Housing: 1970, General Housing Characteristics, Final Report*, HC(11) (San Francisco, Chicago, and Cleveland), tables 18, 23; U.S. Bureau of the Census, *1980 Census of Population and Housing: Census Tracts* (Chicago, Cleveland, San Francisco, and San Jose), table H-1.

had 1980 median incomes below the SMSA average and 101 had incomes above the average; the median incomes of all 122 exceeded the central city median. These same data show that only 7 areas (4 with above-average and 3 with below-average incomes) had a higher percentage of black households than the metropolitan area as a whole; 93 areas had above-average incomes and fewer than 8.1 percent black households.

The predicted distributions of black households in the 123 suburban areas, assuming residential location depends only on household income, are very different from the actual distributions. These estimates indicate that while blacks made up only 1.9 percent of all households in the 93 areas with above-average median income in 1970, they would have accounted for 14.8 percent of the households in these communities if household income had been the sole determinant of residential choice. Analyses published elsewhere show similar results for 12 sub-areas within the central city (Kain 1984).

The last three columns in Table 9.6 show that the percentage of metropolitan-area black households living in the city declined from 91.2 percent in 1970 to 85.1 percent in 1980. Even so, the number of black households living in the central city grew by 21.3 percent between 1970 and 1980, or 65 percent of SMSA growth in black households. The central city share of SMSA black households in 1980 is 33.6 percentage points greater than would be expected from a knowledge of household incomes alone. Finally, the percentage of all black households living in the 12 areas with below-average incomes and fewer than 8.9 percent black households would be 4.9 percentage points greater, and the share living in the 93 communities with above-average incomes and fewer than 8.1 percent black households would be 30.9 percentage points greater, if housing market discrimination had no effect on residence patterns.

The view that racial integration can only be achieved by forcing high-income communities to accept subsidized and other low-income housing (Selig 1984) is not supported by the data in Table 9.6. These and similar analyses suggest that priority should be given to measures that would strengthen enforcement of existing fair-housing laws and assist black households at all income levels to learn about and obtain housing in the nation's increasingly heterogeneous suburban areas. This policy emphasis happens to accord with the Reagan administration's reorientation of Justice Department enforcement efforts toward private discrimination, although not with its tendency to select low-visibility cases and to accept lenient settlements, or its decision not to use the effects test.

Appropriations to enforce fair-housing laws need to be increased substantially. The fiscal year 1979 budget provided only $17.4 million for fair housing altogether, compared to more than $300 million budgeted to support equal employment efforts. Appropriations for fair housing were further reduced by the Reagan administration. The highest priority should be given to providing the Justice Department with the staff and resources required to identify, document, and bring lawsuits against a much larger number of private and public actors. The department should be encouraged to use testers and other systematic methods of detecting discrimination and of insuring compliance with consent decrees and judgments. A major increase in Justice Department fair-housing litigation would encourage fair-housing groups to renew their efforts to achieve integrated residence patterns, strengthen the resolve of minority home-seekers to search for housing in predominantly white areas, and legitimize the efforts of private attorneys to bring Title VIII cases.

Recent court rulings providing for the recovery of attorney's fees and the growth in size of fair-housing judgments are beginning to attract the attention both of firms and individuals engaged in discriminatory practices, and of private attorneys. Greater activity by private attorneys in bringing fair-housing cases could make a major difference: a single Cleveland attorney, Avery Friedman, has brought more fair-housing cases in the last eight years than the Justice Department brought for the entire country. Friedman's cases involved private discrimination and typically resulted in small settlements, but he was instrumental in bringing an important pattern case against Ohio's largest residential broker (*Heights Community Congress* v. *Hilltop Realty*) and he has obtained fair-housing awards of up to $50,000 for his private clients. Aided by the efforts of this private attorney and by those of the Cuyahoga Plan and other fair-housing groups, increasing numbers of Cleveland's minority households are learning of and demanding their rights to housing on a nondiscriminatory basis. While it is impossible to determine to what extent the appearance of growing numbers of black households in formerly all-white Cleveland suburbs are due to these efforts, there is good reason to believe they have indeed made a difference.

Awards in fair-housing cases have continued to increase in size; in July 1984, an upstate New York jury awarded a black plaintiff $545,000 in damages for discrimination encountered in attempting to rent an apartment (*Grayson* v. *Rotondale and Son Realty*). This award is on appeal and is likely to be reduced somewhat, but the appeals court did recently approve $120,625 in damages in another fair-housing case (*Phillips* v. *Hunter Trails Community Association*), a reduction of an original award of $252,675.

The analyses presented above suggest that efforts to eliminate racial segregation should emphasize litigation and other measures to eliminate steering, discrimination in mortgage lending, and discriminatory marketing practices by developers and lenders. The Justice Department should also be encouraged to take vigorous action against local governments engaging in practices that limit black Americans' access to housing in their jurisdictions. In addition, a strong argument can be made for requiring, as a condition of receiving federal and state aid, that those suburban communities with many fewer black households than would be expected on the basis of their incomes and other characteristics be required to develop affirmative policies to attract minority residents. Local governments should be given wide latitude in developing programs and policies, but they should be held strictly to numerical goals. Because of the symbiotic character of residential and school segregation, moreover, communities with few black residents should be strongly encouraged to participate in voluntary busing, and, in assessments of their progress in reaching their occupancy goals, they should be credited for their participation in such programs.

With greatly increased staffing and strong support from top policymakers, the affirmative marketing procedures instituted by HUD in February 1972 could make a major contribution to providing minorities with housing opportunities outside the ghetto. Every developer and sponsor participating in a HUD housing program must submit an affirmative marketing plan before the application can be approved. These plans require developers and sponsors to "carry out an affirmative program to attract buyers or tenants of all minority and majority groups" and to state in their plans the number or percentage of units they will sell or rent to minorities. These requirements undoubtedly assisted some minority households in obtaining rental housing outside of black neighborhoods. HUD's affirmative marketing requirement could be a powerful tool for achieving greater residential integration, but to date it has been little more than a paper requirement: HUD has had neither the staff nor the inclination to monitor these agreements.

Although it is true that subsidized housing accounts for a relatively small part of the nation's housing stock, governmental failure to administer these programs in a nondiscriminatory manner, as well as govern-

ment decisions about the siting of public housing projects, has contrib
uted to segregated living patterns. When they design and administer
subsidized housing programs, governments should consider the program's effect on racial segregation.

Housing vouchers, which are less visible and less disruptive than large
projects, could be a powerful tool in achieving less segregated living
patterns. Still in the absence of meaningful efforts to assist minority
households in locating and obtaining units outside areas of minority
concentration, vouchers are likely to reinforce existing patterns of segregation. It is essential that such programs embrace the entire metropolitan
housing market and that local housing authorities (if they administer the
programs) should be required to show that the programs reduce racial
segregation.

While very little of the existing pattern of racial residential segregation
can be attributed to income, several studies (Kain and Quigley 1975;
Schafer and Ladd 1981) have shown that black households are much less
likely to own their homes than whites of the same income and household
characteristics, due to past restrictions on black residential choice and
discrimination by mortgage lenders. Indeed, estimates (based on methods
similar to those described previously for predicting black occupancy in
the absence of housing market discrimination) indicate that more than
800,000 black households living in the nation's metropolitan areas have
been deprived of the benefits of home ownership by housing market
discrimination. These minority families did not obtain the inflation-in-
duced increase in property values and wealth that benefited similarly
situated white families during the past quarter-century. As a result, they
and their children have much less wealth than similarly situated whites
and are less able to trade up to better housing or to become homeowners.
There is much to be said for a program that would recognize the effects of
past housing-market discrimination on black homeownership and wealth
and would assist larger numbers of black households in obtaining homeownership. At minimum, strenuous efforts must be made to insure that
blacks are not discriminated against in their attempts to buy suitable units
outside the ghetto and that discriminatory lending practices are not employed to frustrate their efforts to obtain financing.

TABLE A

Black Households as a Fraction of Total Households,
by Household Income and Type, for All U.S. SMSAs, 1980

Household type and age	Total	Under $5,000	$5,000 to 9,999	$10,000 to 12,499	$12,500 to 14,499	$15,000 to 19,999	$20,000 to 24,999	$25,000 to 34,999	$35,000 to 49,999	$50,000 or more
Married Couple										
15–24	0.078	0.147	0.109	0.087	0.075	0.063	0.052	0.049	0.052	0.081
25–34	0.083	0.161	0.137	0.116	0.103	0.081	0.070	0.069	0.066	0.041
35–44	0.083	0.165	0.159	0.141	0.124	0.104	0.081	0.072	0.065	0.034
45–64	0.074	0.181	0.145	0.123	0.109	0.093	0.075	0.061	0.050	0.031
65 and over	0.067	0.165	0.085	0.061	0.054	0.050	0.049	0.045	0.036	0.020
Male head, no wife										
15–24	0.106	0.155	0.122	0.099	0.090	0.084	0.071	0.064	0.048	0.053
25–34	0.126	0.224	0.176	0.147	0.134	0.112	0.096	0.080	0.056	0.047
35–44	0.161	0.306	0.251	0.214	0.197	0.166	0.126	0.099	0.072	0.042
45–64	0.170	0.297	0.229	0.196	0.181	0.160	0.121	0.098	0.067	0.037
65 and over	0.137	0.209	0.123	0.094	0.090	0.085	0.074	0.068	0.051	0.032
Female head										
15–24	0.211	0.323	0.187	0.141	0.129	0.118	0.107	0.092	0.095	0.118
25–34	0.243	0.380	0.277	0.205	0.180	0.171	0.157	0.133	0.115	0.107
35–44	0.258	0.369	0.311	0.248	0.226	0.202	0.188	0.177	0.157	0.121
45–64	0.192	0.293	0.204	0.162	0.158	0.145	0.141	0.136	0.126	0.106
65 and over	0.100	0.138	0.074	0.068	0.071	0.071	0.068	0.062	0.058	0.036

SOURCE: U.S. Bureau of the Census, 1980 *Census of Housing,* Vol. 2, *Metropolitan Housing Characteristics* (Washington, D.C.: U.S. Government Printing Office), Tables B3, B4, B27, B28, C3, C4, C27, and C28.

REFERENCES

American Civil Liberties Union. 1984. "In Contempt of Congress and the Courts: The Reagan Civil Rights Record." 27 February. Washington, D.C.: ACLU.

American Institute of Public Opinion. 1978. *The Gallup Opinion Index*. Princeton: American Institute of Public Opinion.

Citizens Commission on Civil Rights. 1983. *A Decent Home*. Washington, D.C: Citizens Commission on Civil Rights.

Farley, Reynolds, et al. 1978. "Chocolate City, Vanilla Suburbs: Will the Trend Towards Racially Separate Communities Continue?" *Social Science Research* 7: 319–44.

Farley, Reynolds, Suzanne Bianchi, and Diane Colasanto. 1979. "Barriers to the Racial Integration of Neighborhoods in the Detroit Case." *Annals of the American Academy of Political and Social Science* 441: 97–118.

Feins, Judith D., Rachael C. Bratt, and Robert Hollister. 1982. "Final Report of a Study of Racial Discrimination in the Boston Housing Market." Cambridge, Mass.: Abt Associates.

Friedman, Avery S. 1974. "Federal Fair Housing Practice." *Practical Lawyer* 20, no. 8 (December): 15–26.

Grier, George, and Eunice Grier. 1983. "Black Suburbanization in the 1970s: An Analysis of Census Results." Bethesda, Md.: Grier Partnership.

Hersberg, Theodore, et al. 1971. "A Tale of Three Cities: Blacks and Immigrants in Philadelphia, 1850–1880, 1930, and 1970." *Annals of the American Academy of Political and Social Science* 441: 55–81.

Kain, John F. 1977. "Race, Ethnicity and Residential Location." Pp. 267–92 in Ronald E. Grieson, ed., *Public and Urban Economics*. Lexington, Mass.: D. C. Heath.

———. 1980. "National Urban Policy Paper on the Impacts of Housing Market Discrimination and Segregation on the Welfare of Minorities." Paper prepared for the Assistant Secretary for Community Planning and Development, U.S. Department of Housing and Urban Development, Cambridge, Mass. (mimeo.).

———. 1984. "Housing Market Discrimination and Black Suburbanization in the 1980's." Presented at Chicago Urban League Conference on Civil Rights in the Eighties: A Thirty-Year Perspective." Chicago.

Kain, John F., and John M. Quigley. 1972. "Housing Market Discrimination, Homeownership, and Savings Behavior." *American Economic Review* 62, no. 3: 263–77.

———. 1975. *Housing Markets and Racial Discrimination: Micro-economic Analysis*. New York: National Bureau of Economic Research.

Kantrowitz, Nathan. 1979. "Racial and Ethnic Residential Segregation in Boston, 1830–1970." *Annals of the American Academy of Political and Social Science* 441: 41–54.

Karlen, David H. 1968. "Racial Integration and Property Values in Chicago." Urban Economics Report 7, University of Chicago, April.

Lake, Robert W. 1981. *The New Suburbanites: Race and Housing in the Suburbs.* New Brunswick, N.J.: Center for Urban Policy Research.

Lieberson, Stanley. 1963. *Ethnic Patterns in American Cities.* New York: Free Press of Glencoe.

Miller, James Nathan. 1984. "Ronald Reagan and the Techniques of Deception." *Atlantic Monthly* 253, no. 2: 62–68.

Notes. 1976. "Racial Steering: The Real Estate Broker and Title VIII." *Yale Law Journal* 85: 808–825.

Pascal, A. H. 1967. "The Economics of Housing Segregation." Memorandum, RM-5510-RC. Santa Monica: RAND.

Pettigrew, Thomas. 1973. "Attitudes on Race and Housing: A Socio-Psychological View." Pp. 21–84 in A. M. Hawley and Vincent P. Rock, eds., *Segregation in Residential Areas.* Washington, D.C.: National Academy of Sciences.

Saltman, Julie. 1978. "Cleveland Heights: Housing Availability Survey, February–June 1978, Final Report." Cleveland Heights Community Congress (mimeo.).

Schafer, Robert, and Helen F. Ladd. 1981. *Discrimination in Mortgage Lending.* Cambridge, Mass.: MIT Press.

Schelling, Thomas. 1969. "Modes of Segregation." *American Economic Review* 59, no. 2: 169–85.

———. 1972. "A Process of Residential Segregation: Neighborhood Tipping." Pp. 157–84 in Anthony H. Pascal, ed., *Racial Discrimination in Economic Life.* Lexington, Mass.: D. C. Heath.

Schnare, Ann. 1977. "Residential Segregation by Race in U.S. Metropolitan Areas: An Analysis across Cities and over Time." Urban Institute Working Paper 246–2. Washington, D.C.: Urban Institute.

Selig, Joel L. 1984. "The Justice Department and Racially Exclusionary Municipal Practices: Creative Ventures in Fair Housing Act Enforcement." *U.C. Davis Law Review* 17: 445–504.

Sheatsley, Paul. 1966. "White Attitudes toward the Negro." *Daedalus* 95, 1: 217–38.

Taeuber, Karl E. 1968. "The Effect of Income Redistribution on Racial Residential Segregation." *Urban Affairs Quarterly* 4: 5–15.

Taeuber, Karl, and Alma Taeuber. 1964. "The Negro as an Immigrant Group." *American Journal of Sociology* 64: 374–82.

———. 1965. *Negroes in Cities: Residential Segregation and Neighborhood Change.* Chicago: Aldine.

Taylor, William L. 1984. "Farewell Civil Rights Commission." *The Nation* 238, no. 4: 113, 128–31.

U.S. Commission on Civil Rights. 1974. *The Federal Civil Rights Enforcement Effort—1974.* Volume 2. *To Provide . . . For Fair Housing.* Washington, D.C.: U.S. Commission on Civil Rights.

———. 1975. *Twenty Years After Brown: Equal Opportunity in Housing.* Washington, D.C.: U.S. Commission on Civil Rights.

———. 1979. *The Federal Fair Housing Enforcement Effort.* Washington, D.C.: U.S. Commission on Civil Rights.

Van Valey, Thomas L., Wade Clark Roof, and Jerome E. Wilcox. 1977. "Trends in Residential Segregation, 1960–70." *American Journal of Sociology* 82, 4: 826–44.

Wienk, Ronald, Clifford E. Reid, John C. Simonson, and Frederick J. Eggers. 1979. "Measuring Discrimination in American Housing Markets: The Housing Market Practices Survey." Paper prepared for the Department of Housing and Urban Development, Office of Policy Development and Research.

Yinger, John. 1978. "Racial Transition and Public Policy." John F. Kennedy School of Government Policy Note P-78–1. Cambridge, Mass.: Harvard University.

———. 1980. "On the Possibility of Achieving Racial Integration through Subsidized Housing." John F. Kennedy School of Government Policy Note P-80–2. Cambridge, Mass.: Harvard University.

———. 1982. "Evaluation of the Final Report of a Study of Racial Discrimination in the Boston Housing Market." Cambridge, Mass. (mimeo.).

CHAPTER TEN

Commentary

Michael A. Goldberg

I am struck by the pivotal role the United States federal government plays in any proposed agenda for metropolitan America. Virtually overlooked are the states and the metropoles themselves, including the local governments of which they are comprised. An important, and remarkably widespread, theme concerns the economic efficiencies associated with such a federal role. There is broad agreement that the large federal presence has distorted the allocation of resources in such areas as housing, urban transportation, and environmental protection.

Federal involvement seems to have another frequent deleterious effect: pressure to meet perceived national and regional problems in the short run often leads to long-run inefficiencies. For example, in attempting to assure adequate supplies of residential mortgage funds, deposit-rate ceilings of various kinds were instituted. They in turn led to periodic and rapid flows of funds among financial institutions, creating the need for various liquidity-producing federal institutions such as Fannie Mae, Ginnie Mae, and Freddie Mac. In the end, a rather complicated web of institutions had to be created to handle the side-effects of well-intentioned federal residential mortgage policies. Similarly, the federal aid to urban transportation, while providing relief from traffic congestion and improving access for peripheral lands, had significant longer-run consequences for urban form and particularly for the economic and residential viability of the central city.

Above these specific themes lies perhaps the most striking aspect of all:

the assumption that federal intervention is a completely normal, accepted, and perhaps even preferred state of affairs.

I would like to address this assumption about the desirability of federal urban roles, sketching out in the process an alternative approach to metropolitan federalism and policymaking that has rather different results. I draw my examples from the Canadian context. Canada is in many ways an excellent source of alternatives since it, like the United States, is organized about federal principles, is large in land area, is a democracy based on English legal principles, is an advanced capitalist economy and, finally, is a next-door neighbor. These broad similarities make the differences I will touch on more compelling, and possibly more relevant.

ALTERNATIVE POLICIES

CANADIAN EXAMPLES

The government of Canada has largely been excluded from direct involvement in metropolitan matters.[1] The Canadian constitution assigns responsibility for cities and local institutions exclusively to the provinces. In 1977, there were a mere CDN$209 million of direct transfers from the federal government to local governments, compared with United States federal transfers to cities (excluding special-purpose district transfers, which were also excluded in the Canadian case) amounting to U.S.$11.4 billion in 1978, or more than five times as much on a proportional basis.[2] Canadian federalism generally can be characterized as much more adversarial than its United States equivalent, with the Canadian provinces having a considerably stronger role than United States states.

Against this backdrop, I want to look at examples from two areas where Canadian policy has diverged markedly from that in the United States. The first relates to housing finance and the second to urban transportation.

THE CANADIAN HOUSING FINANCE SYSTEM

Canada's mortgage market provides a direct contrast to the situation that emerged in the United States during the 1960s and 1970s. At that time, United States federal involvement and attempts to pump money into the residential mortgage market set in motion a chain of distortions requiring a series of governmental and institutional responses to get liquidity and funds back into the financial sector. Canada followed a rather simpler path that led to a reduction in federally induced distortions with a corresponding increase in both the stability and the magnitude of lendable mortgage funds.[3]

Up through the 1960s Canada and the United States pursued similar strategies. Broadly speaking, the two federal governments sought to remove imperfections in the mortgage market; to make the morgage instrument more attractive to lenders, by improving liquidity of mortgages and reducing default risk; and to stabilize supplies of mortgage funds available to homeowners and builders.[4] These goals were achieved in Canada initially through the creation of the Dominion Housing Act in 1935, whereby the federal government got involved as a direct and joint lender and changed the mortgage instrument from the earlier balloon-payment mortgage to the present fully amortized mortgage instrument, while increasing lending ratios from the prevailing maximum of 60 percent to up to 80 percent and extending the term from a five-year period to ten years renewable for another ten years. Other federal legislation followed in 1938, 1944, and 1945, culminating in the National Housing Act (NHA) of 1954, which brought in mortgage insurance and enabled the government of Canada and its mortgage institution, the Central Mortgage and Housing Corporation (CMHC) to get out of direct and joint loans and instead insure qualified conventional lenders. Initially, CMHC set the mortgage rate at which it would insure loans. However, by the 1960s it became apparent that setting below-market rates was decreasing the amount of available mortgage credit. Therefore, in 1966 the NHA rate was set by formula as some floating percentage above the long-term Canada bond rate, and by mid-1969 the NHA was freed completely to be set by market forces. In 1967 the Bank Act was amended to allow banks to lend at interest rates above the previous 6 percent ceilings. This led to a massive increase in bank mortgage-lending activity, since the banks had largely been precluded from mortgage lending during the 1960s when mortgage rates rose above the permitted 6 percent level. The final major hurdles toward mortgage-market efficiency were cleared in 1969 when the Canada Interest Act and the National Housing Act were changed to allow borrowers to prepay any mortgage loan after five years, with a three-month interest-rate penalty. This effectively reduced minimum contract periods from 25–30 years to 5 years, although mortgages were still being amortized over periods ranging from 25 to 40 years.

These 1969 amendments were to prove particularly important during the inflationary period of the 1970s, since they created the five-year Canadian rollover mortgage whose interest rate was set entirely by market forces. The five-year rollover made it possible for financial institutions to match the terms of their assets (the mortgages) with the terms of their liabilities (savings certificates), thus greatly reducing lender interest-rate risk. Since deposit rate ceilings did not exist in Canada, this meant that rates for both assets and liabilities could float freely in the marketplace, leaving the equilibration process unencumbered to allow and absorb price changes with relative stability. This served to increase the amount of funds available to borrowers.

Inflation in the 1970s brought new imperfections to light. First, the notorious tilt problem pushed lenders to seek alternative mortgage instruments. Second, the five-year rollover caused considerable difficulty for many borrowers whose mortgages came up for renewal during periods of rising interest rates. Moreover, as inflation increased, loan terms were progressively shortened—all the way down to three months, and, for variable-rate mortgages, to an effective weekly term. Borrowers were therefore being asked to bear interest-rate risk that they were unable to lay off elsewhere.

Recent federal policies have sought to remove these two imperfections. During the 1970s, CMHC experimented with a form of graduated payment loan and also, by insuring such loans, encouraged private lenders to use the GPM instrument. Finally, in 1984 CMHC initiated a mortgage-renewal insurance program to protect borrowers from adverse interest-rate shifts on renewal of mortgage loans.

The net result of these policies has been to remove government-induced distortions from the Canadian mortgage market and greatly to increase the efficiency of that market. Residential mortgage funds have been abundant and relatively stable and in turn have stabilized housing starts, while greatly increasing starts during the 1970s, a period when the United States housing and housing-finance industry suffered so critically from the volatility of interest rates.[5] Additionally, Canadian mortgage-lending institutions experienced none of the liquidity and cash flow crises that plagued the American industry during this era.

My point in describing this experience in Canada is to put the United States situation in sharp relief by demonstrating that it is possible for a federal government to put into motion a series of policies over a three-decade period that reduce market imperfections in a rather straightforward manner, rather than producing the distortions and concatenation of secondary market institutions and instruments that have come to be taken as an unavoidable concomitant of the federal role in the United States.

TABLE 10.1

A Comparison of Forms of Transit, United States and Canada

Characteristic	U.S.	Canada
Public transit		
Revenue miles per capita		
mean	8.7	21.1
standard deviation	6.1	7.4
number of cases	69	15
Service area population to		
metropolitan population		
mean	0.74	0.80
standard deviation	0.19	0.24
number of cases	63	15
Expressways		
Lane miles per capita		
mean	0.0017	0.0004
standard deviation	0.0037	0.0002
number of cases	138	25[a]

[a]Data from Quebec are not included due to their present unavailability. The mean would probably rise with the inclusion of Montreal CMA in particular.

SOURCE: Public transit data: American Public Transit Association, Transit Operating Report, for Calendar/Fiscal Year 1976, Washington, D.C., APTA; J. Sewall, "Public Transit in Canada: A Primer," *City Magazine* 3 (May–June 1978): 40–55. Expressway lane miles: U.S. Department of Transportation, Federal Highway Administration Highway Statistics Division, Washington, D.C., personal communication, January 1979; authors' survey of provincial Department of Highways, 1978.

NOTE: The different sizes of n reflect different data sources and availability of data.

URBAN TRANSPORTATION IN CANADA

Where the foregoing example pointed up a federal presence that reduced market distortions over time (my second theme), the case of Canadian urban transportation provides a striking contrast with that in the United States because the federal government is almost totally absent from the picture (my first theme). Urban transportation is a provincial, regional, and municipal function in Canada, and the lack of federal presence has not impeded either the planning or functioning of the urban transportation system. On the contrary, it could be suggested that the absence of a dominating federal presence results in a corresponding absence of the kinds of distortions and inefficiencies highlighted in Gomez-Ibañez's paper.

Not unexpectedly, the Canadian urban transportation system is quite

TABLE 10.2

Commuter Transportation in Metropolitan Areas,
United States and Canada

	U.S.			Canada	
Mode	1975 (n = 21)	1976 (n = 20)	1975/76 (n = 41)	1976 (n = 10)	1977 (n = 10)
Total auto:	82	76	79	64	65
Drive alone	64	59	62	45	48
Drive with passenger	4	4	4	7	6
Ride as passenger	7	6	7	11	11
Share driving	6	6	6	n.a.	n.a.
Public transit	12	18	15	26	25
Walking	5	5	5	8	8
Other	1	1	1	2	2

SOURCE: U.S. Bureau of the Census, "Selected Characteristics of Travel to Work in 21 Metropolitan Areas, 1975," *Current Population Reports*, Series P-23, No. 68, and "Selected Characteristics of Travel to Work in 20 Metropolitan Areas, 1976," Series P-23, No. 72 (Washington, D.C., 1978); Statistics Canada, Education, Science and Culture Division, "Travel to Work Survey, November 1976," Catalogue 81–001 (November 1977), and "Travel to Work Survey, November 1977," Catalogue 87–001 (September 1978).

different from that in the United States. Much of this difference can, I think, be attributed to the very different behaviors of the federal governments in the two countries with respect to urban transportation. Tables 10.1 and 10.2 provide evidence of a Canadian urban transportation system that, relative to that in the United States, is much more reliant on public transit and correspondingly much less reliant on private automobiles and freeways. Accordingly, automobile ownership in Canada is roughly two-thirds and freeway lane miles per capita are less than one-quarter of what they are in the United States.[6]

Given such differences in urban transportation and travel, we should expect Canadian cities to be denser and more compact than American cities. This turns out to be the case, as the data in Table 10.3 illustrate.[7]

All of this suggests that it is possible to develop and maintain a perfectly efficient urban transportation system in the absence of large-scale federal spending. In many instances, the Canadian systems have been developed and operate without any significant provincial assistance either.[8]

There is an alternative, then, to the continued massive American federal contribution to urban transportation, although it is not clear at this

TABLE 10.3
Density Gradients and Central Densities
in Canadian and American Metropolitan Areas, 1950/51 to 1975/76
(CMAs and SMSAs)

Years	Density gradients		Mean central densities	
	Canada	U.S.	Canada	U.S.
1950/51	0.93	0.76	50,000	24,000
1960/61	0.67	0.60	33,000	17,000
1970/71	0.45	0.50	22,000	13,000
1975/76	0.42	0.45	20,000	11,000

point how the United States government can withdraw, given its past role and the urban form that emerged as a result of its role.[9] My purpose here is not to suggest that the Canadian model is necessarily workable in an American setting but, rather, to demonstrate that successful urban transportation systems can be developed without a federal role. Indeed, there are some benefits of excluding large-scale federal intervention in transportation aside from the efficiency losses brought out in the study by Gomez-Ibañez. Specifically, the more compact urban form that resulted from the Canadian model has considerable advantages in terms of the health of the central city and the efficiency of providing services in the metropolitan region.[10]

CONCLUSIONS

As economists, we have understandably viewed the agenda items for metropolitan America through "economic"-colored lenses. However, what comes out of these articles is a need for revised policies not just with respect to economic policy instruments, but more fundamentally with respect to the conduct of federalism itself in the United States. The problem of federal arrangements appears quite general in this context. Essentially, there are various levels of responsibility and concern. National defense, national transportation systems, and other issues of truly national scope fall within the purview of the federal government. Urban land-use controls and urban parks appear to be best dealt with on a local scale. So far so good. However, lying between these poles are hosts of issues that have both a national and a local component. The national defense Interstate Highway System has had enormous effects on the localities through which it passes. Similarly, locally produced air and water pollution extend beyond the borders of local jurisdictions. In short, there is no unambiguous way to assign each responsibility to one level of government or the other.

This problem is repeated in federal-state interactions, state-local relationships, municipal-neighborhood dealings, and even in neighborhood-household and household-individual dualities. Instead of some optimal mix of higher-level and lower-level responsibilities, it appears that there is a dynamic balance that occurs in the needs and responsibilities of the various levels of government over time. I suggest that it may be time to reevaluate the balance that has emerged in the United States. Not only do federal-state-local relationships need to be reexamined, so do the interactions and dealings among the state-local, metropolitan-local, and state-metropolitan levels. The balance in the United States has tipped well over to the side of the federal government and far from the metropolitan regions and the local governments that comprise these regions. By presenting examples from Canada's federal system I have hoped to demonstrate that quite a different balance of federal-state-local powers and resources is possible, though the final mix that evolves in the United States would have to be congruent with American values, institutions, and needs.

NOTES

1. The details of the division of powers between the federal and provincial governments are set out in Elmer A. Driedger, *The British North America Act of 1867* (Ottawa: Ministry of Supply and Services, 1975). In addition, I have discussed these issues at some length in "The BNA Act, NHA, CMHC, MSUA, Etc.: 'Nymophobia' and the On-Going Search for an Appropriate Canadian Housing and Urban Development Policy," in Michael Walker, ed., *Canadian Confederation at the Crossroads* (Vancouver: Fraser Institute, 1978), pp. 321–60.

2. These data are taken from *Canada Yearbook 1980–81* (Ottawa: Statistics Canada, 1982) and from the *Statistical Abstract of the United States 1982–83* (Washington, D.C.: U.S. Department of Commerce, 1983).

3. For anyone interested in the details of the evaluation of the Canadian housing finance industry there is now a wealth of material. For an early history and evaluation see H. Woodard, *Canadian Mortgages* (Don Mills, Ontario: Collins, 1959). For more recent background see Lawrence B. Smith, *The Postwar Canadian Housing and Residential Mortgage Markets and the Role of Government* (Toronto: University of Toronto Press, 1974); James E. Hatch, *The Canadian Mortgage Market* (Toronto: Queen's Printer for Ontario, 1975); George W. Gau and Michael A. Goldberg, eds., *North American Housing Markets into the Twenty-First Century* (Cambridge, Mass.: Ballinger, 1983); and George W. Gau and Lawrence D. Jones, "The Canadian Experience with Interest Rate Risk and Rollover Mortgages" (Vancouver: Faculty of Commerce, University of British Columbia, 1983).

4. The process for Canada is nicely described in Lawrence B. Smith, "Recent Shifts in Policies affecting Housing in Canada," in Michael A. Goldberg, ed., *Recent Perspectives in Urban Land Economics* (Vancouver: Faculty of Commerce, University of British Columbia, 1976), pp. 114–30.

5. This point is made in well-documented detail in Gau and Jones, "Canadian Experience."

6. For a more detailed discussion of the differences in transportation and their implications for urban form in Canada and the United States, see Michael A. Goldberg and John Mercer, "Canadian and U.S. Cities: Basic Differences, Possible Explanations, and Their Meaning for Public Policy," *Papers of the Regional Sciences Association* vol. 45 (1980): 159–83.

7. The differences in urban density gradients and central densities is the focus of the paper by Barry Edmonston, Michael A. Goldberg, and John Mercer, "Urban Form in Canada and the United States: An Examination of Urban Density Gradients," *Urban Studies* (forthcoming).

8. It is interesting to note that in 1978 Edmonton, Alberta, constructed a 7.7 km light-rail transit system (including 2.0 km in subway beneath the downtown), using Siemens conventional streetcars, for approximately CDN$80 million *without* any significant assistance from either the Canadian or the Alberta provincial government. Calgary, Alberta, constructed a slightly longer system using the same streetcars all at grade, mostly on existing railroad right-of-way, opening the system in 1980 for approximately CDN$100 million with about one-fourth of the total provided by the provincial government. And the province of British Columbia is constructing a completely automated 25 km system at a cost in excess of CDN$1 billion, to open in 1986. In British Columbia, a federal contribution of CDN$60 million was received under the guise of technological and export development, since the system is breaking new ground technologically and it is hoped that it can be exported. Finally, the largest of all Canadian transit systems (and now the second largest in North America), the Toronto Transit Commission, operates on a regional (metropolitan) base overwhelmingly financed locally by the metropolitan government and its own fare revenues and only to a minimal extent by the province. In each instance federal support (with the minor exception noted in British Columbia) is absent for both capital and operating grants.

9. The role of federally supported highways in altering urban form and speeding decentralization at the expense of central areas has been documented in P. de Leon and J. Enns, *The Impact of Highways on Metropolitan Dispersion: St. Louis*, Report P-5061 (Santa Monica, Calif.: RAND, 1973).

10. The issues relating to the comparative health of central cities in Canada and the United States is addressed at some length in John Mercer and Michael A. Goldberg, "The Fiscal Condition of American and Canadian Cities," *Urban Studies* (1984), and John Mercer and Michael A. Goldberg, "Value Differences and Their Meaning for Urban Development in Canada and the U.S.A.," in Alan Artibise and Gilbert Stelter, eds., *Essays in Comparative Urban Development* (Vancouver: University of British Columbia Press, 1984).

Commentary

Theodore E. Keeler

Gomez-Ibañez's informative and insightful paper concludes that benefits from the federal urban highway program have exceeded costs; that benefits from investments in transit, especially fixed rail systems, have seldom equalled costs; that federal programs have probably siphoned considerably more funds away from urban highway users than they have returned in investments and that federal programs bias state and local highway investments toward capital-intensive programs which may not be justified; that federal transit programs have biased incentives toward large, capital-intensive rail systems which are difficult to justify economically; and that federal urban transportation programs overall have not acted in the interests of the areas concerned.

Regarding both the effects of the federal aid program and the undesirability of maintaining the transit portion of it, I am in complete agreement; indeed, I believe there is evidence not mentioned in his paper which strengthens his case.

Regarding the benefits versus costs of urban highways, I believe there is evidence that benefits are even higher than is stated. I have conducted the accounting exercise of comparing highway revenues and expenditures (Keeler, Cluff, and Small 1974). One problem is that many urban roads are financed through subdividers and never show up in the government expenditure accounts. Some additional evidence on willingness to pay is provided by the effects of OPEC and of federal regulation of automobile safety and emissions standards over the past few years. Both have increased the cost of owning and operating a car by much more than anyone has seriously contemplated through increases in highway user charges. Yet auto vehicle-miles traveled have increased strongly and steadily over the past decade. Another indication of very high willingness to pay for the benefits of the private auto in urban transportation comes from travel-demand models in an indirect way. Most urban travel-demand models assume that auto users do not perceive the indirect costs of using their cars (e.g., depreciation, interest, insurance). Yet at least some of these costs are indeed variable with use. When Kenneth Small (1976) included all costs of owning and operating a car in his travel-demand equation, he found extremely high values of travel time—in the neighborhood of $40 per hour for walking and waiting time. What he seems to have identified, once again, is a very high willingness to pay for the benefits of the private automobile, and the evidence implies that whether or not people perceive these costs, it is quite clear that they are willing to pay them. Finally, Timothy Hau (1981) made a detailed benefit-cost analysis of the I-580 corridor in the San Francisco Bay Area, and found that for some bottlenecks of that corridor, additional lanes of highways for auto use could pay for themselves in one year alone, with no discounting. There is, thus, mounting evidence that highways are underbuilt in many metropolitan areas of the United States, and that the highways that exist should not be allowed to deteriorate.

I agree completely with the strong evidence presented by Gomez-Ibañez on the costs and virtues of rail transit versus highway transit and the private auto. But there is also some contradictory evidence; the truth may be more ambiguous than this article implies. Federal programs do divert money from urban systems and do spend it on rural systems; to use an economic term common in the study of regulated industries, the federal highway program cross-subsidizes rural roads with revenues from urban roads. I am inclined to agree that this is a bad thing, but more analysis and evidence are necessary before strong conclusions are possible. We need to go back to subdivider-built urban streets (maintained by local property taxes). These roads do not get federal (or, in many cases, state) money. But they do generate fuel-tax revenues, revenues which are used to cross-subsidize other roads. Thus, to the extent that revenues from users cover expenses for these roads, because they are supported by local property owners, these revenues are siphoned off to pay for rural and suburban roads.

Does this make cross-subsidization bad? There are good reasons to believe that it is bad in this context—it represents a possible misallocation of resources. And the most commonly asserted argument against cross-subsidization, "every tub should stand on its own bottom," is based on a well-founded fear that cross-subsidization will misallocate resources to areas in which benefits do not equal costs. Nevertheless, economic-efficiency arguments can be made for cross-subsidization from urban to rural roads. For example, Walters (1968) suggests that urban roads are subject to constant or decreasing returns to scale, whereas rural roads, because of their indivisibilities and low utilization rates, are subject to increasing returns to scale. Under these circumstances, an efficiency-maximizing pricing scheme could very well generate a surplus from urban roads and use it to subsidize rural roads. It is rather unlikely that the present pricing and investment scheme represents an efficient (or even second- or third-best) policy. Nevertheless, it could be superior in efficiency to a program that did not involve such cross-subsidization.

In terms of distribution, it is unclear whether such cross-subsidization is good or bad. As Meyer, Kain, and Wohl (1965) pointed out, the residents of cities do benefit from the superior intercity transportation generated by improved rural highways. If, as Gomez-Ibañez argues, however, main intercity roads generate positive net revenues, then most of the cross-subsidization goes instead to low-density rural roads whose primary function is local service to rural residents. In that case, the incomes of urban dwellers suffer.

In short, then, although I agree that cross-subsidization is a mistake, I believe that more research is needed on the efficiency of such federal programs.

REFERENCES

Hau, T. D. 1981. "Cost-Benefit Analysis of Urban Highway Pricing and Investment: An Explicit Expenditure Function Approach." ITS Dissertation Working Paper Series, UCB-ITS-DS81-3. Berkeley: Institute of Transportation Studies, University of California.

Keeler, T. E., G. S. Cluff, and K. A. Small. 1974. "On the Average Costs of Automobile Transportation in the San Francisco Bay Area." Berkeley: Institute of Urban and Regional Development, University of California (processed).

Meyer, J. R., J. F. Kain, and M. Wohl. 1965. *The Urban Transportation Problem.* Cambridge, Mass.: Harvard.

Small, K. A. 1976. "Bus Priority, Differential Pricing, and Investment in Urban Highways." Ph.D. dissertation, University of California, Berkeley.

Walters, A. A. 1968. *The Economics of Road User Charges.* Baltimore: Johns Hopkins.

Commentary

Richard F. Muth

It has always been a matter of some anguish to me that I have had to disagree so often with my good friends John Kain and Sherman Maisel. I am therefore delighted to report that there is much in their papers with which I agree. Kain's paper makes many important points about the residential segregation of blacks. First, the segregation of blacks is surprisingly persistent in many cities, despite the progress that has been made during the past two decades in other areas of racial relations in this country. Moreover, to the extent that suburbanization of blacks has occurred it has all too frequently been nothing more than an expansion of central-city black areas beyond the central city's boundaries. Surburban blacks, in my experience, are as highly segregated from whites as their central-city brothers are.

Kain is quite correct, I believe, in rejecting the hypothesis that black segregation is the result of black preferences. What little market data I have seen indicate that blacks pay higher prices for comparable housing in areas adjacent to white residences than in areas remote from them. This suggests to me that blacks prefer integration and are willing to pay for it. Nor can one account fully for black segregation by the lower incomes of blacks. Segregated areas of low- and of high-income whites often exist along with similar black areas in United States cities. Moreover, studies that have controlled for income differences find that segregation indices are only somewhat reduced by doing so. In any case, income differences can hardly account for the concentration of blacks in central cities, for while average suburban incomes do exceed average central-city incomes, the differences are small. In 1979, for example, the average income of white central-city households was $20,103, that of white suburban households $23,720—a difference of only about 16.5 percent.[1]

Kain is, however, mistaken, I think, in arguing that white preferences cannot account for black segregation. He bases his conclusion both on the wrong question and on the wrong kind of data. The appropriate question, it seems to me, is whether a white family would move into a dwelling in a black area, not whether it would move out if a black family moved next door. If whites will not move to an area where blacks live, the area will gradually become black.

Moreover, I tend to be distrustful of attitudinal surveys. I would far rather consider what people have actually done when confronted with an event than their response to a "what if" situation. Casual observation over the years supports the conclusion that few whites move into largely black areas. In addition, the few empirical studies of which I am aware find that whites pay lower prices for comparable housing when adjacent to blacks than when their housing is remote from black areas. This is precisely what one would expect if whites preferred segregation from blacks.

This last point is important because of its implications for Kain's policy recommendations. One fault I find with his principal recommendation is that Kain nowhere provides an explanation for the residential segregation of blacks. He appears to believe that it results primarily from the actions of real estate agents, renting agents, lenders, and others. I find it convenient to characterize his implicit explanation as a villain hypothesis, though Kain does not use this term. Nowhere, however, does he give us any explanation for the villains' behavior. It is possible to explain this behavior as being in the villains' economic interest. If a renting agent, for example, were to have no personal aversion to dealing with blacks or preference for dealing with whites, he might well turn away potential black renters, acting on the well-founded belief that at least some white tenants would move out if a black were to move in. Until the agent could replace those departing with new tenants, a higher vacancy level and thus lower net income would result. Moreover, if whites prefer to live with other whites, it would be difficult to replace white tenants who departed for whatever reason. The building or development would thus tend to become black-occupied.

If my explanation for villains' behavior is correct, then stronger enforcement of so-called fair-housing laws would have little long-run effect.

To be sure, by making the penalties great enough one could certainly change the behavior of rental agents and other villains. One could perhaps even devise incentives to make it less likely that white tenants would move out of a building into which a black family had moved, though I doubt such would prove either practical or politically feasible. I see absolutely no way through fair-housing legislation, however, to insure that whites would rent or buy in largely black residential areas. If I am correct, the residential segregation of blacks arises because blacks will offer less of a premium to live in the vicinity of whites than will other whites. To eliminate black segregation, an increase in the amounts blacks would offer relative to white offers for living among whites would be required. This could be accomplished by subsidizing blacks to live in white areas, by subsidizing whites to live in black areas, or by taxing whites who live in white areas. Of the three, subsidizing blacks might be most acceptable politically.

Certainly, there are strong reasons for preferring integration to residential segregation of whites and blacks. It is much less clear to me what is to be gained from the suburbanization of blacks per se. Casual observation, the small white income differential cited above, and the only study of which I am aware[2] all suggest that suburban blacks are no better off economically because of their location. It is true, of course, that some central cities are now so largely black that some blacks would have to be suburbanized in order to achieve integration. Suburbanization would also tend to divide between central-city and suburban governments the fiscal burden associated with the low incomes of blacks. The latter problem might be handled even more easily, however, by collecting taxes for income redistribution at a higher level of government. Thus, I can see little reason for black suburbanization as distinct from white/black integration.

Maisel's paper, like Kain's, is highly critical of the practices of the Reagan administration. Examined carefully, however, it is not the actions of the administration so much as the recommendations of the President's Commission on Housing that Maisel opposes. It is important to distinguish between the two, I think. The administration has indeed succeeded in cutting back sharply on new production programs, as the commission recommended. The voucher program recommended by the commission, however, is currently no more than a fifteen-thousand annual unit pilot program. The Secretary of HUD, moreover, publicly disagreed with the commission's recommendation for a partial federal preemption of local rent control laws. Interestingly enough, the 1982 federal preemption of so-called "due-on-sale" legislation and court decisions was based upon the same rationale as the rent control recommendation.

One of Maisel's principal justifications for government support of housing is that it has become less affordable in recent years. The data he cites, however, are based on mortgage payments. It is now well understood that these are highly misleading as measures of the costs of occupying a house. Even the Bureau of Labor Statistics has shifted to a rental-value measure in its consumer price index. Because of capital gains, the implicit rental value of homeownership fell sharply in the 1970s. Moreover, the income distribution of new house buyers changed very little during the 1970s and their median age actually fell.[3] It was not until late 1979 that the implicit rental value of homeownership rose sharply, and then the rise resulted from the sharp increase in real interest rates in the economy generally and had little to do with housing per se.

I find Maisel's insistence that a housing program necessarily implies the need for government production to be curious indeed. After all, we do not require the recipients of food stamps to spend them in government grocery stores. Nor do we limit treatment received under Medicare and Medicaid to Veterans Administration or Public Health Service hospitals. Public production might be indicated if increased housing demand from lower-income families would lead to higher housing prices, but evidence from the housing allowance supply experiment refutes this supposition. Likewise, virtually every evaluation concludes that housing produced under public programs has been considerably more costly than comparable housing available on the private market. It therefore seems that more low-income families may be assisted at a given resource cost through voucher programs than through public production.

Regarding housing vouchers, Maisel asks—I presume rhetorically— whether money spent on vouchers might be better spent on other programs. My answer would be, yes and no. As a general rule, income transfers are preferable to in-kind subsidies, and I can think of no compelling reasons why housing is an exception. Most low-income families today live in standard housing or in housing that can be brought up to standard at relatively little cost. Their principal problem, now as it has always been, is low income. Housing vouchers provide them additional funds for the purchase of housing. Moreover, under the proposed voucher program, low-income families need not move to receive assistance if their current dwelling meets program standards. The voucher payment then acts as a straight income transfer. Since I prefer income transfers to in-kind subsidies, I am delighted to call an income transfer a housing program if that is necessary to gain political acceptance.

I fully agree with Maisel's criticism of the President's Commission's stand on the tax issues related to housing. Indeed, I did everything I could as a member of the commission to change, and failing this to moderate, its position on these questions. It was anticipated that savings and loan associations would reduce their mortgage lending as they made use of their newly broadened lending powers. The mortgage-interest tax credit was thus proposed as a means of inducing other lenders to make additional mortgage loans to compensate for the reduction. In my judgment, however, such an inducement is not needed. Mortgage yields will rise and the returns to other kinds of lending fall as savings and loans associations redirect some of their lending. Others will then find mortgage lending relatively more profitable and increase theirs. The principal effect of the mortgage-interest tax credit would be to reduce the yields on mortgages relative to those on other securities. While Maisel, judging from his remarks on federal credit programs, might find this effect attractive, I do not. In my judgment, we have already reduced the cost of homeownership too far relative to the prices of other commodities, principally through the tax treatment of income from owner-occupied housing.

The commission's stand on this last issue is Maisel's strongest indictment against it, and rightly so. He questions, though less strongly than I would, the propriety of calling this treatment a tax expenditure. Given the level of other expenditures, the subsidy to homeowners is clearly paid by taxes collected from renters. Members of the former group living in SMSAs had average incomes of $26,229 in 1979, while similarly located renters' incomes averaged only $15,114.[4] Not only do lower-income families subsidize higher-income ones, but the size of the subsidy grows proportionately with the homeowner's income and thus his marginal tax rate. I find it impossible to conceive of a subsidy/tax scheme that operates in a more perverse manner than the treatment of income from owner-occupied housing.

Given his recognition of the nature of the tax treatment of homeowners, I find it difficult to understand Maisel's denial that our economy has overinvested in housing. His comparison of housing built recently with that in the 1950s is surely flawed because of the postwar housing shortage. Most economists appear to believe that the price elasticity of housing demand is at least .75, and I believe it to be unity. At marginal tax rates of 20 percent, the tax treatment reduces the cost of a dollar's worth of

owner-occupied housing to about 85 cents, since interest costs and property taxes are about three-quarters of housing costs. Thus, because of the
subsidy homeowners consume about 12 to 15 percent more housing than
they otherwise would. And, as several writers have observed, the extent
of the subsidy increases with inflation. It should not be surprising, then,
that we built housing at about a 20 percent higher cost in the late 1970s
than we did in 1965.

It is by no means clear to me that it is desirable to subsidize homeownership. In any case, the tax treatment of homeownership is a highly
inefficient subsidy. Most studies suggest that tax treatment increases the
extent of homeownership only on the order of 5 percentage points, or
from about 60 to 65 percent. At the subsidy rate of 1982, $50 billion in
aggregate, it thus cost about $15,000 annually per additional homeowner.
Surely measures that are more cost-effective and less objectionable on
distributional grounds could be found to stimulate homeownership.

Although I agree with the substance of Maisel's criticism of the commission and the administration on this score, his criticism strikes me as
unfair. To my knowledge, no other administration or presidential commission has spoken out against it. Indeed, not long ago the Senate passed
a resolution favoring the current system by something like a vote of 85 to
0. The only surprising thing about this vote to me was that those few
senators not voting for it did not manage to have their votes recorded as
favoring it. Nothing presents a more challenging political problem than
doing away with a program that benefits two-thirds of the voters.

Yet I see an economically sensible and politically possible way to
change matters. It is, to use that hideous Washington verb, "to grand-
father" existing dwellings when requiring homeowners to report, for tax
purposes, income received from their house. The great political hurdle to
removing the current tax treatment is the fact that doing so would result
in capital losses for two-thirds of the electorate. If it were not required to
report implicit income for dwellings in existence at the time of the change,
these dwellings would be worth more than new ones. The cost of the latter
is fixed by conditions of supply, however. The owners of existing dwellings would thus not suffer capital losses, whether they continued to live
in them or not.

Economically, such a proposal makes perfect sense. Regardless of tax
changes, we cannot get the excess materials and labor expended on existing dwellings out of them and into other uses. The best we can hope to
accomplish is to prevent excess investment in housing in the future.
Moreover, since buyers would be willing to offer more for a tax-favored

dwelling than for a new one, its owner would be forced to consider its opportunity cost to society when deciding whether to remain in it. It seems to me that there are few tasks an economist might take up that would be better for our country or for our profession than to work for the repeal of the current tax treatment of owner-occupied housing.

NOTES

1. Calculated from data in U.S. Bureau of the Census, *1980 Census of Housing*, vol. 2, pt. 1 (Washington, D.C.: U.S. Government Printing Office, 1983).

2. B. Harrison, "The Intrametropolitan Distribution of Minority Economic Welfare," *Journal of Regional Science* (12 April 1972): 23–43.

3. See John C. Weicher, *Housing: Federal Policies and Programs* (Washington, D.C.: American Enterprise Institute, 1980), pp. 104–109.

4. *1980 Census of Housing*.

Commentary

Melvin M. Webber

Gomez-Ibañez has presented a precise analysis of a transport sector's behavior and of the policy implications to be inferred. Despite its analytic elegance, the paper is flawed for having been cast in the antiquated mold of the auto-transit dualism. There is of course a long and distinguished pedigree that lends the credence of tradition to that dualism, but it is no longer a useful distinction for contemporary urban transportation analysis or policy.

Transit vehicles come in many shapes and sizes nowadays, and they support increasingly diverse service modes. Rubber-tired types now range in size from hundred-passenger monsters to vans that carry fewer than a dozen to automobiles with only four seats. Each travels on city streets and highways; each carries paid passengers; each is free-wheeling and able to change route flexibly. Even though not all are commonly understood to be transit vehicles, they all perform public transit services. Vehicles that follow fixed guideways also come in many shapes. There are old-fashioned suburban railroad trains like the Long Island Railroad, new-fashioned suburban railroad trains like BART, trolley cars of various vintages and fashions from the old South Line interurban in Indiana to the new Boeing cars in Boston, so-called people-movers like those at the Dallas–Fort Worth airport and Morgantown, and numerous others on the drawing boards. That heterogeneity and those automobiles used as public transit vehicles have vitiated the transit-auto dichotomy. The tenable and useful distinctions are the operating characteristics of various system types. And then, if there are differences among vehicle types that are now germane, they are the ones between small-vehicle systems and large-vehicle systems.

The strangest feature of contemporary urban-transit policy is that the flood of investment in transit systems is pouring into large-vehicle systems with operating characteristics fitted to batch passenger loads rather than small-vehicle systems suited to steady passenger flows. It is especially strange because most of the planned investment is targeted to the large metropolitan areas of the United States West and South, settlements that are new, built largely since World War II, and built at low residential and employment densities. The counterpart of low density in these places is spatial dispersion of homes and jobs, hence relatively small numbers of travelers making trips having the same origins, destinations, and schedules. A further counterpart is a ubiquitous roadway network, such that all locations are linked directly to all others. When fitted out with sufficient vehicles, that network provides the connectivity that has helped transform once-tranquil urban settlements into some of the most productive centers of economic and social activity.

The waves of modal-choice studies of the past two decades have by now made it unquestionably clear why automobiles have become so popular in these places. Travelers select travel modes with an eye to reducing the combined dollar and time costs of travel. Those modes that come closest to offering door-to-door, no-wait, no-transfer service at tolerable monetary outlay are preferred over those that may be more comfortable, prestigious, or in other ways seemingly more attractive or more efficient. It is now clear that automobiles have become the dominant transport mode, especially in suburban and low-density areas, precisely because they most closely match both travelers' economizing criteria and the spatial dispersion of origins and destinations. Buses, especially small buses, come close to meeting these tests within some locations, but the automobile clearly meets them best. Together, and in combination with the ubiquitous road network, cars and buses provide random access— *direct connection* from anywhere to anywhere.

In this respect, the auto-highway system is analogous to the telephone system, which connects virtually all places directly to all other places, assuring random access. The decentralized locational structure of the modern metropolis effectively requires unconstrained connectivity for single travelers and single callers, wherever they may be located.

The contemporary metropolis of the American West and South differs structurally from nineteenth- and early twentieth-century cities of the Eastern seaboard and Europe. In those older settlements, large concentrations of houses and jobs permit large-batch transit of travelers who move on identical routes and schedules. Those older cities built the successful subway and suburban rail systems that are tied in close symbiosis to their concentrated business districts. They are also the apparent sources of recent crusades to build large-vehicle systems in the South and West. Civic boosters in the new metropolises have heard that subways made the older cities great. Flushed with civic pride and expecting boosts in their local real-estate markets and their local economies, they now want subways too. With encouragement from the planning-and-engineering consultants and the generosity of their congressional delegations, the boosters have by now succeeded in acquiring billions of dollars earmarked for underground rail construction. It matters little whether the subways will accomplish the urban development and transportation objectives that are claimed for them, for these projects have themselves become the ends in view. They are no longer merely transportation-improvement projects; they are monuments fostering civic pride, pawns in complex political games, and sources of considerable monetary gain for some.

If, instead, the real objective were to improve accessibility and mobility, quite different strategies would be appropriate. Improvements to public transit service are mandatory components of such an urban-transportation-improvement strategy. For most metropolitan areas the search for transit-service improvement must inevitably lead to small-vehicle systems, specifically to those whose operating characteristics match the spatial dispersion of homes and jobs and hence spatially and temporally dispersed travel patterns.

Those transit system types will surely include buses of various kinds and sizes and automobiles used in public transit modes—in taxi, jitney, and ride-sharing arrangements. Dramatic reductions in traffic congestion should be readily attainable if car occupancy were to be increased. It is evident that much can be done at low capital cost, simply by offering motorists incentives to share their cars with others, for a vast transport capacity in America is going unused. There are enough front seats in the present automobile fleet to carry the entire population at the same time, but of course most of those seats move about empty. Where incentives are great enough, as they are on the San Francisco Bay Bridge, car-occupancy rates can be hiked appreciably. During the morning westbound peak, cars across the bridge are now carrying an average of slightly more than two persons each, owing at least in part to incentives offered commuters. Motorists can save up to 15 minutes and the 75-cent toll if they carry two passengers, and so they collect two or more strangers at bus stops and

BART stations in a win-win arrangement that benefits all parties, including the solo motorist who experiences lessened congestion.

Small vehicles, such as automobiles and vans, have a large latent utility as public transit and quasi-transit vehicles. The distinctions that cry out for analysis now are multidimensional, touching on the varied capabilities of transport systems operationally to match different land-use patterns and different travelers' assessments of costs. The old dualism between auto and transit will no longer serve. It would have been more informative to have read an analysis by Gomez-Ibañez of the consequences stemming from operating characteristics of various large and small vehicle systems, rather than more on the auto-transit debate.

PART FOUR

Regional Issues

A number of federal programs and policies have effects that vary substantially among regions of the United States. Wallace Oates evaluates federal programs involving the environment. Oates gives reasonably good marks to recent environmental regulatory programs but claims that appreciable monetary savings could be achieved if regulatory programs utilized market-oriented solutions more extensively. Peter Mieszkowski describes the sizable differences in employment and industry effects of the foreign trade deficit on regions of the United States, but suggests that the overvaluation of the dollar has had less effect on the Midwest region than is generally believed. In the Commentary, Paul Portney generally supports Oates' conclusions, though he suggests that Oates' benefit-cost framework ought to include political considerations. Timothy Sullivan reviews the Oates article, suggesting a number of important political constraints that face policymakers who wish to make use of effluent fees or marketable pollution permits. Finally, Jerome Rothenberg comments on the general problem of regional infrastructure. He argues that the federal government has an important role in developing roads, highways, sewers, and river systems but that the role must vary depending on whether a given region is in a period of growth or of decline.

CHAPTER ELEVEN

The Environment and the Economy: Environmental Policy at the Crossroads

Wallace E. Oates

During the past fifteen years, raised environmental consciousness has reacted to growing evidence of environmental damage by generating a flurry of legislation and associated abatement activities to control pollution. Federal, state, and local governments in the United States and public officials abroad have adopted a diverse array of measures to protect the environment. These measures have achieved some success in controlling pollution but, as we shall see, the record is distinctly mixed: levels of certain forms of pollution have fallen discernibly, but other pollutant levels have remained the same or even risen. Pollution control has become costly: during the 1980s the United States is spending over $50 billion a year to control pollution. This has taken a small but measurable toll on the performance of the macroeconomy. Particularly in the context of the general economic slowdown in the past decade both here and abroad, the issue of reconciling our environmental objectives and policies with the goals of continued economic growth and price stability has become a major concern. In June 1984, the O.E.C.D. countries met in Paris to address these issues in a major conference on Environment and Economics.

This moment in the evolution of environmental policy thus appears propitious for a reassessment of our environmental programs to determine their effectiveness and to explore the case for redirection of our policy strategies. This is obviously a tall order for a single observer in one essay, but in spite of the necessarily tentative character of much of the analysis, I undertake here such a reassessment.

A central theme is that polluting activities continue to pose a serious threat to our well-being. Much remains to be done to control a wide range of polluting activities that pose dire risks for society. To achieve this end, we need to employ more sensible procedures for setting environmental-quality standards. In addition, the choice of regulatory instruments for pollution control has resulted in enormous waste: abatement costs far more than is necessary to achieve many of the standards for environmental quality. By redirecting regulatory efforts toward a heavier reliance on economic incentives, we can realize huge cost-savings that will go far to reconcile our environmental objectives with a healthy economy.

BACKGROUND

Concern with environmental degradation has manifested itself in a wide range of legislative measures designed to control various forms of pollution. A brief, highly selective survey of the evolution of some of these measures provides needed background for an assessment of the current state of environmental policy.

Under the Clean Air Act (as amended at various times over the past fifteen years), Congress directed the Environmental Protection Agency (EPA) to set national standards for ambient air quality. The EPA responded in the early 1970s by specifying maximum concentrations for a set of "criteria" air pollutants.[1] The responsibility for attaining these standards was lodged with the individual states. Each state was to design a State Implementation Plan (SIP) for attainment of the primary national ambient-air-quality standards (NAAQS) by 1975. Responding to this charge, the states introduced their own regulatory systems to control waste discharges. These have typically involved estimation of needed reductions in emissions, followed by issuance of individual permits to stationary sources. The states then attempted to develop monitoring and enforcement systems.

To control emissions from mobile sources, the 1970 Amendments to the Clean Air Act mandated a highly restrictive set of auto emission standards involving 90 percent reductions (from 1970–1971 levels) in emissions of three pollutants to be achieved by 1975–1976. It was recognized at the time that these standards were beyond the technical capacity of the auto industry; the premise was that such "technology forcing'" measures would induce the industry to develop the needed control technology within the specified time.

The approach to control of water pollution has been somewhat different. Under the 1972 Water Pollution Amendments, Congress specified two general policy goals: an ultimate objective, eliminating all discharges of pollutants into the navigable waters by 1985; and an interim "fishable-swimmable" goal, protecting waterlife and recreational uses of bodies of water. For obvious reasons, the latter goal has served as the general operational objective. Unlike the Clean Air Act, the states themselves set their own standards for ambient water quality. There is thus an intriguing and important asymmetry in air and water pollution legislation: we have uniform national (minimum) standards for ambient air quality, but self-determined state standards for ambient water quality (more on this issue later).

The general regulatory approach to the control of waste discharges has been similar under the Clean Air and Clean Water acts. It involves specification of technology-based emissions standards for certain classes of polluters and issuance of individual discharge permits to sources. In addition, the federal government has played a major role in funding the construction of municipal waste-treatment plants. Paying up to 75 percent of the cost of these plants, the federal government has spent several billions per year to subsidize construction of new plants.

As the decade of the 1970s progressed, a number of problems and a certain amount of dissatisfaction arose with existing policies. It became clear, for example, that the schedule for meeting mandated objectives was, in many instances, not being met. The auto industry claimed that it was unable to meet standards for auto emissions on schedule; delays and extensions ensued. It also became obvious that many cities would not achieve the NAAQS by the prescribed time. Finally, there was widespread evidence both of long delays in specification of standards and issuance of permits, and of problems of monitoring and noncompliance.

Further amendments to the Clean Air and Clean Water acts were enacted in the late seventies. One provision is of particular interest here. As it became increasingly evident that many cities would be unable to meet the standards for all the criteria air pollutants by the mandated deadline of 1975 (later extended to 1977), an unpleasant confrontation loomed on the horizon. The prospective penalty for "nonattainment areas" was severe: a ban on new sources of emissions or significant expansion of existing sources, implying a virtual cessation to economic growth. Congress and the EPA managed to avoid this confrontation by introducing into the 1977 Amendments to the Clean Air Act a system of "emission offsets." Under the offset provision, new sources could enter nonattainment areas under two conditions: (1) that the new source adopt the most effective abatement technology available; and (2) that existing sources contract emissions sufficiently that a net improvement in air quality would result, i.e., the increment to aggregate emissions from new sources would be more than offset by reduced emissions from existing polluters. As I will discuss later, this admittedly pragmatic response to a potentially serious political confrontation has, somewhat ironically, opened the door to a very promising new approach to the control of pollution: tradable emission permits.

In the early 1970s, the bulk of legislative statutes pertained to the conventional air and water pollutants, but during the decade national attention and legislative activity shifted toward greater concern with "toxic" pollutants. Dramatic and disturbing incidents such as those at Love Canal and Times Beach have increased national awareness of the serious threats posed by such pollutants. New legislative measures were enacted to deal with toxic substances and hazardous wastes: the Safe Drinking Water Act (1974); the Federal Insecticide, Fungicide, and Rodenticide Act (1978); the Toxic Substances Control Act (1976); the Resource Conservation and Recovery Act (1976); and the Comprehensive Environmental Response, Compensation, and Liability Act (1980), which created the Superfund for the cleaning of hazardous waste sites. The basic thrust of these acts is, first, identification and, second, control (or cleanup) of toxic pollutants in the environment.

How successful have these measures been in stemming or reversing ongoing environmental deterioration? Before turning to the trends, a problem of inference requires comment. To evaluate the effectiveness of a policy, we need to know what would have happened in its absence. For example, although one dimension of environmental quality may show no improvement over the past decade, had the policy measure not been introduced the situation might have deteriorated. This issue is particularly relevant here, for the decade of the 1970s was a period of relative economic stagnation encompassing a dramatic increase in fuel prices and changing patterns of fuel consumption that would in themselves have altered levels of emissions of various pollutants. In short, some care is needed in making inferences about the success or failure of policy from environmental trends.

THE STATE OF THE ENVIRONMENT

An examination of the effectiveness of environmental policy as measured by levels and trends in environmental quality reveals a very mixed record.[2] Considerable progress has been made in reducing the levels of urban exposure to several "conventional" air pollutants; in contrast, control of water pollution has been much less effective. Moreover, as noted in the preceding section, the emphasis has to some extent shifted from conventional air and water pollutants to the largely unknown, but potentially insidious, effects of a bewildering array of toxic substances and hazardous wastes.

AIR QUALITY

The effort to improve ambient air quality in the United States has focused on the criteria air pollutants. In 1976, an interagency task force developed a Pollution Standards Index (PSI) that combines the observed concentrations of the criteria pollutants into a single measure. The index is designed so that it will take on a value of 100 or more for a given day if the air pollution level at the site exceeds the primary standard for any of the five criteria pollutants. The PSI thus provides a convenient summary measure by which to examine trends in air quality. The general trend toward reduced air pollution is shown in Figure 11.1, which depicts the average number of days per year that the PSI registered over 100 in a sample of 23 metropolitan areas in the United States. As the figure indicates, this number has fallen from over 90 days in 1974 to about 40 such days in 1981. The extent of improvement has been quite marked in some cities: Chicago, Portland (Oregon), and Philadelphia have recorded reductions since 1974 in the number of "unhealthy" days of 92, 78, and 72 percent, respectively. However, in a few cities, notably Houston, Los Angeles, Sacramento, and San Diego, PSI readings have increased over the past decade.

PSI trends to some extent mask the trends for the individual criteria pollutants. For example, in areas for which consistent monitoring data are available, average concentrations of sulfur dioxide and carbon monoxide have declined by roughly one-third from 1975 to 1982, but measured concentrations of nitrogen dioxide show little change over the period. Total suspended particulates (TSP, thought to be one of the air pollutants most detrimental to health) exhibit a more curious temporal pattern: average concentrations of TSP seem to have remained fairly constant over the 1970s but to have decreased significantly in 1981–1982. It has been suggested that this improvement may represent only a temporary reduction associated with the concomitant decline in industrial production.

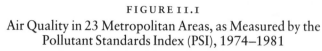

FIGURE II.I

Air Quality in 23 Metropolitan Areas, as Measured by the
Pollutant Standards Index (PSI), 1974–1981

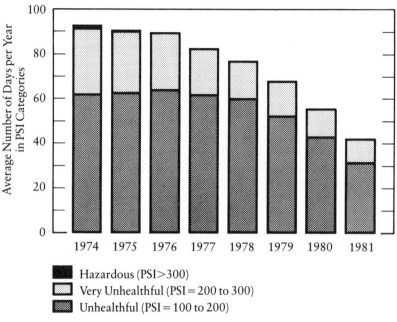

- ■ Hazardous (PSI>300)
- □ Very Unhealthful (PSI = 200 to 300)
- ▦ Unhealthful (PSI = 100 to 200)

SOURCE: Conservation Foundation (1984, p. 88).

The record for air quality, while certainly mixed, does appear on balance to indicate significant improvement in terms of the conventional air pollutants. Overall, air quality seems to have gotten better in the last decade in most of our urban areas.[3] However, in many metropolitan areas the primary standards for air quality still have not been met. Much is yet to be done, and it is likely that the remaining task will be considerably more difficult and expensive than in those cases where the initial effort has already attained the standards.

WATER QUALITY

The trends in water quality in the United States are both less well documented and less encouraging than for air quality. Some striking successes in water-quality management have been recorded: the return of Atlantic salmon to the Connecticut and Penobscot rivers in New England, for example, and the revival of lakes Erie and Ontario. But existing evidence of a more general kind suggests little real improvement in sur-face-water quality over the last decade. Of the conventional pollution indicators (dissolved oxygen, fecal coliform bacteria, suspended sedi-ment, dissolved solids, and phosphorus), the Conservation Foundation reports that "the vast majority of monitoring stations show no significant change in pollutant concentrations between 1974 and 1981, with those showing trends of increase balanced by a comparable number of de-creases" (1984, p. 109). These findings, incidentally, are based on reports from the National Ambient Stream Quality Accounting Network (NASQAN) of the U.S. Geological Survey, which provides "the most consistent and comprehensive information available on specific contami-nants" (Conservation Foundation 1984, p. 107).

The evidence does suggest considerable progress in the control of "point-source" discharges. According to EPA estimates, industrial dis-charges have fallen by 70 percent or more from 1972 to 1977, and some progress has also been made in controlling discharges from municipal wastewater plants, the other major point source. The results from a recent nationwide survey indicate that in spite of an increase of 12 percent in oxygen-demanding pollutants entering municipal plants over the period 1972–1982, the quantity of these pollutants emitted from the plants declined by 46 percent. "Pollutants leaving municipal treatment plants would have been almost twice as high as the amount actually discharged in 1982 if there had been no improvement to the facilities that existed in 1972" (Conservation Foundation 1984, p. 119). Periodic difficulties arise with the efficient operation of these plants, however. In particular, since federal subsidies apply to the construction of municipal waste-treatment plants but not to their operation, many newly constructed plants are not operating properly.

Non–point-source pollution—especially agricultural runoff, but also urban runoff—has proved much more difficult to control. State officials, in fact, most often cite these sources as preventing streams from providing desired services. Runoff from agricultural lands contributes most of the sediment, nitrogen, phosphorus, and organic pollutants entering surface waters in the United States, as well as significant amounts of pesticides, bacteria, and dissolved solids. Development of effective programs for the management of non-point sources is essential if we are to realize any substantial improvement in water quality.

Potentially even more troublesome than the control of surface-water quality is the recently recognized spectre of contamination of our ground-water. Underground aquifers are the primary source of water in many parts of the United States. We do not have comprehensive information on the extent of groundwater contamination, but surveys have uncovered hundreds of cases of well closures as a result of contamination from toxic pollutants. Other groundwater sources have been rendered unusable for most purposes due to saltwater contamination, the presence of bacteria and viruses, the intrusion of nitrates, and radioactive contamination. We are just beginning to get some sense of the magnitude of the problem—and it appears to be getting worse.

TOXIC SUBSTANCES AND HAZARDOUS WASTES

So-called toxic pollutants encompass a very diverse range of substances. They include a vast array of toxic metals, organic toxic chemicals such as pesticides and polychlorinated biphenyls (PCBs), and fibrous minerals such as asbestos. Demonstrable progress has been made in reducing exposure to some of these substances. Lead, for example, was identified fairly early on as an insidious pollutant with debilitating health effects. Widely used as a gasoline additive, in automobile batteries, and in pigments and paints, lead found its way into the human environment through several paths. Existing data indicate that lead production and consumption gradually increased over the 1960s and early 1970s. However, between 1977 and 1982, average concentrations of lead as measured at urban monitoring sites have declined by almost two-thirds. There are similar declines over this period in the lead content in samples of human blood. These results are attributable primarily to the growing reliance on unleaded gasolines; moreover, as older, leaded-fuel cars are retired from use, further declines in lead concentrations should take place.[4]

We have also made major progress in reducing levels of exposure to certain other toxic substances: DDT, PCBs, and asbestos are major cases. But against this record must be weighed environmental calamities such as Love Canal and Times Beach, and the frightening prospect of thousands of chemical and other substances with unknown effects being discharged into the human environment. We have learned that many harmful substances are not effectively neutralized when disposed of in landfills; they do not degrade into harmless materials or stay put at the site. Instead they can infect the environment, with sometimes disastrous consequences, long after their disposal. It is estimated that United States industry currently generates over a ton of hazardous wastes per person per year. Many of these wastes find their way into hazardous-waste disposal sites. EPA reports indicate that there are 16,000 to 22,000 inactive or abandoned sites scattered across the United States that are actual or potential sources of contamination. An extensive effort is now underway to identify these sites and to clean them up, in part with federal support from the recently created Superfund.

Yet more perplexing is dealing with the wide range of substances about whose effects we know virtually nothing. The Conservation Foundation (1984, p. 40) notes that although there are over 66,000 chemicals currently in commercial use in the United States, only a tiny fraction of them have been adequately tested for effects on human health. The Foundation Report concludes:

> For the most part, how to determine, or to adequately measure, many of the effects that toxic substances have on people or on the environment remains a mystery. The continuing discovery of previously unsuspected hazards from various chemicals and other substances underscores this point. The environmental and human health effects of even those substances identified for priority consideration, in general, have not been adequately studied. Moreover, until the present decade, testing of suspected toxic substances was confined largely to acute effects. Only in the last few years have the chronic, long-term effects of exposure to many of these substances been understood. Knowledge of environmental effects, how chemicals are transported through the environment, what biological pathways they follow, and where they ultimately end up is still lacking for most suspected toxic materials. A shortage of trained personnel and the absence of a comprehensive system for storing and analyzing information aggravate the scientific bases for government inaction. (pp. 65–66)

The existing evidence on the state of the environment thus indicates that much remains to be done in the control of the conventional air and water pollutants, in the identification of toxic substances and hazardous wastes, and the regulation of their production and disposal. Environmental policy has made a difference over the past decade. As was noted, intensive abatement efforts have resulted in marked improvements in certain dimensions of environmental quality. Moreover, measures of pollutant concentration indicate that levels of several air and water pollutants have at least not increased over the past decade. In the presence of a growing population and economy, this in itself is some evidence of the effectiveness of environmental policies.[5] But the remaining agenda for pollution control is long; it is one that we cannot afford to ignore.

THE COST OF POLLUTION CONTROL

As Table 11.1 indicates, pollution control is not cheap. By 1980, total expenditures on pollution abatement and control in the United States exceeded $50 billion per year, with the business sector undertaking about

TABLE 11.1

Expenditures for Pollution Abatement and Control
(billions of dollars)

	1972	1975	1980
Pollution abatement			
Personal consumption	$ 1.5	$ 3.5	$ 7.0
Business	11.0	18.1	34.0
Government	4.7	7.6	11.6
Regulation and monitoring	0.4	0.7	1.3
Research and development	0.8	1.1	1.8
Total	$18.4	$30.9	$55.7

SOURCE: Council on Environmental Quality (1983, table A-80).

two-thirds of this spending and the government sector the remaining third. Such spending in 1980 represented about two percent of the GNP in the United States. As Portney (1981) has stressed, total expenditures are not identical with costs in a full economic sense. Firms, for example, may well employ certain of their own resources for abatement activities that are not reflected in actual expenditures. Probably more important, the regulatory system itself may introduce uncertainties and delays that distort economic decisions and generate costs to the economy that do not show up as spending on pollution control. In all likelihood, expenditures to some extent understate the true costs to the economy of reducing pollution.[6]

The past decade has seen troublesome price inflation and a slowed rate of economic growth. To what extent have the costs of our environmental programs contributed to the relatively poor macroeconomic performance over this period? In answering this question, it is important to emphasize the basic, if obvious, point that standard measurement procedures are, in an important sense, biased against environmental programs. Since the GNP does not include imputations for the services of the environment as a public good, benefits from pollution control do not show up as measured increases in real income.[7] Instead we see the effects expenditures on environmental protection have on the pecuniary cost of economic activities and on the price level.

Several studies have explored the macroeconomic effects of regulatory measures for pollution control. One approach has used some of the large quarterly econometric models to estimate the effect of control expenditures on the rates of price inflation and economic growth (see Portney

1981). For example, Data Resources Incorporated has employed its DRI quarterly model to estimate the macroeconomic effects of environmental regulation in the United States. The DRI results indicate that during the period 1970–1987, environmental regulation will increase the average annual inflation rate by about 0.4 percentage points; for the period 1981–1987, the estimated increase is 0.6 percentage points. DRI projects that the average annual growth rate of the GNP will fall by about 0.1 percentage points per year as a result of environmental programs.

While these are certainly not trivial magnitudes, they are not momentous. In one sense, these results should not be very surprising. The primary determinants of the projections of the macroeconomic models are levels of expenditure. Since spending on pollution control is only a minute fraction of total (and marginal) expenditure in the economy, we would not expect to find this category of spending exerting any major effect on macroeconomic variables. However, with its exclusive reliance on expenditures, this approach neglects the possibly larger adverse effects of environmental regulation, involving delays and other modifications to investment decisions. For example, Quarles (1979) has argued that implementation of the Clean Air Act has in many instances created an atmosphere of such confusion and uncertainty that many firms either delayed or abandoned plans altogether for industrial expansion.

Various other kinds of studies have tried to capture some of these effects contributing to the retardation of productivity growth. Denison (1979) has employed his "growth accounting" framework to estimate the contributions of various determinants to the slowdown in productivity growth. Siegel (1979) has used time-series econometric analysis on macroeconomic variables, and Crandall (1981) has made microeconomic estimates for certain industries that were the subject of heavy environmental regulation. Although these studies do not come to precisely the same conclusions, they reveal the same general picture. The impact of environmental regulation on productivity growth is a measurable but not a dominant one. The effects, for example, of the huge rise in energy prices in the early 1970s seem far more important in retarding growth in productivity than do those of pollution-control regulations. Haveman and Christiansen concluded that "little evidence exists to suggest that as much as 15 percent of the overall slowdown [of productivity growth] can be attributed to these [environmental] regulations. A reasonable estimate—but one resting on a good deal of judgment—is that 8 to 12 percent of the slowdown in productivity is attributable to environmental regulation" (1981, p. 74).

Interestingly, studies in other O.E.C.D. countries suggest roughly similar findings. The estimated effects of environmental measures on the rate of inflation (in terms of percentage points per year) are: Austria 0.1 to 0.3, Netherlands 0.1 to 0.6, Japan 0.4 to 0.6, France and Italy 0.1. Likewise, environmental regulations seem to have had minor effects on productivity growth. A recent O.E.C.D. study concluded: "In sum, then, the evidence makes clear that environmental regulations have contributed only modestly to the last decade's fall-off in measured labor productivity growth, and can in no way be considered the driving force behind this reduction" (1984, p. 37).

Thus, the effects of environmental policy on the performance of the macroeconomy over the past decade have been discernible, but modest. Neither in the United States nor in the other O.E.C.D. countries can environmental programs be seen as the major culprit impeding economic growth and the attainment of stable prices. Nevertheless, pollution control is expensive: the United States will probably spend well over $500 billion on environmental programs during the 1980s. For efforts of this magnitude, it is obviously important to marshall our resources in a sensible and efficient way. Large-scale misuse of these resources will undermine our capacity to achieve both environmental and other pressing social goals.

STANDARDS FOR ENVIRONMENTAL QUALITY

CRITERIA

According to basic economic principles, an activity such as pollution control should be extended to the point where marginal benefits equal marginal costs. From this perspective, the environmental authority should set standards for pollutant concentrations in the environment such that the damages from another increment of pollutant equal marginal abatement costs. Of course, the application of this simple dictum encounters formidable obstacles. For many pollutants, we do not have firm scientific knowledge of how emissions from sources translate into pollutant concentrations in the environment, or of how much harm is caused by exposure to various levels of a pollutant. Moreover, environmental degradation results in many so-called intangible damages—aesthetic insults as well as injury to health. This raises all the knotty problems of trying to assess in money terms a very diverse and uncertain range of effects on individual welfare. Steven Kelman (1981) has introduced a more philosophical objection: the act of placing the pollution problem in a benefit-cost framework itself undermines environmentalist values by making environmental quality just another commodity in the marketplace.

In response to these problems and objections to benefit-cost analysis, Congress has been quite explicit in rejecting this criterion for the determination of environmental standards. In the Clean Air Act, Congress instructed the EPA to set standards for ambient air quality "to protect the public health and welfare." This put the environmental authority in an awkward corner. The scientific evidence for most pollutants suggests a continuum of health damages. Low concentrations typically result in modest health effects; with higher concentrations these damages escalate. The EPA, however, has effectively been directed to find a threshold concentration for each pollutant below which there is *no* impairment to health. A very literal interpretation of the Clean Air Act could require concentrations of zero for certain pollutants. This is, of course, infeasible, since it would imply a complete cessation of fuel combustion and various other forms of economic activity.

The EPA has, in fact, had to make compromises. As Crandall and Portney have pointed out, "Economic and other practical considerations are surely taken into account in setting standards, even if no one is willing to admit it" (1984, p. 53). However, the legislative mandate has led to some very difficult and questionable decisions. Crandall and Portney have cited an interesting case. In 1980, the EPA proposed a tightening of the standard for carbon monoxide, intended for the protection of persons with angina pectoris. The definition of whom to protect is important here, for it was argued by others that even the more stringent standard was inadequate to prevent adverse health effects for hemolytic anemics.

> Despite this definition of the sensitive population, there is evidence that the health protection offered by reduced carbon monoxide had a very high cost indeed. According to the Regulatory Analysis and Review Group of the Executive Office of the President, comparison of the 9 parts per million (ppm) carbon monoxide standard that the EPA was proposing with a less strict alternative, 12 ppm, showed that each sick day prevented by the stricter standard would cost the nation between $6,000 and $250,000. Although the health of those with cardiovascular disease is very important, it is far from obvious that the prevention of one sick day is worth $6,000—much less a quarter of a million dollars. (Crandall and Portney 1984, p. 53)

This is not the only case for which the costs of apparently quite marginal improvements are enormous. The issue here is not that modest increments to health are not worth much—on the contrary, we may as a society be willing to make considerable sacrifices for them. The point is, rather, that the determination of standards for environmental quality inevitably involves difficult and unavoidable trade-offs between economic goals, on the one hand, and such goods as health and aesthetics on the other. The argument, incidentally, is not that environmental decisions should be based in any rigid way on a benefit-cost criterion; the available estimates of benefits and costs are typically far too tentative for that. Rather, benefit-cost estimates can provide a rough sense of orders of magnitude that can be extremely valuable in reaching an informed decision. There appears to be a growing realization of this in the policy arena. The General Accounting Office, for example, has recently issued a report (1984) urging the use of benefit-cost analysis for environmental regulations, and at the recent Paris conference of the O.E.C.D. countries sentiment was widespread that, after acknowledging all its deficiencies, "economic analyses of the costs and benefits of environmental policies can aid this decision-making process by permitting aggregation and comparison of the many heterogeneous impacts frequently associated with environmental policies" (O.E.C.D. 1984, p. 90).

When a particular control activity results in reduced illness and/or loss of life, offensive calculations of the monetary value of health and life can be avoided through a cost-effectiveness approach. This can be quite valuable in rationalizing the use of resources across different kinds of abatement efforts. Cost calculations can suggest, for example, that one form of pollution control is significantly more effective per dollar in reducing the incidence of a certain form of illness than another. Especially where a specific pollutant enters the environment through a number of different avenues, such studies can indicate the least costly way to reduce exposure.

In principle, the level of the standard should depend to some extent on the defensive activities available to those who suffer the effects of pollution.[8] Where, for example, insulation can protect against undesired noise, it is a straightforward matter to show that the marginal social damage curve will lie below that where, ceteris paribus, no such defensive activities exist. Moreover, when the standard is set correctly, it can be shown that individual maximizing behavior will lead to economically efficient levels of these defensive activities (Oates 1983). All this depends, of course, on full information both on the range of effects of the pollutants and on the extent of effectiveness of the defensive measures, information which often is far from complete. But the general point remains valid: the availability (and cost) of ways to avoid the effects of pollutants is one determinant of the optimum standard.

Responding to Kelman's philosophical objection to benefit-cost analysis is more difficult. The basic contention is that environmental resources are, in a sense, different from other goods in the marketplace. Many environmentalists believe that people have a basic right to a clean environment, and that pollution is an infringement of that basic right. Moreover, it is feared that placing environmental concerns in the economist's framework of market value will lead to a depreciation in the perceived value of our environmental resources. The claim here is that tastes for environmental quality are, to a significant degree, endogenous, and subjecting environmental standards to the benefit-cost calculus will, over time, reduce the intensity of preferences in support of environmental objectives. Hence, Kelman sees economists as lobbyists for economic efficiency in a political setting where many environmentalists seek to emphasize other objectives.

While Kelman may well be correct in describing the differing perceptions of the various participants in the environmental debate, I have a basic pragmatic difficulty with his philosophical position. Such a perspective does not provide a sound basis for environmental decisionmaking. Instead, it tends to promote legislative pronouncements like that in the Clean Water Act that specifies as an objective "the elimination of all discharges of pollutants into the navigable water by 1985," and the provision under the Clean Air Act for standards "to protect the public health and welfare." As I have argued, these are not operational objectives, and they have put the environmental authority in the difficult position of paying lip service to existing legislation while proceeding, in reality, to make the compromises inherent in environmental measures. It makes more sense, I think, to make the trade-offs explicit so that they can be assessed in a sensible way.

UNIFORM NATIONAL STANDARDS OR LOCAL VARIATION?

An important issue in standard-setting for environmental quality is whether to allow local diversity. Should the central environmental authority establish a single standard binding in all areas, or should regional or local authorities tailor standards to their own circumstances? Interestingly, as noted above, environmental legislation in the United States is not consistent on this matter. Under the Clean Air Act, Congress instructed the EPA to set national minimum standards for ambient air quality, and the EPA responded by establishing maximum levels of concentration for the criteria air pollutants applicable to all areas in the country. States have

FIGURE II.2

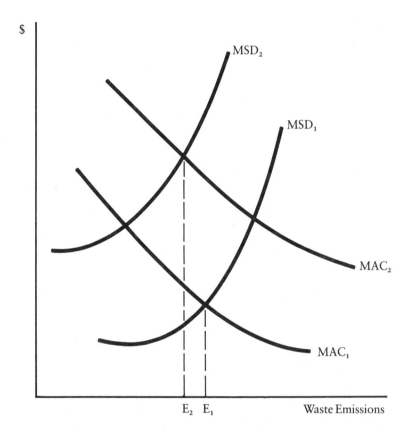

the option of establishing more stringent standards for air quality, but only California has yet chosen to do so. In contrast, under the Clean Water Act, the individual states have the responsibility for setting water-quality standards, although the EPA plays an important role in specifying treatment technology and issuing permits to dischargers. We thus have uniform national standards for air quality but state-specific standards for water quality.

Simple economic analysis again provides a seemingly straightforward resolution of this issue: standards should vary across jurisdictions in accordance with local circumstances. The economically optimal level of environmental quality is that for which the marginal social damages of waste emissions equal marginal abatement cost. Figure 11.2 depicts such an outcome. Suppose that MSD_1 and MAC_1 are, respectively, the marginal-social-damage and the marginal-abatement-cost functions in jurisdiction 1; then the economically optimal level of waste emissions is E_1. Other jurisdictions, however, will typically have different MSD and MAC functions; if, for instance, MSD_2 and MAC_2 are the curves for jurisdiction 2, then local authorities in 2 should set a more stringent standard for environmental quality than in jurisdiction 1 ($E_2 < E_1$).

An interesting question is, would one expect the optimal level of environmental quality to be higher in an urban area or in a less densely populated, rural area? To address this question, we must examine the determinants of the two functions. Since environmental quality is basically a public good, we derive the MSD curve through the vertical summation of individual marginal damage curves. If people's tastes for environmental quality are roughly similar, we would expect a higher MSD curve in a more heavily populated area—reflecting the greater number of people suffering damage from existing pollution. In Figure 11.2, we might associate MSD_1 with the rural area and MSD_2 with the urban area. The MAC curve, in contrast, is a horizontal summation of individual MAC curves. Since a typical urban area will presumably have far more sources of waste emissions than our prototype rural area, we would expect the urban MAC curve to lie to the right of the rural curve. In Figure 11.2, MAC_1 might represent the rural curve, while MAC_2 indicates the comparatively higher level of abatement costs in the urban area for any given level of emissions. We could thus associate MAC_1 and MSD_1 with a representative rural area as compared to MAC_2 and MSD_2 for the urban area. It is now clear that there is no presumption a priori as to whether the optimal level of environmental quality will be higher in urban or rural areas. Both the marginal damages from pollution and the marginal abatement costs are likely to be higher in the urban area, so the outcome depends on the relative magnitudes for a particular case.[9]

The analysis does clearly suggest that the optimal pollution level will vary across jurisdictions. What, then, is the case for uniform national (perhaps minimum) standards? John Cumberland (1979, 1981) has made the case for national minimum ambient standards on two grounds. The first is interregional externalities. Unfortunately, existing political jurisdictions often do not conform at all well to appropriate environmental jurisdictions: pollution generated in one area may well settle elsewhere. This led Cumberland to the conclusion that fully decentralized environmental decisionmaking is likely to result in excessive pollution: "The federal level should set maximum emission or minimum ambient standards to avoid the deliberate or inadvertent tendency of local regions to site detrimental activities on border locations which cause interregional flows to impact inequitably on downstream regions" (1981, p. 8). Second, Cumberland stressed the possibility of "destructive interregional competition." In their eagerness to encourage new business investment and the creation of jobs, state or local authorities may compete with one another in reducing standards for environmental quality so as to reduce costs for prospective business enterprise. The argument here parallels the phenomenon of tax competition among jurisdictions to promote state or local economic development.

Just where all this leaves us is difficult to say. It is really a matter of the comparative magnitude of welfare losses. We know that uniform national standards will entail allocative losses (relative to the first-best outcome), because of the failure to allow local standards to reflect local costs and benefits. But how large are these losses compared to those associated with the likely distortions from interjurisdictional externalities and competition? It is hard to know without careful empirical work to provide a sense of the relevant magnitudes, but let me offer a couple of observations. First, it is not clear that setting minimum national standards is the appropriate response to the problem of interjurisdictional externalities. A national standard for the concentration of a particular pollutant, for example, will not in itself lead one jurisdiction to cease polluting its neighbor. It may simply induce the unfortunate neighbor to reduce its own emissions to offset the unwelcome inflow of the pollutant. What is needed is some mechanism to internalize the externality. This could conceivably take the form of Coasian negotiations between the jurisdictions or, alternatively, of federal intervention to regulate interjurisdictional flows of pollutants (such as restrictions on tall stacks).[10]

The environmental-competition argument is also hard to evaluate. Depreciation of environmental standards will itself impose costs on the local populace, and the extent to which it is in the local authority's interest to promote economic development at the expense of the local environment is unclear. Conceivably, states or localities might choose to compete by offering higher environmental quality. As I noted earlier, no state, save California, presently has ambient-air-quality standards more stringent than the national minima. One might interpret this as an indication that the EPA has set tougher standards than the optimal ones for virtually all states. Alternatively, one could see this outcome as providing support for the interjurisdictional competition argument: states have competed to the fullest extent allowable by holding their standards down to the national minimum.

Although it is admittedly difficult, at this juncture, to reach any firm conclusions on the national/local issue in standard-setting, it is my judgment that some local variation in standards is needed (and, ultimately, inevitable). Several United States cities, for example, are still nonattainment areas for certain of the criteria air pollutants; moreover, it will probably prove infeasible (i.e., too costly) for some of them ever to achieve the standards. I suspect that the optimal level of environmental quality varies widely across jurisdictions and that the welfare losses associated with enforcing a uniform standard are quite large. Greater leeway for tailoring standards to local circumstances is probably in order.

REGULATORY STRATEGIES
FOR CONTROLLING POLLUTION

The second part of the policy problem is the design and implementation of a regulatory mechanism to attain the prescribed standards for environmental quality. Two broad regulatory strategies are available: (1) a command-and-control (CAC) approach under which the environmental authority specifies how polluters are to behave; or (2) a system of economic incentives through which the authority creates economic inducements for abatement activity but leaves polluters free to determine their own responses to these incentives.

Each of the classes of regulatory strategies offers a number of alternative policy instruments (and the distinctions between these policy instruments are important). Under CAC, for example, the environmental agency may prescribe in detail a set of *technology-based standards* that define specific abatement techniques for each source. Alternatively, the agency may simply set *performance standards* consisting of an overall ceiling on emissions for each source, leaving the source to determine the most effective way to meet its emissions limitation. Likewise, economic incentives can take many different forms including effluent charges, marketable emission permits, or various deposit-refund schemes.

COMMAND-AND-CONTROL VERSUS ECONOMIC INCENTIVES

The objective of the regulatory system is to achieve the set of predetermined environmental-quality standards in the least burdensome way. A potential regulatory mechanism thus must be evaluated in terms of its capacity to insure attainment of the standards and to minimize the costs it imposes on society in the course of reaching these standards. In order to minimize aggregate control costs, a regulatory system must satisfy two conditions: (1) each source must meet its own emissions limitation in the least costly way; and (2) the pattern of emissions limitations (or abatement quotas) among polluters must be an efficient one so that savings cannot be realized simply by adjustments to the pattern of waste discharges among sources.

We immediately see a basic difference between the two CAC instruments. Under technology-based standards, the environmental authority must prescribe a specific abatement technology for each source. This makes enormous information demands on the regulatory agency if each source is to employ the least-cost method of pollution control. In contrast, with performance standards the agency need only determine an overall emissions limit for each source; the polluter is left to find for himself the least expensive technique for compliance. Under the performance-standards method, the authority will admittedly not be able to determine the least-cost set of abatement quotas across sources without knowledge of the individual abatement-cost functions, but at least this policy instrument can make use of the cost-minimizing propensity of the individual sources to satisfy the first of the above conditions for minimizing aggregate abatement costs. Moreover, performance standards provide some incentive in a dynamic context for sources to seek new and cheaper technologies to meet their emissions limitation.[11] There is little incentive for such technological change under technology-based standards. Thus a strong case can be made within the CAC framework for the use of performance standards instead of technology-based standards.

However, a properly designed set of economic incentives has the potential to satisfy both of the conditions for cost minimization and to do so with relatively modest informational demands on the regulatory authority. Taking a simple case, suppose that the environmental damages for an increment of emissions are the same across all sources. Then it is easy to show that an effluent charge set so as to restrict aggregate discharges to the level needed to meet the environmental quality standard will generate the least-cost outcome (Baumol and Oates 1975, ch. 10). In this case, the first-order condition for cost minimization is to equate marginal abatement cost (MAC) across all sources. Since cost-minimizing polluters will extend abatement activity to the point at which MAC equals the effluent fee, it follows that the equilibrium outcome will be characterized by the necessary equality of MAC across polluters. Where the marginal damages differ from emissions from various sources as a result of location (or, perhaps, varying chimney heights), the issue becomes somewhat more complicated—a point to which we will return below.

A system of economic incentives can thus promise greater savings in abatement costs than a CAC regime. How large are these potential savings? We now have a substantial body of empirical work that has explored this issue for a considerable variety of air and water pollutants. This work consists mainly of simulation studies that compare the costs of pollution control under different regulatory systems. These studies have two ingredients: a dispersion model of the air shed or waterway that indicates the effect of emissions from each source on pollutant concentrations at the various receptor points, and abatement-cost functions for each source. With these data alternative regulatory "rules" can be simulated to determine the resulting levels of abatement costs and of pollutant concentrations at each receptor point. These simulation outcomes allow us to compare the effects on pollution levels and control costs of a variety of CAC and economic-incentive schemes.

On the whole, these studies suggest very large potential cost savings from properly designed systems of economic incentives as compared to CAC programs. The magnitude of these savings depends on what assumptions are made concerning the form of the economic incentives, and also, of course, on the CAC regime used for purposes of the comparison.

Before turning to the simulation studies, it is worth noting the findings in a survey of the costs of controlling hydrocarbon emissions in a particular metropolitan area. In 1979, a state agency in Maryland collected estimates of abatement costs for a sample of point sources of hydrocarbon emissions in Baltimore. The findings are quite striking. Among the large point sources, for example, unit costs of abatement ranged from $0.06 per pound to $1.55 per pound—a differential in excess of an order of magnitude. The variation in abatement costs among the sources was extremely large, suggesting the potential for large cost-savings from a more efficient allocation of abatement activity among sources.

Some estimates of the magnitude of these potential savings are indicated in Table 11.2, which presents the findings from seven simulation studies of pollution control, five relating to air pollution and two to water quality. The table shows figures for the least-cost solution to the control problem and for a representative CAC system. In some instances the CAC system is modeled on the actual control program (e.g., the state implementation plan, or SIP, for certain of the air pollutants); in other cases the CAC baseline is of a cruder form involving, for example, an assumed equi-proportionate reduction in emissions from all sources. Table 11.2 reveals enormous differentials between aggregate control costs under the CAC system and the least-cost outcome. Aggregate abatement costs un-

TABLE II.2

Aggregate Abatement Costs: Least-Cost Solution
and CAC Outcome (millions of dollars per year)

Study	Pollutant/Place	Least-Cost	CAC
Seskin et al.	Nitrogen dioxide in		
(1983)	Chicago AQCR	$ 9.0	$66.0
Md. Dept. of Economic	Nitrogen dioxide in	1.7	9.9
Community	Baltimore AQCR	0.4	1.2
Development (1982)		0.07	1.5
McGartland and	Particulates in		
Oates (forthcoming)	Baltimore AQCR	27.0	113.0
Atkinson and Lewis	Particulates in		
(1974)	St. Louis AQCR	0.2	2.7
Palmer et al.	Chlorofluorocarbon		
(1980)	emissions in U.S.	110.0	230.0
Kneese et al.	BOD emissions in	1.6	5.0
(1971)	Delaware River estuary	7.0	20.0
O'Neil et al.	BOD emissions in		
(1983)	Fox River	10.3	16.1

NOTE: The pairs of numbers refer to abatement costs for differing levels of environmental quality.
AQCR = Air Quality Control Region.

der CAC are, in every case save one, at least twice as large as under the least-cost solution—and, in certain instances, more than an order of magnitude larger. The first four simulation studies, which examine nitrogen dioxide and particulate pollutants in the atmosphere, find huge differences in control costs between CAC and the least-cost case. The relative differentials, although still sizable, are somewhat smaller for the water-quality simulations (involving BOD emissions). Because the various studies use different environmental objectives and CAC baselines, their findings are not really comparable, but they do provide some rough sense of the large differences between the least-cost and CAC outcomes.

These findings suggest very large *potential* savings from a more efficient system of regulation. However, the results in a sense stack the deck in favor of economic incentives. The real issue is the extent to which alternative regulatory mechanisms have the capacity to realize these potential savings.

EFFLUENT FEES VERSUS MARKETABLE EMISSION PERMITS

While it is possible in principle to design a system of effluent fees or marketable permits that can generate the least-cost outcome, it is usually not a simple matter. For the special case where the effect of a unit of emissions on pollutant concentrations is independent of the location and other characteristics of the source, the solution is fairly straightforward. The environmental authority can either establish a uniform effluent fee at the requisite level to meet the standard or issue the appropriate number of permits (either through an auction or by direct distribution to sources). The permits would be freely tradable among sources on a one-for-one basis (i.e., a permit for one unit of emission would entitle any source to emit a unit of the pollutant). One interesting case of such a pollutant is chlorofluorocarbons (CFC). The effect of CFCs in depleting the ozone layer in the stratosphere does not appear to depend upon where on the earth's surface the discharge occurs; thus a national (or global) market in emission permits would not have to distinguish among sources.

However, for most air and water pollutants, the location of the source (and certain other characteristics such as chimney height) are quite important determinants of the ultimate effect of a discharge on the pattern of pollutant concentrations in the environment. The effect, for example, of a unit of particulate emission will be very different if it is discharged on the windward side of an air shed than if its source is on the opposite, leeward border of the area. Where spatial (and other) characteristics matter, it can be shown that the first-order conditions for cost minimization require that the "shadow price" for waste discharges for each source reflect the relative contribution of that source's emissions to pollution. If source A's discharges result in twice as much pollution per unit of discharge as source B's, then source A should face a "price" twice as high as B's.

The implication is that a cost-minimizing system of effluent charges (aside from our special case of pollutants such as CFCs) must take the form of a differentiated set of charges among sources. While this may not be a troublesome issue in principle, it is a real liability in the policy arena. The environmental agency is unlikely to have the authority to discriminate among sources in the necessary way; "discriminatory" taxes are often either unconstitutional or very unpopular. Suppose the agency is constrained to a uniform fee system—how seriously is this likely to impair the cost-saving capacity of the system? Simulation studies suggest that uniform fee systems may perform quite badly. For a case in point, we return to the study by Seskin et al. (1983, cited in Table 11.2) on nitrogen dioxide emissions in the Chicago Air Quality Control Region. This study estimated the least-cost outcome to entail annual control costs of about $9 million per annum, while under their CAC system, annual costs are projected to be $66 million. In contrast, a uniform fee sufficiently high to attain the environmental standard would result in abatement costs of $305 million! This astonishing result reflects the high degree of "overcontrol" that many sources must undertake in relatively clean sectors of the air shed in order to get sufficient abatement in the "hot spots." Other studies confirm this general result. The failure to make the necessary spatial (and other) distinctions among sources can seriously undermine the efficiency-enhancing properties of a system of economic incentives.[12]

It is a powerful advantage, I believe, of marketable permit systems that they can incorporate these specific characteristics of the sources in a manner that is less objectionable to policymakers. This is accomplished in the following way: all sales of permits among sources are made subject to the constraint of no violation of the environmental-quality standard at any receptor point. This implies that if, as before, source A's emissions are twice as damaging as source B's, then A will have to purchase from B two units of emission reduction to justify an additional unit of discharge of its own. Note that this is equivalent to charging source A a fee on its emissions that is twice as high as B's fee. Moreover, this condition on trades can be, in principle, and has been, in practice, incorporated into exchanges of emission rights. Thus, systems of marketable permits have, in the policy context, a much greater potential for realizing cost-savings than do effluent charges.

Permit systems have four additional and important advantages over systems of fees. First, from the perspective of a regulator, permits promise more direct control over the level of emissions. The setting of fees puts the regulating agency in the less comfortable position of influencing quantity only indirectly, through price. If the fee is set too low, the resulting emissions will be excessive, with the consequent failure to achieve the mandated level of environmental quality. In a policy setting in which the regulator must insure that specified levels of pollutant concentrations are not exceeded (as under the Clean Air Act in the United States), a preference for control over quantity to control over price is easily understandable.

Second, and closely related to the above issue, are the complications that result from economic growth and price inflation. Under a system of effluent fees, continuing inflation will erode the real value of the fee; similarly, expanding production from both existing and new firms will increase the levels of waste emissions if fee levels are held constant. Both these forces will require the fee to be raised periodically if environmental standards are to be maintained. In short, the burden of initiating action under fees is on environmental officials; the choice will be between unpopular fee increases or nonattainment of standards. Under a system of permits, market forces automatically accommodate inflation and growth with no increase in pollution. The rise in demand for permits translates directly into a higher price.

Third, permits are likely to be more attractive to sources than are fees. Somewhat paradoxically, in spite of the large savings in abatement costs relative to CAC, a system of effluent fees can result in much higher costs for polluters. This results from a new form of costs to sources: the fee bill. Not only must polluters bear their costs of abatement, but they must also pay a fee on their remaining emissions. While such payments represent a transfer from the perspective of society, they are nevertheless a cost to sources. Existing simulation studies suggest some rather staggering estimates for potential fee bills. In the RAND study of chlorofluorocarbon emissions into the atmosphere (Palmer et al., cited in Table 11.2), the control costs under a hypothetical CAC program were estimated to be $230 million. A prospective fee program promised large savings in abatement costs—about 50 percent—with control costs projected at $110 million. But the associated fee payments were estimated by the RAND group at $1400 million! These results suggest that a fee program could impose costs on sources over six times as large as the CAC regime. Another study suggests similar findings. The simulations by Seskin and his colleagues (also cited in Table 11.2) for nitrogen dioxide discharges in the Chicago AQCR reach similarly dramatic conclusions: they estimate that fee payments under a system of uniform effluent fees would total $414 million, as compared to total control costs of $132 million under a representative CAC program.

These are troublesome results. For feasible policy reform, we typically search for proposals that represent a Pareto improvement. Based on existing studies, it is hard to believe that a fee system will typically make sources better off.[13] However, a permit system need not impose additional costs on existing polluters. Instead of auctioning off the permits, the system can be set in motion with an initial distribution of permits to sources. Trading can then proceed from this initial allocation. Some have objected on equity grounds to a distribution to polluters of "property rights" to the environment. However, the equity issue is a complex one. We should recall, for instance, that most sources have already been required to institute extensive control measures to reduce their waste discharges. Starting from the existing CAC equilibrium, the proposal is to allocate entitlements only for the remaining, or residual, discharges.

Fourth, the use of permits offers to both regulators and sources the attraction of familiarity. The introduction of a fee system involves a wholly new form of environmental management with uncertain consequences from the perspectives of the administering agencies and polluters. Permits already exist. It would seem a much less radical move to make permits transferable than to supplant permits altogether by a new system of effluent fees.

In a policy setting, a system of marketable permits thus has some compelling advantages over effluent fees. But I do not want to overstate the case. There surely are circumstances under which fees are the more attractive policy instrument. As Weitzman (1974) has shown, where marginal social damages (MSD) are readily measurable and fairly constant over the relevant range, a fee set equal to MSD can be the more effective means for attaining the efficient level of the polluting activity. Harrison (1983) has suggested that this may well be the case for regulation of airport noise. However, my sense is that the range of application for such a use of fees may be rather limited. Particularly when the spatial dimension of the pollution problem is important so that sources must confront different "prices" (as is true for most major air and water pollutants), the design *and* implementation of the requisite fee system are likely to prove very difficult. For these cases, marketable permits represent the more promising approach. From this perspective, it is not surprising to find the evolution of environmental policy taking the direction of marketable permits instead of fees. Two recent innovative programs in the United States, one for the control of air pollution and one for the management of water quality, represent exciting new experiments with the permit approach to a system of economic incentives for protection of the environment.

EMISSIONS TRADING AND THE WISCONSIN TDP SYSTEM

The Emissions Trading Program has its legislative origins in the 1977 Amendments to the Clean Air Act. As was noted above, Congress and the EPA headed off a political confrontation by introducing a provision for "offsets" in nonattainment areas. Under this provision, new sources could enter such areas if their emissions were more than offset by reductions in existing sources' discharges. This authorization for offsets effectively legalized certain transfers of emissions entitlements among sources. The EPA has extended the offset strategy to encompass a broader set of provisions that will facilitate emissions transfers. This framework, now called emissions trading, has three components: bubbles, offsets, and banking. Under the first, an imaginary bubble is placed over a plant or firm with multiple sources of emissions. Instead of meeting technological standards or permit limits on each source under the bubble, the firm is treated as a single unit subject to an overall emissions limitation. Within this overall limitation, the firm is free to determine its own pattern of abatement activity and emissions. The offset policy amounts, in a sense, to an extension of the bubble to encompass trades between firms. A number of administrative restrictions exist on the use of these procedures, but the basic point is that under the bubble and offset policies, firms can trade emissions both within their own establishments and with other firms.

The most recent component of the emissions trading framework is the banking provision. Introduced in 1979, banking allows firms to receive credits for emissions reductions in excess of those required under existing regulations. These credits can be used later by the firm to increase emissions, or they can be sold for use as an offset by another firm.

In spite of the somewhat exotic terminology, the various components of emissions trading are really no more than routine dimensions of a conventional market. The trades permitted under the bubble and offset provisions and the storing of credits under banking all represent standard forms of economic behavior in the marketplace. From this perspective, emissions trading can be seen as a framework for establishing a market in emissions entitlements. A basic limit to overall emissions is set by the predetermined ambient-air-quality standard, and, subject to this limit, firms can trade emissions. However, the emissions trading program is embedded in a broader body of regulations, some of which prescribe technology-based standards and place obstacles in the way of cost-saving trades. Moreover, each state must implement the general framework for emissions trading with its own state implementation plan (SIP). But emissions trading has made real headway in some regions. Nearly all states now have offset provisions in their SIP, and several hundreds of transactions, many resulting in quite large savings, have taken place.

There have been certain impediments, however, to trading in the air-emissions market. Perhaps the most serious is a general sense of uncertainty concerning the nature and life of this new form of property right. Some sources, fearing changes in regulations (perhaps involving more stringent abatement requirements) have been reluctant to part with their emissions entitlements. It is absolutely essential to the proper functioning of these markets that the participants have firm guarantees and full confidence in the validity of their entitlements. With such guarantees and some further experience with trading institutions and procedures, emissions trades should become more widespread.

The new Wisconsin system of transferable discharge permits (TDP), unlike emissions trading, has its origins in a coordinated effort at the state level. Economists at the University of Wisconsin and officials in the Wisconsin Department of Natural Resources have designed the system to regulate water quality on Wisconsin's most polluted stretches of river, notably the Fox River, with its heavy concentration of paper and pulp mills along with several municipal waste-treatment plants.

The system that emerged is a sophisticated form of transferable discharge permits, designed to achieve a target level of water quality of 5 parts per million of dissolved oxygen (DO)—sufficient to sustain fishlife and allow recreational activities on the river. Along the Fox River there are two stationary "sag points," located behind dams, where the DO content of the water reaches its lowest levels. The problem thus becomes one of insuring that the DO content stays at or above 5 ppm at these locations. A model of the river indicates the effect that a unit of emissions from each source will have on the DO level at the sag points. The permit system begins with an initial allocation of allowable discharges (based on historical levels) among the sources that is consistent with achieving the water-quality target. Sources are then free to trade permits among themselves subject to certain constraints, one of which is that they meet the water-quality standard. Note that, as under emissions trading, this constraint implies that permits typically will not be traded on a simple one-for-one basis. Where the pollution constraint is binding, the source whose emissions have a relatively large effect on water quality at a sag point will have to buy permits from other sources in an amount greater than the increase in its own emissions. The Wisconsin system explicitly incorporates the spatial dimensions of the pollution problem in such a way that it has the potential to realize the least-cost pattern of emissions among sources.

Another interesting feature of the Wisconsin permit system is that allowable emissions vary with the river's capacity to assimilate them. This capacity varies widely over the year with changes in river flow and temperature. During the summer, when water flow is relatively low and temperature comparatively high, emissions tend to be more damaging. Under the Wisconsin plan, the level of emissions allowed per permit is itself variable. Such "flow-temperature" permits require sources to adapt their levels of discharges to river conditions. To help accommodate the needed adjustments, the TDP system can allow short-term leasing of permits among sources.

Like emissions trading, however, the TDP scheme is built on a CAC system that requires certain minimum treatment activities on the part of all sources. Nevertheless, the estimated potential savings compared to a wholly CAC regime are substantial—on the order of 80 percent over a crude CAC system that imposes an equiproportionate cutback on all sources.

SOME FURTHER ISSUES

Marketable permit systems thus appear to offer a promising alternative to an exclusive reliance on the CAC approach to regulation. But there are some potential difficulties that need to be resolved. In their important work in California, Robert Hahn and Roger Noll (1983; F. Cass et al. 1982) have explored the extent of distortions that can arise from market imperfections. In particular, the presence of one large polluter with substantial power in the permit market can result in an inefficient pattern of abatement activity across sources. On another issue, Scott Atkinson and Tom Tietenberg (1982) have voiced their concern that proposed market systems, although meeting the formal standards for ambient air quality, may result in degradation of local air quality in places where, under existing CAC systems, it is currently cleaner than the standards require. However, it has been shown that by introducing a further constraint on trading, such increments to air pollution can, in principle, be avoided. In fact, it is not hard to design a marketable permit system that, starting from an initial CAC equilibrium, can bring both improved environmental quality and reduced abatement costs to polluters (see McGartland and Oates forthcoming). Such a system represents a Pareto improvement from the perspectives both of environmentalists and of sources.

Finally, the response of sources to the opportunities for trading in these markets remains to be seen. This, of course, will be the real test of the ability of systems of marketable emission permits to achieve our environmental objectives at relatively low cost. We have had some experience with emissions trading that suggests certain "start-up" problems including reluctance to engage in trades. However, as all this becomes more familiar, these markets should become more active.

MONITORING AND ENFORCEMENT

Discussions of regulatory systems for the control of pollution inevitably come around to the issue of monitoring waste discharges and enforcing effluent limitations. It is tempting to acknowledge the importance of the matter and then to dismiss it on the grounds that it is not really relevant to the choice of a particular regulatory system; after all, any system will require monitoring and enforcement. However, there are some differences. Market-incentive systems require the actual measurement of the quantity of waste discharges, since the fee bill (or, alternatively, the emissions entitlement under a permit system) is based on the actual level of emissions.[14]

In contrast, the monitoring requirements of a command-and-control system will depend on its characteristics. As was noted earlier, technology-based standards specify the use of particular treatment procedures or equipment. For this kind of system, monitoring need only entail periodic inspections to determine that the mandated procedure is in use— measurement of effluents may not be necessary. Performance standards can be more demanding since, like market-incentive systems, they generally refer to actual levels of discharges. Even these general observations mask the range of subtleties and possibilities in monitoring emissions of particular pollutants. Reasonably satisfactory shortcuts to determining levels of waste emissions (e.g., based on the sulfur content of the fuel used) can exist. Or, as in some instances under emissions trading, transfers may be made contingent on the sources' installation of sophisticated monitoring devices. Monitoring and enforcement are serious issues, but it is not my sense that they constitute anything like insuperable obstacles to the introduction of market-incentive schemes. The potential gains-from-trade typically dwarf the costs of even quite sophisticated techniques for monitoring waste discharges.

THE REAGAN ADMINISTRATION RECORD AND SOME CONCLUSIONS

The Reagan administration inherited an array of environmental policies beset with fundamental problems: widespread delays and noncompliance, inadequate monitoring and data systems, unsatisfactory procedures for standard-setting, a command-and-control regulatory system imposing inordinately and unnecessarily high costs on the economy, and lack of a much-needed analytical and research capability.[15]

While these problems are sources of genuine concern, they represented an opportunity for the incoming administration to give a new direction and impetus to environmental management in this country. The Carter administration had already set in motion one important line of reform, the emissions trading program, which introduced the use of market incentives for pollution control with the potential for large savings. Moreover, the two early cornerstones of environmental legislation, the Clean Air and Clean Water acts, were both scheduled to come before Congress for reconsideration during the Reagan term of office. The time was ripe for some fundamental changes in United States environmental policy.

From this perspective, the overall Reagan record to date is distinctly disappointing (although this last year has seen marked improvement). It began with what proved to be unfortunate appointments of key officials, people with little experience in environmental management and with little confidence in the existing staff. The primary concern of the administration seemed to be cutting the EPA budget (which was accomplished) and easing certain standards, rather than a careful reassessment and restructuring of existing programs. The administration pressed for no fundamental reforms in the Clean Air and Water acts when they came up for renewal; there was a virtual absence of legislative initiatives from the executive branch. What took place instead was unproductive haggling over particular environmental standards. Moreover, until quite recently the administration did little to sustain the momentum established under emissions trading for basic regulatory reform involving the introduction of market incentives for pollution control.

The Reagan administration can point only to a few modest successes in environmental policy: some progress in reducing the regulatory backlog with revised effluent guidelines for water polluters and the processing of SIP modifications, and some recent extensions of emissions trading to encompass, for example, a lead-trading policy. On the whole the record is not impressive: it represents a chronicle of "mistaken priorities and missed opportunities" (Crandall and Portney 1984, p. 61).[16]

In consequence, the agenda for the reform of environmental policy in the United States is much the same as it was when the Reagan presidency began in 1980. In my view, the most pressing issues for reform continue to include:

1. Restructuring regulatory mechanisms for controlling waste discharges to embody more efficient techniques for achieving our environmental quality standards. As I have suggested, measures that incorporate economic incentives, particularly systems of marketable emission permits, provide a very promising alternative to an exclusive reliance on traditional CAC policies. Emissions trading and the Wisconsin TDP system represent innovative and important moves in this direction.

2. Introduction of procedures for setting environmental standards that take account of the relevant benefits and costs. This will require identifying pollutants where scientific knowledge is lacking and undertaking the research needed to provide the requisite information.

3. Reassessment of the roles of the various levels of government in standard-setting and in the design and implementation of regulatory systems. My sense is that the attempt to define and enforce uniform national standards for the criteria air pollutants is ill-advised. Environmental measures will, I suspect, better promote the social welfare if they are tailored to local circumstances.

4. Improvement in systems of monitoring and enforcement. As Crandall and Portney (1984) stress, there exists widespread noncompliance with existing standards—just how wide is not clear, since the monitoring system is at present inadequate to make such a determination. We need to develop an effective nationwide system of monitors for ambient environmental quality, and also more reliable techniques for measuring and testing the discharges of individual sources.

This juncture in the evolution of our environmental policies presents real opportunities for redirection of efforts in ways that can both improve environmental quality and reduce the burden of the regulatory system on the economy.

ACKNOWLEDGMENTS

I am grateful to Paul Portney, John Quigley, Daniel Rubinfeld, and Timothy Sullivan for valuable comments on an earlier draft and to the National Science Foundation for its support of my research into environmental policy.

NOTES

1. The six criteria air pollutants are sulfur dioxide, total suspended particulates, carbon monoxide, nitrogen dioxide, ozone, and lead.

2. This section draws heavily on the Conservation Foundation report (1984) and on the recent annual report by the Council on Environmental Quality (1983).

3. One caveat here is that the nationwide monitoring network is far from adequate. As Crandall and Portney (1984) stress, we cannot have complete confidence in reported readings, because of deficiencies in both the number of monitors and their reliability. Crandall

(1983) is also skeptical of progress as measured in terms of the PSI because, as noted, trends in certain of the air pollutants can pass unnoticed.

4. In a recent move the EPA, reversing an earlier position, has proposed yet more stringent lead standards. This decision is apparently based on a reassessment of the serious health effects of lead (particularly on children in the central cities) and on some evidence suggesting that progress in reducing lead emissions is being undermined by the continued use of older cars, the disconnection of auto emissions-control systems, and illegal use of leaded fuel. The distinction, incidentally, between the criteria air pollutants and toxic substances is not altogether clear; this is illustrated by the inclusion of lead as both a criteria air pollutant and a toxic substance.

5. As was noted earlier, however, not all the improvement can be attributed to policy. Some of the changes in air quality, for example, resulted not from the Clean Air Act but from increases in fuel prices and economic fluctuations that caused reductions in consumption of fuels, and consequently in emissions of certain pollutants.

6. As Portney (1981) has noted, however, in certain instances reported pollution control expenditures may exceed actual spending, for sources may overreport control activities to emphasize how burdensome existing regulatory measures are.

7. It is quite possible for increased environmental degradation to raise the GNP as individuals spend more to defend themselves against damage. See Peskin (1981) for a careful treatment of the relationship between the national income accounts and the quality of the environment.

8. Typically, individuals can mitigate the effects of existing pollution in a number of ways ranging from various sorts of cleansing devices to changes in location or even in occupation to reduce exposure. Such defensive measures obviously vary widely in their cost. Putting it slightly differently, Paul Portney has suggested to me a kind of continuum in the extent of the voluntary character of exposure to pollutants. At one end of the spectrum are activities such as smoking which are wholly by individual choice, while toward the other end is ambient air pollution where exposure is much more difficult to avoid.

9. As Daniel Rubinfeld has pointed out to me, if environmental quality is a normal good and if urban residents have lower incomes on average than rural residents, it is possible that the MSD_1 curve could lie above the MSD_2 curve. The higher willingness-to-pay of rural residents would, in such a case, more than offset their fewer numbers. For some evidence on this relative to clean air, see Harrison and Rubinfeld (1978).

10. Daniel Rubinfeld has suggested to me that existing tort law specifies property rights in such a way that the Coase approach might work under certain circumstances. One possibility within states is nuisance suits across jurisdictions.

11. However, the incentive for innovation in abatement technology under performance standards can easily be eroded if sources have reason to believe that improved abatement techniques will induce the environmental authority to tighten the standards.

12. A feasible compromise might be for the environmental authority to divide the air shed into zones and set a different effluent fee for each zone. Even this is unlikely to be fully satisfactory, however, for the impact of sources within the same zone can differ significantly as a result of source-specific characteristics such as chimney height or the exit velocity of the pollutant.

13. It is possible to design a fee system that is less burdensome to sources by assigning to each source some allowable level of emissions and assessing fees only on discharges in excess of the baseline. For such a proposal see Crandall (1983, ch. 10).

14. In fact, fee systems may demand considerably more refinement in monitoring than marketable-permit systems. Continuous monitoring to determine total discharges over a period will typically be needed to calculate the fee bill. Under a permit system, periodic checks to insure that the emissions entitlement is not being exceeded may be sufficient.

15. The discussion of the Reagan record in this section draws heavily on the excellent paper by Crandall and Portney (1984).

16. But I again note the recent improvement in EPA performance under the direction of its new administrator, William Ruckelshaus. Of particular importance is the effort to initiate cleanup of some of the most serious hazardous-waste sites.

REFERENCES

Atkinson, S., and D. Lewis. 1974. "A Cost Effectiveness Analysis of Alternative Air Quality Control Strategies." *Journal of Environmental Economics and Management* 1: 237–50.

Atkinson, S., and T. Tietenberg. 1982. "The Empirical Properties of Two Classes of Designs for Transferable Discharge Permit Markets," *Journal of Environmental Economics and Management* 9 (June 1982): 101–121.

Baumol, W., and W. Oates. 1975. *The Theory of Environmental Policy.* Englewood Cliffs, N.J.: Prentice-Hall.

Cass, G., R. Hahn, R. Noll, et al. 1982. *Implementing Tradable Permits for Sulfur Oxides Emissions.* Environmental Quality Laboratory Report 22–2. Pasadena: California Institute of Technology.

Conservation Foundation. 1984. *State of the Environment: An Assessment at Mid-Decade.* Washington, D.C.: Conservation Foundation.

Council on Environmental Quality. 1983. *Environmental Quality, 1982.* Washington, D.C.: U.S. Government Printing Office.

Crandall, R. 1981. "Pollution Controls and Productivity Growth in Basic Industries." Pp. 347–68 in T. Cowing and R. Stevenson, eds., *Productivity Measurements in Regulated Industries.* 1981. New York: Academic Press.

———. 1983. *Controlling Industrial Pollution: The Economics and Politics of Clean Air.* Washington, D.C.: Brookings.

Crandall, R., and P. Portney. 1984. "Environmental Policy." Pp. 47–82 in P. Portney, ed., *Natural Resources and the Environment: The Reagan Approach.* Washington, D.C.: Urban Institute.

Cumberland, J. 1979. "Interregional Pollution Spillovers and Consistency of Environmental Policy." Pp. 255–81 in H. Siebert et al., eds., *Regional Environmental Policy: The Economic Issues.* New York: New York University.

———. 1981. "Efficiency and Equity in Interregional Environmental Management." *Review of Regional Studies* 10 (no. 2): 1–9.

Denison, E. 1979. "Pollution Abatement Programs: Estimates of Their Effect upon Output per Unit of Input, 1975–78." *Survey of Current Business* 59 (August 1979): 58–59.

Hahn, R., and R. Noll. 1983. "Barriers to Implementing Tradable Air Pollution Permits: Problems of Regulatory Interactions." *Yale Journal on Regulation* 1, 1: 63–91.

Harrison, D. 1983. "The Regulation of Aircraft Noise." Pp. 41–144 in T. Schelling, ed., *Incentives for Environmental Protection.* Cambridge, Mass.: MIT.

Harrison, D., and D. Rubinfeld. 1978. "Hedonic Housing Prices and the Demand for Clean Air." *Journal of Environmental Economics and Management* 5: 81–102.

Haveman, R., and G. Christiansen. 1981. "Environmental Regulations and Productivity Growth." Pp. 55–75 in H. Peskin et al., eds., *Environmental Regulation and the U.S. Economy.* Baltimore: Johns Hopkins.

Kelman, S. 1981. *What Price Incentives? Economists and the Environment.* Boston: Auburn.

Kneese, A., et al., eds. 1971. *Managing the Environment: International Economic Cooperation for Pollution Control.* New York: Praeger.

Maryland Department of Economic and Community Development. 1982. *Emission Trading to Reduce the Cost of Air Quality in Maryland.* Annapolis: Department of Economic and Community Development.

McGartland, A., and W. Oates. Forthcoming. "Marketable Permits for the Prevention of Environmental Deterioration." *Journal of Environmental Economics and Management.*

Oates, W. 1983. "The Regulation of Externalities: Efficient Behavior by Sources and Victims." *Public Finance* 38, 362–75.

O'Neil, W., et al. 1983. "Transferable Discharge Permits and Economic Efficiency: The Fox River." *Journal of Environmental Economics and Management* 10: 346–55.

Organization for Economic Cooperation and Development (O.E.C.D.). 1984. *Environment and Economics: Issue Papers.* Paris: O.E.C.D.

Palmer, A., et al. 1980. *Economic Implications of Regulating Chlorofluorocarbon Emissions from Nonaerosol Applications.* Santa Monica: RAND.

Peskin, H. 1981. "National Income Accounts and the Environment." Pp. 77–103 in H. Peskin et al., eds., *Environmental Regulation and the U.S. Economy.* Baltimore: Johns Hopkins.

Portney, R. 1981. "The Macroeconomic Impacts of Federal Environmental Regulation." Pp. 25–54 in H. Peskin et al., eds., *Environmental Regulation and the U.S. Economy.* Baltimore: Johns Hopkins.

Quarles, J. 1979. *Federal Regulation of New Industrial Plants.* Environmental Reporter Monograph 28. Washington, D.C.

Seskin, E., et al. 1983. "An Empirical Analysis of Economic Strategies for Controlling Air Pollution." *Journal of Environmental Economics and Management* 10: 112–24.

Siegel, R. 1979. "Why Has Productivity Slowed Down?" *Data Resources Review of the U.S. Economy* 1, 59.

U.S. General Accounting Office. 1984. *Cost-Benefit Analysis Can Be Useful in Assessing Environmental Regulations, Despite Limitations.* Washington, D.C.: U.S. General Accounting Office.

Weitzman, M. 1974. "Prices vs. Quantities." *Review of Economic Studies* 41: 477–91.

CHAPTER TWELVE

The Differential Effect of the Foreign Trade Deficit on Regions in the United States

Peter Mieszkowski

The past fifteen years have seen dramatic changes in the composition of the United States work force. Many economists, labor leaders, and politicians are especially concerned about the declining share of jobs in manufacturing industries, since historically this sector has sustained and expanded the American middle class. Despite this concern, the Reagan administration's international economic policy seems to be exacerbating this trend and injuring those regions of the country that depend most heavily on manufacturing.

As early as 1981, several economic indicators suggested that a change was occurring in the position of the United States in the world economy. The real trade-weighted value of the dollar reached its highest level in seven years. During the next two years, the dollar appreciated by 17 percent, while the recession failed to remove a historically large trade deficit, and this imbalance grew worse with the recovery. In early 1984, the real value of the dollar was 23 percent above the 1973 level, and the trade deficit on merchandise account was at an unprecedented annual rate of $130 billion.

These facts indicate that American companies that compete in home markets with foreign manufacturers—the *import competing sector*—and companies that compete in foreign markets with local manufacturers— the *export sector*—are having great difficulty selling their relatively expensive products. In response, they will decrease production and hire fewer factors, including labor. Conversely, a reduction in the trade deficit will increase domestic employment.

This paper investigates the magnitude of these effects. Under different economic assumptions, we examine the increase in employment, by region, effected by policies that could be undertaken to reduce or eliminate the merchandise trade deficit. First, however, a word is in order about the economic context that conditions these employment effects. The high value of the dollar is not the only source of problems for the manufacturing sector, nor is it the sole cause of the trade deficit: long-term economic trends must also be recognized. In addition, the high value of the dollar is itself a result of the high level of real interest rates. This is due in part to the enormous budget deficits which have been a part of President Reagan's domestic policy. An improvement in the balance of trade can only occur pari passu with policies that affect these other factors.

STRUCTURAL PROBLEMS IN MANUFACTURING, STRUCTURAL TRADE DEFICIT, AND CURRENT ADMINISTRATION POLICY

In 1950, 33.7 percent of the jobs in the nonagricultural sector were in manufacturing. By April of 1984 this share had fallen to 21.4 percent. Whether the drop results from productivity growth or industrial demise, jobs in manufacturing have become more difficult to find. Although manufacturing employment has rebounded significantly from the 1982 recession, total employment in this sector during April 1984 was 19.7 million, down from 21.0 million in 1979.

The regional implications of the decline in manufacturing employment attributable to current policy are important economically as well as politically. Consider, however, the broader context of regional employment trends. Mieszkowski (1979) documented the shift in employment away from the Northeast and North Central regions toward the South and West. The development of the West was explained as due to the migration of people into a richly endowed and underdeveloped region. This population growth allowed the West to become less specialized, broaden its industrial base, and take advantage of economies of scale and urban agglomeration in consumption and production. The development of the South relative to the North was explained in terms of the classical adjustment mechanism. Lower nominal wages and lower energy and land costs attracted capital to the South, leading to the development of a strong industrial base. The demand for labor grew large enough during the 1970s to reverse the well-established postwar migration of people from the rural South to the industrial North. Table 12.1 illustrates this regional

TABLE 12.1
Employment in Manufacturing by Region
(thousands)

Region	1967	1977	1984*
Northeast	1,562	1,390	1,445
Mid Atlantic	4,360	3,617	3,152
East North Central	5,151	4,974	4,130
West North Central	1,206	1,297	1,278
South Atlantic	2,502	2,823	2,997
East South Central	1,092	1,328	1,789
West South Central	1,083	1,442	1,537
Mountain	315	461	572
Pacific	2,050	2,255	2,481
Total	19,321	19,587	19,381

*March estimate.
SOURCE: U.S. *Department of Labor*, Bureau of Labor Statistics, *Employment and Earnings*, various issues.

shift in manufacturing employment. This table also suggests that the manufacturing sector is especially important in the Midwest and Mid Atlantic regions. The number of employees on nonagricultural payrolls has increased significantly from early 1979 to early 1984 in large Sunbelt states such as California, Florida, and Texas, while employment in virtually all Midwest states has declined during this period, with the largest declines occurring in manufacturing. The well-publicized plant closings have been concentrated in these regions.

At the international level, current trends contrast more sharply with previous experience. The United States typically shows a deficit in merchandise trade—the *trade balance*—and this is usually offset by a surplus in services—the *services balance*. For example, the average trade deficit for the 1970s was 0.5 percent of Gross National Product, while the average current account balance—the sum of the trade and services balances—for the same period was virtually zero. However, the average trade deficit has recently exceeded 1 percent of GNP, and the capital inflow to finance the deficit has actually reversed the direction of aggregate capital flow.

The capital inflow to finance the deficit is important. In 1982, gross savings were $406 billion (after subtracting a federal deficit of $147 billion), and gross domestic investment was $415 billion, resulting in net foreign investment of $9 billion. During the fourth quarter of 1983, gross savings increased by $119 billion to $533 billion, resulting in a net capital inflow of \$49 billion. The 1984 *Economic Report of the President* cites the rising trade deficit and associated capital inflow as "the most dramatic recent development in U.S. international economic relations" (p. 42). There is an unprecedented demand for dollars on the international markets, and it is this demand, induced by the high real interest rates, that produces serious problems for the manufacturing sector.

EMPLOYMENT EFFECTS OF A CHANGE IN THE TRADE DEFICIT

How does a change in the overall trade balance affect employment levels for manufacturing in different regions? The answer to this question depends on specific assumptions about the state of the economy and the differences in the industrial structure of the regions.

Recall the basic income identity involving an open economy:

(1) $Y = C + I + G + X - M$
   Y = gross national product or domestic output
   C = domestic consumption
   I = domestic investment
   G = domestic public expenditure
   X = exports
   M = imports

Economists typically refer to $(C + I + G)$ as domestic absorption and $(X - M)$ as the commodity account. Obviously, if there is a deficit on the commodity account, then $X - M < 0$ and domestic product, Y, will be smaller than domestic absorption. Also, if the economy is operating at full employment, then a decrease in this deficit must be accompanied by a decrease in domestic absorption, because domestic output cannot increase.

This last observation implies that assumptions about aggregate employment will be critical to the analysis, and suggests separate treatment of two different cases.

> *Case 1*: Reduce the trade deficit when the economy is not at full employment.

Suppose that government decreases the trade deficit by some arbitrary amount, say \$40 billion, and that domestic absorption remains unchanged. As a policy matter, the government could increase taxes and use the proceeds to decrease the federal deficit, thereby causing the real

TABLE 12.2

Employment Related to Manufacturing Exports
by Region, 1977 (thousands)

Region	Total non-agricultural employment	Manufacturing employment	Direct export-related employment	Indirect export-related employment	Total export-related employment	Export-related employment as % of total employment
U.S.	89,369	19,590	1,990	1,274	3,264	.036
New England	5,257	1,390	156	76	232	.044
Mid Atlantic	14,794	3,617	361	211	572	.039
East North Central	17,220	4,974	556	292	848	.049
West North Central	7,398	1,298	123	106	236	.031
South Atlantic	13,995	2,706	230	178	385	.029
East South Central	5,405	1,328	106	77	183	.034
West South Central	8,820	1,444	133	120	253	.029
Mountain	4,133	463	48	46	94	.023
Pacific	12,325	2,254	269	176	435	.036

SOURCE: U.S. Department of Commerce, Bureau of the Census, 1977 *Census of Manufactures*. Vol. 1: *Origins of Exports of Manufactured Products*, pp 12–1 to 12–43.

interest rate to decline. This in turn would cause a capital outflow, depreciation of the dollar, and a fall in the trade deficit. Of course, the tax increase would diminish consumption, which is a component of domestic absorption; we assume that either monetary policy stimulates investment or else government expenditures increase to keep absorption constant. Total domestic output rises by the change in the trade deficit.

The procedure to estimate the effect of this policy change is straightforward. Export-related employment in the manufacturing sector has a direct and an indirect component. To determine the former, we use the report prepared by the Bureau of the Census (1977) on the origin of the exports of manufactured products for 1977. Manufacturing establishments were required to report total shipments and the value of products shipped for export. These data were reported by two-digit manufacturing industry by state. We estimate the direct export-related employment, by industry and by state, from the relation: direct export-related employment is to total employment as the value of export shipments is to the value of all shipments.

The indirect component consists of the supporting employment generated in manufacturing by exports, and the employment related to manufactured exports in nonmanufacturing industries such as trade, business services, transportation, and so on. We use the figures (U.S. Dept. of Commerce 1974) which derive from the 1972 input-output table.

As is shown in Table 12.2, less than 4 percent of all nonagricultural jobs in 1977 were attributed to exports; that is, on the national level, exports make only a small contribution to overall employment. In contrast, nearly 17 percent of all jobs in manufacturing in 1977 could be attributed to exports. Notice that the Midwest, and especially the East North Central region (which is specialized in machinery and transportation equipment) is relatively more dependent on export trade than the less industrialized states of the Southwest and Mountain regions. This variation may well produce differences in the burden each region carries from the loss in export-manufacturing jobs, although the secular trend in the movement of manufacturing industry toward the South and West should attenuate these differences over the long run. Estimates based on any cross-section will thus provide upper bounds of the differential effects on regions of a decrease in the trade deficit.

Now, $40 billion corresponds to a 20 percent increase in 1984 export volume. Since 1977, the volume of exports has risen by about 15 percent, and output per worker in manufacturing has also increased by 15 percent. Therefore, a 20 percent increase in export volume will lead to about a 20

TABLE 12.3
Projected Levels of Employment Related to Manufacturing Exports,
Case 1 (thousands)

Region	Direct and indirect employment related to manufacturing exports, 1977	Employment w/20% increase in exports	Employment w/20% increase in exports + 20% decrease in imports
U.S.	3264	3910	4561
New England	232	278	325
Mid Atlantic	572	686	800
East North Central	848	1018	1187
West North Central	229	275	321
South Atlantic	408	490	571
East South Central	183	220	256
West South Central	253	303	354
Mountain	94	113	131
Pacific	445	534	623

SOURCE: See text for sources and methodology.

percent increase in the 1977 level of total export employment. If in addition there were a 20 percent decrease in the volume of imports, this 40 percent improvement would balance the 1984 current account. Unfortunately, the census study presents no information on imports or import-competing industries. Since the United States imports many of the same commodities it exports, such as chemicals, transportation equipment, and machinery, we make the strong assumption that the import-competing industries are the export industries. (The alternative treatment of the employment effects of reduced imports would require an analysis on a commodity-by-commodity basis.) The effects of this change, which approximate the effects of a devalued United States dollar, are calculated by doubling the regional employment effects from the 20 percent increase in exports. These results appear in Table 12.3.

For the nation, the elimination of the current account deficit, assuming a constant level of domestic absorption, increases employment by $(4,561 - 3,264) = 1.3$ million workers. This is not a large percentage of the current nonagricultural employment of 92.9 million, but it is large relative to the employment increase of 3.3 million that occurred between the recession year of 1982 and April 1984.

As expected, the most significant employment effect of a weaker United States dollar is found in the East North Central region, where the estimated employment increase in 339 thousand. At present, the level of employment in this region is 15,775 thousand, down from a peak of 16,728 thousand in 1980. So the 339,000 jobs that would result from a devaluation equal 36 percent of this recent decline in employment, a substantial improvement for the region.

These conclusions must be qualified. First, the value of exports and imports as a percentage of GNP increased by 20 percent between 1977 and the first quarter of 1984, so these estimates may understate the current significance of foreign trade on employment. Similarly, by assuming that domestic absorption is constant, we are not allowing for multiplier effects induced by export-related employment in the locally produced non-tradable industries such as services, housing, and retail trade.

However, as noted above, the analysis ignores variation in export and import price elasticity of demand by commodity group. It assumes, in effect, that export and import volumes by commodity change in the same proportion in response to a devaluation of the dollar. Of course, many commodities, such as textiles, apparel, steel, and automobiles, are subject to quotas and "voluntary" agreements limiting imports into the United States. Similarly, American exports of agricultural commodities are restricted by foreign governments. If these trade restrictions remain in effect, then the price sensitivity of various imports will be slight and the quantity of restricted commodities may be less affected. Consequently, the employment effects calculated for industries such as apparel, textiles, and automobiles are probably biased upward.

Case 2: Reduce the trade deficit, keeping output constant.

In this analysis, we assume full employment, or a policy strategy that holds domestic output constant. The trade deficit is decreased by $40 billion (Policy A), and another change (Policy B or Policy C) is undertaken to offset the improvement in the trade balance, keeping gross national product constant.

The policies considered are:

> Policy A: A $40 billion improvement in the trade balance resulting from a $15 billion increase in exports and a $25 billion decrease in imports (so GNP rises by $40 billion). The calculation is for manufactured exports and imports, and the weights for deliveries

by two-digit manufacturing industries are calculated from *1984 U.S. Industrial Outlook*, tables 3 and 5, which show the industrial sources of exports and imports.

Policy B: A $40 billion decrease in personal consumption. The industry weights are calculated from input-output information on deliveries to personal consumption by industry in the *Survey of Current Business*, April 1979.

Policy C: A $40 billion decrease in gross private fixed capital formation. Industry weights are found in the same source as weights for consumption.

In each case, three separate calculations were required to determine the effect on employment:

1. Each policy indicates the source of a change in aggregate demand, but only a portion of this new demand stimulates each industrial sector and two-digit manufacturing industry. These fractions must be determined. In the language of input-output analysis, the change in deliveries to final demand attributable to each policy must be inferred. These are the "weights" referred to above; they are calculated from available input-output information.

2. An input-output table is used to calculate the direct and indirect employment effects from (1). These are estimated at the national level, by two-digit manufacturing industry.

3. The national totals, are then disaggregated to the nine census regions. For manufacturing, it is assumed that changes will be proportional to employment for two-digit manufacturing by region in 1977—that is, if in 1977 employment in the East North Central region in primary metals was 40 percent of the national total, we assume that 40 percent of the increases in employment in primary metals will occur in this region.

The total national employment effects of each of these policies, by major industry, are reported in Table 12.4. Since column A shows the smallest total, we conclude that the overall employment effects from increases in manufactured exports and decreases in imports are smaller than those induced by consumption and investment. The employment changes resulting from these policies are distributed very differently over the industries. Foreign trade is the most manufacturing-intensive, while a decrease in consumption leads to relatively little manufacturing unemployment.

TABLE 12.4
Employment Effects by Industry for Three
Alternative Policies (thousands)

Industry	Policy A	Policy B	Policy C
Agriculture, forestries, fisheries	53	102	13
Mining	65	26	31
Construction	23	37	678
Manufacturing	1487	612	1213
Transportation	68	84	140
Communications	15	41	31
Utilities	13	227	9
Wholesale and retail trade	119	473	294
Finance, insurance, real estate	77	384	101
Business services	84	111	217
Other services	76	564	74
Government enterprises	27	63	26
Total	2107	2724	2832

NOTE: Policy A: $40 billion improvement in foreign trade balance.
Policy B: $40 billion increase in consumption.
Policy C: $40 billion increase in investment.
SOURCE: See text for sources and methodology.

Investment goods require a large amount of construction labor and manufacturing employment.

We now focus strictly on manufacturing industries and add the regional dimension. Table 12.5 reports employment effects of Policy A disaggregated by two-digit SIC code for each of the nine census regions.

One important and somewhat surprising result is that employment effects of eliminating the trade deficit are generally quite diffused among regions. The implied employment increase in manufacturing of 1.487 million is 7.67 percent of total manufacturing employment in April 1984. The estimated employment increase for the East North Central region of 397,000 is 9.5 percent of manufacturing employment in this region. However, between 1977 and 1984, the share of manufacturing in employment of the East North Central region fell 25.4 percent, to 21.3 percent, so the trade-induced employment effect in this region would now be proportionately smaller and possibly equal to the national average.

On the other hand, domestic absorption does not change in Policy A, and so we have not allowed for regional multiplier effects. The employment increase related to export growth will induce employment in housing, services, and trade as the new manufacturing workers spend their

TABLE 12.5

Estimated Employment in Manufacturing Induced by $40 Billion Change (Exports $+$15 B., Imports $-$25 B.) in Foreign Trade Balance (thousands of persons)

Sic code	Industry	N.E.	M.A.	E.N.C.	W.N.C.	S.A.	E.S.C.	W.S.C.	Mt.	Pac.	Total
20	Food	2.0	6.8	10.3	5.9	6.3	2.9	4.9	1.5	7.8	48.3
21	Tobacco	–	0.1	–	–	1.1	0.3	–	–	–	1.5
22	Textile mill	3.8	7.1	1.1	0.5	34.7	5.4	1.1	–	1.1	54.8
23	Apparel & textile	4.6	27.7	6.4	3.7	19.4	12.9	7.4	2.8	7.4	92.2
24	Lumber & wood	1.5	2.2	4.4	1.8	6.2	3.7	3.7	2.2	10.6	36.3
25	Furniture	0.1	0.4	0.7	0.1	1.0	0.4	0.3	–	0.5	3.7
26	Paper	2.7	4.4	5.9	1.2	4.0	1.7	2.0	0.3	2.5	
27	Printing	1.2	4.6	4.1	1.6	2.1	0.9	1.2	0.5	1.2	17.6
28	Chemical	3.8	20.9	5.2	4.8	20.0	9.5	12.4	1.0	4.8	82.3
29	Petroleum & coal	0.5	3.5	5.2	1.2	0.7	0.5	8.9	0.7	3.7	25.0
30	Rubber	4.2	7.4	15.8	2.8	5.1	3.3	3.3	0.9	4.7	47.5
31	Leather	8.3	8.0	4.0	3.3	2.7	3.3	2.0	–	1.7	33.3
32	Stone, clay, glass	0.8	3.5	4.5	1.0	2.3	0.8	1.3	0.7	1.5	16.6

33	Primary metal	6.4	38.3	65.5	6.4	12.8	11.2	8.0	1.6	11.2	161.3
34	Fabricated metal	4.7	9.4	21.7	4.1	4.1	3.5	4.7	–	5.9	58.1
35	Machinery (exec. elect.)	20.1	40.3	88.2	25.2	17.6	10.1	20.2	5.0	25.2	252.1
36	Electric equip.	20.7	43.6	59.7	13.8	23.0	13.8	13.8	6.9	32.1	227.3
37	Transportation equip.	11.8	19.6	76.4	15.7	15.7	7.8	9.8	3.9	37.2	197.9
38	Instrument	8.4	17.4	10.1	2.8	3.4	1.1	2.2	2.8	8.4	561.7
39	Misc. mfg.	8.9	13.3	7.9	3.0	3.9	2.5	3.5	1.5	5.4	49.7
	Total employment change, Policy A	114.5	278.6	397.2	98.9	186.2	95.6	110.5	32.3	172.8	1,486.8
	Total employment change, Policy B	44.5	118.8	134.7	40.3	99.7	46.8	48.3	13.1	65.8	612.1
	Total employment change, Policy C	87.3	207.4	373.6	85.9	130.2	68.8	87.6	26.6	145.6	1,213.0
	Total employment manufacturing, April 1984	1,445.0	3,152.0	4,130.0	1,278.0	2,997.0	1,789.0	1,537.0	572.0	2,481.0	19,381.0

SOURCE: See text for sources and methodology.

TABLE 12.6

Estimated Employment Effects by Region of Alternative
$40 Billion Increases in Final Demand for Manufacturing
(thousands of persons)

Region	Exports	Automobiles	Steel
Northeast	114.5	93.6	70.1
Mid Atlantic	278.6	223.7	343.1
East North Central	397.2	501.7	582.2
West North Central	98.9	98.9	70.3
South Atlantic	186.2	152.3	130.6
East South Central	95.7	81.1	102.4
West South Central	110.5	89.4	86.0
Mountain	32.3	25.2	18.5
Pacific	172.8	196.7	118.4
Total	1486.8	1462.5	1521.6

SOURCE: See text for sources and methodology.

incomes. If a differential favoring the Midwest exists, the effects of a change in the trade balance on overall employment will be larger than these calculations suggest.

POLICIES TO PROTECT SPECIFIC INDUSTRIES

The employment decline in the iron and steel industry and the foreign penetration of the American automobile market are well known. For the last several years the Japanese automobile industry has voluntarily restricted its exports to the United States. Congress is currently considering a five-year 15 percent quota on steel imports. A recent Congressional Budget Office study (1984) concluded that the quota would generate offsetting losses in the rest of the economy, and there is little prospect that the quota would reverse the secular decline in the industry.

The employment effects of a general policy to improve the merchandise account are diffused throughout the national economy, but presumably protection of specific industries such as steel and autos would have a more concentrated employment effect in the important steel- and automobile-producing regions, the Mid Atlantic and East North Central regions.

To test this proposition we calculate the industry employment effects by region for $40 billion increases in exports (imports), steel and automobiles. These results are reported in Table 12.6.

The overall employment changes are quite similar for the three types of change in final demand. For the foreign trade or exports change the Mid Atlantic and East North Central regions gain 675.8 thousand jobs, or 45.5 percent of additional employment. For an expansion of automobiles the employment gain for the East North Central region becomes larger, but for the Mid Atlantic it is smaller. When the steel industry expands, the employment change in the two principal industrial regions is 925.3 thousand, or 61 percent of the total change in manufacturing employment.

These results are open to interpretation. My conclusion is that while policies that are industry-specific do result in more concentrated changes in employment by region, the difference is not sufficiently large to warrant deviation from a neutral policy that seeks to improve the general competitiveness of American industry in the world economy. Very large weight has to be given to employment changes in specific regions to justify the distortionary effects of quotas on steel or automobiles.

REGIONAL EFFECTS OF INCREASED DEFENSE EXPENDITURES

If the goal were merely to stimulate employment in manufacturing industries, the government could undertake a variety of other activities. The methods used in the previous analyses can be used to address questions about the regional employment effects of other policies, for example, defense procurement.

In this general spirit is the study of transfers by Golladay and Haveman (1977). They carried out a detailed regional analysis of the introduction of a negative income tax. The purpose of this change is to lessen various regional differences, and their principal conclusion is that the direct benefits of transfers that occur primarily to poor areas, the South in particular, are offset by employment gains in the industrial areas. The wealthy who pay the taxes to finance the income transfer consume relatively more textile and apparel products and low-wage service products. Increased spending by low-income consumers increases the demand for goods produced by high-skilled workers located in the Northeast and North Central states.

The calculations by Golladay and Haveman utilize regional input-output tables constructed by Karen R. Polenske (1980). An unpublished study by Martin Holmer (1978) also uses the Polenske (1980) tables in analyzing the regional economic effect of increased civilian procurement by the federal government, and increased military procurement. For

TABLE I2.7
Regional Distribution of
Expenditures on Military Procurement (as percentage)

Census region	CSA data 1975	Census data 1975	CSA 1982	Assumed 1982
Northeast	23.1%	26.2%	26.0%	29.0%
North Central	16.7	20.1	17.0	21.0
South	29.2	19.6	27.0	18.0
West	31.0	34.1	30.0	32.0

SOURCE: 1975: Holmer (1978), table 2. CSA 1982: Community Services Administration, *Statistical Abstract of the United States, 1984*, table 562.

Assumed 1982: Calculated from Census-type data extrapolating from Holmer's (1978) calculation.

1975, Holmer compares Community Services Administration (CSA) data on military procurement for primary contracts with census data that report military production under prime contracts and subcontracts. These data are reproduced in Table 12.7.

We want to calculate the impact on employment in manufacturing industries, by region, of a $40 billion increase in military procurement. We assume that the policy is implemented in 1982, but all calculations, as before, are in 1972 dollars. As before, we use the 1972 input-output table to determine the increased manufacturing employment for the nation. The total increase is 1.47 million jobs, which is virtually the same as the results of a $40 billion increase in export-related employment (cf. Table 12.5). Of these, 838 thousand, or 57 percent, are estimated to result directly from the increased procurement.

We then allocate the 1.47 million new jobs across the nine census regions. The indirect employment is allocated exactly as before. The direct component is allocated according to the information on the regional distribution of primary contracts and subcontracts in 1982 (the last column of Table 12.7). Table 12.8 shows the estimated regional distribution of increased defense-related manufacturing employment of 1.47 million. These estimates strengthen the presumption of employment benefits from increased defense procurement in the Pacific and Northeast regions. In contrast, the East North Central region gains significantly more from foreign-trade-related employment (397 thousand) and investment (374 thousand) than from defense procurement (289 thousand).

TABLE 12.8

Projected Regional Distribution of New Jobs Due to $40 Billion
Increase in Military Procurement (thousands)

Northeast	166	East South Central	43
Mid Atlantic	225	West South Central	93
East North Central	289	Mountain	48
West North Central	120	Pacific	315
South Atlantic	155		

CONCLUSIONS

Although I have taken a number of shortcuts in deriving results, some reasonably firm conclusions can be drawn from the estimates.

First, if the objective of policy is to stimulate employment in manufacturing at the possible expense of total employment, the dollar should be devalued and foreign trade stimulated. A more expansionary monetary policy accompanied by a tax increase would increase employment in manufacturing relative to employment in services and trade. Lower real interest rates that stimulate investment would also help manufacturing and construction.

The overall or absolute employment effects of trade expansion depend critically on the degree to which resources are fully utilized. A favorable change in the United States trade balance, without changes in domestic absorption $(C + I + G)$ will lead to employment changes that are not spectacular relative to total employment but that are significant relative to cyclical swings in employment and do represent a substantial proportion of recent employment declines in the industrial heartland, the East North Central region.

As the economy moves toward full employment, trade expansion policies will be accompanied by deflationary policies. The *overall* employment effects of trade expansion and the reduction of consumption are ambiguous even for the export-specialized regions of the Midwest. If excess industrial capacity is concentrated in the Midwest, selective financial policies that stimulate exports could expand employment without requiring offsetting deflationary fiscal change.

Another result is that the differential effects on regions of policies to expand exports and/or contract imports is quite small. If the dollar were devalued, manufacturing employment in Michigan and Ohio would increase somewhat, but the relative employment increase in manufacturing in these states is not significantly larger than employment in the Pacific region and the textile-producing regions of the South. The importance of manufacturing employment is higher in the Midwest, especially in Michigan, where manufacturing employment is 31 percent of total employment (the national average is 21 percent).

The roles of international trade and the overvalued dollar in the decline of employment, especially in manufacturing, in the Midwest relative to other regions has been overstated. I make this conclusion tentatively, as the evidence is fragmentary, our estimates are made without information on interregional trade flows, and regional multiplier effects are not accounted for.

Finally, our calculations confirm the differential benefits of increased defense procurement for the Pacific and Northeast regions. The proportionate effect on employment in manufacturing resulting from increased defense is much larger in these regions than in the Midwest and Mid Atlantic regions.

ACKNOWLEDGMENTS

Financial support from the Rice Institute for Policy Analysis is gratefully acknowledged. I am indebted to my colleague Gordon W. Smith for suggesting the topic of this paper, and for his comments. Keun Huh and Bo K. Huh provided excellent research assistance. The exposition was greatly improved through the efforts of Paul Rothstein.

REFERENCES

Congressional Budget Office. 1984. "The Effects of Import Quotas on the Steel Industry." Washington, D.C.: U.S. Government Printing Office.

Economic Report of the President, 1984. 1984. Washington, D.C.: U.S. Government Printing Office.

Golladay, Frederick L., and Robert H. Haveman. 1977. *The Economic Impacts of Tax-Transfer Policy.* New York: Academic Press.

Holmer, Martin. 1978. "Preliminary Analysis of the Regional Economic Effects of Federal Procurement." Paper presented at the Conference on Inter-regional Growth in the American Economy, sponsored by the Committee on Urban Public Economies, Baltimore, May 5–6.

Kaldor, Nicholes. 1970. "The Case for Regional Policies." *Scottish Journal of Political Economy* 17: 337–47.

Lawrence, Robert Z. 1984. *Can America Compete?* Washington, D.C.: Brookings Institution.

Mieszkowski, Peter. 1979. "Recent Trends in Urban and Regional Development."

Pp. 3–39 in Peter Mieszkowski and Mahlon R. Straszheim, eds., *Current Issues in Urban Economics*. Baltimore: Johns Hopkins Press.

Polenske, Karen R. 1980. *The U.S. Multi-Regional Input-Output Accounts and Model*. Lexington, Mass.: Lexington Books.

Richardson, J. David. 1983. "International Trade Policies in a World of Industrial Change." Pp. 135–58 in *Industrial Change and Public Policy*. Kansas City: Federal Reserve Bank of Kansas City.

U.S. Department of Commerce. Various issues. *Survey of Current Business*.

———. 1984. *U.S. Industrial Outlook*. Washington, D.C.: U.S. Government Printing Office.

U.S. Department of Commerce, Bureau of the Census. 1977. *Census of Manufactures*. Vol. 1: *Origins of Exports of Manufactured Products*. Washington, D.C.: U.S. Government Printing Office.

U.S. Department of Commerce, Bureau of Economic Analysis. 1972. *Input-Output Structure of the U.S. Economy*. Washington, D.C.: U.S. Government Printing Office.

CHAPTER THIRTEEN

Commentary

Paul R. Portney

Oates' paper is commendable in a number of respects. First, in his discussion of United States environmental policy, he actually presents data on changes in environmental quality. While this might appear unexceptional, most discussions of environmental policy lack any mention of what the policies have or have not done to improve ambient environmental conditions. And the EPA, forced by the press of new legislation to look ahead constantly, has yet to look back at the link between policies pursued in the past and changed environmental conditions. This is unfortunate, because one simply cannot ascribe all environmental improvement to date—or lack of improvement, for that matter—to past policies. As Oates notes, too many other factors have changed to permit a *post hoc ergo propter hoc* argument to go unchallenged. I hope that subsequent analyses of environmental policy follow Oates in discussing actual environmental trends and the role of policies in those trends.

Oates' discussion of effluent charges and marketable permits is commendable for its pragmatism. Let's face it: the choice between these two incentive-based approaches to pollution control will not hinge on Weitzman's (1977) astute observations about the relative costs of errors under both in an uncertain world. Rather, marketable permits are likely to prevail, as Oates observes, because they look more like the current regulatory system than would a full-blown system of effluent charges, and because they have practical advantages as well. This is an important observation since it is a necessary, though hardly sufficient, condition for policy change in Washington that an idea be explicable in two minutes or less. Similarly well taken in Oates' paper are his points about the importance of location in pollution control, an importance often overlooked in discussions of environmental policy reform.

One other example of pragmatism's effect on the pursuit of efficiency may be instructive; it also helps link Oates' article with those of Kain and Mieszkowski. I refer to the role of employment considerations in policy design. For instance, potential job losses among miners of high-sulfur coal had a substantial effect on EPA's final 1978 source performance standard for coal-fired electricity generation plants (see Ackerman and Hassler 1981). Briefly, that standard was tailored so as not to displace high-sulfur coal miners from their jobs, but at an *annual* cost-per-job-saved of $350,000 to $700,000 (Portney 1982). The current debate in Congress over acid rain control has taken the same form. The leading acid-rain control bill in the House of Representatives this past year mandated the same technological removal of sulfur dioxide from the largest existing power plants as was embodied in the 1978 standards for new plants. Once again this was done to protect the jobs of high-sulfur coal miners, and once again this would have come at a very high cost to society (Portney 1983). The important point is that those costs can be illuminated and the debate forced to take place in this harsh light.

This point is relevant to Mieszkowski's article. He points out the regional employment effects of policies designed to reduce the United States trade deficit. These policies have costs, of course. In the same way that the FTC has estimated the total social costs associated with import restrictions (Morkre and Tarr 1980) and divided into these totals the estimated numbers of jobs protected so as to calculate costs-per-job-saved, so too could Mieszkowski. This would not only put in perspective his clear discussion of regional employment gains (and their costs) but would also allow these to be compared with the costs of other job-creating or job-protecting measures. If we set out to be protectionists, we ought to be as cost-effective at it as possible.

This point ought also to be borne in mind as we think about rebuilding urban infrastructure. A major attraction of programs to undertake such rebuilding has nothing to do with the fear of interrupted water supplies, bad roads, or crumbling sewers, serious though these problems may be. Rather, it is the prospect of the employment gains that might result and the political benefits they will confer on sponsors. To take a case in point, between 1972 and 1981 the EPA expended nearly $40 billion in grants to local communities to construct sewage treatment plants. Many of these plants have never worked very well and violations of discharge permits at such facilities continue to be widespread (GAO 1983). Nevertheless, the program is still going strong today—if at a slightly reduced level—because it is such a large provider of jobs. Again, the trick in policy analysis is to calculate the net positive environmental benefits resulting from the program (if any), attribute the rest to job creation, and calculate a cost-per-job-created so as to render the environmental (or, indeed, any infrastructural development) program comparable to other employment creation or protection programs. This theme lies just beneath the surface of the Oates, Mieszkowski, and Kain articles.

In the balance of my comments I would like to elaborate on or depart from several points raised in Oates' paper. First is the distinction he correctly draws between the conventional air and water pollutants—at which were directed most environmental regulatory activity during the 1970s—and the so-called hazardous or toxic pollutants, about which we are hearing more and more. While the latter do include some potentially very serious health hazards, I believe a careful reading of health studies suggests that the risk remaining even after control of several conventional pollutants may far exceed that associated with a number of toxic air and water pollutants. Therefore I hope that the increasing attention given to toxic pollutants does not divert attention from the more serious but perhaps less exotic health hazards with which we have dealt only in part. Moreover, since we currently spend over $50 billion annually controlling conventional pollutants, and since the opportunities for cost savings through reform are so great, it would—as Oates points out—be expensive indeed to give up now on reforming our means of controlling conventional pollutants.

My second observation concerns an important prerequisite for the system of marketable permits Oates recommends. One reason real estate markets work well is the security of title in, say, a house on Grizzly Peak here in Berkeley I own and am willing to sell to you (would that this were so!). Similarly, marketable pollution permits will only be freely exchanged if there is a comparable security in title. There must be virtually no chance of permits being confiscated once they have been issued or purchased. This is a real fear of some polluters who are considering reducing emissions and "banking" them while awaiting a buyer. Moreover, EPA's national emissions "inventory"—an inventory of who is *estimated* to be emitting how much of each of the criteria pollutants, rather than a monitored record of *actual* emissions—is too speculative ever to serve as the legal basis for a full-blown system of tradable permits.

My final observation concerns the possibility of geographically varying environmental standards, a subject Oates deserves credit for raising. Indeed, this is the part of his paper perhaps most relevant to a conference on metropolitan America. For those to whom environmental policy is not a daily concern, I should point out that no subject is more taboo than this. The notion that people should be free to choose the level of air or water quality they want—just as they choose public school quality, the protection afforded them by police and fire departments, and so on—is upsetting to many actors in the environmental arena.

This distress, to the extent that it reflects fear about interregional externalities, is perfectly reasonable. Acid rain serves as an excellent example of the export of air pollution, not only across regions but across national boundaries. Other air or water pollutants, however, are of the "hot-spot" variety and do not migrate far. In these cases, opponents of local choice claim, regions eager for economic growth will compete for degradation and at least some will become pollution havens. Yet this flies in the face of evidence—advanced in other forums by these same individuals—that environmental values are widely and deeply held and will not be easily compromised, even for economic gain (see the Harris polls of 1981 and 1982). I strongly suspect that this latter view is the correct one and that more latitude should be granted airsheds or watersheds to decide on minimum ambient standards. If some choose a lower level of environmental quality, so be it—as long as they do not "air mail" it elsewhere. One useful piece of evidence in deciding how likely this would be would be estimates of the welfare costs currently associated with a uniform national approach.

In conclusion, let me reiterate my view that Oates' paper is a clear and sensible overview of United States environmental policy. It combines the analytical insights of an economist with the pragmatism that comes of living within twenty miles of the Capitol.

REFERENCES

Ackerman, Bruce, and William Hassler. 1981. *Clean Coal/Dirty Air*. New Haven: Yale.

General Accounting Office. 1983. "Wastewater Dischargers Are Not Complying with EPA Pollution Control Permits." Report GAO/RCED-84-53.

Morkre, Morris, and David Tarr. 1980. *Effects of Restrictions on U.S. Imports*. Staff Report of the Bureau of Economics to the Federal Trade Commission.

Portney, Paul. 1982. "How Not to Create a Job." *Regulation* (November/December): 35–38.

————. 1983. "Making Sensible Environmental Policy: The Case of Acid Rain."
    Washington, D.C.: Resources for the Future.
Weitzman, Martin. 1977. "Prices and Quantities." *Review of Economic Studies*
    41: 477–91.

Commentary

Timothy J. Sullivan

Oates' article brings the reader to a summit from which he or she can gain an excellent, and sobering, view of the achievements and the issues affecting environmental policy in the United States. The article assembles information from a wide variety of sources, both government documents and foundation reports, to demonstrate that for $50 billion a year, the United States has achieved modest improvements in air quality and has stopped the rise of deterioration in the quality of lakes and rivers. That seems like a lot of money, but Oates puts the cost of environmental controls in perspective: analysts estimate that this expenditure has caused the average annual growth of output to fall by 0.1 percent per annum.

The article moves downward from this grand picture, to analyze the costs of alternatives to current command and control regulations, most notably effluent fees and a system of marketable pollution permits. In my view, it is in this discussion of effluent fees and marketable permits that this article offers the freshest insights. Although in theory either effluent fees or marketable permits can harness the energies of the market to produce the least-cost abatement of pollution, these alternatives differ substantially on a number of critical political, institutional, and bureaucratic levels. Oates identifies four reasons why permits are superior to fees:

1. Permits promise the regulator more direct control over the level of emissions.

2. Permits avoid the need for constant price readjustments.

3. Permits can readily avoid the staggering redistributional effects that a uniform effluent fee would produce. Achieving the level of abatement of NO_2 now produced in Chicago by a command-and-control strategy costing $66 million per year would require industry to pay effluent charges of $303 million a year. These charges would induce private expenditures of $9 million per year to meet the current level of abatement. Although the effluent fees are transfers rather than costs, these sums are staggering. Their size raises substantial political doubts about the acceptability of effluent fees.

4. Finally, permits are a regulatory instrument familiar to regulators and firms that pollute. Indeed, the EPA requires a permit for almost everything it regulates.

Although Oates hesitates to claim to have demonstrated that economists' hopes for effluent fees are false, any analyst who has read this paper will find the message between the lines daunting: If you choose effluent fees to achieve current air and water quality goals, you will not know in advance what emissions will total; you will need political authority to collect taxes that dwarf the current outlays for pollution control; periodically, you will need to increase these charges—and remember, your agency has no experience in collecting taxes. To a practicing policy analyst, further discussion of effluent fees would seem a costly luxury.

By the conclusion of this article, Oates has descended from the elegance of economic theory into the morass where policy analysts work. He worries about the consequences thin markets and noncompliance might have on his marketable rights proposal. Here ideal solutions meet brutal realities. This is an area of inquiry more familiar to the policy analyst and the regulatory bureaucrat. The perspective of the regulatory practitioner suggests that permits will have value only if a monitoring and enforcement system can protect their value. Marketable permits will require an information system that updates records quickly. Finally, the program will require even better monitoring of air quality to insure that emission rights reflect the actual damage done to an airshed, based on the plant location, topology, and local winds. These tasks are difficult, both on an intellectual and a policy level. Some will even require the hard physical work of climbing smokestacks to check what comes out.

I have been working with Andy Gunther, a graduate student who spent a summer climbing smokestacks for the California Air Resources Board. Gunther participated in a study of air pollution in the Los Angeles and San Francisco airsheds, and I looked over his shoulder. In California, the

Air Resources Board regulates the work of regional air quality management districts, much as the United States Environmental Protection Agency oversees the regulatory programs of states. In brief, the study found that 31.7 percent of the stationary sources in the Los Angeles Basin failed to comply with their permit conditions. In the San Francisco Bay Area only 8.3 percent failed to comply. Gunther sought to explain these drastically different compliance rates for identical regulatory programs. His report analyzed the enforcement and monitoring system used in the two localities. It found that the Los Angeles and San Francisco Air Quality Management Districts differed greatly in the ratio of inspectors to sources, the quality of testing equipment, and the percentage of random inspections. This study holds lessons for proponents of marketable permits. Monitoring compliance with the terms of permits that are routinely exchanged and have a monetary value will create an even tougher task. Before one can tap the energies of the market, one must solve the less exciting problem of enforcement.

Regulation by command-and-control strategies is never easy. It becomes possible only through adoption of a number of shorthand rules and pieces of regulatory folk wisdom. Prominent among the shorthand rules is the 90–10 rule, taken from business. The environmentalist's version is that 90 percent of the pollution is caused by 10 percent of the sources. Of the 200,000 existing stationary sources of air pollution, 23,000 produce 85 percent of all stationary source emissions. Similar numbers hold for the generators of hazardous wastes. This folk wisdom makes gigantic regulatory tasks seem much more manageable. Further, all power plants are more or less the same. Unlike cars, they do not move around. They are maintained by engineers. Not many new ones are built. These folk rules and helpful accidents seduce regulators, many of whom are engineers, into thinking that a direct solution to pollution problems is possible. It is not inconceivable that engineers could review the pollution control technologies and the 23,000 stationary sources in this country and make reasonable recommendations. Oates' presentation, however, suggests that this has not happened.

To counteract the pull of established beliefs, regulators will need a set of rules, often only rules-of-thumb, to guide them in their choices of tools for correcting the market failures that produce pollution. These rules-of-thumb must incorporate an assessment of the market efficiency of each regulatory technique, and an analysis of the political and administrative tasks each technique requires. In the EPA, many regulations are written in a windowless shopping mall in southwest Washington by individuals whose daily work places them in a regulatory and bureaucratic thicket. The view from the regulation writer's desk is not long. Oates' article provides one rule-of-thumb that can help these regulators address the problems of air and water pollution: consider marketable permits as seriously as you consider engineering solutions. More rules-of-thumb are needed for the tasks that lie ahead.

Commentary

Jerome Rothenberg

Our cities are growing old, and with them the infrastructure that provides the foundation to support an advanced production-consumption society. The bill to replace this infrastructure could be in the hundreds of billions of dollars. Where could such enormous sums of money come from? How can city governments meet their needs with declining federal assistance?

The argument is often couched in all-or-nothing terms that are highly misleading and do not illuminate the variety of circumstances involved in judging the adequacy of infrastructure. My own research does not establish that there are no large and lumpy financing needs for local infrastructure, but does emphasize the infrastructure investment in an intricate complex of technological factors and a rich repertoire of types of governmental action.

INFRASTRUCTURE NEEDS AND FINANCING

I use the term *infrastructure* loosely to refer to public services that require a high capital intensity, using capital that has considerable durability, and especially—though not exclusively—where physical networks are involved, i.e., systems providing transportation, water, sanitation and, perhaps, education.

The technology of such service provision requires in varying degrees central production facilities, an arterial distribution system, and a capillary distribution system. These differ markedly with regard to aging, durability, and adjustments to greater and lesser capacity.

Increased wear and ineffective maintenance mean a rising cost of supplying any particular quality level of the service. This implies a rise in price relative to public and private services that have a lower capital intensity. Optimal budgeting of resources, then, calls for decreasing quality levels of the infrastructure services as they age. Permitting the fall in service quality levels with increased age is thus a deliberate, rational response to aging, and not necessarily cause for alarm.

The optimal timing of replacement, the alternative to maintenance for any particular portion of infrastructure capital, depends on the durability of the capital; on changes in the wear-offset capabilities of maintenance with aging; and on credit conditions, or changing input prices, or even trends in technological change.

Since capital components will typically differ in the determinants of replacement timing, investment demand at any one time will refer to only part of the capital relevant to the service, and the magnitude of the demand will depend on the relative importance of the various capital components for that service. Accommodation takes a number of forms, involving operating and maintenance inputs, delay of replacement, retirement without replacement, or replacement to an expressly designed smaller overall scale. All of these fail to pinpoint a changed capacity structure to meet new needs; furthermore, all involve lagged adjustment—and the overhead, arterial, and capillary components differ very substantially in both regards. Moreover, the savings from these adjustments would be small for a considerable period, rising only gradually. Indeed, savings may achieve significant magnitude only when substantial *increased* spending is made to replace the overall facility with an expressly designed smaller-scale one.

These meager aggregate payoffs—the outlay savings—from current and investment adjustments face a community whose aggregate and per-capita-tax-base wealth is declining. The resulting discrepancies between needs and financing are likely to be resolved by starving service levels and postponed replacement. These discrepancies appear to stem largely from differences in the technology of service provision among the components of capital. The possibility of discrepancy seems least for capillary capital and greatest for central overhead capital. More generally, the possibility of needs-financing difficulties for any service depends on its relative weighting of all three capital components. Large-scale economies and intricate network characteristics are potentially troublesome; simple additive capital technology is likely to be much less so.

INTERGOVERNMENTAL POLICY:
A TYPOLOGY FOR INTERVENTION

My analysis has indicated that infrastructure investment needs are not uniform, and they do not inherently constitute social problems. The context of these needs helps to determine their size and kind, and the *willingness* of the electorate to undertake the project (not their "ability to afford" them, which is a much fuzzier notion). Three elements are most salient in defining the context:

1. Service type—the size and nature of scale economies; separability among operating processes, and of the distribution of services to beneficiaries; and extent and degree of interdependence of network characteristics.

2. Age of infrastructure—the age of the stock as a whole. This is a composite of the ages of the different types of capital, each of which will usually have undergone a series of replacements, additions, and modifications. As the overall "effective age" increases, maintenance outlays, and savings on maintenance, become larger, service quality becomes more variable, and replacement decisions become more urgent.

3. Growth situation—whether the local population is stable, growing, or declining. Degrees of growth and decline are significant due to lags and unevenness in adjustment. Growth facilitates the meeting of infrastructure needs (except possibly in extreme cases of new-community spurts). A stable population generates sporadic needs for significant capital outlays, and some of these may lack the critical consensus necessary to finance them. Decline creates genuine problems for separate infrastructure services, because the quick adjustments possible are grossly inadequate and save little in outlays to offset the decline in tax base; more adequate long-term adjustments are notoriously lumpy and delayed, and require large *additional* outlays.

Intergovernmental policy attention seems most warranted, then, for cities with much old infrastructure capital that are declining significantly in population, to help finance high-scale, high-network services. Such attention seems least warranted for moderately growing cities that have a fundamentally modern infrastructure, to help finance essentially additive services. The corollary is that there is no overall need for intergovernmental help to finance infrastructure investment per se.

INTERGOVERNMENTAL POLICY:
ISSUES IN IMPLEMENTATION

The need for brevity limits me to suggesting some initial guidelines for the more detailed policy examination that would be necessary to implement desirable intergovernmental intervention.

An acceptable adaptation to population decline, especially with aged capacity, might well be to allow service levels to decline well below those of a normal aging strategy. But this may be a crude adjustment, given the complex natures of the public services being provided, and the inability of local governments to tax public benefits perfectly. Population and business migration may thus generate real fiscal externalities among localities. In two respects this adaptation may create important corollary difficulties: (1) in compromising income-distribution goals; and (2) in preventing outside beneficiaries from participating in the allocation or financing decisions.

The political rejection of apparently warranted large-scale replacement, in the context of either stable or declining populations, may leave the community with infrastructure systems that are increasingly obsolete in size, configuration, and technology. This can, at worst, aggravate the community's problems, or, at best, prevent it from being aided by more appropriate design and technology. The decision is whether to face a moderate, unattractive hurdle early, in order to avoid a much higher, much more unattractive hurdle later. Given the bias in public incentives, this kind of intertemporal passing of the buck is hardly surprising. Intergovernmental intervention should be designed to create incentives for local governments to take such salubrious hurdles early.

Three broad problems arise in gauging the role of intergovernmental intervention: (1) internal allocative distortions relating to maintenance and the timing and character of investment; (2) internal income-distribution deterioration, both within the present generation and across generations; and (3) systemwide allocative distortions. The first refers mostly to needs-financing discrepancies; the second refers to intertemporal and interpersonal shifts; the third refers to problems of jurisdictional spillover benefits and tax incidence (especially concerning highways, bridges, and water supply). The urgency and direction of intervention from higher governmental levels should be evaluated in terms of the degree to which each of these types of allocational and distributional difficulty is involved.

Where intervention is being considered to correct intertemporal, intergenerational distortions, the federal or state government need not resort to outright subsidy. A corrective instrument might be an exceptionally favorable long-term intergovernmental loan. This would alleviate the present generation's concern that they would be financing future generations.

Where interpersonal distribution difficulties, or interjurisdictional allocative difficulties are involved because of the slippage of service quality over time, higher levels of government, or even other affected jurisdictions at the same level, could purchase higher levels or wider distribution of infrastructure services from the service-providing jurisdiction. Determination of the amount to be purchased and the appropriate price would require a searching analysis of the gains and costs of various resource-use patterns.

ACKNOWLEDGMENTS

The author wishes to thank the Center for Real Estate and Urban Economics, University of California, Berkeley, for financial support. Much of the analysis is based on my "Technology of Infrastructure Services, and the Demand and Supply for Infrastructure Investment," MIT Working Paper No. 356, November 1984.

PART FIVE

Overview

*In conclusion, John Quigley and Daniel Rubinfeld dis-
cuss the role of the federal government in the various
programs within the domestic budget. They summarize
the arguments for a reduced federal role that runs
through a number of the chapters in the book. In several
cases they make contrary arguments. They also suggest
that reducing the role of the federal government is not
likely to generate large budgetary savings, especially in
the short run. If the problem of the federal deficit is to be
resolved, tax reform and/or tax increases will be necessary, they argue, and they propose a number of changes
that would increase the tax burdens of wealthy
households.*

CHAPTER FOURTEEN

Domestic Priorities in Our Federal System

John M. Quigley and Daniel L. Rubinfeld

During the 1980 and 1984 presidential campaigns, debates about federal domestic policy have concentrated on defining the appropriate roles of the national and lower levels of government in raising revenues, in setting spending priorities, and in managing individual programs. In part, the discussion has been framed in moral and ideological terms. Largely, however, the focus has been on the relationship between federalism and economic efficiency, both allocative efficiency in the choice of levels and types of spending by public agents and private decisionmakers, and productive efficiency—the elimination of waste, fraud, and bureaucratic ineptitude.

Choices made by the executive and legislative branches of government during the 1980s have substantially reduced the federal government's role as raiser of revenues and have significantly altered fiscal relations among levels of government. One major outcome of these fiscal choices has been the increasing prominence of the federal budget deficit—which, under current conditions, is both large and enduring.

The need to deal with this large deficit will require Congress and the president to confront the options for making further cuts in the federal budget and more generally for reducing the scope of federal domestic activity. The magnitude of the deficit, now projected at some 5 percent of GNP for the next decade, provides special motivation for this book's examination and evaluation of the domestic portion of the federal budget, while changing federal and state fiscal relations motivate a detailed analysis of the domestic programs undertaken by federal, state, and local governments.

The administration's New Federalism initiative is perhaps the best place to begin this discussion. The 1982 Reagan budget message suggested a "swap" of federal and state functions, with the federal government assuming control of Medicaid while relegating responsibility to the various states for food stamps and Aid to Families with Dependent Children (AFDC). At the same time, it was proposed that some sixty-one other federal programs in education, community development, transportation, and social services be returned to the states, with funding during the transition to be provided by a new federal trust fund.

The intent of the administration's current proposals can be debated, but the discussion in this volume makes it clear that the New Federalism was motivated not by normative or efficiency notions about the appropriate locus of program responsibility but, rather, by a simpler motive—a perceived opportunity to cut the domestic federal budget. The administration had clear plans to reduce the Medicaid program once it came under federal control, and although the Reagan program involved a substantial federal (as well as state) government role, that role did not have direct budgetary consequences.

Coupled with the strong stance taken by the Reagan administration on the New Federalism, the magnitude of the current budget deficit raises a number of issues of fact and interpretation: (1) Have the recent trends in the financing of programs by state-local governments and the transfer of fiscal responsibilities during the first Reagan term marked a move away from government spending, or simply a readjustment of program responsibility and financing from the federal to the state and local levels? In other words, is the new federalism simply an anti-government program, or does it represent a serious movement toward fiscal reform? (2) Should the role of the federal government in the regulation of the domestic economy be diminished? If so, should these regulatory and oversight functions be performed by lower levels of government, or should they be relegated to the private sector? (3) If domestic programs are to be further restructured in the interests of economic efficiency, how should that restructuring take place? If program changes are to be made, what opportunities for savings in federal budgetary dollars will arise?

These and related issues have appeared and reappeared in the preceding chapters. In this brief concluding chapter we highlight some of what we have learned and add our own interpretation. We examine critically the notion of fiscal federalism and investigate reforms that would be consistent with federalist principles and would save budgetary dollars.

A budgetary perspective on federal programs is a good starting point. Table 14.1 presents the 1983 federal domestic budget broken down by program area. Social security, by far the largest of the income security programs, is currently financed by a trust fund and raises a host of separate questions. In addition, specific campaign promises by President Reagan make it less likely that social security will be reevaluated during the president's second term. Given the domestic focus of our discussion, we ignore expenditures on national defense and consider net interest and veterans' payments to be "uncontrollables" (even though there are current proposals to cut back Veterans Administration health benefits). It is important to note that of the total federal budget of $820 billion, $216 billion goes to defense, space, and international affairs and $245 billion to social insurance. Net interest amounts to about $94 billion, and veterans' benefits to $26 billion. As a result, our scope for evaluation—the domestic portion of the federal budget not involving social security, veterans' benefits, and interest—totals approximately $239 billion.

STABILIZATION

The normative issue of the appropriate allocation of budgetary functions between the federal and state-local sectors is one which has been discussed throughout the history of our nation by politicians and for nearly that long by political scientists and economists. The classic economic position concerning stabilization, redistribution, and allocation was summarized by Wallace Oates a decade ago (Oates 1972) and is reinterpreted in this book by Edward Gramlich. Oates and others argued that the central government is generally best suited to address questions of economic stabilization. Local stabilization policies are unlikely to be successful, in part because of high levels of labor mobility in response to local monetary or fiscal policy and, in part because a substantial portion of debt held by subnational governments is external to those governments.

Gramlich raises novel questions about the classic view. He points out that much of the federal debt is external as well and argues that state governments are able to manage regional stabilization policies effectively. Gramlich thus seems generally unwilling to require the central government to undertake regional stabilization policies (including, for example,

TABLE 14.1

Federal Government Domestic Expenditures, 1983

(billions of current dollars)

Function	Total expenditures[a]	Purchases	Transfers plus net interest	Grants
Health, hospitals, medical care	$86.9	$6.9	$57.8	$19.0
Welfare and social services	41.6	1.8	18.9	20.9
Education	14.7	1.5	6.4	6.8
Transportation	22.1	7.3	–	12.6
Housing and urban renewal	13.5	1.0	8.6[b]	3.9
Environment and natural resources[c]	8.7	4.7	–	4.0
Revenue sharing	4.6	–	4.6	–
Other[d]	45.7[e]	26.2	0.4	5.0
Social insurance[f]	245.2	2.1	239.3	3.8
Veterans' benefits	26.0	9.0	16.8	–
Net interest	94.2	–	94.2	–

[a]Includes subsidies less current surplus of government enterprises.
[b]Includes housing subsidies to the poor.
[c]Includes water and sewerage expenditures.
[d]Includes civilian safety, recreation and cultural activities, energy, agriculture, postal service, economic development, and labor training and services.
[e]Includes $20 billion in revenues from sale of power and $14.6 billion in agricultural subsidies.
[f]Includes social security and government retirement programs.
SOURCE: *Survey of Current Business* (July 1984), table 3.15.

the responsibilities once undertaken by the Economic Development Administration). However, the appropriate locus of responsibility for regional stabilization policy depends greatly on the ability of each level of government to manage a stabilization policy and to raise the revenues needed to make such a policy function successfully. In our judgment, though not in Gramlich's, the advantages of federal dominance are substantial. Given the relative ease of mobility of capital and labor among regions in the United States economy, management by the states is likely to be difficult at best and ineffective at worst.

REDISTRIBUTION

The arguments concerning the appropriate allocation of the responsibility for anti-poverty policies and transfer programs are analogous to those regarding stabilization. The economic case for a dominant federal role is based on the central government's ability to raise revenue from a sufficiently broad base and to adopt a policy that does not create artificial incentives for migration and mobility. If tax and redistribution policies are adopted at the state level, migration across state boundaries makes the achievement of any given redistributive goal more costly for society.

A decentralized system also provides a powerful incentive for individual states to offer a relatively low benefit package to those in need, since generous benefits would attract migrants and increase state and local taxes. The result can be a stable outcome in which states provide lower levels of benefits than they would if the level of benefits were determined by statute at the federal level. In contrast, some have argued that a state-local redistributive policy can be important because individuals care more about redistribution among their "neighbors" than among others who live at greater distances. A state government may be better able to determine the wishes of its residents and also to manage the redistribution.

Unlike the architects of the New Federalism proposal, we find the argument for a centralized federal redistribution function persuasive—in part because of the importance of migration incentives, in part because we feel that a national commitment to raising the incomes of the poor is itself a public good and in part because the federal tax structure provides an administratively efficient and mildly progressive vehicle for raising revenue. The recent Reagan administration modifications of redistributive programs are not inconsistent with this normative view. As Danziger and Feaster point out, administration proposals involve federal cuts but do not involve countervailing increases at the state and local levels. The

Reagan program should be viewed, then, as involving a reduction in the national commitment to income redistribution but not as a serious attempt to change the responsibility for it.

Income security and health are redistribution programs that make up a substantial portion of the domestic federal budget. Both AFDC and Medicaid are essentially state-administered programs that are funded jointly by the federal government and by the states. Views about the level of support, and therefore the effect on the federal budget, of changes in programs will depend on notions about the proper level of publicly provided low-income assistance. The broad post–World War II trend toward a substantially increased federal role in low-income assistance has been reversed during the first Reagan term. According to the calculations of Danziger and Feaster, the fraction of United States households officially classified as poor decreased from 14.3 percent in 1967 to 11.4 percent in 1978, a period during which real cash transfers per household increased by 67 percent and real GNP per household increased by 9 percent. In contrast, the poverty rate increased from 11.4 percent in 1978 to 15.2 percent in 1983, while real transfers decreased by 1 percent and real GNP by 7 percent. For fiscal year 1985, the administration has already proposed a reduction of about 12 percent in cash transfer programs and a 29 percent reduction in AFDC assistance, compared with pre-Reagan projections. The reforms already enacted have reduced benefits most drastically for the so-called "working poor."

The analysis projects that the aggregate poverty rate will remain far above the 1978 rate even if the economy were to grow according to the most optimistic of the administration's public pronouncements. Danziger and Feaster argue that AFDC guarantees, which have fallen by more than a third in real terms in the past decade, should be indexed and that a national minimum should be enacted. They suggest that a targeted employment program modeled on the Supported Work Demonstration Program be encouraged and that child-support programs be reformed to generate transfers from absent parents.

Neither Hanushek's nor Wolch's commentary provides comfort for those who would implement these suggestions. In Hanushek's judgment, with a federal deficit that "hovers at 5 percent of GNP for as far as anybody cares to project it," the indexation of benefits is politically unthinkable and targeted employment programs unlikely. Wolch's comments suggest that the data and conclusions of the Danziger–Feaster analysis are far too optimistic for the "truly needy," the service-dependent poor. Those whose only protection is the "social safety net" are substantially worse off under current and projected future policy.

SHIFTING PUBLIC FUNCTIONS

The proper division of functions between the federal and state-local sectors depends largely on a judgment about which level of government is best able to allocate resources effectively. Three options are available—federal responsibility for both revenue and expenditure, state-local responsibility for revenue and expenditure, and federal taxation with grants-in-aid to state and local governments. The first Reagan term was marked, not only by a move to decrease federal expenditures, but also by a shift in the nature of federal grant programs from specific categorical programs to general-purpose unrestricted block grants. The magnitude of grant programs declined substantially. These policies are consistent with a goal of reduced federal spending rather than with an attempt to take full advantage of the federal government's ability to raise revenue, even if those revenues can be allocated more effectively by state and local governments.

The arguments for increased local control of public expenditures are certainly not new, but they have received a good deal of attention recently. As Gramlich sums it up, "Public goods [are] to be provided by the jurisdiction covering the smallest area over which benefits are distributed—that way the public-goods efficiencies are maximized and the effect of taste differences minimized." From this perspective, the intellectual basis for the New Federalism lies in the observation that in our society there are many publicly provided goods that are produced at constant cost and whose benefits are distributed narrowly within a state or within a metropolitan area or other small region. Control over these expenditures by states and smaller units of government allows for variation in the provision of these goods in response to local tastes and incomes. This economic argument does support the New Federalism, at least when there are no economies of scale in production and no paternalistic reasons for providing a given service. But to judge whether such a move makes good economic sense requires a program-by-program examination of the federal domestic budget—to which we will turn in a moment.

The appropriateness of local control of taxes and expenditures depends in addition on the capacity for management, the nature of accountability, and the role of politics at different levels of government. The set of political motives and the general political environment at the federal level are substantially different from those at state and local levels. Thus an important historical argument for an important federal role, including grants with high matching rates, was a presumption that local politicians and public managers are typically less competent and more susceptible to corruption than their federal counterparts. In part, federal financial and regulatory controls were designed to force lower levels of government to act as agents for the national government.

These considerations of political economy are useful in predicting the effects of grant consolidation and the removal of federal restrictions on local government spending. It is difficult to predict the spending effects of a change in the levels and structure of federal aid to states and to forecast decisions of state-local governments to spend out of their locally raised revenue. However, the evidence presented in this volume does indicate that the move to give states full financial responsibility for the AFDC program would reduce spending on welfare by 50 to 95 percent. The analysis of the food stamp program reported by Inman yields somewhat different results. Together, however, the findings indicate that states do link the AFDC benefits they provide with the national food stamp program. For example, if the federal government were to transfer responsibility for the food stamp program to the states, it is projected that state welfare spending would rise by only 50 cents for each dollar decline in federal food-stamp spending. In the aggregate, spending on welfare and food stamps would fall by about one-half, a decrease from $24 billion in 1983 to $11 to $12 billion. Thus, the New Federalism proposals represent a reduction in federal domestic spending and a net decline in state-local spending as well. Those programs that supply transfers to low-income households would provide far less assistance to recipients.

The effects of the "swap" proposed by the proponents of the New Federalism on spending for other programs may not be very different from the effects of low-income assistance. For elementary and secondary education Inman reports that the consolidation of categorical educational aid programs into a single trust fund would lower state support for public elementary and secondary education: "Left on their own, states do not want to maintain spending on public education." The same general argument may well apply to other specific program areas. The move from federal funding of programs to state funding is likely to involve substantial decreases in the overall level of program support. Whether the specific changes proposed under the New Federalism initiative will be enacted is problematic—most political commentators appear to be skeptical. However, regardless of program specifics, the decline in direct federal spending and in federal aid to states and localities is likely to be substantial. In the end, whether such changes are seen to be desirable must depend on our evaluation of the benefits and costs of particular government activities.

ALLOCATION BY FUNCTION

EDUCATION

In 1983 the federal government provided approximately $15.4 billion for education and related programs, $6.8 billion of which involved direct grants to state and local governments. Of the total federal budget for education, $68 million was allocated to elementary, secondary, and vocational education. In November 1984 administration officials proposed modest increases in direct federal assistance for education, in part to provide new support for teacher training in math and science. The administration has also proposed larger indirect increases in federal education subsidies through tuition tax credits for private-school education. Murnane argues that there remains an important federal role in education; we conclude that there are substantial externalities in primary and secondary education.

ENVIRONMENT

During the past ten to fifteen years a growing concern for environmental problems has been coupled with increased expenditures by all levels of government and by the imposition of a complex set of regulations. The federal budget figure for environmental control—approximately $8.7 billion in 1983—is well below the true expenditures by individuals, business, and government on pollution abatement. It appears that the choice of policy instruments for achieving abatement goals has been quite wasteful. If greater reliance were placed on the use of economic incentives, huge cost savings would result.

Compare the aggregate abatement costs under a command-type system of standards (similar to the current set of federal and state regulations) to the least-cost abatement program using effluent fees, emission fees, or marketable permits. Oates estimates the savings in achieving a nitrogen dioxide standard in the Chicago air-quality-control region to be about 80 percent; estimated savings for particulate emissions in Baltimore are similar. These savings are typical, argues Oates. Most of the reductions in cost that he documents would accrue directly to consumers and businesses and a substantial portion of the over $10 billion of government abatement expenditures could be reduced as well. Paul Portney and Tim Sullivan suggest that these examples overstate the actual gains achievable from a system with more rational economic incentives. However, in our view the case for a system of marketable permits would be powerful even if the gains were only a third as large as Oates claims.

These proposals are not likely to affect the federal budget greatly, but the Oates analysis of these regulatory reforms has important implications for the debate about federalism. The issue is whether uniform national standards ought to be set or whether the Environmental Protection Agency (EPA) should foster state and local diversity in standards. Currently, EPA sets minimum air-quality standards (i.e., maximal concentrations for pollutants), and only California has adopted more stringent standards. Water pollution, on the other hand, is regulated almost entirely by the states, with much variation in state-by-state standards. The argument for diversity is that states are better able to respond to the differential demands of their citizens for pollution abatement and to account for the differences in the cost of abatement as well.

Why, then, have national standards? How important is the inefficiency of tax competition emphasized by Gramlich? It is possible, indeed likely, that states would set lower standards to avoid losing businesses and tax revenues to competing states. Moreover, there is growing evidence of externalities across states because emissions in one state actually harm those in another. The argument for central control, whether or not there are uniform standards, seems to us to be compelling. The principles of the New Federalism are inconsistent with the environment goals of our society, or so they seem to us. In any case, substantial federal budgetary gains are unlikely to be achieved even if the appropriate policy reforms are made.

HOUSING AND RACE

The problems of inadequate housing and race are often discussed simultaneously. The residential segregation of urban blacks has remained at relatively high levels despite general improvements in income. We are optimistic about the prospects for reducing the levels of racial segregation in the housing market, in part because of the recent willingness of the courts to enforce fair-housing laws (and award damages) and in part because of the trends in the 1980 census reported by Kain.

Kain's policy recommendations involve little budgetary cost—the 1983 budget for fair-housing enforcement was less than $20 million—but would involve a more visible commitment by the federal government. It is impossible to attribute the existing pattern of racial residential segregation to income, so we cannot expect expanded housing programs per se greatly to affect the level of residential segregation by race.

An expanded role for the federal government in the housing area is supported in the analysis presented by Sherman Maisel and is disputed in the commentary by Richard Muth. Maisel points out that the 1982 Report of the President's Commission on Housing urges a greater reliance on the private market to deal with housing problems. This commission recommended, for example, that housing production subsidies be ended and that non-entitlement voucher programs of aid to the poor be introduced. The commission also urged a reduced role in the provision of homeowners' mortgage insurance and a restructuring of the thrift industry to reduce the regulation of housing finance and building. The implications for fiscal federalism were mixed. The commission recommended government aid in the development of new mortgage instruments, urged that favorable tax treatment of homeowners be continued, and recommended that the federal government act to override local preferences with respect to zoning, building codes, and especially rent control.

Maisel clearly supports a strong federal role in the housing market. To some extent he bases his arguments on the externalities generated by housing. This point is generally conceded. However, Maisel goes on to argue that a federal role is necessary to insure the "affordability" of housing for the average American household. On this point, controversy is generated between Maisel and other contributors to this volume. Maisel concludes that housing is not affordable by many who are elderly, families with female heads, and large minority families. In addition, young moderate-income first-time buyers have difficulty because of the mortgage tilt (high real payments early in the mortgage life and low payments later) and the high real interest rates resulting from current policy. We agree with Maisel's characterization of the situation, but we conclude that this "affordability problem" is merely a symptom of inadequate income and that the federal role ought to be restricted to treating the problem of low incomes, irrespective of an individual's housing situation.

TRANSPORTATION AND INFRASTRUCTURE

The role of the federal government in providing transportation should be seriously diminished or at least redirected. The analysis by Gomez-Ibañez takes as given the notion that government ought to be involved in surface transportation—the question is simply one of allocation of function. It appears, however, that the rationale for a federal role in urban transportation is weak. In addition, the structure of federal grants for Interstate Highway construction and for urban mass-transit capital projects, with their high matching rates, have been seriously distorting. In fact, the analysis of urban mass-transit assistance by Gomez-Ibañez seems to be a case study of an inefficient fiscal structure.

In analyzing transportation and other infrastructure policies, it is worth distinguishing between the capital and the operating portions of the budget. During the past several years, there have been alarming reports of deterioration of the public infrastructure. The Joint Economic Committee (JEC 1984), the Congressional Budget Office (CBO 1983), and the Advisory Commission on Intergovernmental Relations (ACIR 1984) have documented the sizable infrastructure needs of the 1980s and 1990s. The Joint Economic Committee points out, for example, that state and local infrastructure outlays on transportation (highways, bridges, etc.), water supply and distribution, and wastewater collection and treatment have declined from 2.2 percent of GNP in 1961 to 1.9 percent in 1981. Basic infrastructure needs are concentrated primarily in the Northeast and the Midwest, where the public facilities are in most need of modernization.

Federalism is central to analyzing public infrastructure investment. It could be argued, after all, that the diversity of problems is best handled by the individual states—as Gomez-Ibañez concludes for fixed-rail transit systems. The JEC argues that the financial problems and uncertainties involved make it imperative that the federal government provide financial assistance. According to the JEC, state and local governments should assume primary responsibility for the management, financing, and development of public infrastructure, but the federal government has a vital role in setting standards and in guaranteeing continuing aid in response to short-run, localized economic problems.

In addition, the benefits of some types of infrastructure development are so broad that management at the state level is unlikely to recognize all externalities appropriately. Rothenberg's commentary supports this by stressing the intertemporal as well as interjurisdictional externalities.

These certainly exist in water-resource development; navigational projects, and flood control, which affect many states over a substantial period of time. Both types of externalities are also present, as Oates points out, in waste-water treatment and disposal.

The federal role in infrastructure planning and investment could be facilitated simply by redirecting some portion of the large urban mass-transit subsidy program to more general urban capital-investment programs. An alternative would be to increase the highway trust fund itself and to redirect its spending priorities. The trust fund is financed by excise taxes, principally on gasoline and motor fuels. These excises are quite low by international standards, and the *ad valorem* tax level has declined substantially during the past decade. Even a modest increase in the gas tax, coupled with a more liberal interpretation of eligible uses of trust fund revenues, would go far toward eliminating the urban infrastructure problem.

A CHANGING CONSENSUS

In broad summary, the articles presented in this volume do reflect a changed consensus about the appropriate structure of American federalism. Economists seem somewhat more willing now than they were in the early 1970s to devolve program authority and financial responsibilities from the federal government to state and local governments. In particular, the contributors to this volume seem less concerned by the equity or price-equalization arguments for intergovernmental revenue-sharing or for matching grants. They are more tolerant of regional variations in the tastes for public output, such as clean air and water, even when these tastes are purely income-determined. These views may well reflect a shifting professional consensus.

THE BUDGET DEFICIT

Although the authors of many of the articles in this volume have questioned the current federal role in a number of domestic public programs, major budgetary reductions are not achievable in the short run, either from a further devolvement of responsibility or from further reductions in domestic programs. (Recall that the domestic budget less social insurance interest and veterans' benefits is only $239 billion.) Some increase in federal revenues is possible, however, largely by removing a variety of federal tax-code-generated subsidies to upper-income households.

Removal of the federal subsidy for homeowners, arising because imputed rent is untaxed, could raise about $50 billion in federal revenue and would be consistent with a stronger government commitment to noninterference in housing transactions. The only practical way to compensate for the unique treatment of owner-occupied housing would be to disallow deductions for mortgage interest payments. If, instead, mortgage interest deductions were capped at some reasonably high level, the reform could be targeted to generate revenues from higher-income taxpayers. For example, in 1981 the Congressional Budget Office reported that capping deductions at $10,000 a year would affect less than one-half of one percent of taxpayers, yet would generate revenues of about $2 billion, largely from higher-income households. Such a move would apparently be widely supported by economists.

Removal of the current tax exemption for the obligations issued by state and local governments would be clearly consistent with the devolution of fiscal responsibilities and would raise about $20 billion in federal revenues. The current system whereby lower levels of government issue general and special-purpose obligations exempt from federal taxation is subject to two criticisms. First, these obligations are owned primarily by financial institutions and wealthy taxpayers and the system provides a direct subsidy to those households whose marginal tax rate exceeds that of the average household. Second, by reducing state and local governments' costs for borrowing, the tax exemption encourages "too much" public investment. We are unpersuaded by the second argument, in particular with the implication that economic efficiency requires public investment to earn the pre-tax rate of return in the private economy, but we see the first criticism of the current system as a powerful one. The cost of this provision to national taxpayers, about $20 billion, exceeds the value of the exemption to state and local governments, estimated to be about $8 billion. The same subsidy could be provided far more cheaply and efficiently through a federal capital grant to lower levels of government than through the exemption mechanism. The net savings from this reform would be $12 billion. If across-the-board removal of this exemption is considered too difficult politically, we would support its elimination on all but general-revenue obligation bonds.

Similar reasoning underlies our support of the repeal of the current federal deduction for certain state and local taxes. Removal of this provision of the federal tax code would encourage the adoption of more efficient user charges rather than taxes where appropriate, and would also increase federal revenues by about $29 billion by taxing more affluent households. From the viewpoint of local governments, the same subsidy can be provided through a federal grant, more efficiently and equitably than under the current system, at a cost of about $8 billion. Thus elimination of the current deduction for state and local taxes would raise about $21 billion net of an equivalent grant to state and localities.

Together these reforms, which appear to be consistent with the spirit of the New Federalism, could increase federal revenues by something like one-third of the current differences between projected federal revenues and expenditures.

The financial conclusion may be too optimistic, however, especially if provision is made for a gradual introduction of these desirable reforms. Immediate elimination of the homeowner subsidy or the tax-exempt status of municipal bonds would have powerful and immediate effects on the value of housing and commercial capital. Dislocation associated with abrupt changes in investment incentives would be substantial. Step-by-step increases in tax obligations for the purchase of new municipal obligations or newly completed dwellings (as suggested by Muth) would prevent sharp drops in housing prices and bond prices. These types of incremental staging of programs would also assist in generating political support for reform, since they would preserve the benefits currently accruing to middle- and upper-income households.

These plans would also mean, however, that the increased revenues from such reforms would scarcely be felt during the Reagan administration.

REFERENCES

Advisory Commission on Intergovernmental Relations (ACIR). 1984. "Financing Public Infrastructure." June. Washington, D.C.: U.S. Government Printing Office.

Congress of the United States, Congressional Budget Office (CBO). 1983. "Public Works Infrastructure: Policy Considerations for the 1980's." April. Washington, D.C.: U.S. Government Printing Office.

Congress of the United States, Joint Economic Committee (JEC). 1984. "Hard Choices: A Report on the Increasing Gap between America's Infrastructure Needs and Our Ability to Pay for Them." February 25. Washington, D.C.: U.S. Government Printing Office.

Oates, Wallace E. 1972. Fiscal Federalism. New York: Harcourt, Brace, Jovanovich.

Contributors

HENRY J. AARON is Senior Fellow, The Brookings Institution.

GEORGE F. BREAK is Professor of Economics, University of California, Berkeley.

PAUL N. COURANT is Professor of Economics, University of Michigan.

SHELDON DANZIGER is Director, Institute for Research on Poverty, University of Wisconsin–Madison.

DANIEL FEASTER is a graduate student in economics, University of Wisconsin–Madison.

MICHAEL A. GOLDBERG is Professor of Urban Land Policy, University of British Columbia.

JOSE A. GOMEZ-IBAÑEZ is Professor of Urban Planning and Public Policy, Harvard University.

EDWARD M. GRAMLICH is Professor of Economics and Public Policy, University of Michigan.

ERIC A. HANUSHEK is Deputy Director, U.S. Congressional Budget Office, and Professor of Economics, University of Rochester.

ROBERT P. INMAN is Professor of Finance, Economics, and Public Policy and Management, University of Pennsylvania.

JOHN F. KAIN is Professor of Economics and City and Regional Planning, Harvard University.

THEODORE E. KEELER is Professor of Economics, University of California, Berkeley.

SHERMAN MAISEL is Professor of Business Administration, University of California, Berkeley.

JULIUS MARGOLIS is Professor of Economics, University of California, Irvine.

PETER MIESZKOWSKI is Professor of Economics and Finance, Rice University.

RICHARD J. MURNANE is Associate Professor of Education, Harvard University.

RICHARD F. MUTH is Professor of Economics, Emory University.

WALLACE E. OATES is Professor of Economics, University of Maryland.

PAUL R. PORTNEY is Senior Fellow, Resources for the Future.

JOHN M. QUIGLEY is Professor of Economics and Public Policy, University of California, Berkeley.

JEROME ROTHENBERG is Professor of Economics, Massachusetts Institute of Technology.

DANIEL L. RUBINFELD is Professor of Law and Economics, University of California, Berkeley.

DAVID STERN is Associate Professor of Education, University of California, Berkeley.

TIMOTHY J. SULLIVAN is Assistant Professor of Public Policy, University of California, Berkeley.

MELVIN M. WEBBER is Professor of City Planning, University of California, Berkeley.

JENNIFER R. WOLCH is Assistant Professor of Urban and Regional Planning, University of Southern California.

Compositor: Wilsted & Taylor
Printer: The Murray Printing Co.
Binder: The Murray Printing Co.
Display: Sabon
Text: 10/13 Sabon